Animals

OXFORD **PHILOSOPHICAL** CONCEPTS

Animals

A HISTORY

Edited by Peter Adamson and G. Fay Edwards

OXFORD
UNIVERSITY PRESS

OXFORD

UNIVERSITY PRESS

Oxford University Press is a department of the University of Oxford.
It furthers the University's objective of excellence in research, scholarship,
and education by publishing worldwide. Oxford is a registered trade mark of
Oxford University Press in the UK and certain other countries.

Published in the United States of America by Oxford University Press
198 Madison Avenue, New York, NY 10016, United States of America.

© Oxford University Press 2018

Library of Congress Cataloging-in-Publication Data
Names: Adamson, Peter, editor; Edwards, G. Fay, editor.
Title: Animals : a history / edited by G. Fay Edwards and Peter Adamson.
Description: New York : Oxford University Press, 2018. | Includes
bibliographical references and index.
Identifiers: LCCN 2017036011 (print) | LCCN 2018004743 (ebook) |
ISBN 9780199375998 (online course) | ISBN 9780199375981 (updf) |
ISBN 9780199375967 (cloth : alk. paper) | ISBN 9780199375974 (pbk. : alk. paper)
Subjects: LCSH: Animals (Philosophy)
Classification: LCC B105.A55 (ebook) | LCC B105.A55 A74 2018 (print)
| DDC 113/.8—dc23

1 3 5 7 9 8 6 4 2

Paperback printed by Webcom, Inc., Canada
Hardback printed by Bridgeport National Bindery, Inc.,
United States of America

Contents

Series Foreword

Oxford Philosophical Concepts (OPC) offers an innovative approach to philosophy's past and its relation to other disciplines. As a series, it is unique in exploring the transformations of central philosophical concepts from their ancient sources to their modern use.

OPC has several goals: to make it easier for historians to contextualize key concepts in the history of philosophy, to render that history accessible to a wide audience, and to enliven contemporary discussions by displaying the rich and varied sources of philosophical concepts still in use today. The means to these goals are simple enough: eminent scholars come together to rethink a central concept in philosophy's past. The point of this rethinking is not to offer a broad overview but to identify problems the concept was originally supposed to solve and investigate how approaches to the concept shifted over time, sometimes radically. Recent scholarship has made evident the benefits of reexamining the standard narratives about Western philosophy. OPC's editors look beyond the canon and explore their concepts over a wide philosophical landscape. Each volume traces a notion from its inception as a solution to specific problems through its historical transformations to its modern use, all the while acknowledging its historical context. Each OPC volume is a history of its concept in that it tells a story about changing solutions to its well-defined problem. Many editors have found it appropriate to include long-ignored writings drawn from the Islamic and Jewish traditions and the philosophical contributions of women. Volumes also explore ideas drawn from Buddhist, Chinese, Indian, and other philosophical cultures when doing so adds an especially helpful new perspective. By combining scholarly innovation with focused and astute analysis, OPC encourages a deeper understanding of our philosophical past and present.

One of the most innovative features of Oxford Philosophical Concepts is its recognition that philosophy bears a rich relation to art, music, literature, religion, science, and other cultural practices. The series speaks to the need for informed interdisciplinary exchanges. Its editors assume that the most difficult and profound philosophical ideas can be made comprehensible to a large audience and that materials not strictly philosophical often bear a significant relevance to philosophy. To this end, each OPC volume includes Reflections. These are short stand-alone essays written by specialists in art, music, literature, theology, science, or cultural studies that reflect on the concept from their own disciplinary perspectives. The goal of these essays is to enliven, enrich, and exemplify the volume's concept and reconsider the boundary between philosophical and extra-philosophical materials. OPC's Reflections display the benefits of using philosophical concepts and distinctions in areas that are not strictly philosophical and encourage philosophers to move beyond the borders of their discipline as presently conceived.

The volumes of OPC arrive at an auspicious moment. Many philosophers are keen to invigorate the discipline. OPC aims to provoke philosophical imaginations by uncovering the brilliant twists and unforeseen turns of philosophy's past.

Christia Mercer

List of Contributors

PETER ADAMSON is a professor of Late Ancient and Arabic philosophy at the LMU in Munich. He is the editor of another forthcoming volume in the Oxford Philosophical Concepts series, *Health: The History of a Concept*, and the author of the book series *A History of Philosophy without Any Gaps*, also published by Oxford University Press. Two volumes collecting his papers on Neoplatonism and philosophy in the Islamic world appeared recently with the Variorum series published by Ashgate.

DEBORAH J. BROWN is a reader in philosophy at the University of Queensland and director of the University of Queensland Critical Thinking Project. She is the author of *Descartes and the Passionate Mind* (Cambridge University Press, 2006) and numerous articles in early modern philosophy.

AMBER D. CARPENTER is an associate professor at Yale-NUS College. After a PhD at King's College London and scholarly publications on Plato's ethics, moral psychology, and metaphysics, an Einstein Fellowship enabled her to begin research into Sanskrit philosophy, focusing on Buddhist materials. Her book *Indian Buddhist Philosophy* appeared in 2014. She continues to publish on Greek philosophy and, increasingly, on Greek and Indian Buddhist philosophy together. She collaborates with Rachael Wiseman on the Integrity Project and is currently coediting a volume of *Portraits of Integrity*.

G. FAY EDWARDS completed her doctorate in ancient philosophy at King's College London in 2013 and took up a position as an assistant professor of philosophy at Washington University in St. Louis until late 2015. She has published papers on Plato, Porphyry, and the Stoics and is the author of "How to Escape Indictment for Impiety: Teaching as Punishment in the *Euthyphro*" in the *Journal of the History of Philosophy*.

ROBERT GARNER is a professor of politics at the University of Leicester. He has published widely on the ethics and politics of animal protection. His books include *Animals, Politics and Morality* (Manchester University Press, 2004), *Animal Ethics* (Polity, 2005), *The Political Theory of Animal Rights* (Manchester University Press, 2005), and *A Theory of Justice for Animals* (Oxford University Press, 2013). He is currently working on a Leverhulme Trust–funded project on the intellectual history of animal rights.

DEVIN HENRY is an associate professor of philosophy at the University of Western Ontario. He received his PhD from King's College London. He is the author of several articles on topics in Aristotle's philosophy of natural science (including classification, teleology, and biology), as well as Plato's late epistemology. He is currently working on a book on Aristotle on substantial generation.

PATRICK KAIN is an associate professor of philosophy at Purdue University. After receiving his PhD from the University of Notre Dame in 2000, he has worked extensively in ethics and modern philosophy, focusing especially on Kant. He is the coeditor of *Challenges to Moral and Religious Belief: Disagreement and Evolution* (Oxford University Press, 2014) and *Essays on Kant's Anthropology* (Cambridge University Press, 2003) and the author of numerous articles on Kant, including "Self-legislation in Kant's Moral Philosophy" in *Archiv für Geschichte der Philosophie* and "Kant's Defense of Human Moral Status" in *Journal of the History of Philosophy*. He was a Humboldt Fellow in Marburg in 2003.

PAUL KATSAFANAS is an associate professor of philosophy at Boston University. He has published a number of articles on action, ethics, moral psychology, and nineteenth-century philosophy. He is the author of two books: *Agency and the Foundations of Ethics: Nietzschean Constitutivism* (Oxford University Press, 2013) and *The Nietzschean Self: Moral Psychology, Agency, and the Unconscious* (Oxford University Press, 2016).

PHILIP KITCHER, the John Dewey Professor of Philosophy at Columbia University, is the author of seventeen books and numerous articles. His most recent books include *Life after Faith: The Case for Secular Humanism* (Yale University

Press, 2014) and, coauthored with Evelyn Fox Keller, *The Seasons Alter: How to Save Our Planet in Six Acts* (Norton/Liveright, 2017).

JEREMY B. LEFKOWITZ is an associate professor of classics at Swarthmore College. He received his PhD from the University of Pennsylvania in classical studies in 2009 and was awarded a Rome Prize from the American Academy in Rome in 2015–16. His recently published work on the ancient fable includes "Grand Allusions: Vergil in Phaedrus" in the *American Journal of Philology* and "Aesop and Animal Fables" in the *Oxford Handbook of Animals in Classical Thought and Life.*

CECILIA MURATORI is a research fellow at the University of Warwick. She is the author of *"The First German Philosopher": The Mysticism of Jakob Böhme as Interpreted by Hegel* (Springer, 2016) and coeditor of *Ethical Perspectives on Animals in the Renaissance and Early Modern Period* (SISMEL, 2013). She is a co-curator of the exhibition *All in All: The Conceptual World of the Mystical Philosopher Jacob Böhme* (Dresden National Museum, 2017).

SABINE OBERMAIER is an associate professor of medieval German literature in the German Department at the Johannes Gutenberg University of Mainz. Her research interests are in Middle High German "poetry on poetry" (*Von Nachtigallen und Handwerkern: Dichtung über Dichtung in Minnesang und Sangspruchdichtung*, Niemayer, 1995); in medieval fables, notably of Indian origin (*Das Fabelbuch als Rahmenerzählung*, Winter, 2004); and in animal lore (*Tiere und Fabelwesen im Mittelalter*, de Gruyter, 2009; the Animaliter Project, and a number of papers on this subject).

ALLEN F. ROBERTS is a professor of world arts and cultures and a coeditor of the journal *African Arts* at UCLA. His books and museum exhibitions include *Animals in African Art* (Prestel, 1995), *Striking Iron: The Art of African Blacksmiths* (forthcoming 2018), and, with Mary Nooter Roberts, *Memory: Luba Art and the Making of History* (Prestel, 1996) and *A Saint in the City: Sufi Arts of Urban Senegal* (UCLA Fowler Museum, 2003).

JAMES SIMPSON is the Donald P. and Katherine B. Loker Professor of English at Harvard University. He was formerly a professor of medieval and Renaissance English at the University of Cambridge. His most recent books are *Reform and Cultural Revolution*, being volume 2 in the *Oxford English Literary History*

(Oxford University Press, 2002), *Burning to Read: English Fundamentalism and Its Reformation Opponents* (Harvard University Press, 2007), and *Under the Hammer: Iconoclasm in the Anglo-American Tradition* (Oxford University Press, 2010). He is currently writing *Permanent Revolution: Surviving the Long English Reformation.*

HELEN STEWARD is a professor of philosophy at the University of Leeds. She is the author of *The Ontology of Mind* (Clarendon Press, 1997) and *A Metaphysics for Freedom* (Oxford University Press, 2012) and has published many articles in the philosophy of action, the philosophy of mind, and in the metaphysical and ontological issues that bear on these areas. She recently completed an AHRC Fellowship on a project entitled "Persons as Animals" and is currently working on the idea of representational content in animal cognition.

HOU-MEI SUNG is the curator of Asian art at the Cincinnati Art Museum. Since receiving her PhD from Case Western Reserve University, she has held positions in museum and academic fields in Asia and the United States. She has organized numerous exhibitions, including *Roaring Tiger, Leaping Carp, Realms of Immortals*, and *Masterpieces of Japanese Art*, and has over fifty publications, including *The Unknown World of the Ming Court Painters* (Liberal Arts Press, 2006), *Decoded Messages: The Symbolic Language of Chinese Animal Painting* (Yale University Press, 2009), and *Forbidden City: Treasures from the Palace Museum, Beijing* (Virginia Museum of Fine Arts, 2014).

JUHANA TOIVANEN is a researcher at the University of Gothenburg and a member of the research program Representation and Reality: Historical and Contemporary Perspectives on the Aristotelian Tradition. He specializes in medieval philosophical psychology and political philosophy. He has published a monograph, *Perception and the Internal Senses* (Brill, 2013), and several articles on medieval philosophy of mind. He is currently working on theories of the internal senses between 1200 and 1350, and also preparing a monograph on medieval conceptions of human sociability.

Animals

OXFORD **PHILOSOPHICAL** CONCEPTS

He who understands baboon would do more towards metaphysics than Locke.
—CHARLES DARWIN

Introduction

Peter Adamson

Recently two humans, Thomas Thwaites and Charles Foster, independently hit upon the idea of trying to live as nonhuman animals, respectively a goat and a badger. They found the task challenging but also life-enhancing: Foster acquired the ability to navigate in the forest by scent alone, while Thwaites actually built prosthetic limbs with which he could navigate hillsides on all fours. They even adopted the diet of their chosen species, though Thwaites found that he had to prepare grass in a pressure cooker to make it edible for his human digestive system. We can't say for certain what Aristotle would make of all this, but it's hard to believe he would be impressed. Paradoxically Aristotle was simultaneously the ancient philosopher most interested in animals at an empirical level and an early proponent of the long-lived assumption that humans, as *rational* animals, are beings of an entirely different order, superior to other living things.[1] Both features of his thought come together when he encourages his reader to investigate and appreciate animals, even if some of them may be "meaner (*atimoteron*)" than others.[2] From Aristotle's point of view, the undertakings of Thwaites and Foster might seem to take the spirit of discovery too far, deliberately identifying themselves with creatures who are worse than they are.

In the popular imagination, the history of philosophy is associated less with the enthusiastic side of Aristotle's approach to animals and more with the disdainful side. This is evident from a recent book entitled *Are We Smart Enough to Know How Smart Animals Are?* by the primate researcher Frans de Waal. In response to what he sees as the tide of philosophical opinion, de Waal tells us about elephants, magpies, and apes who recognize themselves in mirrors, with one ape even using a mirror to clean out her ear with a straw; wasps who can tell each other apart by facial markings; a bird who can fashion a straight wire into a hook for use as a tool; a sea lion who reasons that if A is equivalent to B and B equivalent to C, then A is equivalent to C; the coordinated hunting tactics of eel and coral trout; the ability of the octopus to open screw-top jars; two dolphins who rescue a third from drowning; and a chimpanzee who acts like Dick Cheney (more impressive than it sounds). Any reader will come away from the book astonished by the capacities of animals and disappointed in their fellow humans for failing to appreciate those capacities.

In particular they will be disappointed by humans who lived before Darwin. With the honorable exception of David Hume—who is praised by de Waal for his suggestion that similar animal and human behaviors must spring from the same internal causes—premodern thought about animals is assumed throughout to have been benighted and simplistic. De Waal speaks of a "pre-Darwinian mindset, one uncomfortable with the notion of humans as animals," and remarks that refusing to admit the continuity between animals and humans is "essentially pre-evolutionary."[3] In his eagerness to warn us against underestimating the animals around us, he underestimates the humans of the past.[4] For it turns out that the nature and capacities of animals, and the question of what they share with us, have been contested matters since Aristotle's own day and throughout the history of philosophy.[5]

Nowadays intense philosophical reflection is being devoted to animal cognition, the ethical treatment of animals, and the fact that humans too are animals.[6] But none of this is entirely new. To take the third issue first, ancient and medieval philosophers, far from being "uncomfortable" with admitting the animality of humans, made it central to their anthropology. This went far deeper than the ubiquitous definition of humans as "rational animals." Drawing on ideas in Plato and Aristotle, the lower aspects of the human soul were assumed to be aspects possessed by nonhumans also. Thus the lowest and middle parts of the soul could standardly be called "vegetative" and "animal." The psychological overlap between these different kinds of souls made it easier to conceive of human-animal transmigration, something we readily associate with Indian thought but which is also mentioned several times by Plato. As G. Fay Edwards explains in this volume, some ancient thinkers (like Plutarch) drew what may seem to be the obvious conclusion: in killing an animal, you may be killing a former human, even a reincarnated member of your own family. On the other hand, as Amber Carpenter points out, the philosophical and especially ethical implications of the doctrine are not so clear. Thinking that a chicken may once have been an ancestor of mine could give me a reason not to eat it. Equally it might inspire me to kill the chicken so as to free my ancestor's soul from its unfortunate current incarnation. Still, a belief in transmigration across species does fit well with the idea that humans and animals have very similar souls. Perhaps an animal soul is simply a human soul that is temporarily unable to exercise reason?

This of course brings us to the question of animal cognition and the contrast between rational humans and irrational beasts. There is no denying that this contrast has been a recurrent assumption in the history of philosophy. Particularly notorious is Descartes, who seems to go even further than Aristotle by making animals autonoma with no mental life whatsoever. Again, though, things are not so simple. In antiquity some argued against the Aristotelian and Stoic claim that only humans are capable of reasoning and of language. There are stretches of Porphyry's *On Abstinence from Killing Animals* that read like an ancient Greek version of de Waal's paean to animal intelligence, full of anecdotes about the clever things done by birds (he had a talking pet partridge) and other creatures. In the Islamic world the philosopher al-Rāzī, discussed in Peter Adamson's chapter in this volume, dismissed Galen's claim that animals cannot think, giving the example of a mouse who cunningly dips its tail into a bottle full of oil and then licks the oil off.[7]

As for Descartes, his position was by no means uncontested in his own time. As Deborah Brown discusses in her chapter, it was subjected to "swift and widespread rebuke,"[8] and she mentions other modern figures, such as Montaigne, who could be listed along with Porphyry, al-Rāzī, and Hume as proponents of cognitive sophistication in animals. Brown argues, however, that we should not underestimate Descartes's own contribution to this debate. His sustained defense of the automata theory of animals raises questions about the extent to which human behavior too is automated. In portraying animals as complex machines, Descartes was not so much assigning an unprecedentedly low value to animals as voicing unprecedentedly high expectations about the capabilities of machines.

In fact it would be astonishing if premodern philosophers had been unaware of the complexity of animal behavior.[9] After all, animals were ubiquitous in their societies, not only as house pets (Descartes himself, we are glad to report, had a dog named Monsieur Grat, meaning "Mr. Scratch") but also as livestock, beasts of burden, and so on. How did they explain the impressive feats animals perform on a regular basis, despite their insistence that only humans are rational and can "think"? Effectively there were two strategies: arguing that lower faculties like sense-perception and imagination allow the animal to do more than you might expect, and granting animals additional, higher capacities that still fall short of reason.

A good example of the former strategy would be a passing comment by Dante, who says in his *Convivio* that while animals may seem to talk

or think, actually "they do not possess the power of reason... [but]
merely reproduce what they see and hear."[10] As Devin Henry explains
in this volume, we see something similar in Aristotle, who invokes the
faculty of *phantasia* (usually translated as "imagination," though this is,
in fact, rather too narrow) to explain such phenomena as animal
memory. Here we may see early intimations of the kind of thinking
embodied by "Morgan's Canon." Named after Conwy Lloyd Morgan,
the Canon encourages us to explain animal actions on the basis of
"lower" psychological faculties whenever possible. In this volume
Helen Steward offers a discussion of the powerful criticisms that have
been aimed at this rule and considers whether there is anything still to
be said for it.

Yet the alternative strategy of granting higher faculties to animals was
popular long before the critics of Morgan's Canon came along. A particularly influential contribution was made by Avicenna, who postulated a
capacity called "estimation" (in Arabic *wahm*, translated into Latin as
aestimatio) to explain how animals can perceive and react to nonsensory properties, like the hostility of the wolf noticed by the alarmed
sheep, an example mentioned in several chapters in this volume. It is
worth noting that, according to Avicenna and the many thinkers in the
Islamic and Latin Christian worlds who followed his lead, this same
faculty is also possessed by humans. Functionally speaking, a similar
role was played in the nineteenth century by the concept of drive or
instinct. Paul Katsafanas's piece is devoted to this notion and further
undermines any neat division of philosophy about animals into two periods, before and after the advent of Darwinism. In fact the idea of
drives had already emerged in eighteenth-century philosophy, paving
the way for more gradualist ideas about the relationship between human
and animal—not only because humans too have drives but also because
drive-motivated activities may involve various sorts of cognition, something incompatible with Cartesian automatism about animals.

Again, though, we should be wary of assuming that gradualism, the
admission of continuity between animals and other classes of being,

emerged only in the past two centuries. At the lower end Aristotle already recognized the difficulty of differentiating between plants and animals: there are some rudimentary animals that lack most of the senses and the capacity for locomotion. He was more optimistic about drawing a firm line at the upper limit, refusing to grant animals what Henry here calls "full-blown rationality." But later thinkers in the Aristotelian tradition worried about intermediate cases. A particularly odd example is the supposed "pygmys" discussed by Albert the Great, which appears in the paper by Juhana Toivanen. The same dilemma was posed again when Europeans discovered the New World and encountered cannibals: Were these individuals to be conceptualized as human or animal? By exploring this blurry border in her chapter, Cecilia Muratori gives us further evidence that, as she puts it, "well before Descartes the question of whether there is a radical differentiation or elements of continuity between humans and animals was a topic of debate."

Of course these questions about the human-animal divide have practical implications and consequences. Historically humans have frequently justified violence and enslavement of other humans on the basis that their victims are "barbaric" or less than fully rational. It has been even easier to extend the same rationale to animals. Clearly the rise of gradualism has put pressure on this way of thinking. As Philip Kitcher remarks in his chapter, once we are convinced of the continuity between animal and human, we should be encouraged to "expand the moral community" to include nonhumans. The current debate as to just how, and why, we should do this is discussed by Robert Garner, who shows how such disparate moral and political theories as utilitarianism, contractarianism, and interest-based ethics have been brought to bear on the issue. It seems fair to say that nowadays the question is not *whether* animals have any moral claim on us but rather *how much* of a moral claim they have. In particular Garner considers whether there can be any sound basis for putting a higher moral value on human life and interests than we put on animal life and interests. Some philosophers do

so, he tells us, on the grounds that animals are not persons, or have no—
or reduced—rights, while other philosophers argue that like interests of
humans and animals should be given equal consideration.

But again, these are not entirely new developments. The eighteenth-
century utilitarian Francis Hutcheson proposed that animals may have
rights, as Patrick Kain discusses in his chapter. And already in antiquity
contractualism was a context for discussion of animal ethics. Admittedly
this discussion was one intended to justify the killing of animals: some
Hellenistic philosophers (mentioned and criticized by Porphyry) contended that the inability of animals to make binding agreements puts
them outside considerations of justice. On the other side of the debate,
a variety of reasons were given for vegetarianism and, in general, better
treatment of animals. Both Edwards and Carpenter show that, while an
appreciation of animals' cognitive abilities may have played some role in
antique debates, it was not necessarily the central consideration. Jain
and Buddhist monks avoided harming animals in pursuit of the broader
virtue of nonviolence (*ahiṃsā*), while a Platonist might adopt vegetarianism simply to weaken the body's influence on his soul. Several remarkable discussions from the medieval Islamic world are similar, in
that they offer a surprising rationale for benevolence toward animals,
namely that we should show providential care and mercy to them in
imitation of God's treatment of us.

Between these ancient and medieval discussions on the one hand,
and Darwinian gradualism on the other, the most notable figure in
animal ethics is inevitably the most notable figure in ethics full stop:
Immanuel Kant. Kain offers a correction to the standard picture of
Kant's stance on animals. According to the usual reading, since Kant
denies that irrational creatures can be "ends in themselves," we can have
no duties to animals, and the only reason to treat them well is as a kind
of training for ourselves. According to this "brutalization argument," a
person who beats his neighbor's dog may wind up beating his neighbor, and this is why we should discourage people from beating dogs.
Kain, however, points out that, for Kant, animals do "engage morally

significant feelings," not just because they are aesthetically pleasing and impressive but because they can suffer. This stops short of allowing that we have full-blown duties *to* animals as opposed to duties *regarding* animals. Yet our moral reactions to them are grounded in their natures and capacities, not only in our own need to develop good moral habits.

Before we dismiss as retrograde Kant's denial that we have duties *to* animals, we should reflect on the fact that, for Kant, having a duty to someone implies that that someone is also a moral agent, and then ask ourselves whether animals can be such agents. (This is closely related to the aforementioned question of whether animals are persons.) We might say that a dog is cowardly or a fox sneaky, but normally we do not assign moral blame when we do so. Why not? A common assumption throughout the history of philosophy is that animals immediately respond to their environment without pausing for evaluation or forward planning—and this has often been deemed necessary for moral responsibility. Indeed even al-Rāzī, of the mouse-tail-in-oil example, urges humans not to be like animals who immediately pursue any pleasure put before them.

In fact, though, this assumption is false: experiments have shown that many animals are capable of deferring self-gratification for the sake of a later reward. Yet the idea that animals are not moral agents is one of the last redoubts of nongradualism. Even a fervent proponent of animals' cognitive sophistication and moral worth may hesitate to claim that animals can themselves be morally responsible for what they do. Certainly the vast majority of philosophers covered in this book would consider humans unique among animals in this respect. When these philosophers advise us not to act like animals (as they frequently do), they are not necessarily telling us not to be stupid or crude but are rather telling us to live up to ideals to which animals are simply not held.[11] Indeed all the thinkers in this book have lived up to at least one such ideal—for humans philosophize about animals, but as far as we know, they do not philosophize about us.[12]

CHAPTER ONE

Aristotle on Animals

Devin Henry

ANIMAL PSYCHOLOGY

Animals are living things, and Aristotle takes living things to be primary examples of "natural" substances.[1] A natural substance, according to Aristotle, is a substance that has within itself a principle of change and rest (or "nature"), which is an intrinsic cause of its characteristic patterns of behavior (*Physics* II 1). In *Physics* II 2 Aristotle argues that each natural substance has two natures, a material nature and a formal nature, and that it is the job of the natural scientist to investigate both (194a12–15). The formal nature of a living thing is its soul (*Parts of Animals*, I 1, 641a21–27), which Aristotle treats as a set of capacities that the living body has for executing various kinds of life functions. Together these capacities constitute the essence of a living thing (*On the Soul*, II 1). According to *On the Soul*, the animal soul is constituted by two main parts. The souls of nonhuman animals have (1) a nutritive part, which houses their metabolic and reproductive functions, and (2) a sensory part, which constitutes their essence (it is what makes a living thing an animal). Human souls include, in addition, (3) a rational part that sets them apart from all other animals.[2] However, unlike the Stoics, Aristotle assigned to the sensory part of the soul a wide range of complex psychological functions and so was able to afford even nonhuman animals a rich cognitive life. In this section I want to set out the basic architecture of the animal soul before going on, in the next section, to reflect on how Aristotle thinks the lack of reason impacts the moral status of animals other than humans.

First, all animals have the capacity for sense-perception. Sense-perception by definition has three kinds of object: proper sensibles, common sensibles, and so-called incidental sensibles (*On the Soul*, II 6). Proper sensibles are properties that can affect only a single sense modality (color for vision, odor for smell, sound for hearing, etc.) and where no error is possible, while common sensibles are those that can affect, and so are common to, multiple senses (number, shape, size, motion and rest). Aristotle says that of these first two kinds of sensible each is perceptible "in virtue of itself" (418a8–9). By contrast, incidental sensibles are not perceived in themselves but only in virtue of being "accidents" of things that are directly sensible. It is not entirely clear what Aristotle means by incidental sensibles or what the nature of incidental perceiving turns out to be.[3] What we are told is this:

> I call a sense object incidental, e.g., if the white thing is the son of Diares. For one perceives this incidentally because what is perceived [the son of Diares] belongs to the white thing only incidentally, and that is why [the sense] is not affected by the sense object insofar as it is that sort of thing. (*On the Soul*, 418a20–24)

The second sentence can be glossed by saying that sight is not affected by the sense object seen because it is the son of Diares but because it is white. In other words, Aristotle thinks I do perceive the son of Diares, but I perceive this object not in virtue of that property but in virtue of its color, which directly activates my senses. It is in this sense that Aristotle says of proper and common sensibles that each one is perceptible "in virtue of itself," while the other is perceived only "incidentally," namely, because what is perceived in this case (the son of Diares) is also accidentally something white (cf. 425a24–28). What is important for my purposes is that Aristotle treats incidental perception as an act of perception and not an inference; it is an affection of the sensory rather than rational part of the soul. This allows nonhuman animals, despite lacking the rational part, to have incidental perceptions so that the content of their experience is not limited to what is immediately given in sensation.[4] A lion tracking a gazelle across the savannah does not just see a brown shape in motion but sees food, prey, or even a gazelle. This is, of course, controversial. But Aristotle nowhere says that incidental perceiving requires rationality of any sort.[5]

Aristotle also affords some animals a function he calls *phantasia*, which is a capacity for producing, storing, and recalling mental images.[6] In *On the Soul* III 3, he describes *phantasia* as that capacity in virtue of which things appear to an agent (428a1–2). Aristotle not only includes under this description the sorts of appearances that arise in the absence of external stimuli (e.g., images that occur in dreams) but also those we experience under normal perceptual conditions (e.g., he attributes the fact that the sun appears to be a foot in diameter to *phantasia*, 428b3–4). Although it is often translated simply as "imagination," some scholars (not unreasonably) characterize *phantasia* more broadly as a capacity for mental representation.

Now Aristotle denies that *phantasia* is a function of reason, including belief.[7] While he insists that thinking requires mental images (*On the Soul*, 431a14–9, 431b2–10; *On Memory*, 449b31–450a1), the ability to generate, store, and manipulate them does not belong to the rational part of the soul. Aristotle holds this position on the grounds that some nonhuman animals possess *phantasia*, despite lacking the rational part of the soul. But he also denies that *phantasia* is identical with sense-perception. For example, when I form an image in my mind of a fox wearing socks and attend to his orange fur and blue socks, I do not literally *see* the image. For, properly speaking, sensations occur when my sense organs are acted on by the sensible properties of external objects. However, *phantasia* is a function of the sensory part of the soul (*On Dreams* I) and has its causal history in immediate sense-perceptions (*On the Soul*, III 3, 429a2–3). When an animal perceives a sensible object, that object sets up a "motion" in its sense organs, which travels down to the primary sense organ where it generates perception (see *On Sleep*, e.g. 455b10–11, and *On Dreams*). In animals with *phantasia* a second "motion" arises alongside the original, which is retained by the sense organ. These "residual motions" are stored and can be redeployed later in the form of mental images of the original sense object (e.g., as in dreams or memory).[8]

Phantasia makes possible a whole host of other cognitive activities that enrich the mental lives of the animals that have them. Most important among these is memory. Aristotle is explicit that some non-human animals have the capacity to form memories, and so their encounter with the world is not limited to the present (*On Memory*, 450a15–22).[9] For those that lack this additional psychological function the world just disappears when their senses shut off. Such animals, Aristotle says, have no knowledge outside sense-perception:

> In those animals that have sense-perception, in some not only does a sense-perception arise but it is also retained, while in others it is not retained. In those where the sense-perception is not retained there is no knowledge[10] outside of sense-perception (either no knowledge at all or none concerning the part that is not retained). But some can still hold it in their soul even after perceiving them. When this occurs, there is then a further difference: in some an account (*logos*) comes to be out of the retained sense-perceptions, while in others it does not. (*Posterior Analytics*, II 19, 99b36–100a3)

The last part of this text refers to the capacity that some animals have to systematize their memories into what Aristotle calls an "experience" (*empeiria*): "Thus from sense-perception comes memory (as we call it) and from many memories of the same item comes experience; for memories that are many in number form a single experience" (100a3–4; see also *Metaphysics* I 1, 980b29–981a12). According to Alexander of Aphrodisias, Aristotle denies that nonhuman animals have the ability to develop experiences since they lack reason (*On Aristotle Metaphysics*, 4, 15–7). "For experience," he says, "is already rational knowledge of some sort" (4, 23). Yet in *Metaphysics* I 1, Aristotle explicitly says that nonhumans do have "a small share in experience" (980b26), which I take to mean they have a limited share in it.

Imagine a young rabbit that is attacked by an owl for the first time. Since rabbits have *phantasia*, the perception of this event is retained in the rabbit's soul as a memory image whose content corresponds to that particular event. Over time the rabbit comes to acquire more memories of the same kind representing different attacks by different owls. If I am right, then Aristotle thinks that the rabbit has the cognitive machinery necessary to connect those many memories into a single mental representation of owls as predators.[11] In what sense is this experience limited? While Aristotle does not say, it will at least be limited in the sense that it does not involve the sort of universals required for scientific understanding and craftsmanship.[12] For he denies that nonhuman animals are capable of grasping universals.[13] For this reason the content of the rabbit's experience (whatever it includes) will be substantially different from that of a human being. It is only in the case of human beings that experience leads to the kind of grasp of universals that is necessary for science and the productive arts (*Posterior Analytics*, II 19, 100a3–b5). This requires what Aristotle calls *nous*, which is a state of the rational part of the soul.

The capacity for sense-perception, which all animals have, also entails desire (*orexis*) and a sense of pleasure and pain (*On the Soul*, 414b1–6,

431a8–14). Now Aristotle typically distinguishes three forms of desire: (1) sensual appetite (*epithumia*), (2) wish (*boulēsis*), and (3) decision (*proairesis*). Appetite is a non-rational desire for food, drink, and sex, while wish and decision are both types of rational desire that are directed toward an agent's conception of the good. Wish is a desire for certain ends—ultimately for happiness, which Aristotle thinks is the supreme end of all our actions—while decision is a desire to execute those actions that deliberation has shown to be the best means for achieving those ends (*Nicomachean Ethics*, 1111b26–29, 1113a14, *Eudemian Ethics*, 1226b7–17, *Magna Moralia*, 1189a7–11).[14] Aristotle says:

> Since the object of a decision, which is desired as a result of deliberation, is among the things that are up to us, decision turns out to be a deliberative desire for things that are up to us; for when we have decided [to do X] as a result of deliberation, we desire [to do X] in accordance with our wish [for Y]. (*Nicomachean Ethics*, II 2, 1113a9–12).[15]

Since wish and decision are the province of reason, and since Aristotle denies reason to nonhuman animals, it follows that only humans are capable of these kinds of desire. Nonhuman animals, though they have appetites, are incapable of having wishes and making decisions about how best to satisfy them.

While Aristotle went quite far in affording nonhuman animals such complex cognitive resources, and though (as we shall see) he has much to say about animal intelligence, especially in the biological works, he is categorical that they lack reason. Only humans have the rational part of the soul, which incorporates various mental functions such as discursive thinking (*dianoia*), abstract thought (*nous, noeisis*), deliberation (*boulēsis*), practical wisdom (*phronēsis*), and calculation (*logismon*). Aristotle even denies that nonhuman animals have the ability to form beliefs (*doxa*) (e.g., *On the Soul*, III 3, 428a18–24)[16] As we shall see, all of this has significant implications for his views about the moral status of nonhuman animals.

ARISTOTLE'S ETHOLOGY

In *History of Animals* VIII Aristotle outlines his view of animal behavior. According to this view, "the behavior of all animals, including humans, is determined by a set of dispositions that collectively determine how the animal's capacities for feeling and doing will be exercised on a given occasion."[17] Aristotle refers to these dispositions collectively as states of character and argues that the same sorts of character traits can be found in human and nonhuman animals alike (588a17–b3, translated below). Some of these are states that the ethical works identify as moral virtues and vices (e.g., courage, cowardice, spiritedness). Perhaps even more surprising is the fact that in the biological works Aristotle appears to have no trouble ascribing various rational capacities to nonhuman animals, including practical wisdom, sagacity, and intelligence.[18]

Aristotle's student Theophrastus took this seriously and argued that nonhuman animals are akin to humans in their ability to engage in reasoning (Theophrastus ap. Porphyry, *On Abstinence*, 3.25).[19] I shall return to Theophrastus below. For now we can simply note that if, in assigning reasoning to animals, Theophrastus intends to make animals rational, then he explicitly contradicts his teacher. For in the *History of Animals* Aristotle is clear that when he does speak of animal intelligence he is talking about something that is only analogous to human reason:

Some of these traits differ relative to humans by the more and less, in the sense that humans exhibit them to a greater extent relative to animals (for some of these sorts of things are present more in humans, some more in the other animals), while others differ by means of analogy. For example, just as we find skill, wisdom, and sagacity in humans, so too in some of the animals there is some other natural capacity of this sort. (*History of Animals*, VIII, 588a21–26)

This is an important qualification. Aristotle remains consistent throughout that nonhuman animals lack reason. Instead what they have is "some other natural capacity" that is only *analogous* to reason. They are analogous, I want to suggest, in that both cause behavior exhibiting the same teleological (means-end) structure.

In the *Physics*, Aristotle argues that all goal-directed processes, whether natural or the result of skill, exhibit the same teleological structure where the intermediate steps occur for the sake of the end that results (199a9–19). "This is most obvious," he says, "in animals other than humans; for they make things neither by skill nor as a result of inquiry and deliberation, which is why people wonder whether it is by reason or some other capacity that these animals work, e.g. spiders, ants, and the like" (199a20–24). Consider the spider. The purpose of her web is obviously to catch bugs; that is its end. When she constructs her web, the intermediate steps she performs are organized for the sake of that end. But this means-end structure is not the product of deliberation; the spider does not literally calculate how best to achieve that end. Rather, Aristotle thinks, her goal-directed behaviors are caused by a certain natural capacity that is the counterpart of human reason. On this reading the "practical wisdom" of nonhuman animals is analogous to human practical wisdom because it causes behavior with the same means-end structure.

But Aristotle does think that nonhuman animals possess some states of character that, in humans, are associated with ethical virtues (e.g., courage, anger, spiritedness).[20] They simply differ by degree "in the sense that humans exhibit them to a greater extent relative to animals (for some of these sorts of things are present more in humans, some more in the other animals)." However, even in these cases Aristotle denies that the states of character possessed by nonhuman animals qualify as genuine virtues. Instead he refers to them as the "traces and seeds" of virtues:

The actions and ways of life of animals differ according to their character and food. Even in the majority of other [sc. nonhuman] animals there are traces of the modes connected with the soul, which are more clearly differentiated in humans. For just as we pointed to resemblances in the organs, so in a number of animals we find in them cultivation and wildness, gentleness and harsh temperament, courage and cowardice, fear and confidence, spirit and roguishness, and, concerning intelligence, sagacity. Some of these traits differ relative to humans by the more and less, i.e. humans exhibit them to a greater extent relative to animals (for some of these sorts of things are present more in humans, some more in the other animals), with others differing by means of analogy, e.g. just as there is skill, wisdom, and sagacity in humans, so too in some of the animals there is some other natural capacity of this sort. This sort of thing is most evident when we consider the case of children when they are young. For in children it is possible to see traces and seeds (*ichnē kai spermata*) of what will later become fixed states of character, though at that time their soul hardly differs from that of the beasts, so that it is not unreasonable if some traits are identical in the other animals, some nearly the same, while others are present only by analogy. (*History of Animals*, VIII, 588a17–b3)[21]

Again in *History of Animals* IX 1 Aristotle says:

These latter animals appear to have a certain natural capacity corresponding to each affection of the soul—to practical wisdom and guilelessness, courage and cowardice, gentleness and harsh temperament, and to other sorts of character states. Some also have a share in learning and teaching, some from one another and others from humans, namely, those that have the ability to hear, and not merely those that can hear sounds but those that can distinguish the difference between signs.... The traces of these character states are more or less visible everywhere, but they are most conspicuous where character is more developed, and most of all in humans. For the nature of humans is most perfect, and consequently the above states of character are most conspicuous in them. (608a12–17, b5–8)[22]

Both children and nonhuman animals are said to possess the "traces and seeds" of virtue; however, in the latter case they do not develop into genuine virtue. Why not? To answer this we need to turn to the *Ethics*.[23]

In *Nicomachean Ethics* VI 13, Aristotle tells us that virtues of character exist in two stages of development: natural virtue and full-fledged virtue. The natural virtues, which are said to be present in children and nonhuman animals from birth, seem to correspond to those natural capacities that *History of Animals* VIII refers to as the "traces and seeds" of virtue. The *Nicomachean Ethics* discussion fills out the *History of Animals* picture by adding that, in the case of humans, the natural virtues develop into full-fledged virtues because humans have practical wisdom:

> In all of us each of the states of character are present somehow by nature; for we have just, temperate, courageous, and other such states of character already from birth. But, nevertheless, we are investigating something else, what is good in the proper sense (*to kuriōs agathon*), and the sorts of states that are present in another way. For the natural states of character are present even in children and beasts, but without reason they appear to be harmful. But this much seems clear, that just as a strong body moving without sight can happen to take a strong fall because of the lack of sight, so too here. If, however, a person acquires intelligence, it makes a difference to his actions; for the disposition that is like virtue [sc. natural virtue] will at that point be virtue proper. So, just as there are two species of belief, cleverness and practical wisdom, so there are two species of virtue in our character, natural virtue and virtue proper, and virtue proper does not arise without practical wisdom. (1144b3–17)

According to Aristotle's picture, then, some animals have from birth a natural disposition toward justice, temperance, courage, and so forth. He is clear that these dispositions develop into full virtue only in human beings, however, because only human beings have practical wisdom, which is necessary for the perfection of virtue proper.[24]

ANIMAL LOCOMOTION AND VOLUNTARY ACTION

The final capacity of the animal soul to discuss is that of locomotion. Aristotle treats the ability to move from place to place as an essential part of the animal soul: "The soul of animals is defined by two capacities: the capacity for judgment, which is the work of thought and sense-perception; and the capacity for locomotion" (*On the Soul*, III 9, 432a15–17). The basic psychological causes of animal motion are the same for human and nonhuman animals. The object of desire is either directly perceived by the animal or else represented to it as a thought or mental image (phantasma).[25] The perception, thought, or image of the object then triggers the faculty of desire, which in turn causes the animal to move. Aristotle develops this model of animal motion in *On the Soul*, III 9–11 and *Movement of Animals*, 6–7.

It is clear that these two factors, desire and thought, are responsible for producing motion, if, that is, one posits *phantasia* as a kind of thinking process. For men often follow the appearances (*phantasiai*) contrary to knowledge, and in nonhuman animals there is neither thinking (*noēsis*) nor calculation (logismos), but only *phantasia*. Both of these, then, thought and desire, have the capacity to effect movement. [In the case of humans] the thought in question is the practical mind, which calculates for the sake of something....And every desire is for the sake of something; for the thing at which desire aims is the starting-point of the practical mind, while the last step [in deliberation] is a starting-point of action. So these two, desire and practical thinking, appear quite reasonably to be the things responsible for initiating movement. For the object of desire effects motion, and on account of this thought moves the agent because the object of desire is the starting-point of this. But *phantasia*, too, when it causes motion, does not effect motion without desire. That which moves, then, is a single capacity, namely, desire. (*On the Soul*, III 10, 433a10–21)

We see that the things that move the animal are thought, *phantasia*, decision, wish, and appetite. All of these are reducible to thought or desire. For both *phantasia* and sense-perception cover the same ground as mind, since they are all faculties of judgment (though differing according to distinctions stated elsewhere).[26] And wish, spirit, and appetite are all forms of desire, while decision is something common to intellect and desire (*Movement of Animals*, 6, 700b16–25).[27]

When a lion encounters a gazelle, perception directly triggers the appetite, which moves the animal toward the object. No thought processes intervene. While humans may also act immediately on perception or appearance, thought can also trigger movement. In these cases the object of desire is first set up in the mind as a goal to be achieved, which forms the starting point of deliberation. The practical mind then calculates the best means of acquiring that object. The conclusion of this process is a decision—a rational desire—which then moves the agent. In both cases the object of desire moves the animal as a final cause, while desire (which is "primed" by sense-perception, thought, or *phantasia*) moves it as an efficient cause.

Despite the fact that Aristotle compares the motion of animals to automatons (*Movement of Animals*, 7), which may give the impression that he thinks of them as mere machines in the Cartesian sense,[28] he is explicit that nonhuman animals are capable of acting voluntarily (*Movement of Animals*, 11, 703b2–4; *Nicomachean Ethics*, III 2, 1111a25–26, b6–9). This makes them responsible for their movements in a more robust sense than inanimate objects. While the fire may be causally responsible for the blaze, it does not do so voluntarily. By contrast, when a tiger kills a chimpanzee Aristotle thinks there is a real sense in which her actions are voluntary.

Now, on Aristotle's account, in order for an action to be considered voluntary it must satisfy two conditions: (i) the origin (*archē*) of the action must be "internal" to the agent,[29] and (ii) the agent must know (*eidoti*) the particulars surrounding the action (*Nicomachean Ethics*, III 1, 1111a3–21). Aristotle's account of animal motion helps explain why he thinks the behavior of nonhuman animals satisfies these conditions. Consider our tiger again. There is a sense in which she knows the particulars of the situation insofar as Aristotle treats sense-perception and *phantasia* as a kind of knowledge (432a15–17, 433a10–13; cf. *On Generation of Animals*, I 23, 731a34): she perceives (via the common sense: *On the Soul*, III 1–2) that she herself is a tiger; she correctly represents (via *phantasia*) the animal she is stalking as food rather than, say, her cub; and she grasps (via memory and experience) that biting its throat will kill it (cf. 1111a3–20). So there is a sense in which she knows what she is doing when she acts. Second, the causes of her movements are various internal mental states—her perception (or *phantasia*) of the chimp and the desire it triggered—which satisfies the first condition: the origin of her action was "internal" to her.[30]

While Aristotle is explicit that nonhuman animals are capable of voluntary movements, their behavior does not count as "action" (*praxis*) in the robust sense. An action, in this sense, is a voluntary behavior that expresses the agent's decision to pursue a certain end, and decision, Aristotle says, "is not shared by things that lack reason" (*Nicomachean Ethics*, III 2, 1111b12–13). As we have seen, a decision is a rational desire formed on the basis of deliberation. Since nonhuman animals lack reason, they do not have the ability to engage in the kind of means-end reasoning process that issues in a decision.[31] Therefore they cannot be said to act. We attribute *praxis* to adult humans alone: "Humans, when they reach a certain age, have both [sc. reason and desire], to which we assign the ability to act. For we do not use this term of children or beasts but only of the human being who acts through calculation" (*Eudemian Ethics*, 1224a27–30). For this reason Aristotle denies that nonhuman animals can be happy (in his technical sense). While horses and dogs may be able to achieve some kind of well-being that is proper to their species, this well-being does not raise them to the level of true happiness.

Aristotle, we have seen, accepts that the dog who bites a child does so voluntarily, even if its conduct does not count as action in the full sense. But does he think the dog is morally responsible for its behavior such that its conduct warrants blame? There are two ways to interpret Aristotle on this question. On one reading, Aristotle has a rather thin concept of moral responsibility that equates it with voluntary conduct.[32] On this reading an agent is morally responsible for doing X just in case X was done voluntarily. Aristotle does give some indication that voluntariness is necessary and sufficient for praise and blame, and therefore for moral responsibility. For example, in *Nicomachean Ethics* III, he says that praise and blame are bestowed only on voluntary behavior, while involuntary behavior is excused or pitied (1109b30–35; cf. 1110a31–32). Again in *Nicomachean Ethics* V, he says that what makes an action right or wrong is determined by its voluntariness or involuntariness: "for when it is voluntary it is blamed and is, at the same time, an unjust action" (1135a19–21). On the thin version of the concept, then, nonhuman animals can be held morally responsible for their conduct, and thus merit praise or blame, to the extent that they are in control of their behavior.

Others argue that Aristotle has a more robust concept of moral responsibility that excludes the behavior of nonhuman animals. Alexander, for example, argues that moral responsibility requires the conduct in question to be "up to" the agent and claims that this applies only to rational agents. Specifically he thinks this requires that the agent have the power to deliberate between alternatives[33] and decide whether or not to perform the action:

> For activities that are "up to" the agent are only found among those things that come to be in accordance with a rational (*logikēn*) impulse. And rational impulse only occurs in things capable of deliberation and decision, that is, in the impulse of human beings when it comes to

be as a result of those things. For the activities of other creatures that are done in accordance with impulse are not like this because with them it is no longer the case that they have the power of also not doing the activity that is according to impulse. (*On Fate*, 33, 205, 16–206, 5)

More recently Susan Meyer has argued that the Aristotelian concept of moral responsibility is even richer than this. On her reading, Aristotle holds that the only agents who merit praise or blame, and are thus morally responsible for what they do, are those whose features properly subject them to the demands, expectations, and evaluations of morality.[34] One of these is that the agent be capable of voluntary action. But not all voluntary agents are morally responsible for their voluntary actions. Those actions must also flow from a virtuous or vicious character: "Briefly put, Aristotle thinks we are morally responsible for all and only those actions of which our moral character is the cause."[35] Since, as we have seen, nonhuman animals are incapable of developing virtues and vices (even if they possess the "traces and seeds" of them), they are not properly subject to the demands, expectations, and evaluations of morality.

THEOPHRASTUS ON THE ETHICAL TREATMENT OF ANIMALS

Aristotle does not have a lot to say about our moral responsibilities toward nonhuman animals, but he does make at least two passing remarks that are of some relevance to the topic. First, he denies that there can be either friendship or justice between humans and nonhuman animals because we share nothing in common with them (*Nicomachean Ethics*, VIII 11, 1161a31–b3). Second, and more importantly, he argues on teleological grounds that we are justified in hunting animals and otherwise using them as we see fit, whether for food, for clothing, or as tools:

> In a like manner we may infer that, after the birth of animals, plants exist for their sake, and that the other animals exist for the sake of

humans, the domesticated for their use and food, and the wild ones, if not all of them, then at least the majority of them, for their food and clothing and various tools. Now if nature makes nothing incomplete or in vain, the inference must be that all animals exist for the sake of humans. So, from one perspective, the art of war is a natural art of acquisition, for the art of acquisition includes hunting, which we ought to practice against wild animals, and against men who, though intended by nature to be governed, will not submit to rule; for war of such a kind is naturally just. (*Politics* I 8, 1256b15–25)

Writing in the context of the ethics of animal sacrifice, Aristotle's associate Theophrastus argues against this position on a variety of grounds.[36] For example, he claims that sacrificing animals is unjust and impious because it causes them harm insofar as it deprives them of life (and presumably we have a moral obligation not to harm other living things). Moreover, if someone should object (along the lines of *Politics* I 8) that the gods gave us animals for the sake of our personal use, Theophrastus argues that it is still wrong because it is impious to harm the property of another (the gods):

For nothing ought to be so noxious to all things as sacrifice. But if someone should object that the gods gave animals to us for our use, no less than the fruits of the earth, it does not follow that they are, therefore, to be sacrificed. Because in so doing they are harmed inasmuch as it deprives them of life. For sacrifice…is something pious. But no one acts piously who extracts a benefit from things that are the property of another, whether he takes fruits or plants from one who is unwilling to be deprived of them. For how can this be pious when those from whom they are taken are harmed? (Theophrastus ap. Porphyry, *On Abstinence*, 2.12.13 ff.)[37]

By contrast, Theophrastus argues that when we eat fruit we do not thereby deprive the plant of life. For we typically do not kill plants by taking their fruit. Moreover when we sacrifice animals or use them for food the animals are unwilling participants in the act (and presumably we have a moral obligation not to do something to another living thing against its will).[38] But, again, when we take fruit it is not given unwillingly, since the plant would have dropped it anyway.[39]

Finally, Theophrastus argues that, pace Aristotle, there is something common between humans and nonhuman animals and so there can and ought to be justice between us. This is perhaps the most important argument. Theophrastus holds that humans are closely akin to and have an affinity with nonhuman animals in two respects. First, we share our proximate matter in common insofar as our bodies are composed of the same basic tissues (flesh, bone, sinew, etc.). Second, and more important, humans and animals share several soul functions in common, including reasoning and calculation:

The principles of the bodies of all animals are naturally the same. I do not mean the first elements of their bodies [sc. earth, air, fire, water], since plants also consist of these; rather, I mean the seed, flesh, and class of connate humors that is inherent in animals. But animals [including humans] are much more allied to each other through naturally possessing souls that are not different from each other, I mean in appetite and anger, and besides these, in reasonings, and, above all, in the senses. But just as with their bodies, so too with respect to their souls, some animals have them more, but others less perfect, yet all of them have naturally the same principles.[40] And this is evident from the affinity of their passions. If, however, what we have said is true, that the genesis of the character of animals is of this sort, then the whole race of them exhibits intelligence, but they differ both in terms of their training and in the blend of their primary elements. And if this be admitted, the genus of other animals has an affinity and is allied to us.... Hence, since animals are allied to us, if it should appear, according to Pythagoras, that they are allotted the same soul that we are, he may justly be considered as impious who does not abstain from acting unjustly towards his kindred. (Theophrastus ap. Porphyry, *On Abstinence*, 3.25)

Sorabji takes the key claim here to be that animals enjoy a natural kinship with us because they can engage in reasoning and so should be afforded the same ethical considerations as all rational beings.[41]

But, as we have seen, Aristotle is also willing to talk about animal intelligence without implying that animals have reason. When the spider constructs her web or the sparrow builds his nest, Aristotle freely speaks of them as exercising practical wisdom, cleverness, and sagacity. Yet he is explicit that their behavior is the effect of "some other natural capacity" that is only the analogue of human reason. They do not possess rationality in the proper sense. There is no reason to suppose that Theophrastus contradicted Aristotle on this front. (There is certainly no textual evidence to suggest that he thinks nonhuman animals also have the rational part of the soul.) Nor does he need to ascribe them rationality for his affinity argument to go through. For among those "common" features that Aristotle recognizes are those that are common by analogy (*Parts of Animals*, 645b27). Thus when Theophrastus says that the whole race of animals are akin to one another because they share reasoning in common, he could still hold, as Aristotle does, that the intelligence of nonhuman animals is only analogous to human reason. This may be a strong enough affinity in his mind to justify extending moral considerations to them without having to afford them full-blown rationality.

CHAPTER TWO

Reincarnation, Rationality, and Temperance

PLATONISTS ON NOT EATING ANIMALS

G. Fay Edwards

The two figures that come most immediately to mind when considering what Platonists have to say about animals are Plutarch and Porphyry.[1] Like many philosophers before them, both of these Platonists were vegetarian, but unlike their predecessors, each sets out numerous arguments in favor of the practice in their writings.

These arguments are many and varied. We are told that we should be vegetarian because killing and eating animals makes us more likely to kill and eat human beings, because human beings may reincarnate as animals, because animals are rational creatures that are owed moral consideration from humans, and because meat-eating has negative effects on the bodies and souls of human meat-eaters. Notably, while in some cases meat-eating is presented as wrong because of what it does to animals, in others it is so only because of what it does to human beings. The different arguments thus paint quite different pictures concerning the place of animals in Platonist thought.

In this chapter I analyze several core arguments for vegetarianism that are given by Plutarch[2] and Porphyry and suggest that these thinkers are, in fact, more concerned about the effect that meat-eating has on human beings than they are about the effect that it has on nonhuman animals. If I am right about this, it means that although their position certainly results in practical recommendations surrounding the treatment of animals, it is wrong to suppose, as some have, that these Platonists are particularly sympathetic toward the animals themselves.

REINCARNATION: VEGETARIANISM FOR THE SAKE OF OTHER HUMANS

By the third century AD, vegetarianism seems to have become something of a hallmark of Platonism, with several prominent Platonists—including Xenocrates, Polemo,[3] Plutarch, Plotinus,[4] and Porphyry—having adopted a vegetarian diet on philosophical grounds. In adopting this diet, they consider themselves to be continuing an ancient and pious tradition, which goes right back to the first humans in the "golden age" of humankind.

This mythical period of human history, first mentioned by Hesiod in *Works and Days* (lines 109–20),[5] is said to have been a time, long ago, during which people lived an idyllic existence in peace and harmony and the earth produced food for them in abundance without the need for labor on the land or competition for resources. The people of this time reportedly neither killed nor ate animals and offered only bloodless sacrifice to the gods (Plutarch, *On Flesh-Eating*, 993ac; Porphyry, *On Abstinence*, 1.13.1–5, 3.27.10, 4.2.1–6; Plato, *Laws*, 782c).[6] Since these ancient people are regarded as models of piety by later thinkers, their adoption of a vegetarian diet is taken to be a strong point in its favor (Porphyry, *On Abstinence*, 1.13.1–5). Yet little in what is said suggests that these people were vegetarian out of a concern for animals. Instead they seem to have been vegetarian because the abundance of plant food made it unnecessary for them to eat animals to survive,[7] and to have avoided animal sacrifice because they regarded blood as unsanitary and thus not fit as an offering to a deity (Plato, *Laws*, 782c; cf. *Cratylus*, 397e–8b).

Although not part of the golden age themselves, the pre-Socratic philosophers Pythagoras and Empedocles are presented as having returned to its ancient and pious ways by refraining from eating, and discouraging the killing of, animals.[8] Again these thinkers are so revered by the Greeks of antiquity that their mere adherence to a vegetarian diet is regarded as a point in its favor (Porphyry, *On Abstinence*, 1.26.2–3). Their names repeatedly arise in Plutarch's and Porphyry's texts as philosophers whom the Platonists take themselves to be emulating.

We are given more information about why these philosophers were vegetarian than we are about the people of the golden age. One reason, which is attributed to Pythagoras by both Plutarch and Porphyry, is the belief that killing and eating nonhuman animals makes humans more likely to kill and eat their fellow human beings and, conversely, that abstinence from these actions toward animals makes abstinence in these actions toward humans more likely. There is a sense, in our texts, that humans may become desensitized and/or habituated to behave toward humans in the ways that they persistently behave toward animals.[9] We should be vegetarian, on this line of reasoning, simply because it makes us more likely to treat our fellow human beings with respect.

Notice, then, that the wrongness of killing and eating animals, in this case, comes from the wrongness of killing and eating other human beings, and that it is really *humans*, and not animals, that are of moral concern here. Indeed, if we knew that human actions toward animals really had no impact on human actions toward other humans, then this argument would give us no reason at all not to kill and eat nonhuman animals.

Another, better known reason for vegetarianism that is attributed to both Pythagoras and Empedocles in our texts is a belief in the doctrine of human-animal reincarnation.[10] According to this doctrine, human souls can come to dwell inside the bodies of nonhuman animals after the death of their human bodies (and vice versa). Plato too sometimes appears to ascribe to this doctrine,[11] though it is never invoked as a reason to avoid eating animals in the dialogues.

One way to understand reincarnation as a reason to avoid killing and eating animals is to suppose that it makes animals, for the purposes of moral consideration, count as humans, insofar as there is (or might be) a human soul within every animal body. The thought would then be that, since it is wrong to kill and eat human beings, it will also be wrong to kill and eat animals *qua* reincarnated human beings.[12] This makes one's actions toward animals wrong not because such actions make one more likely to behave in a certain way toward human beings, as on the previous line of thought, but because they really *are* actions toward human beings—that is, bodies with human souls.

A different way of understanding the doctrine appears in Plutarch and Seneca, however. Both of these thinkers present reincarnation as grounds for vegetarianism, not because it means that animals have human souls but because it means that some animals have the souls of a special group of human beings—namely, one's former friends and family members. Thus Plutarch reports that the worry is that by killing and eating animals, you might end up killing and eating "your mother, or father, or some friend or child" (*On Flesh-Eating*, 997e; cf. 997f, 998f), while Seneca similarly claims that reincarnation makes people worry that they might be guilty of parricide (*Epistles*, 108, 19). This understanding fits well with a famous anecdote about Pythagoras, in which he stops someone from beating a puppy on the grounds that he recognizes the voice of a former human friend in its cries (Diogenes Laertius, *Lives*, 8.36).

On this understanding it seems that it is wrong to kill and eat not all human beings, as on the first understanding, but rather only our own human loved ones, and that it will be wrong to kill and eat nonhuman animals not *qua* reincarnated human but, instead, *qua* reincarnated friend or family member. This results in abstention from killing and eating all animals, however, insofar as one cannot tell which animals have the souls of one's former loved ones and which do not (unless, of course, one is Pythagoras!).

Notice that, on either of these understandings of reincarnation as a reason for vegetarianism, the wrongness of killing and eating animals is dependent on the status of animals as reincarnated humans—be it any human or only humans to whom one bears a special relationship. As such, reincarnation also fails to make animals *qua* animals worthy of moral concern.

Despite its philosophical pedigree, later Platonists—like Plutarch,[13] Iamblichus,[14] Proclus,[15] and perhaps also Plotinus[16] and Porphyry[17]— appear to have been skeptical of the possibility of literal human-animal reincarnation. Nonetheless in *On Flesh-Eating*, Plutarch presents human-animal reincarnation as one of the central reasons for adopting a vegetarian diet.

Unlike many of Plutarch's other works, *On Flesh-Eating* is a treatise rather than a dialogue and purports to express Plutarch's own views. It is unique in his corpus in that it is the only work in which he expressly argues in favor of adopting a vegetarian diet. The work presents vegetarianism as the original and ancient diet of humankind, with the initial move to meat-eating being attributed to a lack of plant food produced by famine and war. Plutarch suggests that meat-eating in his time (when plant food is, once again, abundant and easily procured) is perpetuated by the gluttony of human beings, who eat meat purely for pleasure (993a–994a). Alongside these claims he offers human-animal reincarnation as a consideration in favor of adopting a vegetarian diet, but gives it only in the form of a "better safe than sorry" argument.

Imagine, Plutarch says, that a warrior who is about to kill someone in full armor is greeted by cries of "Hit him! He's your enemy" on one side and "Don't strike! He is your son" on the other (998e). The best course of action for the warrior, Plutarch argues, is to spare the individual, since he cannot be completely certain that it is not, in fact, his

son (however unlikely this actually is); far better, he thinks, to leave
one's enemy alive than to risk murdering one's own son by mistake. Yet
this, Plutarch argues, is precisely the situation that we find ourselves in
with respect to animals. On the one side, we have philosophers, like
the Stoics, exclaiming "Kill it! It's only a brute beast," while on the
other, we have Pythagoras and Empedocles saying "Stop! What if the
soul of some relative or friend has found its way into this body?"
(998f). Just as in the case of the warrior, Plutarch argues, we ought to
spare every animal, since we cannot be certain that any one animal
does not possess the soul of a deceased human relative, however unlikely this may actually be (and Plutarch seems to think it is rather
unlikely; 998df)—any risk at all that we could be accidentally murdering and feasting on our own human kin is, in Plutarch's eyes, simply
too great.

Notice that Plutarch's concern here is again with how we are behaving toward other human beings, however, and not with how we are
behaving toward the animals themselves. On this reasoning, if we
could be certain that any particular animal did *not* possess the soul of
one of our dead human relatives, then we would have no reason at all
not to kill and eat that animal.

It is less clear what Porphyry makes of reincarnation as an argument
for vegetarianism. Among Porphyry's works we find an entire treatise
devoted to arguing in favor of the practice of vegetarianism, entitled
On Abstinence from Killing Animals (henceforth *On Abstinence*).[18]
This treatise is addressed to a fellow Neoplatonic philosopher, Firmus
Castricius, who has reportedly begun eating meat again after a period
of abstinence (1.1.1). In it Porphyry chastises Firmus for jettisoning "the
ancestral laws of philosophy" (1.2.3) and resolves to prove to him that
vegetarianism is an essential part of the philosophic life and that the
many arguments that are given against vegetarianism by their opponents (such as the Stoics, Peripatetics, and Epicureans) can all be an-
swered convincingly (1.3.2). This project leads Porphyry to cover huge
swaths of material and to include arguments that proceed from a variety

of different philosophical commitments and that work in a multitude of different ways. Yet despite this, Porphyry never once argues that it is wrong to kill and eat animals on the grounds that they have (or may have) literally human souls.

The closest we get to an appeal to the doctrine of reincarnation comes in Porphyry's attack on the Stoics in book 3, where he points to Pythagoras's belief that animals and humans have "the same soul" and are "kin" to one another (3.26.1; cf. 1.19.1) in his argument that animals are of moral concern for humans. These statements may be intended to recall the doctrine of human-animal reincarnation to which Pythagoras subscribed. Yet in his *Life of Pythagoras*, Porphyry presents Pythagoras's belief as being that reincarnation is made possible by the similarity of human and animal souls, and while he says that Pythagoras was vegetarian, he does not say that this was because of his belief in reincarnation (s.19). This difference in emphasis may make for quite a different understanding from what we have seen thus far. It may be that Porphyry thinks it is this similarity of soul that is supposed to make it wrong for us to kill and eat animals, on Pythagoras's view, and not the status of animals as reincarnated humans. That is, animals may be worthy of moral concern because they possess, not literally human souls, but rather the feature that makes human souls worthy of moral concern. Understood in this way, human-animal reincarnation itself does not give us a reason to abstain from killing and eating animals; rather the similarity of soul that makes reincarnation possible does.

Notice that, on this understanding, the concern for our kin that was present in Plutarch's use of the reincarnation doctrine is still a central factor, but in this case it is most certainly animals *qua* animals that are regarded as kin to humans and thus of moral concern. If this is the correct way to understand Porphyry's argument, then it may mark a move away from human actions toward animals being wrong solely on the basis of the effect they have on human beings, and toward a position in which animals are considered worthy of moral concern in themselves.

ANIMAL RATIONALITY: VEGETARIANISM FOR
THE SAKE OF NONHUMAN ANIMALS

The question of whether or not animals are rational arises in the ancient debate on vegetarianism because some theorists—most notably the Stoics—believe that animals are owed moral consideration from humans if and only if they are rational. What the Stoics mean when they say this is that animals must be rational in order to be capable of being wronged by humans and for there to be a demand on humans to avoid wronging animals in their actions. Since the Stoics also accept that, if animals were owed moral consideration from humans, it would be wrong for humans to kill and eat them, proof of animal rationality would commit the Stoics to vegetarianism on their own principles of morality. Yet, of course, the Stoics actually believe that animals are irrational and, therefore, not owed moral consideration from humans. This means that, on their view, nothing that humans do to animals—including killing and eating them—wrongs the animals themselves.[19]

In response to the Stoics, representatives from other ancient schools, including Plutarch, Porphyry, and Sextus Empiricus, present arguments in favor of granting rationality to animals—although only Porphyry explicitly uses this material as part of a wider argument in favor of vegetarianism.

The most extended treatment from Plutarch comes in his dialogue *The Cleverness of Animals* (henceforth *Cleverness*). The bulk of this work consists of a debate between the characters Aristotimus and Phaedimus, concerning whether land or sea animals are "cleverer." Both characters present a vast array of examples of the behavior of land and sea animals, with Aristotimus arguing that his examples prove that land animals are highly rational and intelligent while sea creatures are irrational and stupid (965e–75c), and Phaedimus arguing exactly the opposite (975c–85c). In most cases the characters recount examples of animal behavior and move on without any reflection on what each example is supposed to show, and having so many varied examples makes it difficult to understand what we are supposed to make of the evidence from Plutarch's perspective. This problem is compounded by the fact that the characters often disagree with one another,[20] with what they themselves said previously,[21] and with what is said in Plutarch's other works.[22] Although *Cleverness* ends with the question of whether land or sea animals are cleverer being left to the audience, Autobulus's closing remark, "By combining what you have said against each other, you will together put up a good fight against those[23] who would deprive animals reason and understanding" (985c), has led most scholars to think that Plutarch himself believes these arguments prove that all animals are rational.[24] Occasionally scholars also take Plutarch to be committed to thinking that animal rationality makes animals worthy of moral concern,[25] and thus that it has implications for the behavior of humans toward animals.

Many of Plutarch's examples in *Cleverness* are repeated, and added to, by Porphyry in his treatment of animal rationality in book 3 of *On Abstinence*. Earlier, in book 1 of this same work, Porphyry recounted the Stoic argument that we cannot wrong animals by killing and eating them because animals are irrational (1.4–6), and the argument of book 3 constitutes his reply to this—viz. that animals are rational, and thus that (on the Stoics' own principles) we should not kill and eat them after all (3.1.4). As with *Cleverness*, a huge amount of empirical evidence is offered here with little reflection on what it actually shows, and as a consequence it is difficult to determine what Porphyry himself really thinks. Yet, as with Plutarch, most scholars have taken book 3 to commit Porphyry himself to the belief that all animals are rational, and since his argument appears as a part of *On Abstinence* they often take him to be committed to the further view that this rationality makes it wrong for humans to kill and eat animals.[26]

Among Plutarch's and Porphyry's evidence for animal rationality we find claims that animals employ syllogisms;[27] count;[28] perceive;[29] experience pleasure, pain, and other emotions (e.g., anger, fear, envy);[30] that they remember,[31] make meaningful vocal sounds,[32] employ and teach skills,[33] live in groups and defend one another,[34] live with and defend humans,[35] love their offspring,[36] display virtue and vice,[37] go mad,[38] plan ahead,[39] and use the different parts of their bodies (e.g., teeth, hooves, and claws) appropriately.[40] It is not immediately clear, however, how the presence of each of these many behaviors and capacities is supposed to prove that animals are rational.

There are two questions that we might ask about Plutarch and Porphyry at this juncture: (1) Do they really believe that all animals are rational? and (2) Supposing that they do, does animal rationality provide us with a central reason for adopting a vegetarian diet, on their view? Let us take each of these questions in turn.

A thorough analysis of each piece of evidence in favor of granting rationality to animals and what it shows about our Platonists' attitudes on this matter is beyond the scope of this chapter. In answering the first question, then, I limit myself to a few general remarks about how we should approach these texts, followed by a more in-depth discussion of just two pieces of evidence: animal syllogisms and animal capacities for sense-perception and emotion.

To begin, the dialectical context of Plutarch's and Porphyry's arguments for animal rationality ought to make us cautious about accepting these arguments as a straightforward portrayal of their own beliefs. It is clear that at least some of the evidence given by our Platonists is supposed to attack the Stoics on their own grounds, by using Stoic (and not Platonic) tenets against them, and it may be that all of the arguments are supposed to work in this fashion. Such a strategy is employed by Plutarch throughout *On Stoic Self-Contradiction*,[41] so it would not be strange to find him employing a similar strategy here. The appeal to the fact that animals know how to use their body parts correctly (*On Abstinence*, 3.26.7–10), for example, is a clear reference to the Stoic doctrine of appropriation (*oikeiōsis*), which, in Stoic (and not Platonic) theory, forms the basis of justice. So too both Plutarch and Porphyry appeal to Stoic definitions of things like sense-perception, emotion, planning, memory, and even rationality itself[42]—the point being that the way the Stoics (but perhaps not the Platonists) define these things makes animals rational. If the arguments make use of Stoic premises to which our Platonists are not committed, however, they will tell us little about our Platonists' own commitments with respect to animal rationality.

A further reason for caution is that our texts do not present one consistent position on what rationality is and what consists of convincing evidence that animals possess it. Thus, for example, the argument of Strato that sense-perception requires intellect, and is thus a rational capacity (which would make animals—who perceive—rational), is immediately dismissed by the phrase "but let us suppose that sense-perception does not require intellect to do its job" (Plutarch, *Cleverness*, 961b = Porphyry, *On Abstinence*, 3.21.9). So too, immediately after offering evidence of mythical animals in conversation with humans as proof of their rationality, Porphyry suggests that we dismiss such stories "due to our natural trait of incredulity" (*On Abstinence*, 3.4.1). Similar shifts throughout our texts make it impossible to read them as mere straightforward statements of the Platonists' own beliefs concerning animal capacities.

In addition very similar evidence is offered by Sextus Empiricus in his *Outlines of Scepticism*, where it is purportedly argued—again, in response to the Stoics—that rationality should be granted to animals (1.65–77). Yet of course Sextus is a skeptic and thus cannot be committed to this position himself; his point (though not explicitly stated) must be merely that there is as much evidence in favor of granting rationality to animals as there is against it (and thus that we should suspend judgment). It may be that Plutarch's and Porphyry's arguments are part of a wider trend to attack the Stoic position on animal irrationality without thereby committing oneself to the position that all animals are rational.

A final reason to be cautious about attributing such a position to our Platonists is that it breaks with what has, by this time, become a long-standing philosophical tradition, whereby humans are differentiated from animals by the human possession, and animal lack, of reason.[43] In particular the position that all animals are rational lacks a clear Platonic precedent, since Plato himself never says that animals are rational[44] and, in fact, often seems to assert the opposite.[45] In the *Republic*, for example, animals are appealed to as a way of distinguishing the spirited from the rational part of the soul, apparently on the grounds that they possess the former but not the latter (441ab). So too in the *Symposium* it is said that, while all animals go to great lengths to protect their offspring, only humans do so due to reasoning (207ac). Again the *Laws* says that courage can be seen in animals only because it does not require reason (963e), while the *Cratylus* says that "the name 'human' signifies that the other animals do not…reason about anything they see," whereas humans do (399c). Finally, the *Philebus* (15d–17a) and *Protagoras* (321cd) suggest that reason and wisdom (respectively) are a gift from the gods to humans alone, while the *Phaedrus* says that animals cannot possess language because they have not seen the forms (249b).

With this in mind, let us turn to an examination of two pieces of evidence that are given in favor of attributing rationality to animals by Plutarch and Porphyry—animal syllogisms and animal sense-perceptions and emotions—and try to determine what our Platonists are really committing themselves to in the course of these arguments.

Syllogisms

The most famous example of an animal syllogizing is that of the so-called dialectical dog. Originally put forward by the Stoic Chrysippus, the story goes that a hunting dog is pursuing prey and comes to a three-way junction in the road. Sniffing for the scent of its prey down two out of the three available routes and finding none, the dog is said to proceed down the third route *without sniffing*. This example appears in texts on both sides of the animal rationality debate,[46] with everyone apparently agreeing on the facts of the animal's behavior.

When the example appears in Plutarch's *Cleverness*, the character Aristotimus tells us "the dialecticians" assert that the dog is employing a "multiple disjunctive argument," reasoning that "the prey went either this way or that way or the other way, but it did not go this way or that way, so it went the other way" (969b) (that is, "either p or q or r, but not p, and not q, therefore r"). A similar account of the dog's syllogism appears in both Porphyry and Sextus.

The point, Aristotimus explains in *Cleverness*, is that sense-perception is responsible for supplying only the "minor" premises— that is, "not p" and "not q" (no scent here, no scent there)—while *reason*, which is here treated as a distinct and higher-level capacity than sense-perception,[47] provides the major premise "either p or q or r" and deduces that r on the basis of this plus the information provided by sense-perception (969b).

Other, less well-known examples of the same sort also appear in *Cleverness*. The Thracians, for example, are said to use foxes to determine whether a frozen river is safe to cross, since foxes will put their ear to the ice and proceed to cross only if they cannot hear the noise of the water running beneath—a behavior that signals to the humans that the icc is, or is not, thick enough to take their weight. The foxes are said to reason that "what makes noise must be in motion; what is in motion is not frozen; what is not frozen is liquid; what is liquid gives way" (969ab). This, Aristotimus explains, is not due to "the irrational action of sense-perception; it is, rather, a syllogistic conclusion developed from the evidence of sense-perception" (969a). As with the dialectical dog, the point is that sense-perception tells the fox only that there is, or is not, noise coming from under the ice—it is reason's grasp of the relationship between noise and stability, combined with this perceptual observation, that determines the fox's behavior.

Another example of the same thing is that of dogs and crows that drop stones into pots of liquid in order to raise the level of that liquid so they can drink it (*Cleverness*, 967ab; cf. 972b). Aristotimus explains that this behavior is due to the animal's "knowing that lighter substances are forced upwards when the heavier settle to the bottom" (967b). Again the thought is that reason grasps the relationship between heavy and light and puts this together with perceptual observations (that these stones are heavy and this liquid light) to determine the animal's behavior. Notice that in these examples reason is responsible for a creature's grasp of general logical or conceptual truths,[48] as well as its ability to apply logical rules to deduce valid conclusions from these truths combined with information provided by the separate and irrational capacity of sense-perception. These high-level capacities of recognizing and applying genuine logical and conceptual relationships look likely to be definitive of rationality for both the Stoics, for whom an empirically acquired collection of concepts constitutes reason, and the Platonists, for whom an innate knowledge of the transcendent Platonic forms (such as Motion and Rest) may do so. It seems as though the understanding of relationships between concepts for the Stoics, or forms for the Platonists, is regarded as necessary for enabling an individual to see relationships of entailment that make inference and argument possible. It seems, then, that both schools will have to admit that animals are rational if they agree that animals do indeed employ the sorts of syllogisms that are attributed to them in the preceding examples.

It is well known that the Stoics deny that animals employ syllogisms. In the case of the dialectical dog, Sextus says that the Stoics claim it is only "as if" the dog syllogizes (*Outlines of Scepticism*, 1.69), while Porphyry records the Stoic retort that the dog behaves in the way it does "by nature" (perhaps, instinct) (*On Abstinence*, 3.6.4, 3.10.1). The other examples of animal syllogisms would, presumably, be dismissed in the same way. What is less well-known is that Plutarch's *own speaker*, Aristotimus, denies that the dialectical dog syllogizes. Immediately after describing the dog's syllogism, he asserts that, in fact, this description "is both false and fraudulent; for it is sense-perception itself, by means of tracks and changes, which indicates the way the creature fled, without bothering with disjunctive propositions" (*Cleverness*, 969b).[49] That is, there is no syllogism in the dog's mind, and its behavior can instead be explained by sense-perception (and not reason), since it notices perceptual—although nonolfactory—changes to the route (perhaps footprints, broken twigs, and moving undergrowth) that indicate which way its prey went. We can imagine a similar, perceptual explanation being given for the behavior of the other animals as well.

The thought here seems to be that syllogizing really is too advanced a capacity to be granted to animals and that the dog's behavior can in fact be explained by the lower, irrational capacity of sense-perception. Add to this the fact that both Plutarch and Porphyry only ever say that other philosophers claim that the dog employs a syllogism, and it starts to look unlikely that these Platonists really intend to grant that animals syllogize and are rational—in the sense of understanding and employing conceptual relationships—on the basis of this kind of evidence.

While it may seem bizarre for our Platonists to include in their argument claims that they think are fallacious, a possible explanation for this is that they are employing an argumentative strategy, common in the Stoic school, whereby the inclusion of more arguments (however weak) is supposed to increase the persuasiveness of one's overall case.[50] It may be that the Platonists believe that whereas they can, themselves, explain the special psychological capacities of humans, as opposed to animals, by appeal to the former's special acquaintance with the Platonic forms, the Stoics cannot, on account of their denial of the existence of these entities.

Sense-Perception and Emotion

Another argument for animal rationality we find in Plutarch's and Porphyry's texts—and one that should strike us as surprising given what we have just seen—appeals to the fact that animals possess the capacities for sense-perception and emotion. Animals, we are told, see colors, hear sounds, taste flavors, smell scents, and so on, as well as growing angry, afraid, envious, delighted, distressed, and other things of that nature. All of this is supposed to be demonstrated by the characteristic behaviors of animals, such as their ability to navigate their environment (sense-perception), their propensity to stand and fight (anger) or run away when threatened (fear), their competition for mates (envy), their being summoned by music (delight) and corrected by punishment (distress), and so on (Porphyry, *On Abstinence*, 3.8.1–6; Plutarch, *Cleverness*, 961df = Porphyry, *On Abstinence*, 3.22.3–5). Porphyry, for his part, also appeals to the expert testimony of Aristotle in support of his position (*On Abstinence*, 3.6.5–7, 3.7.1, 3.8.6, 3.9.5, 3.12.4), since in numerous passages Aristotle grants that animals possess genuine sense-perception and emotion.[51] Both Porphyry and Plutarch are clear that animals have exactly the same capacities for these things as humans do, and not mere analogs of the human capacities, and the point is said to be that sense-perception and emotion are themselves rational capacities, and thus that animals, since they possess these capacities, must also be rational.

Yet there is something decidedly odd about sense-perception and emotion being given as proof of animal rationality by our Platonists, since the usual school line is that such capacities belong to the lower, irrational soul-part, as opposed to the higher, rational soul-part that is in contact with the Platonic forms. Thus while Plutarch and Porphyry seem genuinely committed to the position that animals have the very same capacities for sense-perception and emotion as humans do, their own position appears to be that these capacities are irrational—even in humans (see, for example, Porphyry, *On Abstinence*, 1.30.1–7, 1.33.3–6, 1.34.7, 3.19.3; Plutarch, *On Common Conceptions*, 1058ef).

Furthermore, as we have just seen in our analysis of animal syllogisms, some arguments in our texts actually rely on exactly this kind of opposition between reason and sense-perception in order to make a case for animal rationality. The same can also be said of emotion, which in these arguments is presented as a rational capacity but elsewhere appears as a distinct irrational force that opposes reason—as in *Cleverness* when the crocodile is said to act on the basis of reason, as opposed to emotion, when it protects only the bravest of its offspring while destroying the rest (982d; cf. Porphyry, *On Abstinence*, 3.19.3). Thus some of the arguments for animal rationality require the irrationality of sense-perception and emotion to go through, while others depend on the rationality of these very capacities. Since these positions are contradictory, Plutarch and Porphyry cannot be committed to both at once.

In fact this is symptomatic of the dialectical nature of Plutarch's and Porphyry's arguments. What is going on here is that they are responding to the position of some Stoics, who denied that animals possessed genuine sense-perception and emotion, and granted them instead only analogs of these human capacities.[52] This is because, on their Stoic view, these capacities are rational, and thereby inaccessible to irrational animals.[53] It is this position that Porphyry and Plutarch are complaining about when they state, "Some people foolishly say that animals are not pleased or angry or afraid, but that...the lion is '*quasi*-angry' and the deer '*quasi*-afraid'...that neither do they see or hear, but '*quasi*-see' and '*quasi*-hear'...these assertions, as any sensible person would be convinced, are...contrary to the obvious" (*Cleverness*, 961f = *On Abstinence*, 3.22.5). In response to this Stoic position, Plutarch and Porphyry argue simply that animals really do possess exactly the same capacities for sense-perception and emotion as humans do. The point is that, since these are, according to some Stoics, rational capacities, and since animals really do possess them, then animals too must be rational beings. Thus Plutarch and Porphyry claim that "because every animate creature is perceptive by nature...it is also not plausible to require that an animate creature should have...an irrational aspect—not when one is debating with people who think that nothing shares in sense-perception unless it also shares in understanding" (*Cleverness*, 960de = *On Abstinence*, 3.21.4).[54] That is, when one is in conversation with the Stoics, who hold that sense-perception is a rational capacity, one must conclude that all animals are rational, since all animals possess the capacity of sense-perception by definition. Exactly the same analysis can be given of the arguments concerning the animal capacity of emotion.

What Does This Tell Us about Platonists' Views on Animal Rationality?

In answer to our first question concerning whether the Platonists really believe that all animals are rational, what we have seen in the preceding passages should make us quite cautious. Indeed it seems to me that they are more likely to be trying to trap their Stoic opponents into having to admit that animals are rational, while thinking that they, as Platonists with the forms at their disposal, can allow animals to have many capacities in common with humans, without thereby needing to grant them rationality.

This brings us to our second question, whether animal rationality provides us with a central reason for adopting a vegetarian diet, according to our Platonists. If I am right that they do not believe that animals are rational, then the answer to this question will be negative. However, for the sake of argument, we might still ask whether animal rationality *would* provide us with a reason for vegetarianism, on Platonist principles.

Taking Porphyry first, the point of his argument for animal rationality in book 3 of *On Abstinence* is certainly that it has vegetarian consequences for some understandings of ethics. Porphyry himself says as much, arguing that once animal rationality is proven, his "opponents" (i.e., the Stoics) will be committed to granting that animals are of moral concern (3.1.4, 3.18.1), thereby making them vegetarian. However, in the same book Porphyry tells us that, as far as he is concerned, the Stoic approach to ethics is wrong. Porphyry's opposing view, as I understand it, is that one's killing and eating of animals is wrong whether or not animals are rational, because it brings about, or results from, a disordered soul state, in which the rational part of one's soul is not appropriately in control of the lower, irrational parts (3.26). What this means, in straightforward terms, is that it is the relationship between an agent's action and his or her motivations and desires that makes an action ethical or unethical, on Porphyry's view. Porphyry's point, in making an argument for animal rationality in book 3 of *On Abstinence*, is, I suggest, that animal rationality would have vegetarian consequences for the Stoic approach to ethics.[55]

Unlike Porphyry's, Plutarch's arguments for animal rationality are not designed simply to make a wider point in favor of adopting a vegetarian diet. Nonetheless twice in *Cleverness* Plutarch's characters point to a link between animal psychological capacities and the ethical treatment of animals. On the first occasion Autobulus suggests that animal rationality need not make it unethical to kill injurious animals, while taming and making use of gentler animals as human helpers (964ef). The implication appears to be that animal rationality may make it unethical to kill and eat gentle animals that do humans no harm. On the second occasion it is Aristotimus who claims that those who deny that animals are owed moral consideration from humans are correct with respect to sea animals, who, according to him, are irrational and stupid (970b). Again this suggests a link between the psychological capacities of animals and human ethical obligations toward them— which might extend to all animals if one's belief is, in fact, that all animals are rational. Yet *Cleverness* does not present a consistent picture on this matter, since elsewhere in the same work Autobulus notes that animal rationality has been presented as a point in favor of the practice of hunting, since it makes animals harder to catch and thus makes hunting a better exercise for human wits (960a). It is this point that frames the whole discussion in this dialogue, with Aristotimus's arguments for the greater rationality of land animals being presented as a defense of land animal hunters (965f–6a) and Phaedimus's arguments being presented as a defense of fishermen (975c).

Plutarch's other two works that are of relevance here are *On Flesh-Eating* and *Beasts Are Rational*, both of which—unlike *Cleverness*—contain extended arguments in favor of adopting a vegetarian diet. However, neither of these works argues against the human consumption of animals on the grounds that animals are rational. Instead their focus is on reasons for vegetarianism that concern the effect that meat consumption has on human beings. On balance, then, it looks as if we would be going beyond our texts to think that a central reason for vegetarianism in Plutarch's philosophy is the rationality of animals.

If I am right so far, then Platonists like Plutarch and Porphyry do not themselves consider facts of animal psychology to provide a reason in favor of adopting a vegetarian diet. So too, while we have seen one argument against meat-eating from Plutarch, concerning human-animal reincarnation, we have not yet seen the arguments that constitute Plutarch's and Porphyry's core reasons in favor of adopting a vegetarian diet. Let us now turn, then, to considering what our Platonists' central reasons are for thinking that eating animals is wrong.

TEMPERANCE: VEGETARIANISM FOR THE SAKE OF OURSELVES

In addition to Pythagoras and Empedocles, Platonist philosophers like Plutarch and Porphyry also believe that vegetarianism is endorsed by the ultimate authority figure: Plato himself (Plutarch, *On Flesh-Eating*, 996b; Porphyry, *On Abstinence*, 1.36.1, 1.37.1, 1.39.3–6). Indeed in *On Abstinence*, Porphyry claims that being vegetarian is necessary for philosophers, especially Platonists (2.3.1), since one cannot achieve the goal of philosophic life while eating meat (1.48.1, 1.57.2). Nonetheless it is rare to find overt references to vegetarianism in the Platonic corpus.

One place in which vegetarianism does explicitly appear is *Republic II*, when Socrates first describes the life of the citizens in the ideal city. These citizens have a frugal and simple manner of living; they drink wine and have sex in moderation, sleep on uncomfortable-sounding beds, and consume a diet consisting of wheat and barley loaves, olives, cheese, boiled roots and vegetables, figs, chickpeas, beans,[56] myrtle, and acorns (372ad). They do not, however, eat any meat[57] or make use of other luxuries (*opsa*), such as "perfumed oils, incense, prostitutes and pastries" (373a). Socrates clearly approves of this manner of living;

he describes the city that adopts it as "healthy" (373b) and says that its citizens will live to "a ripe old age" in "peace and good health" (372d).

Unfortunately Socrates offers only a few frustratingly brief remarks as to why meat and other luxuries are excluded from this city. It is because, he explains, they (a) are not "necessary," (b) are productive of bodily illness, and (c) require the provision of many resources; for example, meat requires livestock, animal handlers, chefs, and cookware (*Republic* 373c; cf. 404cd; *Gorgias*, 464d, 465a, 501ae, 521d–2a). This, however, is all the explanation we get. Socrates does not explain exactly what each reason means, why it matters, or how it relates to the other reasons. Notice, in particular, that no special reason is given for excluding meat from the city, and that any worries about the animals themselves seem very far from Socrates's mind.

This *Republic* passage is the only place in the Platonic corpus in which vegetarianism is explicitly recommended, and yet thinkers like Porphyry, and perhaps also Plutarch and Plotinus, seem to believe that the central tenets of Platonic ethics necessitate vegetarianism. Reading the *Republic* passage alongside other central ethical texts in the Platonic corpus, such as the *Phaedo*, enables us to understand why this is the case. In the *Phaedo*, philosophers are said to prioritize the needs, desires, and pleasures of their soul over the conflicting needs, desires, and pleasures of their body (63e–9d). As a part of this project they are said to avoid "the so-called pleasures" of food, drink, and sex (that is, all the "pleasures concerned with service of the body"), "except insofar as one cannot do without them" (64de)—that is, except insofar as they are necessary. While this may, at first, sound like a recommendation concerning only food quantity (such that one should eat as much as is required to remain alive and no more),[58] when read in combination with the *Republic* passage it sounds like a recommendation to avoid certain kinds of food as well. For, as we have seen, the *Republic* says that particular foods—such as meat and pastries—are unnecessary, and thus, in conjunction with the *Phaedo*, it seems that the person who aims to live well must avoid these kinds of foods.

All three reasons for abstinence from meat that appear in the *Republic* form central and recurrent themes in Plutarch's and Porphyry's arguments for vegetarianism (Plutarch, *On Flesh-Eating*, and *Beasts are Rational*, 991ad; Porphyry, *On Abstinence*, 1.27.1–1.47.4). To begin with, both Platonists repeat the *Republic's* reason (a) when they claim that meat is eaten by humans (or, for Porphyry, just philosophers)[59] not out of necessity, since humans (or philosophers) can survive perfectly well on plant foods alone. Instead Plutarch and Porphyry claim that meat is really eaten out of a desire for bodily pleasure, being used as a relish (*opson*) on top of otherwise perfectly adequate food, simply to make a meal more enjoyable for the consumer (Plutarch, *Cleverness*, 959e, and *Beasts are Rational*, 991bd; Porphyry, *On Abstinence*, 1.37.3, 1.38.2, 1.41.2, 1.45.4, 1.46.2, 1.54.2, 3.16.1, 3.19.1, 3.20.6, 3.26.5, 3.27.1). Yet bodily pleasure is regarded by the Platonists as something bad and (as far as possible) to be avoided, on account of its ability to distract one's higher soul from its proper activity of contemplating the Platonic forms. Since meat is not a necessary part of our diet, the additional pleasure that is brought to a meal by its inclusion is completely avoidable, and this makes meat-eating a matter of intemperance for Plutarch and Porphyry (Plutarch, *On Flesh-Eating*, 965a, 966ef, 998ef, 999b, and *Beasts are Rational*, 991c; Porphyry, *On Abstinence*, 1.2.3, 1.45.4, 1.46.1, 3.16.1, 3.18.5).

Plutarch even complains about ancient practices that involve considerable animal cruelty on the grounds that they stem from human intemperance—that is, a desire for bodily pleasure—and not from necessity. He speaks, for example, of the practice of "thrusting red-hot spits into the throats of swine so that by the plunging in of the iron the blood may be emulsified and, as it circulates through the body, may make the flesh tender and delicate," as well as the practice of jumping on the udders of sows about to give birth so that the offspring will be blended together with milk, and so too the practice of sewing up the eyes of geese and cranes in order to make their flesh more appetizing (*On Flesh-Eating*, 996f–997a). He complains not so much about the suffering caused to the animals, however, as about the fact that humans are acting in these disgusting ways, not because they need to in order to stay alive but simply out of a desire to increase the bodily pleasure that they experience during a meal (997a).

In her examination of Porphyry's arguments for vegetarianism, Catherine Osborne complains that the argument from necessity "achieves too much." Osborne points out that, since no particular foodstuff is necessary for health and sustenance, the same argument can be deployed against everything that we might eat, and thus, absurdly, leave us with nothing to eat. So, for example, one does not need to eat carrots in order to survive, therefore carrot-eating is an unnecessary pleasure that ought to be avoided. Repeat this argument for every possible food, and we are left to starve.[60] Yet Plutarch and Porphyry seem to be thinking in terms of categories of foodstuffs rather than individual foods, and to suppose that the argument from necessity rules out meat as a category, but not plant foods. Thus Porphyry says that "a meat-eater needs inanimate foods as well, but someone satisfied with inanimate food needs half as much" (*On Abstinence*, 1.48.4). When we consider the fact that the Greek diet in antiquity was largely made up of plant-based food, with a small portion of meat on top to serve as a relish, we can see how it seemed possible to Plutarch and Porphyry to survive on the plant-based food alone without the meat relish, but not the other way around.

Plutarch and Porphyry also agree that eating meat is not only unnecessary for a healthy life but that it is actually preventative of it, since meat-eating is the cause of illness and disease in human bodies (Plutarch, *On Flesh-Eating*, 998c, and *Beasts are Rational*, 991b; Porphyry, *On Abstinence*, 1.47.1–2, 1.52.1–3)[61]—reflecting reason (b) in the *Republic*. Porphyry, conversely, claims that a vegetarian diet not only does not cause disease and ill health but that it causes and preserves health in the body and, indeed, cures illnesses where present (*On Abstinence*, 1.2.1, 1.52.1, 1.53.2–4). Although, as we have seen, good Platonists are supposed to fulfill the needs of the soul—as opposed to the body—first and foremost, Plutarch and Porphyry are clear that disease-producing foods should be avoided and health-preserving foods taken instead, not because of their effect on the body as such but because a sick body makes the higher soul's characteristic activity—of contemplating the Platonic forms—difficult or impossible (Plutarch, *On Flesh-Eating*, 995f–996a; Porphyry, *On Abstinence*, 1.53.2). Thus if one is going to live a good, philosophic life, one must take adequate care of one's body.

Porphyry also worries in *On Abstinence* about the many resources that are required for maintaining oneself on a diet that includes meat; one needs, he tells us, slaves and chefs to prepare and cook the meat (which cannot be eaten raw, unlike plant food), riches to pay for it (since meat was prohibitively expensive in ancient times), doctors to cure the diseases that are produced by meat consumption, and excessive belongings (such as pots, pans, and cooking utensils) (1.46.2–1.47.4). This reflects reason (c) in the *Republic*, but Porphyry also appears to think that it makes meat-eating incompatible with the recommendation in Plato's *Theaetetus* that we become "like god" (176b; cf. *Republic*, 613b), for one of god's primary qualities is self-sufficiency—that is, needing nothing outside of himself. The more external things we need, Porphyry thinks, the less true we are to this central, Platonic maxim (1.37.4, 1.54.6, 1.56.1, 3.27.1–4). Both Plutarch and Porphyry also echo the *Republic* in their banning of other luxuries, such as perfumes and pastries, for precisely the same reasons as they ban meat (Plutarch, *On Flesh-Eating*, 999ab; Porphyry, *On Abstinence*, 1.41.2).

There are two prolonged presentations of meat-eating as an act of human intemperance in Plutarch's writings. In *On Flesh-Eating*, the gluttony of meat-eating is presented alongside human-animal reincarnation as a central reason for adopting a vegetarian diet, while in *Beasts Are Rational* the intemperance of human meat-eating appears as part of a wider (tongue-in-cheek) argument that nonhuman animals are more virtuous than humans. The two sections bear a striking resemblance to one another and appear to reflect Plutarch's own beliefs.

Beasts Are Rational depicts the mythical Odysseus in conversation with a human comrade who has recently been turned into a pig (named Gryllus) by Circe. Circe has agreed with Odysseus that she will restore his comrades to human form if this is what they themselves desire. Gryllus, however, turns out to be reluctant to change back. He argues that animal life is better than human life since animals exceed humans in virtue—for animal souls, he says, produce virtue "spontaneously and naturally," while human souls produce it only with great effort and training (986f–987b). Gryllus provides empirical evidence of animal behavior, which is contrasted with the corresponding human behavior, to demonstrate that this is the case.

A large section of Gryllus's argument concerns the temperance of nonhuman animals and the comparative intemperance of humans. In the course of this section Gryllus divides desires into the following three kinds[62]: (i) natural and necessary, e.g., the desires for food and drink; (ii) natural and unnecessary, e.g., the desire for sex (989bc); and (iii) unnatural (and unnecessary), e.g., the desire for luxurious items like gold, ivory, fine robes, tapestries, and perfumes (989cf, 990bc). Gryllus tells us that being temperate involves having no type (iii) desires at all, while having and fulfilling type (i) and (ii) desires only to a limited extent (989b).

To prove that nonhuman animals possess temperance so defined, Gryllus points out that, in contrast to humans, animals have no type (iii) desires at all; pigs, for example, do not care for gold and riches and are content with mud to sleep in rather than handsome robes (989f). With respect to type (ii) desires, Gryllus tells us that animals indulge them only occasionally and "without irregularity or excess" (989f; cf. 990e). As proof of this point, he discusses the sexual behavior of nonhuman animals. Animals, he claims, do not have sex once the female is pregnant (990cd),[63] do not engage in homosexual behavior (990d),[64] do not have sex at all times of the year (but only in the spring, i.e., the mating season), and do not have sex with humans (991a, 988f).[65] Humans, by contrast, engage in sex even when the female is pregnant, have sex at all times of the year, and indulge in homosexual activity (990de) and bestiality (990f). The point is that animals limit themselves to sex for the purpose of producing offspring and avoid sex that cannot achieve this goal, while humans indulge in sex that cannot result in offspring, thereby exceeding the limit that ought to be placed on this natural desire. They do so, of course, for pleasure and therefore act intemperately.[66]

Most important for us, however, is what Gryllus says about type (i) desires for food and drink. According to him, animals pursue only those foods that are "naturally suited" to them (by which he seems to mean foods that preserve their health) and go outside of this remit only when absolutely necessary—that is, when their survival depends on it. Thus, he tells us, animals like wolves and snakes eat meat simply because it is the diet that is proper to them and that preserves their constitutions (991d),[67] and while birds and dogs have sometimes gone beyond what is natural for them and consumed human flesh, they have done so only due to a scarcity of their natural foods (991a). Humans, on the other hand, are said to "eat everything" (991c), regularly indulging in foods that are not naturally suited to them (i.e., those that make them ill), doing so not out of necessity—that is, when their lives depend on it—but for the sake of the pleasure they enjoy as a result of it (990f–991c; cf. Porphyry, *On Abstinence*, 3.20.6). Gryllus's own example of such an unnatural food for humans is meat (991bc). Meat-eating is, then, clearly presented by Gryllus as an act of human intemperance.

This presentation reflects comments in Plutarch's *On Flesh-Eating*, where meat-eating as an act of intemperance is the central concern. After presenting us with a potted history of how meat-eating came about as a result of food shortage, Plutarch laments the fact that meat-eating has now become a habit for human beings, who, despite no longer needing to eat meat in order to survive, continue to do so out of gluttony (993c–994a). Notably in this text, Plutarch allows that eating meat sometimes is necessary even for humans, and he is forgiving of meat-eating under these circumstances (966f), but since this is not usually our situation nowadays, he presents animals as pleading with humans, "I do not ask to be spared in case of necessity; only spare me your arrogance! Kill me to eat, but not to please your palate!" (994e). In this work Plutarch makes clear that precisely the same reasons that ought to result in abstention from meat ought also to result in abstention from products such as perfumes and cakes (999ab).

All of this closely reflects Porphyry's concerns in the sections of *On Abstinence* in which his own views are being expounded. In book 2 Porphyry presents the same historical picture as Plutarch, according to which humans, who are originally vegetarian, first began to eat meat as a result of hard times, but then carried on eating meat out of intemperance (2.5.1–2.14.3). In book 1 Porphyry argues that it is impossible to achieve the goal of the philosophic life while eating meat, on the grounds that meat is more productive of bodily pleasure than is vegetarian food (1.46.2) and that bodily pleasure distracts our higher soul from the contemplation that is characteristic of the philosophic life (1.41.1–5). He, like Plutarch, allows that people who need to eat meat in order to survive may do so, but he argues that philosophers, generally speaking, are not among them (4.21.1–2).[68]

Alongside his recommendations of vegetarianism in these passages, Porphyry, like Plutarch, makes other ethical recommendations that steer philosophers away from anything that is especially provocative of bodily pleasure. He recommends the avoidance of exciting sights and sounds, encountering attractive members of the opposite sex, sex itself, drinking wine, making use of perfumes, and overeating, all on the same grounds that he recommends abstinence from meat (1.33.6–1.34.3, 1.41.2–4, 1.46.1). His presentation of these precepts as stemming from the same Platonic ethical considerations suggests that there is nothing particularly special about the avoidance of meat in Porphyry's mind; meat-eating is simply one of a number of things that makes philosophical contemplation difficult. As with Socrates in Plato's *Republic*, worries about the animals that are being eaten seem very far from Porphyry's mind.

At least some of Porphyry's "ordinary man" opponents think it is a
bad thing to be deprived of the bodily pleasure that meat-eating produces, apparently because they think—wrongly, in Platonists' eyes—
that bodily pleasure is a good to be pursued (*On Abstinence*, 1.24.1). Yet
the case is more complicated for the Epicureans, who think that only a
certain type of pleasure is to be pursued, and for the Stoics, who regard
pleasure as something morally indifferent and thus to be actively neither pursued nor avoided. Porphyry in *On Abstinence* argues that the
Epicurean good is best achieved by the adoption of a vegetarian diet,
since this causes least disturbance and fulfills only natural and necessary desires rather than desires for luxury, as per Epicurean principles
(1.48.1–1.54.6). As a result, Porphyry claims, adopting a vegetarian diet
is the best way to experience the particular kind of pleasure at which
the Epicureans are aiming. Clearly not all Epicureans agree, however,
since Porphyry himself records an Epicurean argument that human
advantage is secured by the use of some animals as food (1.7.1–1.12.7,
esp. 1.12.1).

Plutarch's report of the Stoic position tells us that at least some
Stoics agreed with the Platonists that it was necessary to abstain from
pastries and perfumes (*On Flesh-Eating*, 999ab). Although their reasoning is not explained, presumably the thought is that, since such
things are consumed purely for the sake of pleasure, consuming them is
incompatible with the Stoic belief that pleasure is indifferent and is a
mark of intemperance. Plutarch complains, however, that the Stoic
avoidance of pastries and perfumes is inconsistent with their continued consumption of meat, since the very same considerations that
result in these items being banned ought also to result in vegetarianism. If Plutarch is accurate in his report that some Stoics avoided pastries and perfumes but continued to consume meat, then it seems that
these individuals must have fundamentally disagreed with his Platonist
line that meat was eaten purely for pleasure; the Stoics, after all, agree
with him that gluttony is damaging for the soul of the glutton.[69] It may
be that these Stoics believed that, in eating meat, humans were fulfilling

their role in the order of nature, since lower animals exist in order to feed humans,[70] and that any pleasure that came about as a result of that was unproblematic. Interestingly, however, some later Stoics are in complete agreement with the Platonists and recommend abstention from meat as part of a wider asceticism they believe accords with Stoic principles.[71]

CONCLUSION

The upshot of all this is that, as I understand them, Plutarch and Porphyry are vegetarians not so much out of concern for the welfare of animals as out of concern for the welfare of human beings—and, in particular, ourselves. In the course of their arguments for vegetarianism, they offer all sorts of reasons that appeal to opponents with different kinds of philosophical assumptions. However, ultimately their main motivations for recommending a vegetarian diet appear to stem from the concerns they find in Plato, and these concerns have little to do with the experiences of the animals that are killed and eaten. Instead our Platonists' concerns are that one does only what one needs to do in order to maintain oneself in bodily existence, and no more. Meat-eating is thought to go beyond this remit in that meat (unlike plant food) can be done without and results in disturbances in the body that make our higher souls' contemplative activity difficult or impossible. While our Platonists' beliefs have clear practical implications for the treatment of animals, with both Plutarch and Porphyry supposing that it is unethical for (at least certain groups of) humans to kill and eat animals, these practical recommendations hinge on what these practices mean for human beings, not on what they mean for the animals themselves.

Reflection

LISTENING TO AESOP'S ANIMALS

Jeremy B. Lefkowitz

𝕪

The legendary Aesop, whom Herodotus (*Histories*, 2.134) places on Samos in the sixth century BCE, did not write a single fable with his own hand. The fables that have survived under his name were written in the centuries after his death, composed by a diverse set of writers who labeled their stories "Aesop's" with little concern for historical accuracy. We are left with hundreds of tales and anecdotes scattered across the remains of classical literature, in both Greek and Latin, in prose and in verse, each one with murky origins and dubious links to the life of Aesop.[1] While this state of affairs poses significant challenges for the philologist and the textual critic, the openness of the fable tradition, along with its simple style and moralizing tone, make Aesop a useful point of reference for investigations of early Greek thought.

The philosophical content of Aesop's fables is perhaps best described as "popular" or "applied" ethics.[2] Like other ancient satirical genres (e.g., iambography, Greek comedy, Roman satire), fables describe and condemn common varieties of misbehavior, especially greed, hypocrisy, vanity, and deceit.[3] But two salient features set the fable apart from other forms of moralizing literature: (1) the drawing out of an explicit message in the form of a moral[4] and (2) the use of talking animals as protagonists. The aim of this brief reflection is to explore the relationship between these

two aspects of the fable by looking at the role played by animals in
the genre's moralizing program. Why do animals feature so
prominently in Aesop's fables? And why do they talk?

According to our ancient sources, the fable's use of animals
primarily serves to underscore the fictionality and lightness of the
stories.[5] The risibility of the humanized animal allows the fable to
make its point without boring or insulting an addressee. So, it
follows, while calling someone an ass might reasonably cause
offense, fable tellers can be more effective and more politic by
offering advice or criticism with a made-up story. Take, for example,
this excerpt from "The Ass in the Lion's Skin" (Perry, 188):[6]

An ass put on a lion's skin and went around frightening the other
animals (*ta aloga zoa*). He saw a fox and tried to terrify her, too.
But she happened to have heard his voice and said to him, "I can
assure you I would have been afraid of you, too, if I hadn't heard
your braying." So it is that some ignorant men who create an
impression of being someone by their outward elegance expose
themselves by their own talkativeness (*glōssalgias*).[7]

By bringing to the fore the fictitious nature of the story, animal
fables entertain and establish that the only possibility of serious
meaning is the interpretation; the auditor must listen to the moral
and decide if the fable applies.[8]

No ancient writers (and few modern critics) seem to think of
Aesop's talking animals as having anything at all to do with real
animals. But it is worthwhile to reflect on why fable, one of
the world's earliest forms of ethical literature, turned to
anthropomorphized animals for its chief protagonists.[9] That is, we
can think of the fable animal as a particularly early and dynamic
instantiation of an ancient preoccupation with tracking the
boundaries between human and animal. The polysemy of the
well-known Greek conception of *logos* is essential here; it can

denote (among other things) "speech," "conversation," "reason," and
(significantly) "story" or "fable."[10] While the animal world was
believed to be governed by appetite and self-interest, humans have
the capacity to use reason (*logos*) and thus to settle conflicts with
conversation (also *logos*) and mutual persuasion.[11] Aesopic fables
(called *Aisopeioi logoi*) play with the multiple meanings of *logos* by
having animals use human speech to appeal to the laws and customs
that govern human society. More often than not, however, the
animals' attempts at persuasion fail and give way to natural
instincts.

As a typical example, in the fable of the "Wolf and Lamb" from
the *Collectio Augustana*,[12] the wolf's search for a just (*eulogos*) cause
to devour the lamb is met with the lamb's readiness to defend itself
with words (Perry, 155):

A wolf saw a lamb drinking from a river and decided to find a just
cause for making a meal of him. So from where he stood upstream
he began to complain that the lamb was muddying the water and
not letting him get a drink. When the lamb said that he was no
more than touching the water with his lips and that besides, from
where he was standing downstream, he couldn't possibly disturb
the water above him, the wolf, failing in this complaint, said, "But
last year you made unpleasant remarks about my father." Then,
when the lamb said he wasn't even a year old, the wolf said to him,
"Am I to be cheated out of eating you just because you are so glib
(*apologiōn*) with your excuses?"
The fable (*logos*) shows that those who are set on doing wrong are
not to be deterred even by a legal argument (*dikaia apologia*).

According to the moral, the fable is about the futility of using
words to persuade those who refuse to listen to legal (or just)
arguments. Greek ideas about what separates the human from the
animal map directly onto the narrative: Aesop's animals may

paradoxically have the power of speech (*logos*), but the fable's (human) addressee must use reason (*logos*) to recognize and learn from the wolf's refusal to listen.

Even when the issue does not arise so explicitly, the gap between talking animals and listening humans appears to be built into the very structure of Aesopic fable. Fable animals are usually motivated only by predatory or survival instincts; they constantly resort to violence despite their ability to converse with one another. The attached morals then deliver their messages by marking the transition from animal fiction to human lesson, as in the following examples:

So it is with men, too. Those who give up what they have in hope of greater things are ill-advised. ("Hawk and Nightingale," Perry, 4)

So it is with men, too. It behooves men of sense not to undertake anything until they have seen where it leads. ("Fox and Goat in the Well," Perry, 9)

So it is with men, too. Liars always show off most when there is no one to discredit them. ("The Fox, the Monkey, and His Ancestors," Perry, 14)

It is just the same with men: some of them pretend to be suffering while others are doing the work. ("The Oxen and Squeaky Axle," Perry, 45)

A number of different formulaic phrases introduce morals in our surviving collections (e.g., the common Latin phrase *fabula docet*, "The fable teaches"), but these above, attached to fables in the *Collectio Augustana*, begin with phrases (e.g., *houtōs kai tōn anthrōpōn*) that spell out how we humans are meant to learn from the fictionalized animals: sometimes we behave like animals, but we must use our more robust possession of *logos* to improve ourselves.

By toying with the conventional role played by *logos* in separating human from animal, fable implies that there are some humans who,

left to their own devices, would prefer to live like animals. This idea
surfaces most explicitly in a pair of fables on the origin of humans:

"Zeus, the Animals, and Man" (Perry, 311)
They say that creatures were first fashioned and that gifts were
bestowed on them by god: strength to one, speed to another, wings
to another; but man stood there naked and said, "I am the only one
you have left without a gift." Zeus said, "You are ungrateful
although you have been granted the greatest gift of all, for you have
received reason (*logos*), which prevails among gods as it does
among men, is more powerful than the powerful, and swifter than
the swiftest." Then, recognizing his gift, man went his way in
reverence and gratitude. That although all rational (*logō*) beings are
honored by god, some men are unappreciative of this honor but are
rather jealous of dumb and irrational (*aloga*) beasts.

"Prometheus and Men" (Perry, 240)
At the direction of Zeus, Prometheus fashioned men and beasts.
But when Zeus saw that there were more of the irrational (*aloga*)
animals, he ordered him to destroy some of the beasts and make
them over into men. When he did as he was told, it turned out that
the ones who had not been fashioned as men from the start had
human form but were bestial in spirit (*tas de psuchas thēriōdeis*). The
fable has a lesson for men who are bestial (*thēriōdē*) and ill-
tempered.

These fables on human origins shed light on some basic
assumptions that seem to underwrite the use of talking animals
throughout the tradition: animals are "irrational" (*aloga*) and
"dumb"; humans, though "naked" when compared to the physical
gifts of the other creatures, have been given "reason" (*logos*) to
compensate for their relative weakness; despite the gift of reason,
certain humans nonetheless have "beastly souls" and are prone to
imitating animal behavior.

It is also tempting to read these tales as accounts of the origins of fable, which, after all, makes animals' limited participation in *logos* into a tool for teaching right and wrong behavior. In granting animals a share of *logos*, Aesopic fable necessarily blurs the lines between human and animal and, however playfully, hints at a continuum of human-animal behavior. On some level every animal fable challenges us to confront our conceptions of what exactly separates humans from animals. As a *logos* meant to be spoken and heard, each fable insists that it is our responsibility to listen and learn from its funhouse version of animal behavior. But amusing or not, fable animals are inevitably implicated in broader commitments to the human-animal binary; our understanding of those commitments can be enriched if we listen carefully to Aesop's talking animals.

CHAPTER THREE

Illuminating Community

ANIMALS IN CLASSICAL INDIAN THOUGHT

Amber D. Carpenter

Animals are everywhere throughout classical Indian literature. They are found in law books and ethical codes; they populate the major epics; they figure as stock examples in philosophy—the rope mistaken for a snake (or, more dangerously, the other way around), and the dewlap as the characteristic mark of the cow; and of course they are familiar as the main characters of the rich Indian fable literature, about which I will have more to say. What we do not have, however, is anything tying all of this animal talk into a single discourse.

One significant reason for this is that the Indians, unlike their European counterparts, did not make the barbaric mistake.[1] The Indians do not typically get overly exercised about locating, repeating, and emphasizing "the fundamental" difference between humans and other animals, lumping all nonhuman animals together as if they were much the same compared to how different they are from human beings. And when occasionally the matter of human distinctiveness does arise, the

Sanskrit (and Pāli) texts do not show anything like the almost obses-
sive concern the European tradition has had in particular with whether
animals are *rational*.[2]

In Greece we find Hesiod, standing at the front of the European
tradition's thinking about animals, claiming, "This law for man was established by the son of Chronos: that fish and beasts and flying birds
eat one another, since right (*dikē*) is not in them; but to mankind he
gave right which is by far the best" (*Works and Days* 10.277–80[3]). For
Aristotle, only humans can be properly happy (*eudaimon*), since that
blessed state requires something of a rational appreciation of the good
or the fine for its own sake as the reason for one's actions. When he
turns to psychology, if Aristotle thinks humans are special it will be in
virtue of a certain special form of intelligence, *nous*; and the Stoics
banish animals beyond the circle of justice because they cannot put
together a grammatically correct sentence.[4]

In particular, what the European tradition is anxious about is what
makes "them" different from "us," in virtue of which we are allowed to do
whatever we like with them. They don't have justice; they can't enter into
an agreement; they are machines. This should not just salve our guilty
consciences but illuminate what is so special about us. We cannot do to
humans what we can do to other animals because humans are not machines; we have a moral sense; we can enter into meaningful agreements
with each other; we have opposable thumbs. The "barbaric mistake"
underwriting this instrumentalization of animal-talk for the sake of dis-
covering the "uniquely, truly human" is that there is *nothing* that all nonhuman animals have in common—except that they are not human. They
are not a genuine kind. So there is an important sense in which, in this
tradition, we are not thinking about *animals* at all, and it is perhaps no
wonder that trying to discover the human through examination of the
nonhuman should end (and go on) in irresolution and frustration.

Now the Indians were perfectly capable of having a "humans are distinctive"–type thought, and when they do, it is not an altogether unfa-
miliar thought. Here is a Hesiod moment from the *Hitopadeśa*, written

sometime between the eighth and twelfth centuries of the Common Era but drawing on much earlier didactic tales and fables, particularly from the third century BCE *Pañcatantra*[5]: "Food, sleep, fear, and sex are common to humans and beasts.... Dharma is the distinctive quality without which human beings are the same as brutes."[6] *Dharma*, like Hesiod's *dikē*, eludes satisfactory translation in a single English word; both are to be located in the area of what we in English would today call "the moral," specifically associated with what is fitting, right, appropriate, just, and to be done. Like Hesiod for the Greeks, the *Pañcatantra* and texts like it were widely taken as sources for practical advice about how to live and who to be, about what outlook to adopt in life. In fact the *Hitopadeśa*, like the *Pañcatantra* it draws on, is explicitly didactic, classified as *nītiśastra*—that is, advice for how to get on with others, and get on in life, so as to survive and flourish as much as possible. These two collections, like the even earlier Buddhist *Jātaka*[7] tales they are sometimes based on, have almost entirely nonhuman animal characters.

Now the thought picked out in *Works and Days* and in the *Hitopadeśa* is strikingly similar, and probably touches on something that many feel "intuitively" correct: for all our similarities, whatever they may be, with other animals, there is after all something that distinguishes human beings from other animals; if we try to pinpoint what it is, it is to be found somewhere in the region of our own appreciation of *moral* right and wrong, a sense of justice and fairness, that we do not expect other animals to have or to hold themselves to. It is a sense of right and wrong that cannot be traced to biological flourishing and success, and can even come into conflict with it.[8]

So consider the Hesiod quote again: animals eat one another; humans do not. From a survival point of view, such abstemiousness seems inexplicable and squandrous. Break an egg in a henhouse, and the hens will sensibly help themselves to the nutrient-rich egg. We would be horrified if humans did the equivalent. This sense of restraint— of there being certain things *we just don't do*, even if they might give us a material advantage—is what makes us human, and different from all other animals.

The Indian texts, as the *Hitopadeśa's* observation makes clear, were perfectly capable of recognizing this sort of difference. For the Buddhists, at least, animals were notorious committers of incest and cannibalism in particular,[9] and this view was shared widely beyond Buddhist popular thought. It is *humans* who may not eat each other or sleep with their mothers or brothers. The Jains, Hindus, and Buddhists all recognize some way in which *dharma*, understood as virtue, is not applicable to animals—but, as we will see, this is not a hard and fast rule, and all three of these Indian traditions at certain points back away from or even eschew altogether the claim that morality is the exclusive prerogative of the human.[10] The tradition did not speak with one voice on the issue and, more important, it did not make heavy weather of the claim one way or another. The *Hitopadeśa* quote stands out to those coming to the question of animals with an agenda set by the European tradition (or coming from Hesiod directly). But it is far from the dominant or even a central *motif* in classical Indian thought about animals. That *dharma* is for humans is a defeasible generalization, and not a hard and fast rule, for the observation was not made in the service of a theory of human nature in the first place.

However broadly acknowledged, here is what the acknowledgment of virtue and morality as special to the human did not do: it did *not* license us to suppose that whatever it was that made humans the same as each other and different from other animals entitled us to exclude animals from our moral world and our moral consideration. If anything, having *dharma* does the opposite: it imposes a new set of restrictions on our behavior, not just vis-à-vis each other but overall, vis-à-vis other animals and the environment generally.

The fact that classical Indian thought about animals does not focus on identifying the unique feature of the human has typically been traced to the difference in background cosmologies between Greece and India and to the Indian cosmology of rebirth in particular. There is likely a measure of truth in this, and I will explore in what senses there is a plausible connection between rebirth cosmology and the relative absence or weakening of human exceptionalism. That animal rationality in particular is not an issue of concern can be traced, I will suggest, to the popularity and pervasiveness of the fable in Indian culture. Both of these operate as forces for supposing that when we do think about animals, it is not to learn *by contrast* about the human but to learn by communion.

REBIRTH AS GROUNDS FOR CONCEPTIONS OF NONHUMAN ANIMALS

A cosmology of rebirth looks to be part of the pan-Indic cultural background nearly as far back as we can go. While there were categories of living beings (gods, humans, ghosts, animals, hell-beings is one popular Buddhist division),[11] these categories were always seen as bridgeable through rebirth.[12] What happens now to be a human life could become any kind of nonhuman life next time around. If we are familiar with the minority Pythagorean tradition in ancient Greek and Roman thought, then we might suppose there is a direct line from a belief in rebirth to a thoroughgoing nondistinction between human and non-human animal. Xenophanes recounts a story told of Pythagoras taking pity on a puppy being beaten in the street; he asks that the beating stop because he recognizes in the dog's cry the voice of a deceased friend.[13] If the beast I am beating, exploiting, about to step on, or about to eat might be my deceased grandfather, then there is as much absolute prohibition against eating or beating it as there is against eating or beating my grandfather.

But there is in fact no direct line from interchangeability to empathic kindness to nonhumans. And considered in the abstract, there is no reason why it should be so. If the scorpion is no different from the human (in whatever the relevant respect is meant to be), then the human is likewise no different from the scorpion. Of itself the nondistinction would speak no more in favor of kindness to animals than in favor of brutality to humans. But even if the scorpion *is* your beloved grandfather, with the usual valence that is thought to have, until we know the quality of his scorpion life (and perhaps many other things besides) we cannot say whether we would not be doing Grandpa a favor to step on him and thus relieve him of his scorpion existence.[14]

What does the work in the Indic traditions is not primarily rebirth but nonviolence (*ahiṃsā*). While the Jains can perhaps be credited with initiating emphasis on *ahiṃsā*,[15] and with taking it most seriously, Buddhists and Hindus agreed (in their different ways) that nonviolence was a paramount virtue.[16] It is because of a prior commitment to nonviolence that the continuity between human and nonhuman expressed in a rebirth cosmology will not in fact tell in favor of generalized disregard. Against the thought Xenophanes presents regarding Pythagoras, the value of *ahiṃsā* in classical Indian thought was not usually argued on the grounds that some animal lives might once have been human lives, for in that way the principle could protect nonhuman animals only once it had been established to apply to humans—and it would make for heightened interest in techniques for determining which animals had previously been human (inedible) and which had not (edible). Such an interest is wholly lacking in the various classifications of animals according to their edibility.[17] Rather the principle comes first—"No breathing, existing, living sentient creatures should be slain, nor treated with violence, nor abused, nor tormented, nor driven away. This is the pure, unchangeable, eternal law which the clever ones, who understand the world, have proclaimed"[18]—and applied to human and nonhuman animals alike. Because the specialness of humans is neither presumed nor invoked as the basis for *ahiṃsā*, it is evident without further comment that nonviolence applies wherever violence is possible, and violence is possible wherever harm is possible. Harm (as opposed to mere damage) is possible wherever there is sentient life, so that the pressing need is to determine the extent of sentience.[19] Here indeed is where we find vigorous dispute and discussion within the classical Indian tradition.[20]

This did not ensure peaceable coexistence between animal kinds, not even between the human and nonhuman. In spite of the widely shared agreement that nonviolence is better, and alongside a cosmology of transient identities crossing permeable boundaries, ancient India was an agrarian society, with plenty of use for domesticated animals; it was a martial society, with plenty of use for horses[21] and elephants—and occasion enough to kill both human and nonhuman animals; it was a hierarchical society, wherein a certain class of people amused itself in the hunt; and it was for many centuries a place of animal sacrifice. In the face of stricter Jain and Buddhist interpretations of nonviolence, those who followed the ritual practices of the Vedas gradually preferred dough stand-ins for the ritual animal sacrifices, but they had already found ways to reconcile animal slaughter with the nonviolence principle: according to the ancient *Laws of Manu* (5.39),[22] "killing in sacrifice is not killing," and "violence (*himsā*) ordained by the Veda is really *ahimsā*."[23] Elsewhere the *Laws of Manu* put ritual animal sacrifice and complete abstention from meat-eating on a comparable moral footing: "A man who abstains from meat and a man who offers the horse sacrifice every year for a hundred years—the reward for their meritorious acts is the same" (V.53).[24]

Besides a certain ambivalence regarding *ahimsā*, we can see here that how humans treat nonhuman animals is not a categorically different matter from how humans interact with each other. Just as nonviolence does not necessarily preclude just war, so too it does not necessarily preclude human employment of nonhuman animals in agriculture, nor their sacrifice in ritual. The question of how humans may treat nonhuman animals, just as the question of how they might engage with other humans, was treated as a question of what is *dharma* and *adharma*—where *dharma* may prescribe specific behaviors with respect to specific species of animal but refrains from instituting categorical distinctions between human and nonhuman as such. In the particular requirements or permissions of *dharma*, each species may be treated in its own right, but there is no categorical difference between humans

and "the rest." Basic principles by which humans are bound, such as
ahiṃsā, are valid across the board, even if the nature of the correct application may be tied specifically to context: killing a horse is wrong,
just as killing a person is wrong, but a soldier killing in war may be
dharma, just as slaughtering a horse in a Vedic ritual may be *dharma*.[25]

Thus when the Buddha objected to practices of animal sacrifice in
Brahmanical society, this was as much on account of its inefficaciousness as on account of cruelty to animals—indeed part of its cruelty
might be said to be due to its inefficaciousness, just as practicing austerities is self-cruelty because release from suffering is not thereby attained.[26] In spite of commitments to universal care (*karuṇā*) and
loving-kindness (*maitrī*), the earliest Buddhists were not vegetarians.[27] They considered not killing the animal oneself or having it
killed for one sufficient to satisfy the requirement of nonviolence.[28]
Eating leftover, donated meat was *not*, in their view, the equivalent of
eating one's kin or another human. The Jains, more thoroughgoing in
their interpretation of nonviolence, criticized the comparatively lax
Buddhists accordingly.[29] But this was a variation in the interpretation of the demands of *ahiṃsā* and not of the nature or implications
of rebirth.[30]

This universal scope or the lack of categorical distinction between
the human and nonhuman is not derived from a rebirth cosmology by
first assuming the specialness of humans. It is based on the vulnerability to harm that is shared across species, regardless of their various distinct qualities and capacities—and regardless of what they might have
been before or might be after their deaths. There is simply no straightforward line from rebirth cosmology to conceptions of or attitudes
toward animals.[31] This does not mean, however, that there are no lines
to be drawn at all, or that Olivelle is wrong to call rebirth "the most
significant religio-cultural belief that is connected to animal anthropomorphism"[32]; it is certainly relevant to attitudes toward, and thinking
about, animals.

REBIRTH ARTICULATING THE HUMAN BY
COMPARISON, NOT CONTRAST

Instead of reasoning from "rebirth" to any specific attitudes toward animals, we should consider the picture the rebirth cosmology presents as a whole. A division of possible realms for rebirth—human, animal, god, etc.—represents a way of conceiving the human condition. Humans live and move within a world populated by other animals. These other animals are not just the backdrop against which the truly important action of human life takes place. They are, on the contrary, equally pursuing their lives. That is, the interchangeability aspect of rebirth makes it natural to conceive nonhuman animals as *having lives*, in the relevant sense: having projects, plans, wishes, desires, relationships, and so on. These relationships are with other animals of their kind or not, and may sometimes be relationships with human animals. Among the many nonabsolute taxonomies of animals in Sanskrit literature, one significant (though not exhaustive) distinction is between village animals, wild animals, and farm animals that do not quite count as either. From this relation to human habitation follows a host of specific rules about how humans may or may not, must or must not interact with, treat, or consume the various animals so classified.[33] Conceiving the cosmos as one in which lives extend over multiple and various incarnations means conceiving the human world as fundamentally a *shared* world, and shared not just with other humans but also with nonhuman animals. These creatures are on the same journey as we are, are liable to the same conditions and pressures as we are. To think about them is to think about us, not by contrast but by comparison.

While it is largely agreed that an animal form of life is a less desirable one than a human form, this is mostly thought to be due to differences in degree rather than in kind. Nonhuman animals tend to be liable to greater pain and suffering than humans, with less opportunity for mitigating or eliminating that suffering. (Gods, by contrast, are comparatively less liable to pain than human beings.) Thus Jains, Buddhists, and Hindus all take a dim view of animal incarnation, and it is not infrequently presented as a punishment or an evil consequence for someone who has behaved badly in a human incarnation.[34] Most animal lives are considered to be full of discomforts that affect human lives rather less; the domesticated ones labor as beasts of burden, for instance, and the wild ones live in constant fear of not having enough to eat or of being eaten themselves.[35] Perhaps more important, animal lives are thought of as miserable because animals are considered to have no options. This is related to the question of whether animals have *dharma*.[36] On the whole, nonhuman animals are thought to lack the capacity to, for instance, refrain from violence or revise their conception of the good so that they do not live in constant fear. Lacking a capacity for revising one's desires and restraining one's impulsive behavior, and perhaps lacking a sense of right not driven by natural necessity, is a disadvantage that makes life on the whole more miserable and less desirable than a human life—even than an impoverished and difficult human life.[37]

In fact, however, the view of animal moral capacities was much more complex and ambiguous in the various Indian traditions. In a way we should expect this—within a cosmology of reincarnation, coupled with a moralized doctrine of *karma* (as it was in classical India), if animals (and other beings) cannot behave morally, it looks as if they could never be reborn in a better estate; this would have obvious awkward implications about the direction the world is heading. More important, the exclusion of animals from the possibility of engaging in ethical behavior would be such a massive constraint on the interchangeability aspect of the system as to render it virtually meaningless. If damnation were permanent, or if it were just the effects of *karma* without the possibility of generating fresh action, we would no longer be conceiving of nonhuman beings as participants in our shared world.

So while the official line in Hinduism is that "only human beings, in the ordinary course of things, have access to *mokṣa* or *mukti* (spiritual liberation)"[38]—and indeed this is sometimes, as with Śaṅkara, restricted still further to only well-born male humans—the tradition nevertheless abounds in tales of extraordinary animals that were able to rise above their expected station and behave in morally exemplary ways, and some that were able even to attain liberation.[39]

For the Buddhists likewise animals "are not considered to be capable of growth in the *dhamma* and the *vinaya* [monastic discipline],"[40] but this excludes them from activities that certain classes of human beings are excluded from in the same clause. So beings vary in their moral-spiritual capacities, but not according to their status as human or otherwise. And Buddhist texts are nevertheless explicit and consistent in treating animals as, in a sense, ethical beings: nonhuman animals can be reborn in a better station in the same way that any living being might be reborn in a better station, namely, as the natural consequence of living an ethical life, where that is primarily understood as acting out of care and concern for others.[41] Still more, animals might live *exemplary* lives. "That animals as well as humans are considered capable of truly ethical behavior is underlined by a striking passage from the *Vinaya Piṭaka*," writes McDermott:

> Here a partridge, a monkey, and a bull elephant are pictured as having undertaken the five moral precepts, and living together, "courteous, deferential, and polite to one another." Their life-style is referred to as "Partridge Brahma-faring," and set up as a model of morality upon which even the Buddhist *bhikkhu*s should pattern their lives.[42]

Nonhuman animals are considered sufficiently like the human sort in kind, and in situation, that they may act as role models for how humans ought to live.[43] At their worst, animals are beings of the same sort, just less wise, more violent, and unhappier than humans, so that they are appropriate beings toward whom *śīla* (right and restrained conduct, speech, and livelihood) is to be expected.[44]

... But Can We Eat Them?

While animals may be on the same journey as humans, and while this set Buddhists against the sacrificial practices of their Brahmanical contemporaries, we noted earlier that this was not originally seen by Buddhists as a reason to refrain from eating them. Instead, and reflecting the Buddhist emphasis on intent and disposition, one may not *kill* living beings for the purpose of eating them (or for any other purpose) nor have them killed or even knowingly allow them to be killed for one's sake. "Meat should not be eaten when it is seen, heard or suspected to have been killed for one," the Buddha is recorded as saying (*MN* 55); if one does not see or hear or suspect that an animal has been killed for one, then if meat is given, one may eat it. This disregard for actual suffering or harm caused, regardless of intentions, was severely criticized (mocked, even) by the more austere Jains.[45] It had, however, a distinct practical advantage among a community committed to living exclusively on alms within a meat-eating society.[46] Moreover such pragmatic accommodation looks less ridiculous when we recognize that the Buddhists are not attempting to set one principle of right (intention) over another (outcomes); the Buddhist project—perhaps the Indian project of moral thinking *tout court*—was not a quest for a decision principle or a source of normativity. This is no doubt related to the relative lack of presumption about the categorical specialness of human beings.[47] At any rate, for the Indian Buddhists, moral thinking is in the service of our quest for moral improvement and ultimately for liberation, and for that, the focus is rather on who and how to *be*. The Buddhist interpretation of *ahiṃsā* is that we should live and be in such a way that we intend no ill or harm to any living being, directly or indirectly.

In fact this Buddhist emphasis on the cardinal dispositions of loving-kindness, equanimity, care,[48] and sympathetic joy led very naturally to an ethic that disregards differences in animal kinds when considering how to engage with others. Of course how one *expresses* loving-kindness, say, to a human being may differ from the expression of loving-kindness toward a vulture, but in every case loving-kindness is what is called for—and similarly for the other virtuous dispositions (*brahmavihāras*).[49] It should be no surprise, then, that Buddhism did ultimately come to advocate vegetarianism, and not just as a monastic discipline but as a moral precept for all (albeit a precept liable to violation). The Mahāyāna movement, which, among other things, drew the ambitions of monastic life into the daily lives of nonmonastics, seems to have initiated the commitment to refraining from eating animals even if they were not killed for one's own sake.

The eighth chapter of the *Laṅkāvatāra Sūtra* is an instructive text in this regard,[50] although this chapter is possibly later than the rest of the (probably) third-century CE text. The chapter consists of a series of reasons why one should not eat meat. The appeal throughout is to care and have concern for living beings: anyone who cares for the welfare of other beings would not eat animals because.... One of the most charming reasons is that meat-eating makes you stink. This is not a problem because other human beings might be offended by your body odor; it is a problem because animals with much more discerning senses of smell will immediately detect your scent as "meat-eater," and therefore as a possible danger to themselves. "If this is a meat-eater, it might eat me!" think all the small furry creatures in your surroundings. Even if you have no intention of eating rabbit, or that particular rabbit, for dinner tonight, it is cruel and thoughtless to walk around striking terror into the heart of every living being around you. Restraining one's appetites is a courtesy to others.

A second striking argument is a slippery slope argument. If you start by eating animals of any sort, the thought goes, you will eventually turn to eating forbidden or filthy animals, and may well even find yourself eating human flesh.[51] This is backed up by, on the one hand, a story of a notorious king who apparently did just that and, on the other hand, by a claim about the psychology of meat-eating. By eating meat one develops a taste for it and simultaneously desensitizes oneself to what one is doing in eating meat (to the fact that it is a dead animal, a stinking corpse, you are eating). This instigates a kind of craving for new, fresh, intense meaty flavors, unchecked by a natural repugnance, which has been blunted; this in turn leads to further and more various meat consumption, and so on.[52] The point of interest here is the emphasis on mental training. Eating meat cultivates and perpetuates a psychological disposition and outlook, and this is what is particularly pernicious about it.

Finally there is the *Laṅkāvatāra Sūtra*'s argument from rebirth. The text argues that since all beings have been reborn innumerable times, there is no way to know that any given animal is not a close relation to you at some point in the process. This is the argument for vegetarianism that one expects within the context of rebirth cosmologies; it trades on the strong intuition that eating your kin is obviously appalling, and of course on a literal notion of rebirth. But the text then does something more interesting: it juxtaposes this with the oft-repeated observation that the Buddha, and anyone striving for the enlightenment he reached, regards all living beings as his only child.[53] Here the claim is precisely *not* trading on a literal notion of rebirth. The Buddha does not think all beings were, in some incarnation, his only child. Rather, knowing this not to be literally the case, he nevertheless regards them with the intense affection and concern that parents typically have for their only child. This is the recommendation of a stance to adopt toward all creatures (and not a claim about essences, either similar or different). We do not see ourselves as radically distinct, but as radically—intensely, closely—related. Starting with an appeal to literal rebirth, in a culture where that is a going item, gets one to begin to see what adopting this outlook means. One of the difficulties of non-rebirth cultures, then, is how to get a foothold in radical relatedness.[54]

The Jains were the most systematic in extending the nonviolence principle to every living thing and had the widest understanding of what was alive. This difference was indeed based on a distinctive cosmological picture, but not on any variation of a theory of rebirth.

The Jains opted for a single, stable, and exhaustive taxonomy of living beings, organizing them according to the number of sense faculties they have. Plants have one sense faculty (touch); mammals, birds, and fish have all five (touch, taste, hearing, sight, smell); and various insects and smaller creatures have various subsets of these.[55] This taxonomy, however, does not establish a normative ranking; creatures with more sense faculties are not thereby more worthy.[56] These characterizations are purely descriptive. Anything with any sense faculty is capable of suffering or flourishing in some respect, and the classification of living beings according to their sense faculties provides valuable information about *how* they can be helped or harmed—and so what may and may not be done with or to them. This classification of living beings enables Jainism to establish "a truly unprecedented philosophical foundation for compassionate behavior toward animals."[57]

Arguing against their non-Jain contemporaries that more care must be taken to avoid harming all sorts of living beings, the Jains generally presented arguments from virtue and character rather than from the basis of the natures of living beings.[58] Violent is as much a bad thing to *be* as violence is bad to *do*. That is, the fact that it harms others is not the foremost consideration against violence—after all, harming others is the point of violence, so pointing out that my violence harms others has not yet given me a reason to desist. A hostile mentality itself is not an edifying one. Violence is counterproductive; over the long run it does not help to achieve one's aims; it is frowned upon or sanctioned by gods or society; having hurtful intentions, and then especially acting on them, does violence to *myself*. The Jains share with the Buddhists an emphasis on character, on what sort of person I become through either careful or aggressive behavior toward others, both human and nonhuman.

Like the Buddhists (and, to some extent, the Hindus), the Jains fill their texts with stories of animals behaving morally. As with the Buddhists, their behavior determines their next incarnation, which can be either good or bad; that is, being an animal does not mean that one is bound to act viciously. In fact these stories even depict animals

as *choosing*, and so as responsible for their acts even on a more robust
account of moral responsibility.[59]

In sum, a rebirth cosmology does not of itself determine that we
owe animals the same treatment we owe other humans, and it does not
entail that we cannot distinguish between the moral relevance of killing a person and the moral relevance of killing a rat. Taken as a logical
proposition, almost nothing follows from a commitment to rebirth.
Taken, however, as a description of the human condition, the cosmology of rebirth offers a depiction of that situation in which there is
nothing distinctively human about it. Humans do not act out the lead
roles on a stage set by a relatively undifferentiated nonhuman environment. Animals, and indeed all living beings, are part of our shared
world; anyone might occupy interchangeably any position within this
shared world. Where all animals (or living things) are interchangeable,
identity is fluid, not essential. That is a fact about the human condition, and the fact is, it is not a distinctively *human* condition at all. All
animals are on the same journey or in the same predicament; their suffering takes different forms, and the resources they can bring to difficulties differs. This is what is precious in a human incarnation: our
resources, should we choose to use them, are so much more varied and
effective. But these additional resources bring with them additional
responsibilities: it is much easier for human beings to restrain their desires and not act out of fear than it is for a tiger, and so it is more incum-
bent upon us to do so. Doing so, at the same time, gives us easier access
to the fruits of virtue. But these differences are generally thought of as
a matter of degree, and there is no great pressure to hunt down some
essential difference that marks out humankind.

FABLES

The metaphysics or cosmology did not work alone in creating the sense
of a shared world and shared condition between humans and other
animals. Indeed if the foregoing is correct, even the apparently

metaphysical and cosmological works in a more literary fashion—suggesting and articulating an outlook and way of relating—than by providing grounds for inescapable conclusions. We should not consider principles like *karma*, *ahiṃsā*, and *karuṇā*, then, independently of the explicitly literary works that encoded these principles and provided opportunity for their concrete engagement and exercise.

From the perspective of ancient Indian literature, it is a striking fact that there are no talking monkeys in the *Iliad*. There are no snake kings or eagle heroes, no helpful mice or shifty jackals.[60] If animals exist in the ancient Greek literary world, they are the backdrop against which the real action of human life takes place, or props in an act of human madness; significantly, they do not take on speaking roles.[61] In ancient India, by contrast, although in an oral tradition it is impossible to be certain, it looks as if the practice of sharing tales involving talking animals is perhaps as old as the cosmology of rebirth. Stephanie Jamison has argued, for instance, that although there are no animal fables proper in the *Ṛg Veda*, we see in certain passages evidence that such stories were told and expected to be familiar to the audience of the *Ṛg Veda*.[62] Talking animals are not only very old, but were also extremely widespread. The sheer quantity and pervasiveness of animal fables is difficult to overestimate. The earliest surviving collection we have may be the voluminous *Jātaka* tales, stories of the previous lives of the Buddha, likely composed around the fourth century BCE. Some of these previous lives are as a human or a god, but very many are nonhuman animal incarnations. For these tales Buddhists likely drew in part on an existing body of stories already familiar to their audience and reworked them to serve the purpose of describing the Buddha's long journey to enlightenment as a series of studies in particular virtues. When Buddhism was at its height in India—let us say, from around the period of the Buddhist convert emperor Aśoka (third century BCE), who unified much of India, and for the next seven or eight centuries—these stories would have been very widely known. *Avadāna* tales collected and circulated during this time, sometimes featuring virtuous animals,[63] and the so-called "commentary" on the *Dhammapadā* of the 5th Century C.E. consisted of morality tales, some involving animals.[64] Some stories were taken up and reworked into non-Buddhist animal fables and included in the (third-century BCE?) *Pañcatantra*, a massive collection of animal tales, organized as sage practical advice, particularly on how to be successful in one's dealings with others.[65] Some of these are in turn taken up by the *Hitopadeśa* (eighth–twelfth century CE), a similar sort of text, which also incorporates animal fables from other unnamed sources. There is also the eleventh-century CE *Kathāsaritsagara*, the *Ocean of Rivers of Stories*, the largest compilation of Sanskrit tales and fables, several of which involve animals as primary characters (some of these taken from the *Pañcatantra*). With so many talking animals about, it would have been most incongruous to argue that the *essential* difference between them and us—the difference that casts them outside considerations of right and wrong—is their irrationality.

This is even more so since the talking the animals are depicted as engaging in is invariably of a practical sort (asking, What ought I to do? What is the good thing to do, or the right choice?) and often collaborative (What should *we* do?). These fables involving talking animals have an avowedly didactic role and seem always to have been recognized as such. In keeping with this didactic function, narratives of talking animals engaged in practical reasoning were popular and practical—a part of the everyday fabric of life and upbringing in the broadest sense, not reserved for the rarified domain of the literary elite.

But the very fact that these tales should illustrate moral or practical advice for the human, social world raises the ready objection that such tales are not, in fact, about animals at all. Since the animals talk like humans in order to teach us about humans and being human, perhaps we should say the *Jātaka* tales, for instance, present animals as "mere vehicle[s] for human traits" rather than treating "animals as subjects" in their own right.[66] Such fables are anthropomorphizing, the objection goes, indicating much concerning what their audience thought about human social life, perhaps, but nothing at all about what or how they thought about animals. After all, we are not to suppose that an ancient Indian listener conversant in these fables would have supposed of any actual mouse she encountered in the pantry that it might indeed speak to her.

Now there is a curious feature of this anthropomorphizing objection. The very notion of anthropomorphizing presumes we have a distinct and stable notion of the human—of human character and social life—which we then foist upon our nonhuman animals and that we have a definite sense of "the other" animals as necessarily quite distinct from humans in just these respects, so that granting them these "human" characteristics can only be foisting on them something that does not properly belong there. But if our starting point is not the assumption of radical difference, then it is more difficult to articulate the objection *as* an objection. It is true that in these fables, familiar characteristics or traits are isolated and identified particularly with certain animals. The jackal is "the epitome of greed and cunning"; the crow is "smart and curious"; the ass is interested only in food and sex.[67] But what we have here is not so much anthropomorphism as caricature: the distilled forms of virtues and vices are presented and deployed to didactic effect. These caricatures are used not just as particular anecdotes to distill and advertise the folly of pride, say. They are also used cumulatively to argue over many instances for general points: that creatures behave according to their nature, for instance, or that fate does (or does not) determine one's actions. So the story of the carnivorous lion is not taking the lion to stand for a person of a particular kind; it is taking a stand in an argument about the scope of choice, for anyone. Nature made the lion carnivorous, says the story, and it is futile to ask him to be nice and vegetarian. Similarly the lesson states that human individuals or even classes have their natures, and one cannot expect them to suddenly change these or act out of character.[68]

Both storytellers and audiences knew the animals whereof they spoke. In fact to serve their didactic function the animals of the tales *cannot* be a mere blank onto which human features are inscribed. They must be sufficiently similar to human beings in relevant ways and similarly situated. The similarity thought relevant here is not in biological functioning or bodily parts but rather in what might be very broadly characterized as moral situation. Nonhuman animals have natures (*svabhāva*), for instance, just as we do, which they can conform to or try to act against. Having distinctive natures, in their case as in ours, is immediately related to having related duties and propensities (*svadharma*).[69] They are the bearers of the consequences of their actions, just as we are; they have mental states that affect their actions and choices, and are in turn affected by them. These are not picturesque ways of thinking about animals, but thoughts about what animals are actually like. Of course the particular natures ascribed to each kind of animal are, to a certain extent, something the storytellers project onto each animal. And yet the storytellers and their hearers were also acute observers of nature, so that the characters they gave their various animals are recognizable from observation of actual animals, their characteristic reactions and behaviors.[70] The storytellers did not *project* the eternal enmity of the snake and the mongoose onto those poor creatures; they discovered it there, in the observed behavior of the animals, and used it for their storytelling. Nor did narrators *project* subjective mental states such as fear, care, cooperation, aggression, cunning onto empty ciphers; they had experience of animals as subjects and could rely on their audience having the same.

This is why, curiously, we can see that the lessons in a fable may also go the other way; rather than observations about human interactions being projected onto animals so that they can mirror it back to us, we see observations from the animal world turned to lessons for the human world. One example is the proverb repeated in the *Pañcatantra* that "there can be no friendship between grass-eaters and meat-eaters, between a food and its eater" (e.g., *Pañcatantra* II, 9).[71] Here it is animals informing the human world rather than presumptions about humans coloring in otherwise uncharacterized animals. The instruction, illustrated of course with colorful stories, is to look about you in the natural world; see how there is no friendship between the grass-eating animals and the meat-eating animals? There can be no friendship between food and its eater, between two parties, the one of which survives at the cost of the other. So think: when someone offers friendship, is he in a position to offer it? Can he be trusted? If his interests are fundamentally at odds with yours, then do not expect friendship— even if he promises it, and even if he genuinely intends to extend it. If a person cannot survive without consuming you, you will find that, at some point, you have become his supper. Such an implicit line of reasoning relies on an appreciation of the continuity between the human condition and the nonhuman, on a view of whatever lives as essentially in the same situation and liable to the same concerns and constraints.

Sometimes the lessons are not to be carried over from animals to humans in any obvious way at all. The animals remain animals. Take this example from the *Jātaka* tales. The Buddha, in a life prior to his awakening (when he was just a *bodhisattva*), is living as the king rat among a community of rats.[72] A jackal pretends to be very holy, practicing austerities, and persuades the king to allow him to act as sentry when the rats leave their nest to search for food. After several rats have gone missing, it is discovered that the jackal has been using his post as sentry to pick off the last rat through the door when they return each evening. So far, so familiar. The *Bodhisattva* (who will become the Buddha), currently the rat king, then lunges on the wicked jackal and slits open its jugular so that the jackal dies. It is very unclear what lesson is meant to transfer from this heroic mouse escapade to the human world, particularly in terms of teaching Buddhist values of compassion and nonviolence. The story seems simply to recognize that it is in the nature of a *rat* to react murderously to threats and treachery. Taking on board that there is something characteristic of rats in the episode, we can then consider this as a (ratty) expression of the virtue of individuals in community looking out for and defending each other and acting on each other's behalf.

What is going on in such stories, and generally in these animal fables, is not so much anthropomorphism *instead of* taking the animals as subjects (an unhelpful dichotomy) as a lack of recognition of a significant gulf between animals and humans. This is a fitting literature for a cosmology of interchangeability, but it also reinforces, explores, and deepens the sense of commonality, of animals as our fellows— some of them rascals, some of them friends, all of them trying in a way compatible with their natures and naturally given resources to find a way to live a satisfying life in a world populated with many and various other creatures trying to do the same.

CONCLUSION

In Indian classical literature, philosophical, legal, and literary, there is a great deal to be said about specific kinds of animals and forms of interaction appropriate to different specific animals, including the human. But there is not so much evidence of that presumption of a fundamental difference between human and nonhuman forms of life that allows us in English, for instance, to use the word "animal" simply to mean "nonhuman animal."

This means that the concept of the animal is not best suited to explore the nature of the human by *contrast*. Instead we more often find a background presumption of a common condition: whatever lives seeks to sustain its life, wants pleasure and not pain, wants its desires and aims satisfied rather than thwarted. Differences in animals, including the human animals, are then just so many differences in opportunities for pleasure and avoiding pain, abilities to conceive of desires and satisfy them, and forms of vulnerability in having these ambitions frustrated. The many tales of talking animals both express and sustain this basic orientation toward commonality, and they enable us to illuminate the human social world not because the animals are anthropomorphized but because reality is not anthropocentric in the first place.

Instead of seeing the doctrine of rebirth as a reason or ground for assimilating animals to humans, we should see it as expressive of an understanding of fluid and temporary identities, each of which is a variation on a single common condition. A cosmology of rebirth works together with its popular literature to create a sensibility of awareness to the aliveness of things. Both the cosmology and the sensibility, however, require independent appreciation of the badness of violence, the value of *ahiṃsā*, before we can begin to put these together into prescriptions for attitudes or behaviors toward nonhuman animals. Animals are, at bottom, less fortunate versions of ourselves, and if there is anything distinctive of the human role in this relationship, it is that we can perhaps appreciate this fact and possibly even extend sympathy on its basis.[73]

Reflection

THE JOY OF FISH AND CHINESE ANIMAL PAINTING

Hou-mei Sung

Representations of animals in traditional Chinese painting are
among the oldest known motifs and are filled with rich symbolic
implications. Animal paintings make animals a part of the
harmonious existence of all living beings in the universe. To the
Chinese, animals are more than merely beasts in nature; they are
living symbols with philosophical, historical, and metaphorical
associations. This explains why in early Chinese painting animals are
typically portrayed with distinct attitudes or in particular poses, for
example, dragons emerging from the clouds, tigers roaring with the
wind, cranes calling toward heaven, carp leaping above the waves,
and minnows darting playfully among water weeds. Many of these
early conceptual depictions of animals were directly linked to the
ancient Chinese *yin/yang* cosmologies, Daoism, and Confucianism.
Each animal provides unique insights into this rich and constantly
evolving historical and cultural context.[1] I will use a few Chinese
Song dynasty (960–1279) fish paintings for illustration.

By the tenth century Chinese fish painting had already
developed into a fully established and independent subject. It
gained increasing popularity through a new aesthetic standard set
by the rising scholar-elites and their influential participation in art.
According to descriptions of lost paintings as well as those that

have survived, the most prevalent Chinese fish painting themes that emerged during this time were *Fish and Weeds* (*Yuzaotu*) and *Fish at Play* (*Xiyutu*). Both depict minnows swimming joyfully in water. The concepts underlying both themes can be traced to two ancient Chinese philosophical classics; respectively, *The Book of Odes* (*Shijing*), the oldest collection of Chinese poetry (eleventh to seventh centuries BCE), compiled by Confucius, and *Zhuangzi*, the Daoist text written by Zhuiangzu (ca. 369–286 BCE). The *Fish and Weeds* theme was directly inspired by a chapter of this name in *The Book of Odes*, in which the image of fish swimming among weeds was used as a metaphor for the people living under a wise ruler. The second theme, *Fish at Play*, focuses on fish swimming joyfully in water. The concept underlying this theme can be traced to a debate between the Daoist philosophers Zhuangzi and Huizi on "the joy of fish" as they stood on the bank of the Hao River.

ZHUANGZI: See how the minnows [*tiaoyu*] come out and dart around where they please! That's what fish really enjoy!

HUIZI: You are not a fish, how do you know what fish enjoy?

ZHUANGZI: You are not I—so how do you know I don't know what fish enjoy?

HUIZI: I am not you, so I certainly don't know what you know. On the other hand, you're certainly not a fish—so that still proves you don't know what fish enjoy!

ZHUANGZI: Let's go back to your original question, please. You asked me how I know what fish enjoy—so you already knew I knew it when you asked the question. I know it by standing here beside the Hao.[2]

While this dialogue may sound more like an exercise in logic between the two Daoist masters, the image of minnows swimming joyfully in water subsequently became synonymous with Zhuangzi's philosophical emphasis on spiritual freedom. Zhuangzi's contemplation on the "joy of fish" was extremely important for early Chinese fish painting. It triggered a new trend of illustrating swimming fish in water, as seen in both *Fish and Weeds* and *Fish at Play*, instead of the dead "kitchen fish" practiced by many earlier painters.[3] Moreover the direct association with Zhuangzi's "joy of fish" is indicated by the type of fish portrayed: the *tiaoyu*, a long, slender member of the minnow family.[4] The *tiaoyu* is mentioned specifically in the text of Zhuangzi quoted above. It is therefore not surprising that most of the extant fish paintings attributed to Song or earlier artists all portray this particular kind of fish (fig. 3R1—see art insert). These paintings also follow, in various degrees, a consistent set of aesthetic values, techniques, and expressions in representing the lively and graceful movements of the slender minnows in water. The same depiction and aesthetic values can also be found in the opening section of the early twelfth-century handscroll, *Fish Swimming amid Falling Flowers* (fig. 3R2—see art insert). Here the artist enhances the playful mood of the swimming minnows by adding a branch of blooming peach blossoms and portrays the minnows chasing after the fallen petals. This seasonal touch colored the "joy of fish" ideology with both poetic sentiment and the passage of time. The lyrical transformation also reveals the high level of sophistication of Song fish painting, in its content as well as its technique, which captured the realistic features of both the darting movements of the fish themselves and the elusive nature of the aquatic environs.

Thus as early as the Song dynasty (960–1279), the realistic depiction of the aquatic world of fish had already served to express the ideals of the two leading Chinese philosophies: Confucianism, which emphasizes achieving social harmony through a hierarchical and orderly human relationship, and Daoism, which seeks natural harmony by following one's innate nature and the natural order of the universe. On the one hand, the image *Swimming Fish* refers to the "joy of fish" concept associated with the Daoist philosophical text of Zhuangzi, symbolizing the leisurely spiritual freedom of an untethered life. On the other hand, the depiction of *Fish and Weeds* readily reminds one of the Confucian-based interpretation of "the unbound joy of life under a wise ruler."

The "joy of fish" concept continued to play a role in later Chinese fish painting. Even when the leaping carp replaced the minnows and became the dominant fish painting theme after the twelfth century, the "joy of fish" motif continued to be used. It served either to enrich the narration or to complement the new political message expressing the Chinese people's indignation and defiance under the Mongolian-ruled Yuan dynasty (1279–1368) (fig. 3R3—see art insert).[5]

Although the "joy of fish" depiction of the Song dynasty represents only a chapter in the early stage of Chinese fish painting's evolving symbolic language, its conceptual depiction and rich content provide viewers insight into the philosophy and contemplative moods of the Song scholar-elite. While the darting movements of the minnow evoke the seasonal moods of the Yangzi River region, the "joy of fish" ideology and its association with the "unbound joy of the free and unburdened life of a great man"[6] led viewers to a "world of joy," offering a reprieve from the stressful burdens and responsibilities of daily life.

CHAPTER FOUR

Human and Animal Nature in the Philosophy of the Islamic World

Peter Adamson

Humans are, according to the traditional philosophical definition, "rational, mortal animals." Here "rational" does the crucial role of differentiating us from nonhuman animals. Though this notion did not go unchallenged in the ancient philosophical tradition, there was no medieval Arabic translation of such exceptional works as Porphyry's *On Abstinence from Killing Animals*, which appears to grant nonhuman animals a share of rationality. As a result the medieval Arabic reader would have heard the Hellenic philosophical tradition speaking unanimously and drawing a firm dividing line between the human and the animal, with rationality as the basis for drawing that line. On the other hand, the canonical definition also recognizes that humans belong to the genus of animals. This suggests that we share a good deal with nonhuman animals. Then again, the philosophical tradition of the Islamic world is often, and rightly, seen as intellectualist: scientific knowledge is identified as the highest goal of human life. So one might expect the

representatives of this tradition to make little of our animal nature and
instead to focus on the intellective power through which we achieve
knowledge, a power possessed only by human animals.

But this expectation is not borne out. Philosophers working in
Islamic lands did explore the "animal" aspects of human nature, and
did so precisely because of their intellectualism. In epistemology, scientific understanding was seen as the human activity par excellence. Yet
most humans fail to engage in this activity because of the stringent requirements that must be satisfied if cognition is to count as true understanding. This suggests that most people are effectively living a life of
nonhuman animals in human bodies. Similarly in ethics a life devoted
to reason is constantly recommended in philosophical literature, but
the same literature laments that few people live up to that ideal. Again
it would seem that most humans are leading lives consonant with their
animal, rather than their human, nature. Thus to understand the psychological and ethical condition of most people, these philosophers
needed to consider the psychological and ethical condition of nonhuman animals.

We can find rather extreme statements to this effect in Arabic philosophical literature. The starkest examples I know are both found in
commentaries on Aristotle, in the first case a commentary on part of
the *Metaphysics*, written by the Christian philosopher Yaḥyā Ibn ʿAdī:

> The activity of humanity (*fiʿl al-insāniyya*), through which every
> single person is a human, is proper to it [sc. humanity]. It is intellect
> in actuality, which does not belong to them [sc. the people who are
> ignorant of nature]. Thus they do not deserve the name of "people"
> (*al-nās*). Just as a hand, when it lacks its proper activity, is not in
> truth a hand, so with the eye and the ear. And in general, every es-
> sence that lacks its proper activity lacks its own proper existence
> along with the lack of [the activity]. Therefore it does not deserve
> the name of that essence; if it is called by that name, it is so called
> without deserving it. Thus, the Philosopher does not include among

"people"—i.e. among those who are truly people because they do have the activity of proper humanity—those who resemble people by their bodily form, but lack the proper activity of humanity.[1]

And in the second case Averroes's commentary on the *Physics*:

The name "human" is predicated equivocally of a human being who is perfected by a speculative science and of one who is not perfected by it or who does not have aptitude to be perfected by it. Similarly the name "human" is predicated equivocally of a living and dead human being, or of a rational human being and one that is made of stone.[2]

While these are particularly striking passages, they are not unrepresentative. As we'll see toward the end of this chapter, the Andalusian Muslim thinker Ibn Bājja agreed that humans who pursue a bodily life are effectively living as nonhuman animals.

You might expect a philosopher who believes that many people are ethically on a par with nonhuman animals to form benevolent views concerning animal ethics, precisely because of the similarity between humans and animals. After all, I am not morally permitted to abuse or eat my human neighbor whose lack of interest in philosophy and science, and whose devotion to pleasure and desire, mean that he is no better than a cow. So why would I be permitted to abuse or eat a real cow? In fact, though, discussions of animal ethics in the Islamic world hardly ever invoke the shared nature of human and nonhuman animals. Instead we find philosophers following up hints in authoritative religious texts and stating that the correct attitude toward God and oneself implies, as a kind of corollary, a relatively gentle approach toward animals. This will be the thrust of the first section of the chapter, "The God's-Eye View."[3] By contrast, when our philosophers are discussing humans instead of animals, the point about shared animal nature does play a significant role. This will emerge in the second

("Two Three-Part Souls") and third ("Living as a Human") sections. In the second section I look at the development of psychological theories that recognize significant overlap between animal and human cognition. As we will then see in the final section, philosophers in the Islamic world urge us to lead lives devoted to the one faculty that is *not* shared with animals, namely reason or intellection.

THE GOD'S-EYE VIEW

While the Qur'ān frequently presents animals in a positive light, the point of this is not so much to celebrate animals as to celebrate their Creator.[4] Animals are referred to as a "sign" of God's power (e.g., 42:29, 45:4) and as created by God (e.g., 43:12, 88:17). They also provide proof of God's benevolence, in that He provides for them, just as He does for humans (29:60, 67:19). However, animals are also said to be created for the benefit of humans, as in these verses:

> And the grazing livestock He has created for you; in them is warmth and [numerous] benefits, and from them you eat. And for you in them is [the enjoyment of] beauty when you bring them in [for the evening] and when you send them out [to pasture]. And they carry your loads to a land you could not have reached except with difficulty to yourselves. Indeed, your Lord is kind and merciful. And [He created] the horses, mules and donkeys for you to ride and [as] adornment. (Qur'ān 16:5–8)[5]

This same chapter of the Qur'ān mentions cattle (16:66) and bees (16:68–69), alongside plants, as things created for man's benefit. Other passages, several of which use the term "livestock" (*an'am*), confirm the subservience of animals to humans (22:33, 23.21, 36:71, 40:79, 43:12), as does a verse stating that God has preferred humans to other creatures (17:70).

Equally telling are verses denouncing some humans as being no better than, or even worse than, animals:

Do not be like those who say, "We have heard," while they do not hear. Indeed, the worst of living creatures (*dawābb*) in the sight of Allah are the deaf and dumb who do not think (*lā yaʿqilūna*). Had God known any good in them, He would have made them hear. (Qurʾān 8:21–24)

Here the word *dawābb* indicates that animals are being spoken about (cf. use of the singular version of the noun *dābba* at, e.g., 6:38, 29:60, 31:10, 45:4). Similarly at 7:179 we are told that those who are heedless of God are worse than livestock. While such verses suggest a disapproving attitude toward animals, there are also indications that God considers them to have an appropriate relationship to Him, and one for which they will be rewarded. Perhaps the most remarkable such hint is the following verse: "And there is no creature (*dābba*) on [or within] the earth or bird that flies with its wings except [that they are] communities like you. [...] Unto their Lord they will be gathered" (Qurʾān 6:38). This verse seems to hold out the prospect of an afterlife for animals. Furthermore certain animals, especially birds, are said to exalt God and pray to Him (24:41, 21:79, 34:10, 38:19).[6] So despite Qurʾān 8:21–24, quoted earlier, animals can even be seen as setting an example for us to follow rather than a low standard we must rise above. If even the birds worship God, then how much more should humans, capable of thought and favored above other creatures, do so?

These themes are confirmed by the *ḥadīth* (reports about the deeds and sayings of the Prophet). For instance, there is a *ḥadīth* stating that a man who showed kindness to a dog would be blessed, whereas a woman who mistreated a cat will go to hell.[7] It should be noted, however, that Muḥammad's wife ʿĀʾisha, a significant authority when it came to the reliability of *ḥadīth*, dismissed this notion as preposterous: "A believer is too dear to God to be tormented on account of a cat."[8] Muslim theologians, meanwhile, followed up the Qurʾān's suggestion that animals will have an afterlife, and even engaged in detailed discussion of the nature of that afterlife. For instance, the early, admittedly rather idiosyncratic theologian al-Naẓẓām believed that even vermin like scorpions will be admitted to paradise, but freed from their bodies.[9] Theologians of the Muʿtazilite school held that God must obey certain moral and rational norms in His dispensation of reward and punishment, and applied this point to animal eschatology. Animals who suffer will be compensated in the afterlife, for instance with food, while animals that have dealt suffering to others will have to redeem themselves by being serviceable. Again the point is illustrated with scorpions, who are put to work tormenting sinners in hell to compensate for the pain they caused while alive.[10] None of this should be taken to imply that animals bear moral responsibility. Rather the Muʿtazilites simply wished to ensure that suffering never occurs without being somehow balanced in the long run by God's justice.

We can detect an echo of these ideas in the doctor and unorthodox thinker Abū Bakr Ibn Zakariyyāʾ al-Rāzī (d. 925). He debated with Muʿtazilite opponents and in some cases adopted their ideas, if only for the sake of more effective dialectical engagement. This may help to explain his unusual (indeed, in the philosophical tradition nearly unique) interest in the topic of animal suffering. The key text here is a passage from his *Philosophical Life* (*al-Sīra al-falsafiyya*), a work in which al-Rāzī defends himself against unidentified opponents who have accused him of hypocritically failing to live as an ascetic, as a philosopher should.[11] Al-Rāzī responds by arguing in favor of a moderate rather than ascetic life and mentioning a range of other ethical maxims he follows. One of these is as follows: "We ought never to cause any pain to anything capable of sensation, unless it is deserved, or in order that by this pain we can avert some other pain which is worse" (100). He chooses his words carefully here. "Anything capable of sensation" obviously includes animals as well as humans, while excluding plants. Indeed al-Rāzī immediately goes on to provide examples of behavior that violate the maxim by abusing animals, such as taking pleasure in hunting and overworking beasts of burden.

It is, however, consistent with the maxim that one may, for instance, overwork a beast in certain circumstances. Al-Rāzī's example is riding a horse to death while pursued by enemies, in order to save one's own life (104). This is justified by the fact that the human's life is more valuable than the horse's—especially, al-Rāzī adds, if the human is of particular benefit to society! Similarly it is acceptable to kill certain animals, namely carnivorous ones and pests like snakes and (this may sound familiar) scorpions. The reason is that these animals themselves cause "great harm" without being serviceable in any way, so that their very existence is a bad thing (104).[12] Al-Rāzī adds that killing these animals frees them from their bodies, which offers them a release similar to the deliverance of souls from human bodies, a goal frequently mentioned in his ethical teaching (105). This passage encouraged later critics to complain that al-Rāzī was endorsing a theory of animal-human transmigration, but I have elsewhere expressed skepticism about this.[13] He may have meant that such animals could get better bodies in the afterlife, an idea that had previously been proposed in Islamic theological circles. Or perhaps he meant simply that nonexistence would itself be a kind of deliverance for carnivores and vermin.

It's worth noting that al-Rāzī has no objection whatsoever to *using* animals, for instance as beasts of burden, only to causing them unjustified suffering. In fact his other surviving treatise on ethics, the *Spiritual Medicine* (*al-Ṭibb al-rūḥānī*), says that humans' possession of reason (*ʿaql*) makes us better than irrational animals (*al-ḥayawān ġayr al-nāṭiq*). It is for this reason "that we rule and control them, subjecting them to us and directing them in ways conducive to our advantage as well as theirs" (18). This passage shows some concern for animal welfare as such, since we are told to pay heed to animals' advantage, not just to our own. But the emphasis is on the fact that it is appropriate to implement animals for our own benefit. In the *Philosophical Life*, such practices are again endorsed, along with another warning not to cause needless suffering:

One ought not to eradicate beasts of burden and herbivores, but rather work them gently, as we have mentioned, using them as food as little as possible, not breeding so many that one has to slaughter them in large numbers. Instead, one should do this with a purpose in mind, and in accordance with need. (105)

In fact al-Rāzī hesitates over the question of whether one can justify eating meat. He again mentions the freeing of animal souls as a possible justification for this, but adds that some philosophers (including Socrates) have been in favor of vegetarianism.

These passages may suggest that al-Rāzī thought about animal welfare in utilitarian terms, like a medieval Peter Singer. He seems to approach the whole topic from the point of view of minimizing pain and suffering and maximizing benefit for both animals and humans. However, the core maxim that instructs us to avoid causing pain is no ethical first principle. Rather, if we look to the context we see that al-Rāzī treats it as an implication of a more basic maxim: that we should take as our model God, who (as the Muʿtazilites argued) hates undeserved suffering. We can therefore see al-Rāzī's discussion as an application of the Qurʾānic teaching that God watches over animals as well as humans, combined with Plato's famous injunction (*Theaetetus* 176b, quoted explicitly at *Philosophical Life* 108) to "imitate God insofar as possible."

The influence of the Qurʾānic outlook on animals is more obvious in what must be the most famous work on the subject in the Muslim philosophical tradition: one of the *Epistles* of the Ikhwān al-Ṣafāʾ, or "Brethren of Purity."[14] This elusive group of tenth-century thinkers produced epistles on a wide range of philosophical and scientific topics. Their treatment of animals takes the form of a parable in which the animals of the world approach the king of the *jinn* to complain about their mistreatment at the hands of humans. Much of the epistle is taken up with speeches by various animals, as they rehearse the arguments they may use to persuade the *jinn* to take their side. A trial then ensues, in which the animals have the better of the argument for the most part but then lose on something like a technicality. Even if most people are not good for much, truly holy individuals are found only among humans, and never among animals (313/277–78).

The Brethren do give other reasons to see humans as superior to animals. A preface to the fable asserts the traditional teaching that humans alone are rational (65/5) and also argues that the animals must be for the sake of humankind, since animals were created first and "whenever one thing is for the sake of another, its existence is prior" (68/8; cf. 106/45 for animals having existed before Adam did). Within the fable, meanwhile, the animals are made to admit that God has subjugated them to humans, but only for the sake of benefiting humans and "not in order that they be our masters and we their slaves" (106/44–45). Here the animals are echoing the Qur'ānic passages mentioned earlier, which emphasize that God has put certain animals, such as horses, cattle, and bees, at the disposal of humans (a position reminiscent of the Stoics). But they are also quick to allude to other verses, for instance those that describe birds as praising God with their song (302/263). By extension the cricket is also said to acknowledge the oneness of God (301/261–62). Indeed one could consider the entire fable a vivid, literary exploration of the idea found in verse 6:38 of the Qur'ān: each kind of animal has its "community." The Brethren present the various types of creature (e.g., birds of prey and insects) in turn, allowing them to describe their divinely appointed gifts and the relationship they would see as appropriate to humankind.

Entertaining though it is, the Brethren's epistle on the animals stops short of encouraging its readers to reconsider their attitude toward animals, as al-Rāzī had done. To my knowledge, the most significant later case of a philosopher who does do this is Ibn Ṭufayl (d. 1185). A thinker of Andalusia who was a contemporary and associate of the more famous Averroes (d. 1198), Ibn Ṭufayl is known almost solely through his work *Ḥayy ibn Yaqẓān*.[15] It imagines a child, the title character, growing up alone on an island and becoming a fully realized philosopher and mystic. Actually, "alone" is not quite right. Though there are no other humans, the island is populated with many animals, and

Ḥayy's moral and intellectual progress is charted in terms of his changing relationship to those animals. At first he effectively lives as an
animal rather than a human. He is brought up by a gazelle and identifies with her and later her whole kind (37); he also learns to imitate the
calls of animals (28) and sees himself as being, if anything, inferior to
them given his lack of protective hair and natural weapons (29).

An early turning point is reached when he dissects his mother-
gazelle's body to locate the cause of her lethal illness. From here on, he
becomes increasingly "human," for instance by learning to use fire to
cook food and arming himself with artificial weapons and clothing.
His scientific explorations of the world around him lead him to the
conclusion that all animals share a nature grounded in the same kind of
"spirit" (rūḥ, cf. Greek *pneuma*: warm air or breath that pervades the
body). Ibn Ṭufayl emphasizes the unity of the animal genus by comparing this substance to a fluid that is divided into portions as it is received in each animal, including Ḥayy himself (46, cf. 39 for the idea
that Ḥayy, like his mother, has a "vital heat" centered in the heart).[16]
But it is not the discovery of this shared nature that leads Ḥayy to form
benevolent views toward animals. To the contrary: because he is still
living a fundamentally bodily existence, Ḥayy treats the animals as a
resource to be exploited.

Things change again when he comes to the realization that there is a
divine First Principle, which providentially steers the cosmos using the
heavenly spheres as an instrument. Animals are invoked as signs of this
providence:

> [Ḥayy] proceeded to contemplate all types of animals, and how "He
> gave each thing its nature (*khulq*), and then gave guidance" (Qur'ān
> 20:50) in its use. Had He not guided the animals to use those organs
> that were created (*khuliqat*) for them in the ways that provide the
> benefits for which they were intended, animals would not have ben-
> efited from these organs and they would have been most burden-
> some to them. Thereby, [Ḥayy] came to know that He was the most

generous and most compassionate. (*Ḥayy ibn Yaqẓān* 70, Khalidi
trans., modified)

Next Ḥayy comes to see it as imperative to his own perfection that he
should imitate the heavens and likewise become an instrument of the
divine plan. This is explicitly labeled as a goal that animals cannot
pursue: they think only of nourishment and other bodily goods (77).
Thus it is precisely because he is *unlike* an animal that Ḥayy undertakes
to show care for the animals—and for the same reasons, plants—on his
island. He becomes not just a vegetarian but a fruitarian (that is, he
endeavors to eat only what can be harvested without killing the plant).
He shifts water courses and shade to benefit plants and comes to the
aid of wounded or hungry animals (89).

Assuming that this passage is to be taken at face value (it may be, to
some extent, intended as comedy), Ibn Ṭufayl is proposing an approach to animal ethics that goes beyond what we find in al-Rāzī. This
is, however, only a rung on the ladder of Ḥayy's moral and intellectual
improvement. Within only a few pages Ḥayy abandons his care of
plants and animals to devote himself to contemplation of God, taking
up residence in a cave to meditate and leaving all physical concerns
behind insofar as he can (92–93). Finally he achieves mystical union
with God, though his bodily requirements prevent him from maintaining this without interruption. Admittedly Ḥayy still seems to
adhere to the rigorous diet when he ventures forth from the cave for
nourishment. But Ibn Ṭufayl's message is clear: humans can concern
themselves with bodily ends, act as instruments of divine providence,
or pursue the activity of (and ultimately identity with) God. Ḥayy has
moved through these various goals, one after another. While the
second sort of life, which involves devoted care of both plants and animals, is better than the first, merely animal sort of life, it is inferior to
the life of pure contemplation.

This section has shown that medieval philosophers of the Islamic
world did discuss the ethical treatment of animals, sometimes reaching

conclusions that may seem surprisingly modern, as with al-Rāzī's apparent consequentialism and Ibn Ṭufayl's description of a fruitarian diet. Yet in a striking contrast with many modern-day discussions of animal ethics, benevolence toward animals was not justified by appeals to any nature shared between animals and humans. All three of the texts just considered unhesitatingly accept that animals are inferior to humans because of their lack of reason, and see this as justifying the use of animals as means to satisfy human ends, though limits are placed on such use. If a benevolent animal ethics emerged, this was the result of our authors taking the God's-eye view of things and encouraging humans to show the same sort of providential approach to the animal world that God Himself does. But this does not mean that the commonality between humans and animals had no philosophical significance in the Islamic world.

TWO THREE-PART SOULS

To understand why it was indeed significant, we need to say something about the two chief psychological models used by philosophers in this period. These will be well known to anyone who has a passing familiarity with ancient philosophy: the reason-spirit-desire tripartition of the soul from Plato, and the rational-sensitive-nutritive classification of psychological faculties from Aristotle. There were occasional attempts to relate one or the other of these models to Islamic religious texts.[17] Still, the use of these models was a clear inheritance from the Greek tradition and was thus a typical feature of *falsafa*, the tradition of Hellenizing philosophy in Arabic. Representatives of this tradition faced the obvious problem of saying how the two models from Plato and Aristotle relate to one another. Reason is the highest, and distinctively human, part of soul in both cases. This invited readers to do what their syncretic interpretive strategies would have inclined them to do in any case by identifying the two tripartitions, so that Aristotle's sensitive soul is aligned with Plato's spirit and the nutritive soul with desire.

Animals played a key role in this harmonizing move. The lowest psychological faculties recognized by Aristotle are associated with plants: they can engage in nutrition and reproduction but lack any higher faculties. The middle range of faculties, meanwhile, are distinctive of animals. All animals (well, almost all)[18] possess the five senses and are capable of self-motion, but only humans have the further faculty of rational thought. Conveniently, nutrition and reproduction are intimately related to the desires for food, drink, and sex that in any case seem to be the concerns of Plato's lowest, appetitive soul-part. Can we just as plausibly associate the sensitive soul with Plato's spirited soul, which is characterized by love of honor? It was standard to do so in the Arabic tradition, on the basis that the spirited soul is responsible for a range of emotions that are also found in animals, notably anger. This middle faculty is accordingly, and interchangeably, called the "animal" or "irascible" soul.[19]

Though we associate the first, Platonic model most readily with the *Republic*, for the Arabic tradition as for the Latin medieval tradition the more important source was the *Timaeus*. This is significant, because unlike the *Republic* the *Timaeus* associates reason, spirit, and desire with three parts of the body: respectively, the head, heart, and liver (69c–71b). Nor was Plato the only authority to support this view. Galen (d. ca. 216) was, again in Arabic as well as Latin, the crucial source for medical learning. And he had conclusively proved with anatomical experiments performed on animals that the "ruling faculty" is seated in the brain and communicates with the rest of the body through the nerves.[20] Galen did not go so far as to assert that reason or the soul in general was a mere bodily form, pronouncing himself agnostic on this point, which was in any case unimportant for the doctor. But in a work that was well known in Arabic, he did argue that the states of the soul, including the rational soul, are dependent on those of the body.[21]

Here we have a stumbling block for the project of reconciling the Platonic and Aristotelian models. Aristotle explicitly argues in *On the Soul* that intellect—the rational faculty par excellence, if not the only rational faculty—involves no bodily organ. How, then, can rational soul have such a close relationship to the brain? Actually this is a problem even within Platonism. The same passage of the *Timaeus* states that the rational part of the soul is immortal. How can this be if its function is closely tied to the brain, as Galen showed, and the brain is destroyed upon bodily death? Philosophers in the Islamic world dealt with these problems in varying ways. Al-Kindī (d. after 870) composed a *Discourse on the Soul* (*al-Qawl fī l-nafs*), in which he associates the desiring and irascible aspects with body, while making reason an incorporeal and even "divine" substance.[22] In fact he reserves the word "soul" for reason alone, calling irascibility and desire mere "faculties." In a summary of Plato's views on the soul, al-Rāzī agrees that the lower souls are dependent on the body, indeed nothing but "mixtures" of the heart and liver. (Incidentally he calls them "vegetative and irascible," mixing the Aristotelian and Platonic classifications.) He retains the association of reason with the brain too, but the rational soul uses the "mixture of the brain" only as an instrument (28). Since it is not identical with that mixture, it no more needs the brain to survive than a carpenter would need a hammer in order to survive.

For any solution along these Platonic-Galenic lines, which accepts that the rational soul or faculty is above all related to the brain, there is another problem: animals have brains. What use could these possibly serve if animals are irrational? Here the Arabic tradition recognizes a greater degree of commonality between animals and humans than had been acknowledged by the classical philosophical authorities. Actually this process begins in later antiquity, especially with Galen and other writers influenced by him, such as Nemesius of Emesa.[23] The medical tradition was a powerful, perhaps the most powerful factor in convincing medieval philosophers to accept a wide range of faculties as common to both animals and humans. We've already seen, for instance, how Ibn Ṭufayl shows his hero Ḥayy learning about his own body indirectly by dissecting a gazelle. This is a reenactment of Galen's experiments on animals, which he took as evidence for human anatomy.

The relevance of this for our current problem is that authors like Galen and Nemesius inspired philosophers in the Islamic world to grant to animals, and situate in the brains of animals, faculties more advanced than sense-perception but inferior to intellection. Unsurprisingly the doctor-philosopher al-Rāzī again provides us with an example.[24] In an introductory work of medicine, he locates the "animal" (ḥayawāniyya) faculty in the heart, but nonetheless seats faculties in the brain that are clearly possessed by animals, for instance sense-perception and motion.[25] But the brain also houses the higher "governing" (siyāsiyya) faculties, namely imagination, thought, and memory. Here he is talking about human brains, so it's a moot point how many of these higher faculties might be possessed by animals—presumably some animals have at least imagination and memory.[26] We know already, though, that for al-Rāzī animals do not possess intellect or reason itself (ʿaql). It seems therefore that this faculty is distinctive in two ways: it alone belongs to humans, and it does not depend on any bodily organ for its survival, even if it uses the brain as an instrument.[27]

Here we have an anticipation of Avicenna's famous doctrine of the internal senses, according to which our five normal sense modalities (sight, hearing, etc.) are matched by five other "senses" seated in the brain.[28] In addition we can now appreciate more fully the fact that Avicenna illustrates this doctrine with animals rather than humans. He gives the example of a sheep that flees upon perceiving hostility in a wolf. There is no way to explain this unless we grant the sheep some faculty beyond mere sense-perception, because hostility is not a sensible property. So Avicenna postulates such a faculty, one of the internal senses: wahm. This is usually rendered into English as "estimation," following the medieval Latin translation aestimatio.[29] The purpose of wahm is precisely to grasp such nonsensible features of things. Explaining such phenomena as the sheep's retreat from the wolf is one advantage of positing this faculty. Another is that Avicenna can do justice to the idea that animal brains are much like our brains. Wahm and the other internal senses are located in various parts of the brain, and the anatomical distribution in our case is assumed to be the same as in the animal case.

Avicenna may indeed seem to be well on the way to putting animals on a par with humans. If they can grasp nonsensible concepts like hostility, why deny that animals are effectively able to think, and thus that they are rational? But Avicenna is no Plutarch *après la lettre*. He retains a firm dividing line between human and animal cognition. The hostility the sheep perceives in the wolf may be nonsensible, but it is still *particular*. The sheep has arrived at no generalization or, as Avicenna would put it, universal judgment to the effect that wolves are hostile (never mind achieving scientific understanding of wolves' hostility toward sheep). She has merely perceived that this creature in front of her is hostile, and acted accordingly. This way of thinking about *wahm* was not universally accepted. The greatest philosopher of Safavid Iran, Mullā Ṣadrā (d. 1640), argued that the sheep must be grasping universal hostility in some sense because the wolf is perceived as instantiating a general characteristic. Showing the durability of traditional attitudes toward animal cognition, Ṣadrā's commentator Sabzawārī (d. 1878) dismissed this suggestion on the basis that animals are irrational, and any grasp of a universal implies reason.[30]

For Avicenna there were other reasons to insist that *wahm* is restricted to particulars. He proves the immateriality and hence immortality of the human soul on the basis of our grasp of universals. So the epistemic difference between humans and animals is connected to a metaphysical difference between them. Unlike the theologians who envisioned an afterlife for animals, Avicenna saw them as irretrievably corporeal beings who cannot survive bodily death, whereas humans can look forward to an afterlife thanks to their possession of a non-bodily, intellectual faculty.[31] Ṣadrā offered reason to doubt these claims. Unlike the other thinkers we have discussed, he held that lower faculties like imagination and even sense-perception are immaterial. He therefore extended Avicenna's famous "flying man" thought experiment to animals other than humans. In the thought experiment, we imagine that God creates someone in midair, with sight veiled and no other sensory input. Avicenna argued that a person in this situation would nonetheless be self-aware, and Ṣadrā was willing to say that even an animal could do the same despite being irrational.[32]

LIVING AS A HUMAN

We have seen that, even if Avicenna and other thinkers conceded a significant degree of commonality between animal and human cognition, reason and intellection were reserved for humans alone. Intellect was sharply distinguished from even the highest animal faculties, such as estimation and memory, on both metaphysical and epistemological grounds. Now we will see that in ethics too philosophers of the Islamic world tended to believe that humans are distinct from animals only in virtue of our highest psychological capacities. Here we have the normative dimension of the contrast between animals and humans: to live rightly is to live rationally, which means living as humans and not like animals. Unfortunately, many people do not live rationally, so that they are no better than brutes.

To quote just one of many passages making this point, here is Avicenna's contemporary Miskawayh (d. 1030): "Those people whose rational faculty is weak, who are the ones we have described as being at the level of beasts, and in whom the bestial soul is strong, incline towards the desires bound up with their senses, such as food, drink, clothing, and similar pleasures" (*Refinement of Character* 47, Zurayk trans., modified).[33] In fact humans are often worse than animals when it comes to satisfying desires. Whereas animals are instinctually moderate with respect to sexual intercourse and stop eating when their hunger is satisfied, humans often go well beyond what is naturally required in their lust for pleasure. This is a point made by al-Rāzī in his *Spiritual Medicine* (39, 77). At the other end of the ethical spectrum is the reasonable person (*al-ʿāqil*) who is capable of restraining desire, something animals cannot manage: "For the chief way people are better

than beasts is this: the faculty of volition and the dispatch of action
after deliberation. For beasts, being without cultivation, straightaway
when they are called to something by nature, do that thing without
hesitating or deliberating about it" (*Spiritual Medicine* 20). Even if
pleasure were our highest end (which it isn't, according to al-Rāzī), we
would still need to use reason to avoid indulging desires whose satisfaction would bring more pain than pleasure in the long run.[34]

Notice the point that humans, and not animals, are capable of volition or choice (*irāda*). While al-Rāzī mentions this only in passing, in
other authors it becomes the basis for a principled contrast between
animal and human action. Of course this is another borrowing from
the ancient tradition, the most crucial text being Aristotle's *Nicomachean
Ethics*. Developing the famous "function argument" from *Ethics* I.7
and combining it with material on choice from later in the *Ethics*, al-
Fārābī (d. 950) writes:

> Are the instruments given to [man] by nature sufficient for achiev-
> ing the soundness of his body and senses as is the case with all ani-
> mals, plants, bodies and natural bodies and parts? If these two [that
> is, the body and the senses] are themselves the end, and the instru-
> ments he possesses by nature are sufficient for achieving their sound-
> ness, why then were will and choice given to him? (*Philosophy of
> Aristotle* 66–67, Mahdi trans.)[35]

It is because humans possess this characteristic capacity for choice that
we have the potential for virtue and vice. Just as the distinctively human
power for knowledge makes theoretical knowledge available to us and
not animals, so the distinctively human power of choice allows us to
engage in ethical and political life—for better or worse.

An interesting perspective on this point is provided by one of the
last truly Aristotelian thinkers of the Islamic world, the historian Ibn
Khaldūn (d. 1406). He inherits and adopts the contrast between
humans and animals but takes a more descriptive and less normative

approach to this contrast. For him too the political emerges in human life just when life becomes distinctively human rather than animal. This occurs when humans settle down and inhabit cities rather than living like the bedouin. Compared to city dwellers, he says, such nomadic peoples are "on a level with wild, untamable animals and dumb beasts of prey" (§2.2).[36] One might take this to be a mere metaphor, as when he later says that the city dwellers are like domesticated animals in that they become gentle and sociable (§2.15). But he genuinely sees the political life of settled communities as a marker of difference between the animal and the human: "Royal and political authority come to man *qua* man, because it is something peculiar to man and not found among animals" (§2.19). Of course this special feature of humans is related to rationality, which Ibn Khaldūn conventionally reserves for humans alone. This is why humans and not animals engage in the crafts (§5.16) and are able to engage in intellection (§6.6, 14, 22). On the other hand, there is a good deal of variation in the human capacity for such activities, something Ibn Khaldūn compares to the way different chess players are able to see different numbers of moves ahead (§6.2).

The contrast between human and animal is a leitmotif of *Governance of the Solitary* (*Tadbīr al-mutawaḥḥid*) by Ibn Bājja,[37] an Andalusian philosopher who worked just before Ibn Ṭufayl and who is in fact criticized by name in the preface of *Ḥayy ibn Yaqẓān*. The title of Ibn Bājja's work refers to the plight of the perfect, virtuous, philosophical individual who finds himself in a vicious society. In describing this person and the ideal city that could exist if all citizens were of this standard, Ibn Bājja takes up and elaborates on many themes from the earlier writings of al-Fārābī. Among these is the contrast between animal and human. Ibn Bājja follows the traditional line that animals are incapable of accessing intelligibles, which, in his rather idiosyncratic terminology, are called "general spiritual forms." For this reason animals are incapable of "rational activities" and of scientific understanding (§156: *afʿāl fikriyya, ʿulūm*). However, they do grasp "particular spiritual forms." Much like Avicenna's postulation of *wahm* in his account of the internal senses, this allows Ibn Bājja to account for otherwise inexplicable animal behavior. His example is that a mother animal can transfer its affection for its own offspring to other young. Camels will even continue to produce milk for the benefit of a fake offspring, a kind of puppet called a *baww* (§135). This shows that the mother is concerned not just with the particular "corporeal" form of her offspring (which belongs only to that child) but with a *type* of immanent form that can be found also in other particulars.[38]

In addition to these epistemic limitations, animals on Ibn Bājja's view lack any capacity for rational reflection in the practical sphere. This is why animals are not ethical or political agents: "Deliberation, investigation and inference (*al-rawiyya wa-l-baḥth wa-l-istidlāl*) and, in general, thought (*al-fikra*) are used in attaining each of the [ends of political life]. If thought is not used, then the action is purely bestial, with no share whatsoever in humanity" (*Governance of the Solitary* §§150–51). Ibn Bājja seems to anticipate an objection here, to the effect that animals do have ethical dispositions, for instance the vanity of the peacock, the sycophancy of the dog, and the cunning of the fox. He would have good reason to take this point seriously, since Galen used examples like this to prove that "character traits" belong to the non-rational soul.[39] Ibn Bājja does not deny this, but he does deny that it presents a difficulty for his theory (§§152–53, cf. §199). First, the exhibition of such traits can be explained with reference to a grasp of "particular spiritual forms," and he has already admitted that animals are capable of this. Second, animals possess these traits not in the way we acquire our ethical dispositions but simply because of their species membership: all peacocks are vain, for instance. Admittedly there may be exceptions, such as an unusually brave (or cowardly!) lion, but this is merely "accidental." As a result we cannot really call the traits found in animals "virtues" (*faḍāʾil*), except homonymously.

It follows from all this that humans who are living in accordance with their animal nature are not engaging in ethical or political activity. This applies to children, who still act through the "bestial soul"

(§140). With maturity, a properly human life becomes possible, but some adults remain at the level of beasts (§144). This sort of defective human is, we might say, not managing to be a *political* animal: "Clearly someone who has such a bestial action cannot play a role in constituting a city, nor is he any part of a city" (§151). In the worst-case scenario such a poor excuse for a human does not merely make bad choices but fails to choose at all. For Ibn Bājja agrees with al-Fārābī that a capacity for choice is proper to humans, and he infers from this that a human who fails to act in a human way is not even performing voluntary actions:

The actions that are distinctive of humanity are those that are voluntary (*bi-ikhtiyār*), so whatever the human does voluntarily is a
human action.... An irrational animal's action is triggered only by
actions in the bestial soul, and the human can act in this way too, as
when the human flees from something frightening. For this activity
belongs to the human on account of the bestial soul. An example is
someone who breaks a stone that has struck him or a stick that has
scratched him, just because it scratched him. All these are bestial
actions, whereas if someone broke [the stick] in order to avoid its
scratching someone else, or after deliberation that required breaking
it, this action would be human. (*Governance of the Solitary* §§43–45)

He goes on to give a medical example, one of many in the text: if some-one eats prunes for the enjoyment, that is a bestial action, whereas if he does it to regulate his digestion that would be a human action (§46). In general we can say that a bestial action is one that involves no thought process but follows immediately on something like greed, fear, or anger (§47).

So far Ibn Bājja seems to be making the sharpest of contrasts: on one side humans who are using their powers of deliberation and choice to pursue rational ends, on the other side irrational animals and the inadequate humans who act like them. But in fact his view is more nuanced than this. He recognizes that all humans have an animal nature—a "bestial soul" as well as a rational soul—and that this nature is inevitably going to be involved in many of our actions. Consider for instance this observation about the relative frequency of human and bestial actions in defective societies:

> The greater part of [such actions] are both bestial and human. It is rare to find only the bestial without any human [action], because when the human is in the natural state, most of the time and with rare exceptions, even if the cause of his motion is an affection [such as fear, etc.] he cannot help but think about how he should act.... As for someone who acts for the sake of conviction and what is right, without being swayed by the bestial soul or anything that arises in it, such a human ought really to be called "divine." (*Governance of the Solitary* §§48–49)

It is our usual and even *natural* state to be deploying both human and animal soul, both the higher capacity for thought and the lower capacities for non-rational emotion and desire. Even people whose goals befit an animal life will rationally calculate the best way to achieve those goals. To live a life guided purely by rational considerations, meanwhile, would merit the designation "divine"—here Ibn Bājja surely has in mind Aristotle's remarks about the life of pure contemplation in the last book of the *Ethics* (X.7, 1177b).

When philosophers of the Islamic world took an interest in animal nature, it was most often for this reason.[40] They were trying to understand human nature, and they recognized that humans share most of their capacities, and even motivations, with animals. As we saw, reflection on the commonalities between humans and animals was not, as we might have expected, central in discussions of the ethical treatment of animals—even though there were such discussions. Rather it was central to discussions of human ethics. Rationality was seen not just as the distinctive and indeed definitive characteristic of humans but also as the source of moral norms. To be a virtuous person is to subordinate one's animal soul to one's reason, and insofar as one fails to be rational one in some sense fails to be human. Yet human nature includes all those capacities and motives that we share with animals. Hence the paradox suggested by the last passage cited from Ibn Bājja: a purely rational life might seem to be the most purely human life, but in fact it would be more than merely human. After all, people are animals too.[41]

Reflection

OF RAINBOW SNAKES AND BAFFLING BUFFALO
ON A CENTRAL AFRICAN MASK

Allen F. Roberts

Tourist advertisements often depict an Africa filled with an
astounding variety of wildlife, to the exclusion of local people
(except insofar as they may provide "cultural" performances for
safaris). By contrast, over the centuries African artists have depicted
few of the domestic and wild animals whose environments they
share, and the ones that are chosen are often not those emblematic
of Western fantasies. Instead artists have concentrated on a curious
menagerie of aardvarks and antelopes, bats and buffalo, pachyderms
and pangolins, snakes, spiders, and spotted cats. Why are *these*
beasts chosen and not others that may seem so much more
significant to outsiders' eyes? In a famous reflection Claude Lévi-
Strauss recognized that, as key metaphors, "species are chosen not
because they are 'good to eat,' but because they are 'good to think.'"[1]
That is, "signifying animals" are chosen following "age-old
productive and intellective interaction of humans and animals in
Africa" through which "some of the deeper paradoxes of the human
condition can be most profoundly explored and offered up for
meditation."[2]

Let us consider one of the most famous of all African sculptures,
a nineteenth-century helmet mask created and performed by
Luba people of the Democratic Republic of the Congo (DRC).

(Fig. 4R1—see art insert). This astonishing work mixes human and animal attributes and surely must have captivated the Luba individuals who were privileged to perform with it or witness these performances. Subsequently it has captured non-Luba audiences since it was seized in 1896 by Oscar Michaux (a colonial officer of the Congo Free State). Recent research has updated our understanding of how the mask was obtained and came to the collections of Belgium's Royal Museum for Central Africa; sadly, no late nineteenth-century Luba exegeses are known to exist that might explain the mask's iconography, efficacies, and agencies, or indeed how, why, by whom, and when the mask was danced.[3] One is left to propose an archaeology of knowledge from historical and ethnographic fragments.

The nature and symbolic purposes of the helmet mask's anthropomorphic and zoomorphic features have long been debated by scholars, as have the characters and qualities that the mask may have portrayed in performance. For example, the striking coiffure echoes fashions seen in other nineteenth-century Luba sculpture, as well as a few early photographs and drawings depicting Luba and related peoples of southern Congo. To what animal did the "horns" of the hairdo allude—to a ram perhaps? Hardy, fat-tailed sheep were introduced to Central Africa a very long time ago, and Luba cosmogony includes with thunder said by some to be produced. Constantine Petridis writes engagingly of helmet masks with ovine motifs created by other Congolese peoples, for whom a ram is deemed "forceful, dominant, and fertile" and "a visual metaphor of kingship."[4] Such associations and uses in performance may have informed interpretation of the Luba helmet mask, at least for some observers. Might the corniform reference also be to a buffalo, though, since these magnificent beasts were once plentiful throughout the savannahs and forests of the Congo and are depicted in the masks of neighboring peoples?[5]

Buffalo of several subspecies are indigenous to much of the DRC, where they are still sometimes found in large herds despite heavy gun-hunting. Calves and females are generally reddish or "sorrel-colored," while bulls are "almost coal black." Although ordinarily docile, buffalo are notorious for their "deliberate savagery" when provoked. Louis Leakey, the longtime prehistorian of eastern Africa, held that "a wounded buffalo is the most cunning and most dangerous of animals I know," yet, as the adventurer Jean-Pierre Hallet contended, the beasts may not be as "diabolically clever as hunters claim," as they are "really more cow than killer."[6]

Similar ambiguity is to be found in other aspects of buffalo behavior, for they are largely crepuscular, preferring to move about between the hours of dusk and dawn; and although they are mighty, they may virtually disappear in daytime, taking refuge in thickets or mud wallows, where they can submerge themselves almost entirely. Such apparent invisibility can be terrifying if "the animal hides and then surprises the hunter who, thinking it is in front, finds it attacking him from behind. In such manner, the animal is likened to a witch preying upon an unsuspecting foe" among Yaka people of west-central DRC.[7]

So why might the helmet mask's horned coiffure refer to a buffalo in its otherwise anthropomorphic iconography? A first-order hypothesis is that the Luba culture hero Mbidi Kiluwe was so presented, and that the mask's performances followed choreographies inspired by tales of how Mbidi introduced political aesthetics to those who would become known as Luba. The most probable contexts would have been during activities of the Mbudye Society through which such histories are remembered, debated, and performed to our very day.[8] Mbidi Kiluwe is praised as being "shiningly black like the buffalo," and he is understood in Mbudye lore to be descended from an apical ancestress who coupled with a buffalo and/or who may herself have been part human, part buffalo. Furthermore, a century ago Luba youths emerging from

sequestered initiation camps were greeted with the cry "Here are
the buffalo, here are the buffalo!" As they were being transformed
from boys to men, they aspired to Mbidi's values and bearing.[9]

As the Luba Epic goes, Mbidi was a quiet, self-possessed,
handsome man with glowing black skin. He is a member of a genre
of cultural heroes, found throughout Central Africa, of lunar
characters sharing variants of the root -*luwe* in their names. All are
calm, cool, and refined and associated with rain, fertility, and
powerful arcana symbolized by the color black. Mbidi's set of
mythical protagonists are sometimes divided down the body
midline and represented as half-human, half-beeswax. As such,
Mbidi and his fellows personify dichotomous representation and
indeterminacy.[10]

Mbidi came from somewhere in the East and encountered
Nkongolo Mwamba at his heartland kingdom in the region of the
Lualaba lakes of southeastern DRC. Nkongolo was the first Luba
king, but a drunken sot given to all manner of debauchery and
deceit—even matricide. He remains an avatar of excess and is a
member of a Central African mythical genre of immense snakes
that breathe forth the rainbow. Such serpents, sometimes
anthropomorphic, more often not, are solar beings associated with
the dry season, desiccation, sterility, and violent transformation,
as symbolized by the bloody color red. Given their contrastive
characteristics as detailed in narrative and dance, conflict between
Mbidi and Nkongolo was, and is, inevitable.[11]

Mbidi had relations with Nkongolo's sister, and a son named
Kalala Ilunga was born. Kalala eventually decapitated his depraved
uncle and became the model of, and for, political comportment.
Yet, as outlined by the Congolese philosopher V. Y. Mudimbe,
Kalala possessed "conflictual inheritances" of the chaos of
Nkongolo Mwamba and the sacred royalty introduced by Mbidi
Kiluwe. As such, Mudimbe asserts that Kalala presents "a principle
of questioning," for such tensions are "rearticulated and

recomposed" from generation to generation, "realizing and assuming...the opposing expectations of each social formation." The king or his dependent chiefs, then, present a third, mediating category of being.[12] Mudimbe's thoughts, in turn, exemplify an observation by Emile Durkheim made more than a century ago, that in mythologies, "we are continually coming upon beings which have the most contradictory attributes simultaneously, who are at the same time one and many, material and spiritual, who can divide themselves up indefinitely without losing anything of their constitution; in mythology it is an axiom that the part is worth the whole." Indeed, like the Fang people of Gabon as described by James Fernandez, Luba "not only live easily with contradictions, they cannot live without them" as they confront the conflicting choices of everyday life.[13]

In conclusion, the being and behavior of baffling buffalo are "good to think" when applied to the uncertainties of human—and especially male-dominated—endeavors among Luba. Kings and chiefs in southern DRC are understood to be "fathers of their people," who guide, promote, and protect them as best they can. At the same time Luba leaders are feared as the greatest malefactors of the land, for they can be ruthless if provoked, and even when benign (as they usually are) the evil that inevitably exists in their communities must be at their tolerance or, perhaps, to their corrupt profit. Thus leaders present "two faces of the same reality," as Théodore Theuws wrote of western Luba—for paradoxically they embody contradictions of beneficence and brutal self interest inherent in the politics of all human societies.[14] Conundra of the sort were once danced by a man wearing the ambiguously multireferential Luba helmet mask so as to encourage balance of otherwise contrastive and all too often conflicting elements and urges of society.

FIGURE 3R.1: Fan Anren, *Fish and Weeds* (*Yuzaotu*), detail, Song dynasty (960–1279); handscroll, ink and color on silk. National Palace Museum, Taipei.

FIGURE 3R.2: Liu Cai (attr.), *Fish Swimming Amid Falling Flowers* (*Luohua youyu*), Song dynasty (960–1279), early 12th century; handscroll, ink and color on silk. Saint Louis Art Museum, William K. Bixby Trust for Asian Art, 97:1926.1.

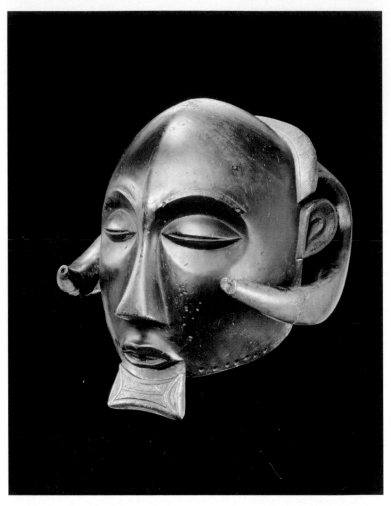

FIGURE 4R.1: Luba helmet mask. Royal Museum for Central Africa, Tervuren, Belgium, object #234.70.

FIGURE 8R.1: Anthropologischer Unterricht (1900). Privatbesitz (but see Althaus and Böller, *Gabriel von Max: Malerstar, Darwinist, Spiritist*, p. 32; Courtesy Galerie Konrad Beyer, München).

FIGURE 8R.2: Selbstbildnis mit Affen (1910), Reiss Engelhorn Museum, Mannheim.

CHAPTER FIVE

Marking the Boundaries

ANIMALS IN MEDIEVAL LATIN PHILOSOPHY

Juhana Toivanen

Medieval philosophers were, generally speaking, not particularly interested in nonhuman animals in their own right, and when they did discuss animals, their aim was to shed light on human nature rather than to understand animals as such. Animals were regarded as "the other" that functioned as a kind of mirror, which enabled philosophers to reveal more clearly what makes human beings special in comparison to the rest of the creation. This does not mean that medieval philosophers never wrote zoological works. They did, and some of them were clearly interested in animals and their psychological abilities for their own sake. Yet in order to understand medieval conceptions of animals, we cannot limit ourselves to materials that relate directly to them. Many important ideas concerning animals can be found in commentaries on Aristotle's *On the Soul* and *Nicomachean Ethics*,[1] in psychological sections of the commentaries on Peter Lombard's *Sentences*,[2] and elsewhere. Even though the tone of these works is clearly anthropological and anthropocentric, the authors often reveal their views on animals while developing their ideas concerning human beings.

My approach in the present chapter is similar to the medieval one, although my aim is squarely opposed to it. Where medieval philosophers discuss animals in order to understand human nature, I endeavor to make medieval conceptions of animals understandable by comparing them to medieval authors' views on human beings. By looking at the various boundaries that were drawn between human beings and animals, we will be able to understand what medieval authors thought about animals—even if they themselves may have been more interested in human beings when they negotiated the exact place of those boundaries.

The chapter is divided into three sections. The first section deals with the metaphysics of the animal soul in comparison to the human soul. I shall underline the radical metaphysical difference between human beings and animals while pointing out certain aspects of medieval views showing that animals were nevertheless considered to be similar to human beings in many respects. The second section is devoted to animal psychology. After presenting the basic framework of medieval faculty psychology and animal psychology, I shall discuss a couple of highly sophisticated abilities that were occasionally attributed to nonhuman animals. The last section briefly approaches medieval conceptions from an ethical perspective by considering animals as moral agents, moral patients, and moral examples.

The following discussion is based on the methodological presupposition that we can understand medieval animal psychology by looking at human psychology insofar as it deals with those psychological powers that medieval authors considered to be common to human beings and animals. In other words, animals and human beings were thought to be similar in relevant respects—to the extent that when humans do not engage in the psychological actions that are proper to human beings, they are very much like other animals. There were authors who thought that our rationality affects the functioning of our lower psychological powers, but it is misleading to think that as rational beings, our mental lives would be completely and radically different from those of other animals. I shall qualify and defend this methodological approach, but it is important to be frank about it from the outset, not least because it explains why the discussion revolves around the demarcation line between human beings and animals. By looking at the differences we are able to see where the similarities end and where they are challenged.

The overall aim of this chapter is to show that medieval views on animals were far more nuanced and heterogeneous than is usually thought. The emphasis is on those aspects of medieval views that portray animals as complex and sophisticated creatures—creatures not as different from human beings as one might expect. It is worth keeping in mind that not every medieval philosopher accepted that animals are capable of all the highest abilities that will be discussed. (At least it is not obvious that they did.) But such abilities were frequently admitted, a point that casts doubt on the recurrent assumption that by downgrading animals, medieval thought underlies modern attitudes that allow their mistreatment. It is true that medieval philosophers were anthropocentric, but their interest in human beings was always a part of a general framework in which human beings were considered to be similar to other animals, or indeed to be animals.[3]

METAPHYSICS

A long tradition stretching from Antiquity to the Middle Ages and beyond unanimously held that all living beings have a soul. In the most general sense of the term, having a soul meant being alive. Various philosophical traditions understood the metaphysical nature of the soul in different ways, but after the reception of Aristotelian natural philosophy during the twelfth and thirteenth centuries, medieval philosophers generally accepted the view that the soul is a form. It is a structural principle that organizes the matter of a body and makes it the kind of body that it is. Every living being, according to them, is a body that is organized in such a way that it is alive and capable of performing various psychological operations. The same metaphysical view applied to all living beings; the bodies of plants, animals, and human beings were organized by their souls.

However, the tradition also saw differences between different kinds of souls. Aristotle distinguished living beings into three major categories—plants, animals, and humans—by appealing to a threefold division of kinds of souls. Plants have a vegetative soul, animals a sensory soul, while human beings are endowed with rational souls. Each of these different kinds of souls enables a certain set of powers that distinguishes it from the others, but on each successive step, from a simpler type of soul to a more complex one, the previous powers are preserved. Animals are capable of all the operations and functions that are attributed to plants, and human beings surpass animals in many ways without losing any kind of power that animals have. The three types of souls form a hierarchy, but they share many central properties.

The sensory soul of animals was understood to be a form, a structural principle that organizes the matter of the body and provides a set of sensory powers for the animal. Unlike human beings, whose souls are immaterial and immortal, animals were taken to be nothing but organized living bodies. The life functions and psychological processes of animals were accounted for by appealing to the movement of matter and material changes in the body, especially in the heart and brain and through them in the veins and nerves. In order to account for the psychological powers, for instance perception and memory, medieval authors appealed to *animal spirit*. We should not be misled by the name, because animal spirit is matter, albeit a special kind of highly refined matter. The fine material spirit flows in the chambers of the brain and in the nerves, and its movement is the material counterpart of psychological functions.[4] Yet it would be misleading to say without qualifications that medieval philosophers defended reductive materialism with respect to animals and their life functions. They were happy to say that all the psychological functions of animals are realized as material changes, as movement of matter in the veins and nerves, but at the same time their theory leaned heavily upon teleological assumptions that are incompatible with modern reductive materialism. The medieval conception of matter cannot be understood without a reference to the form as a structural principle that makes an animal body the kind of body that it is, and the introduction of forms immediately brings final causality, teleology, and even intentionality into the picture. A classic example is the description of anger both as the boiling of blood around the heart and as a desire for revenge or punishment—the cognitive element is indispensable for understanding what anger is.[5] Thus material changes do not explain the higher level phenomena completely. They are but one aspect of complex psychological processes that can be understood only by taking the intentional and cognitive aspect into account as well.[6]

As the soul is the form of the body, it explains why and how the body is capable of doing various things. The soul gives to the body different kinds of powers, which come in accordance to the hierarchy of the kinds of souls. The vegetative soul gives the ability to grow, take on nourishment, and generate new individuals of the same species. In addition to these life functions, the sensory soul of animals provides at least the ability to perceive the world through the external senses but often also other powers, such as memory, imagination, and the abilities to move and have emotions. Thus we find medieval philosophers often making statements such as "An animal is distinguished from a non-animal by the ability to sense and move, as becomes clear from the first book of On the Soul."[7] Finally, human beings were thought to have rational powers and freedom of the will, in addition to the powers they share with animals, because humans have the most sophisticated kind of soul, the rational one.

From early on, medieval philosophers understood this Aristotelian view through a systematic taxonomy that is commonly known as the "Porphyrian tree," the basic principles of which they found in Boethius's (ca. 480–524) translation of Porphyry's *Introduction*. This book is an introduction to Aristotle's *Categories*, and throughout the Middle Ages it was the first book that students read when they started to study philosophy. The central idea in the Porphyrian tree is that all individual beings belong to a systematic hierarchy, which is divided into a descending order of genera and species. The highest genus, substance, is divided into two species: corporeal and incorporeal. These species are in turn divided into subspecies by further distinctions, and so forth, until we arrive at the lowest level of individuals. According to this model, animals belong to the genus of living bodies, and they are distinguished from plants by their ability to perceive. The genus "animal" is further divided into rational and irrational animals. All other animals are irrational; human beings alone belong to the species of rational animals. As the *Introduction* puts it, "Substance is itself a genus. Under it is body, and under the body an animate body, under which is animal; under the animal is rational animal, under which is man; and under man are Socrates and Plato and particular men."[8]

Rationality marks human beings off from other animals. That may not seem to be a big difference (and indeed from certain points of view it is not, as we shall soon see), but there were reasons why medieval philosophers tended to see this difference not only as a matter of being able to *do* more things with one's mind but as a metaphysical difference. The ancient idea that rational thinking cannot be realized in material organs married well with the Christian belief in the immortality and immateriality of the soul. Human rationality was explained by arguing that there is a clear essential difference between human beings and other animals. Medieval philosophers were unanimous that the human soul is an immortal and rational entity, which is created directly by God.[9] The rational soul distinguishes humans from other living beings. We alone, among living bodily beings, belong also to another reality, the immaterial one that lies beyond our visible and tangible world. We alone are capable of intellectual thinking, making free choices, surviving the death of the body, and having a special kind of relation with God. Animals can do none of these things. They are material, mortal beings, incapable of understanding universal essences, and not free in the intended sense.

The view that medieval authors saw a radical difference between human beings and animals is familiar and in many respects true. Yet it is important to keep in mind that within the medieval taxonomy, so clearly depicted in the Porphyrian tree, human beings were counted as animals. Due to the extreme popularity of the *Introduction*, the taxonomy became a truism, to the extent that it was considered a logical truth that the human being is an animal—a special kind of animal, to be sure, but an animal nevertheless.[10] Now there is a crucial lesson to learn from this: even though medieval authors made a clear metaphysical distinction between human beings and other animals, it was always a part of a more general framework based on a similarity between us and them.

I have emphasized the similarities and differences between human beings and other animals because the borderline looks different from different perspectives. From a metaphysical point of view, animals form a clear and distinct group of beings that inhabit this created world. They are distinct from lifeless objects, which do not have souls, and even though they are not so easily distinguishable from plants, metaphysically speaking—the animal soul is not radically different from the vegetative soul, after all—from a psychological and functional perspective also this borderline is rather clear. And finally, animals differ radically from human beings, who are the only bodily creatures capable of turning to the superior intelligible world. Human beings, it was commonly thought, occupy the middle ground between spiritual and corporeal worlds, being members of both.

However, if we change our perspective and concentrate on those differentiating functions that separate human beings from other animals, we face certain philosophically intriguing problems. We may ask in what sense rationality makes us special. Porphyry's *Introduction* and the medieval commentaries on it seem to suppose that every human being has a rational soul even if there is no possibility of actually using the highest rational functions that it provides, for instance due to severe brain damage.[11] However, Aristotle's philosophy offers ideas that easily lead to what might be called "a functional interpretation" of rationality as the essential power that really makes human beings what they are. As is well known, Aristotle argues that things are what they are only when they can perform their functions: an eye that has lost the ability to see is an eye only by name, and a saw that cannot cut wood is not really a saw.[12] It is perhaps easier to give the defining function in the case of an eye than in the case of a complete animal or a whole human being, but in his zoological works Aristotle seems to classify living beings according to the functions they are capable of performing. He hesitates as to whether beings that do not move and perhaps do not perceive should be classified as animals or as plants. Ascidians, sea anemones, sponges, and the like defy clean categorization.[13]

From these ideas it is only a short step to argue that each individual human being may actualize the human essence more or less perfectly, depending on how well he or she is able to use the rational functions that separate humans from other animals. This kind of functional perspective may not have been the mainstream position in the Middle Ages, but it appears occasionally in various contexts. One anonymous author claims:

A human being is chiefly called a human being when he is able to perform his proper operation, which is reasoning (*ratiocinari*). When he cannot do this, he is called a human being only equivocally. The Commentator [i.e., Averroes] attests this clearly in the beginning of the eighth book of Physics. For he says that "human" is said equivocally of a human being who is perfected by speculative sciences and of one who is not perfected, like it is said [equivocally] of a painted and real human.[14]

As the author indicates, this idea originates in Averroes's influential commentary on the *Physics*, which was translated into Latin in the thirteenth century.[15] It was repeated by various medieval authors, who claimed that individuals who do not actualize their full potentiality as human beings are "brute humans" or even simply brutes (*homines brutales, bruti*).[16] Moreover the idea that individual human beings may be less than humans and even worse than any other animal species was a commonplace in medieval commentaries on Aristotle's *Politics*, where it was argued that those who are incapable of living together with other people are beasts, or at least poor specimens of the human species.[17] In line with this view, Peter of Auvergne (d. 1304) claims in passing that "a human being is a human being due to the reason which is in good condition and not corrupted."[18]

Medieval authors did not mean to argue that human beings who are incapable of intellectual thinking would not be humans in the metaphysical sense of not having an immortal rational soul. Rather the claims were usually made in order to show the value of philosophical life. The idea was that individuals who do not lead a life that is proper to human beings as human beings do not live up to their full potentiality and therefore do not actualize the human nature perfectly. This point was first and foremost a normative one, also in the moral sense that human beings should not live like animals but take control over their emotional reactions and actions and cultivate their highest abilities of intellectual thinking. If one fails to live a morally good life, one falls to the level of animals and, in a sense, becomes an animal. In a famous passage of the *Consolation of Philosophy*, Lady Philosophy explains to Boethius:

> And it also follows that whatever falls from goodness ceases to exist, and that evil men cease to be what they were, having by their wickedness lost their human nature, although they still survive in the form of the human body. It is goodness that raises a man above the level of humankind, and it therefore follows that evil thrusts a man down below the human condition, so that he no longer deserves the name of man....All those who have put goodness aside have no

right to be called men anymore, since there is nothing divine about them, but they have descended to the level of beasts.[19]

The fact that these claims are normative, however, does not entail that they are completely metaphorical. When medieval authors claimed that human beings may become animals by failing to live a virtuous and intellectual life, they were serious in the sense that the kind of life they wanted us to avoid was in many ways similar to the life of real nonhuman animals. The Averroist idea shows, if nothing else, that the activities that are proper to human beings and separate us from animals are fairly high in the scale that begins with the vegetative powers and ends with the rational powers. Even though our rationality enables us to overcome certain aspects of our animality, our mental lives are not radically different from those of other animals. This similarity is reflected in the discussions concerning the functional point of view: it is not obvious that we differ from other animals except insofar as we use our rational powers that animals do not have. In our everyday lives we are much like other animals.[20] This is important to keep in mind. It means that the clear metaphysical distinction defended by medieval authors does not translate into a clear psychological distinction.

The bottom line is that in order to understand medieval views on animals, we need not go far. Looking at our own lives stripped of certain rational aspects is a rather good heuristic tool to understand what kind of psychological processes other animals are capable of. That said, it is true that many a medieval philosopher thought our rationality changes our sensory operations. One might argue that our mental lives are in fact radically different from those of other animals, because in our case reason pervades everything else. This argument must be taken seriously, but at the same time it must be remembered that it is by no means clear how medieval philosophers would have responded to it. Arguably there were differing opinions: some authors thought that rationality is an all-pervasive element of our mental lives, while others were willing to give it a more limited role.

A special context, in which the functional perspective was especially important for deciding whether certain beings should be classified among humans or animals, was related to pygmies and various fanciful creatures that populated the medieval imagination.[21] Albert the Great (ca. 1200–1280) and Peter of Auvergne, among others, asked whether pygmies are human beings. In the background of this question was a theological worry. All human beings should be baptized, and the demarcation line between humans and nonhumans was therefore an important theoretical question that potentially had practical implications. As human beings are, by definition, rational animals, the central question was whether pygmies and other borderline cases are capable of using reason.

Opinions differed. An anonymous thirteenth-century author argued that pygmies are as much human beings as anyone who is born of human parents. By contrast, even though other primates appear similar to human beings, they are not. The crucial difference was that "some have the use of reason, such as pygmies, but others do not, such as apes."[22] In sharp contrast to this view, Albert the Great went through a long and tedious path in order to show that pygmies fall short of those rational powers that make us human beings. I shall come back to his view in the next section, but it is important to note that the issue was decided on the basis of the functional perspective, by appealing to the powers and abilities each kind of being has. If there is a being that looks like a human but displays no rational powers, it is not a human being in the proper sense of the term.[23]

Albert's view is objectionable to a modern ear, and for good reason. Luckily we do not need to accept it and its moral implications in order to see what his argumentation reveals about the human/animal boundary. The psychological capacities of pygmies show us how complex functions a creature may have without compromising the distinction between animals and human beings, and therefore medieval discussions concerning pygmies test the demarcation line between rational and irrational animals. Obviously the metaphysical perspective is important, as the crucial difference was between having a rational soul and not having one. Yet the metaphysical and functional perspectives are not distinct from each other because the nature of the soul was inferred partially from the functions that one is able to perform. From this point of view it is possible to declare, as a sixteenth-century philosopher, Antonio Montecatini (1537–99), once did in passing, that "if brute animals were capable of having a mind and learning, they would be human beings, not brutes."[24] Medieval philosophers did underline the metaphysical difference between human beings and other animals, but it is less clear whether this difference translates into a clear psychological distinction. In order to understand medieval conceptions of animals, it is necessary to ask: How far can we ascribe complex psychological operations to animals without making them human beings?

PSYCHOLOGY

As we have seen, animals were defined as living beings capable of perception. This ability separates them from plants. Although this criterion seems to be rather simple at the outset, it involves certain complexities. It may not be obvious, for instance, whether or not a given species *has* the ability to perceive—I already mentioned the Aristotelian borderline cases, such as sea sponges. Even in the case of animals that undoubtedly perceive their surroundings, the cognitive process by which perception takes place is by no means simple. Medieval philosophers were interested in explaining how various modalities of perception differ from each other, what powers of the soul are involved in perception, and which other psychological processes might be found in animals—especially higher ones, such as sheep, dogs, apes, and, sometimes, pygmies.[25]

The starting point is rather obvious. Perfect animals have five familiar external senses—sight, hearing, touch, taste, and smell—by which they perceive their surroundings. Not all animals have all of these, since some species lack one or several of the five senses. Medieval philosophers claimed, however, following a long tradition that stretches all the way to Antiquity, that no matter how simple an animal is, it has at least one external sense: the sense of touch.[26] Being able to feel one's surroundings or the changes in one's body was regarded as an ability that belongs to all animals, and thereby animals were considered able to feel pain and pleasure. Thus, to use a modern term, sentience was regarded as the criterion by which animals were distinguished from plants in the Porphyrian tree.

Touch was considered to be the most material of the senses. It requires direct contact with the object and involves a material change in the body of the perceiver.[27] The other senses were organized into a hierarchy, the peak of which is sight—the most noble of all the senses because the least material of them all. In contrast to the other external senses, sight does not involve any material change in the medium or in the sense organ.[28] Medieval discussions concerning sense-perception centered on sight not only because it was taken to be the most noble of the senses but also because it presented the most challenging philosophical problems.

Another cluster of cognitive powers that animals (including human beings) have is related to post-sensory psychological processes. Animals were thought to be able to remember, imagine, and evaluate whether the objects they perceive are useful or harmful to them. Thus, for instance, a dog recognizes its owner and a sheep immediately knows that a wolf is dangerous when it sees one, even if it has no previous experience of wolves. These psychological abilities are post-sensory in the sense that they either take place after the perception of an external object or add some special element to a bare perception of the perceptible qualities (color, smell, etc.) of an external object. It is possible to see a man without recognizing him as the owner, and it is possible to see a wolf without becoming afraid of it. The additional elements of recognizing and becoming afraid are not parts of a perceptual act in itself, but something that may or may not accompany perceptual acts. Medieval philosophers thought the animal soul must contain a set of post-sensory powers that account for the special features that sometimes accompany perception. These powers were called "the internal senses"—not because they would be means for perceiving something that is internal for the perceiving subject but because their organs are not external and visible.

The idea that the soul has internal senses was not, strictly speaking, a medieval innovation. Aristotle, Galen, and other ancient authors discussed various types of sensory cognition that go beyond simple perception of perceptual qualities. Augustine (354–430) seems to have been the first Latin author to use the term "internal sense" (*sensus interior*),[29] and his psychological ideas influenced medieval views concerning these powers. However, the most important developments of this idea took place in the medieval period. Arabic authors, most notably Avicenna, developed a systematic understanding of the various powers of higher animals and human beings, and medieval Latin authors continued this tradition. It is not an exaggeration to say that in the Middle Ages—both in Arabic and in Latin—the internal senses became the most important powers in the domain of animal psychology. Medieval Latin authors discussed the number of the internal senses, the criteria for distinguishing them from each other, their functions, and their mutual relationships, and much of their psychological discussion revolves around them or at least is connected to them.[30] Even human rationality required appealing to the internal senses due to the widely accepted empiricist idea that all human knowledge either arises from sense-perception or at least requires it as a starting point. Perceptual information goes through the internal senses before arriving at the intellectual level, and the psychological processes that make intellectual understanding possible were not a minor detail in medieval psychological discussions but a central part of them.

This is not a place to provide even an overview of the medieval views concerning the internal senses. Suffice it to say that the list of internal senses that medieval philosophers usually attributed to higher animals included the following powers: the common sense, imagination, estimative power, memory, and, occasionally, cogitative power. Some authors rejected some of these powers as superfluous, and sometimes different terminology was employed, but the overall scheme remained rather stable. Yet we find medieval philosophers presenting various, even radically different views concerning the details of the functions of these powers as well as their mutual relations. One of the more striking suggestions was that the sensory soul includes only one internal sense: the common sense. This suggestion was influenced by Augustine's remarks concerning the centralizing power of the animal soul, but it was defended mostly for philosophical reasons. A proponent of this view, the Franciscan philosopher and theologian Peter Olivi (ca. 1248–98), provided a detailed philosophical analysis of how the common sense is able to perform all the complex psychological operations that are necessary in order to account for animal action. His view was based on the idea that various functions are necessarily connected to each other— that it is not possible, say, to remember an object without imagining it. It was more economical to attribute various functions to one power rather than postulate several powers, and by claiming that there is only one internal sense, there was no problem in accounting for the interconnection of the functions.[31]

The psychological functions that these powers were thought to perform were manifold. Combining and comparing the information received from various external senses, perceiving the so-called common sensibles (figure, movement, number, etc.), imagining objects that are not present, remembering and recognizing past events and objects, evaluating external objects in terms of their contribution to the well-being of the percipient, and second-order perception (that is, perceiving that one perceives) were all thought to be functions that are necessary for explaining animal behavior. The central idea in this kind of psychological approach—commonly called "faculty psychology"—was that if we see a certain kind of behavior in animals, we must attribute to them psychological powers without which the behavior cannot be explained. Thus, because dogs are able to remember that they have been beaten with a stick, and sheep run away from wolves even if they have had no previous experience of them, we must assume that dogs are capable of remembering the beating and sheep are somehow aware of the dangerousness of a wolf in their vicinity, even though they do not suffer pain from the perception. Scientific explanation of these phenomena calls for attributing the corresponding internal senses to these animals.

Human rational powers mark the other end of the spectrum. The rational soul gives human beings a set of abilities that medieval philosophers denied to other animals. A typical list of psychological operations of which animals are incapable would contain at least the following: animals do not understand the essences of things; they do not grasp universals; they cannot speak, for speech is nothing but an external expression of internal rational concepts; they cannot control their emotional impulses but act immediately on the basis of their emotions without the possibility of being checked by reason; they do not have freedom of the will; they cannot reason from premises to a conclusion; and they are not aware of themselves. It is less clear, however, to what extent rationality influences all the lower levels of psychological abilities. Occasionally medieval authors touch upon the role of human rationality in perception, and some differences in the functioning of the internal senses between human beings and other animals were often spelled out.[32] However, a typical approach was (arguably) that our rationality may affect the way we *use* the information that we get from the senses, but the sensory processes as such are similar in human beings and animals. This similarity is significant because it allows us to see what kind of beings animals were thought to be from a psychological perspective.

Rational abilities aside, medieval discussions concerning sense-perception and the internal senses apply to animals even when the author's main intention is to discuss the elementary features of human psychology. Especially when the differences are explicitly taken up and the author explains that human beings are capable of using some of their internal senses in ways that are not possible for animals, it is reasonable to assume that he deems the other operations to be similar. Overall it is clear that animals were not considered to be insensible automata. The difference between humans and animals is more in the level of sophistication. For instance, Thomas Aquinas (1225–1274) argues (following Avicenna) that human beings are capable of imagining things that they have never seen by combining elements from various mental images and actively evoking memories of things they have almost forgotten.[33] We can imagine golden mountains, and we can try to remember what we had for dinner yesterday even if we do not recall it at the moment. By contrast, other animals can imagine only things they have seen before (that is, either a mountain or a pile of gold, but *not* a golden mountain), and they cannot actively search their memories. This difference in psychological abilities is explicitly taken up by Aquinas, who underlines that animal psychology is not, after all, completely alien to human beings. It is but a simpler version of human psychology.

In order to see how sophisticated were the psychological abilities medieval authors attributed to animals, let us look at three examples, which can be found in various medieval authors: (1) the ability to speak; (2) the ability to reason; and (3) a certain kind of self-awareness. My intention is not to claim that these examples would represent typical ways of thinking about animal psychology; rather I take them up in order to show that some medieval philosophers were prepared to concede fairly advanced psychological process to higher animals, and thus to draw the line between animals and humans high. Other authors may have had more restrictive views, but they were nevertheless far from thinking that "animal psychology" is an oxymoron.

(1) The first of these psychological abilities is suggested by Albert the Great. His view is significant, because he explicitly deals with the demarcation line *and* he attributes rather sophisticated abilities to animals. With respect to cognitive operations, higher animals differ from

human beings mainly because they are incapable of understanding universal essences and deducing conclusions from premises.

As we have seen, Albert thinks that pygmies are animals, but he considers them in many ways special among the animal kingdom. Many animals can remember past events and seek things that are not present at the moment, and some are even able to learn from experience. Further, some animals understand human speech and can learn to obey commands.[34] Pygmies are so advanced in both of these skills that they have what Albert calls "the shadow of reason,"[35] a power that is above the estimative power but falls short of being a rational power proper. The former was often used to explain the seemingly rational actions of animals, as well as their ability to know which things in their environment are harmful and which are useful to them. Some of the functions that were attributed to it were complex, but Albert thinks that the abilities of pygmies require a higher capacity.

By the shadow of reason, pygmies can imitate human arts, perform practical reasoning (although incompletely), and even use language: "Some [animals] thrive so much in training the sense of hearing, that they even indicate their intentions to each other—like pygmies who speak although they are irrational animals."[36] Language was usually considered to require rationality, and therefore it was denied to any other bodily creature but human beings. Albert's view is thus atypical, although he sees a difference between human language and the language of pygmies: "And therefore, although pygmies speak, they do not discuss about universal things but rather their voices refer to particular things."[37] Human beings can understand universals and discuss them—that is, we are able to understand essences of things and operate with them—whereas pygmies speak only about particular objects.

Albert's general idea is easy to understand, but his claim about the language of pygmies is problematic. After all, language seems to presume some kind of generality, for otherwise there will be a distinct word for every individual thing in the world, and this makes language use not only superfluous but also impossible. Albert may think that pygmies do have general concepts that refer to several individuals of the same kind without being able to understand the essence of those individual objects.[38] This seems to call for some kind of ability to grasp similarity that is not based on the essences of things. Perhaps Albert thinks that already the sensory soul of animals enables apprehending individuals as belonging to the same species, as well as distinguishing members of different species from each other. This ability would not require understanding the essences of these individuals—after all, understanding an essence of a thing is more like grasping a scientific definition than grasping similarity—and thus it could be attributed to nonhuman animals, which do not have rational soul and reason. This kind of ability could function as the basis of the language pygmies speak.

Unfortunately Albert does not explain his view in any detail, but there are other medieval authors who suggest this kind of idea. An often repeated example, which seems to require the ability to recognize that an object is similar to other objects of the same kind, is a dog that is afraid of *all* sticks because it has been beaten with *a* stick in the past. This Avicennian example was used to prove the existence of one of the internal senses (either the common sense or the estimative power—the dog apprehends the form of the stick and connects it with the sensation of pain, or it apprehends an intention of harmfulness together with the stick it perceives),[39] but for our purposes the crucial point is that animals learn from experience and they learn to avoid certain *kinds* of objects, not only the one individual object that gave them the experience in the first place. Medieval philosophers do not usually discuss the ability to generalize explicitly, but there is at least one author who argues for it while developing his theory of perception. Roger Bacon (ca. 1214–94) attributes it to all animals in his *Perspectiva*:

But it is clear that a dog recognizes a man, whom it has seen before, and that apes and many other animals also do this. And they distinguish between things they have seen of which they have memory, they recognize one universal from another—as man from dog or wood— and they distinguish different individuals of the same species. Thus, this cognition…belongs to brute animals as well as to humans, and therefore it happens by a power of the sensory soul.[40]

The central point here is that animals distinguish one species from another, and apparently they are able to apprehend members of one species as similar to each other in such a way that they are aware of their similarity. Bacon explains that animals differ from human beings because they do this by some kind of natural instinct and not by deliberation, but the crucial point is that animals are able to do this. One way to explain this idea is to say that animals perceive natural kinds, even though they are incapable of grasping universal concepts. They do not understand the definitions of things and cannot form syllogisms, but it seems possible to recognize that two individuals of the same kind are similar to each other without knowing their universal essence.[41]

(2) Another ability that Bacon attributes to animals in the same context is a certain kind of ability to reason. He lists several cases in which animals act in an orderly fashion, making one thing for the sake of another. For instance, he tells a story about a cat that, upon seeing a fish in a large stone container, pulled a stopper and let the water out in order to catch the fish. This kind of process is akin to reasoning, and, Bacon explains, it:

> occurs in an infinity of cases in which brute animals consider many things which are ordered to one thing which they intend to do, as if they were inferring a conclusion from premises. However, they do not organize their reasoning in [syllogistic] mood and figure, and they do not distinguish the end from the first actions. Nor do they perceive that they accomplish this kind of process, because their thinking proceeds as it does by natural instinct alone.[42]

Animals act in certain ways in order to achieve aims that are not an immediate result of their action. However, because they cannot deliberate the process, the situation is beyond their comprehension if they do not immediately see what needs to be done. By contrast, human beings may deliberate the possible courses of action and come up with a solution that was not immediately obvious to them.

It needs to be emphasized that although Bacon and other medieval authors use the term "natural instinct," they do not necessarily mean that animals would be unconscious of their actions. Animals may not be aware of the complex process or of the reasons behind their action; they do not reflect upon various possible courses of action; and they do not decide to perform, or refrain from performing, the action in question.[43] However, these limitations do not mean that they would be unaware of their actions and the objects that are involved in them. Consciousness in animals (or in human beings, for that matter) is evidently a problematic issue, given that medieval philosophers do not identify "consciousness" as a philosophical problem.[44] They do, however, discuss many phenomena that are nowadays considered to be relevant for consciousness, and it is fairly clear that they consider it obvious that cognitive processes involve some kind of phenomenal first-person experience. At least medieval authors think that animals dream, act intentionally, and learn from experience. All of these psychological phenomena are difficult to explain without admitting that animals have some kind of awareness.[45]

(3) A typical limitation that medieval philosophers saw in animals' cognitive abilities was their lack of self-awareness. The metaphysical grounding for this limitation was that material entities cannot turn upon themselves. Because animals do not have immaterial souls, they are incapable of taking their own minds as objects of cognition. They are incapable of thinking of themselves as cognitive subjects. This limitation was related to the idea that animals cannot control themselves the way human beings do, because controlling

one's actions requires the ability to distance oneself from the immediate experiences and emotions.

It is easy to overestimate the significance of the lack of self-awareness in animals, however. Even though medieval philosophers denied to animals a certain kind of intellectual self-awareness, at least some of them were ready to claim that animals are aware of themselves in a simpler way. Such an idea was suggested by Peter Olivi, who argued that animals are aware of their own bodies and the mutual importance of their body parts:

> When a dog or a snake sacrifices one of its members in order to save its head or sacrifices some part in order to save the whole, then it prefers the whole over the part and the head over the other member. Therefore, these animals must have some common power which shows both extremes simultaneously, their mutual comparison, and the preference of one over the other—although it does not do this with the same fullness and degree of reflective judgment as does the intellect.[46]

Olivi's point is that animals appear to protect their vital parts at the expense of other members when they are threatened. A dog avoids being hit in the head by averting a blow with its paw, for instance, and this ability shows that it is on some level aware that the paw is of lesser importance to its well-being than the head. Later Olivi explains that animals are aware of the mutual importance of their body parts because their common sense can turn toward itself in an incomplete way.[47] The distinction between intellectual self-awareness and self-awareness that can be attributed to animals boils down to a difference between having explicit awareness of oneself as a cognitive subject (that is, taking one's mind as an object of a cognitive act) and being aware of oneself as a living, cognitive, and bodily being and a subject of one's cognitive acts. Animals cannot turn their attention to their minds as objects, but the fact that they try to preserve themselves in existence and avoid all kinds of harm calls for some kind of self-awareness. Certain kinds of action cannot be accounted for without appealing to primitive self-awareness.[48]

MORALITY

As animals were considered to have a rather sophisticated cognitive life, one might expect that medieval philosophers would have raised questions concerning their moral status. Morality was, after all, closely related to psychological considerations. However, they usually did not draw the conclusion that the commonalities between humans and animals would give us reason to treat animals more benevolently. The treatment of animals was not considered in moral terms, and the moral status of animals was not seen as a philosophical problem that needs to be treated in any explicit manner. Thus in order to get a hold of the moral status of animals in medieval philosophy, it is necessary to do some interpretative work and read between the lines. One should also keep in mind that there is not much modern research on the moral status of animals in medieval philosophy, and therefore the following points should be taken as preliminary proposals rather than final results.

With this caveat in mind, we may nevertheless approach animals and their relation to morality by using a threefold heuristic model, which helps us to understand how multifaceted the medieval philosophical and cultural imagery of animals was. Animals can be considered moral agents, moral patients, or moral examples.

(1) The first perspective concerning moral agency is by far the clearest of the three. Medieval philosophers were unanimous that animals are not moral agents in the proper sense of the word. The rationale behind this view was that moral action requires psychological freedom. Human beings are moral agents because they have a free will (*liberum arbitrium* or *libera voluntas*) by which they are capable of

choosing their actions. The will was understood as a power of the soul, as a rational appetite or desire, which enables human beings to detach themselves from their immediate emotional reactions and act instead on the basis of rational considerations. Obviously the way this idea was articulated and conceptualized varied from author to author—especially significant was the opposition between intellectualism and voluntarism, which developed in the late thirteenth and early fourteenth centuries[49]—but all accepted that the type of freedom that is required for moral agency comes only with the rational soul.

Without free will, animals are bound to follow their emotional reactions. The behavior of animals is principally caused by desire for self-preservation and pleasure as well as avoidance of harm, which give rise to a variety of emotions: love and hate, desire and aversion, joy and sadness, fear and hope, and so forth.[50] Emotions were considered to be psychophysical phenomena, which involve movements of the animal spirit and the heart but which also include a cognitive element, and they were generally considered to be common to human beings and animals.[51] When an animal perceives an object that is either useful and pleasant or painful and harmful to it, one of its internal senses, the estimative power, apprehends this affective aspect and triggers an emotion. To use the typical medieval example that we already saw, when a sheep perceives a wolf, its estimative power evaluates the wolf as harmful and dangerous, and this evaluative perception gives rise to the emotion of fear. The actions of the sheep are ultimately caused by emotions, and in this case the fear makes the sheep flee the wolf.[52]

A crucial aspect of this general medieval view is that the sheep does not have control over its flight because it is not psychologically free. The emotional responses of animals are automatic and instinctual in the sense that all individuals of the same species react uniformly to similar stimuli. Human beings, by contrast, are able to prevent the emotion from turning into action. Animals can be habituated to some extent, but even then they do not exercise direct control over their actions. Rather their emotional reactions are modified by training, and this modification counts as indirect control at most.[53] It is precisely because animals lack the ability to control their action when confronted with emotional situations that they are not moral agents. They cannot exert cognitive control over their emotions like human beings do, which means that they are not morally responsible for their actions.[54]

In spite of this, medieval times witnessed a practice of prosecuting animals in courts of justice. On the basis of the extant records of these legal procedures it may seem that animals were considered to be legal persons, who can be held responsible for their actions— after all, the procedures were not simply ceremonial, as there are cases in which the prosecuted animals were acquitted. However, it is unclear what we should think about this practice. One possible explanation for the apparent conflict (between the idea that animals are not responsible for their actions and the idea that they can be held accountable for them) is to say that there is a distinction between legal and moral responsibility, which means that animals could be held legally responsible even though they are not moral agents properly speaking. However, we do not know enough of the rationale behind these processes to make definite conclusions, and the only thing we can be fairly confident about is that these records reveal an understanding of the status of nonhuman animals that differs radically from our own.[55]

(2) Another question concerning the moral status of animals pertains to their role as moral patients. One might think that because animals were seen as sentient beings with rather complex mental lives, they would have enjoyed some kind of moral worth and that their treatment would have been regulated by morality. However, this concern was not central in the Middle Ages. Philosophers did not ponder whether animals should be treated

in a special way due to their sentience. Thomas Aquinas, for instance, denies any intrinsic value to animals and thinks that irrational beings are not proper objects of moral concern. Killing an animal is wrong only if it happens to be someone else's property, and the only reason to refrain from cruelty to animals is that it may incline the perpetrator to do the same to other humans.[56]

This does not necessarily mean, however, that animals may be treated in just any way we please. Several medieval authors (including Aquinas) accepted Ulpian's definition of natural law, which they found in an influential collection of Roman law, *Corpus iuris civilis*:

> Natural law (*ius naturale*) is that which nature has taught to all animals; for this law is not specific to mankind but common to all animals, which are born in land and sea, and also to birds...because we see that other animals, wild beasts included, are rightly understood to be acquainted with this law.[57]

This definition suggested that animals participate in the general moral order that regulates the whole creation. Medieval authors were not particularly interested in explaining how animals follow the natural law, and when they took a stand on the issue, they were happy just to say that animals do this by a natural instinct and automatically.[58] This solution obviously leaves many questions open, but it nevertheless shows that the behavior of animals, and the kind of life that is natural for them, was conceptualized in legal and moral terms.

The term *ius* was also employed to denote what we know as a subjective right. A famous proponent of this approach, Jean Gerson (1363–1429), argued that even though rights in a proper sense belong only to rational beings, all creatures have subjective natural rights in a broad sense: the sun has a right to shine, birds have a right to build nests, and so forth.[59] Although this concession does not necessarily imply that preventing animals from following their natural inclinations would be a moral issue—that is, the rights of animals are not claim rights—it is significant that Ulpian's definition was not rejected outright. Animals may not have rights in the same sense as we do, but the language of rights can be applied to them nevertheless.

Whether medieval authors took animals as mere instruments, which can be used to benefit humans without any constraint, is a complicated question. Medieval authors approached this question in the context of a passage from Aristotle's *Politics*, which suggests that plants exist for the sake of animals and that animals exist for the sake of human beings.[60] Regardless of whether Aristotle meant this claim to be taken literally, medieval philosophers were eager to accept it, partly because they found a similar (but not necessarily identical) suggestion in the first book of Genesis, where humans are given dominion over all creation. Yet they felt the need to ask whether it is true that animals and plants exist for the sake of humankind, and although they gave a positive answer, sometimes it was pointed out that there are limitations to the use of animals. So, for instance, Nicholas of Vaudémont, a fourteenth-century Parisian arts master—after claiming that plants and animals can be used to satisfy the needs of humans (food, clothing, etc.)—argues:

> From this it follows as a corollary that if someone appoints plants and animals to any other end than to maintaining human life, he does not use but abuses them. This is clear, because when someone appoints something to an end that is not proper to it, he is said to abuse that thing. Secondly, it follows that if a human being uses plants or brute animals more than is sufficient, he is said to abuse them just like the first one.[61]

Animals may be used to sustain human life, but Nicholas argues that there is a limit in using them. They should not be abused by seeking anything that goes beyond the necessities of life. Nicholas appears to put his argument in moral terms by claiming that even though human beings have the right to use animals, we should not do this more than is absolutely necessary. The argument is surprising, but on the other hand, medieval philosophers believed that although human beings were created to rule other animals, they were also given the task of taking care of God's creation, and the permission to eat animals was received only after the great flood—it was not the practice in the original state of mankind.[62] Moreover, as we have seen, medieval authors were far from conceiving animals as metaphysically equal to lifeless instruments.

To what extent this metaphysical difference, or the psychological abilities of animals, implied anything concerning their moral status is not so clear. Despite Nicholas's concession, animals were not typically considered to be moral patients. When the abuse of animals was criticized, the implication usually was that acting cruelly toward animals corrupts the person who is acting and disposes him or her to act cruelly toward other human beings.

(3) Regardless of their intrinsic value (or the lack of it), animals bear moral relevance in medieval thought in a special way: they were widely used as moral examples. Medieval bestiaries follow the ancient tradition and provide not only descriptions of various species of existent or imaginary animals but also accounts of moral lessons that human beings can learn from them. Different animals represent different virtues allegorically and serve as examples for proper conduct. Certainly the point was not that animals would be more virtuous than human beings, because moral virtue is possible only for rational beings. Rather animals were thought to be created so as to instruct human beings in moral and religious matters.[63]

Another way in which animals served as moral examples is related to the idea that despite their rationality, human beings are also animals. This affinity with other animals and the idea that morality requires us to control our impulses, which stem from our animal nature, meant that animals are like images of what human beings become if they fail to live up to moral standards. We saw something of this already in the first section, when we encountered the claim that human beings who fail to use their reason live the life of an animal. This idea was conceivable partly because animals were considered to be in many ways similar to human beings, a proposal with normative implications. Human beings who fail to control their lives in accordance with rational norms and morality are like animals. By looking at other animals we see what kind of lives those people live who cannot control their emotional reactions. In this sense, animals function as a kind of mirror, "a moral other," which enables us to see what morality requires of us. A person who follows his instincts and emotions without trying to take rational control over them lives the life of an irrational animal and thus allows himself to be dominated by his own animality.

Yet in one sense animals were considered to be better off than immoral human beings. Medieval philosophers emphasize, echoing Aristotle, that human beings who live in separation from other humans due to their deprived nature are bestial and worse than brute animals.[64] Sometimes they suggest that this is true only insofar as the cause for solitude is moral badness. Even vicious humans are better than beasts due to the perfection of human nature, but they are worst of all animals in a normative sense, just because they have the ability to transcend their animal nature.[65]

CONCLUSION

We have seen that medieval conceptions of the relation between animals and humans were multifaceted. The dividing line looks different when viewed from different perspectives. The metaphysical difference is radical and clear, but approaching the boundary only from a metaphysical perspective does not do justice to the complexity of medieval views. Psychological and functional perspective allows us to understand that animals were considered to be sophisticated creatures that are in many respects close to us. Moreover, even though medieval philosophers usually did not consider the moral status of nonhuman animals an important question, it is too simple to say that animals were seen simply as instruments to be used for the good of humans.

The foregoing discussion does not claim to be exhaustive, as it only scratches the surface of the views of a few medieval authors. Moreover I have concentrated on philosophical texts and philosophical conceptions, thereby leaving aside the rich historical material that could be used to reveal medieval attitudes to animals in religious, legal, and medical contexts, as well as in everyday life. The philosophical discussions show, nevertheless, that medieval conceptions of animals share at least one feature: they depict animals as complex creatures. Philosophers were far from thinking that animals are different from us in *all* respects, and the idea that they might be unconscious machines never occurred to them. They attributed a great deal of complexity to animal psychology, and they were able to use animals as the "other" to which human beings can be compared just because animals were considered to be similar to us, yet different in certain relevant ways. Due to this fundamental similarity, medieval philosophers were able to ask what makes human beings special among the rest of the animal kingdom.[66]

Reflection

ANIMAL INTELLIGENCE: EXAMPLES OF THE
HUMAN-ANIMAL BORDER IN MEDIEVAL LITERATURE

Sabine Obermaier

Animals are pervasive in medieval literature. Yet, as in medieval
philosophy, they are rarely considered an object of interest in their
own right. Instead they are invoked as part of humankind's natural
environment or as the property or antagonists of humans. They
appear as metaphors representing human affairs, as indicators of
the status or inner qualities of humans. A key component in the
contrast between animals and humans is the (rational) superiority
of humans.[1] Yet the borders between human and animal could be
blurred,[2] and medieval literary authors sometimes create scenarios
in which animals appear as models for humans to imitate, and this
precisely in the specifically human domains of rationality, ethics,
and faith: animals are depicted as more intelligent, moral, and
pious than their human counterparts. Does this mean that literary
authors display an understanding of animals fundamentally
different from that of their philosophical contemporaries?

THE INTELLIGENT ANIMAL

Walther von der Vogelweide's *Reichston* was written in 1198–1201,
at a time when the German kingship was contested between Philip
of Swabia and Otto IV. In the second stanza,[3] Walther compares

the position of the people at this time to the natural condition of animals. Admittedly no animal life is free of conflict, yet animals show themselves to be more reasonable than humans:

wan daz si habent einen sin:
si dûhten sich zenihte,
si enschüefen starc gerihte.
si kiesent künege unde reht,
si setzent hêrren unde kneht.[4]

And league their purpose to fulfill;
And when the need arises,
They set up strong assizes.
They rule themselves by law and crown,
Raise lords and put the lesser down.[5]

Even the most insignificant of insects (*mugge*) has its (single!) king.[6] Walther here chooses vocabulary that invites us to see animals as engaged in intentional action (*schaffen*: "establishing"; *kiesen*: "choosing"; *setzen*: "determining").[7] They are explicitly granted "sense" (*sin*), which in Middle High German can mean not only "sensation" but also "rational capacity." Such action presupposes free will, which, according to medieval philosophers, is lacking in animals, in particular those animals at the lower end of the order of nature.

THE MORAL ANIMAL

In his Arthurian romance *Yvain*, or *The Knight with the Lion* (written around 1170),[8] Chrétien de Troyes describes how a lion who has served as Yvain's faithful companion after his life was saved by the knight, wishes to commit suicide because he believes Yvain to be dead: "Et s'a talant, que il s'ocie / De l'espee, don li est vis, / Qu'ele et son buen seignor ocis" (verses 3512–14; "And wanted to kill itself with the sword that it thought had slain its master"). The lion is explicitly granted a capacity for free choice, with talk of its *talant* ("wish," verse 3512) and shortly thereafter, *ses voloirs* ("its intention," verse 3520). Fortunately for the lion, Yvain returns before it can act upon its decision. Impressed by the lion's willingness to die in devotion to him, Yvain sees the lion as a model worthy of imitation (verses 3544–51). In the Middle High German version of the story, *Iwein* (written about 1203),[9] the knight praises the lion as an exemplar of unshakeable loyalty:

nû gît mir doch des bilde
dirre lewe wilde,
daz er von herzeleide sich
wolde erstechen umbe mich,
daz rehtriu triuwe nâhen gât.[10]

Now this wild lion,
Who out of heartfelt grief
Was ready to kill himself over me,
Has shown me by his example
That true faithfulness runs deep.[11]

The protagonist admits that, at least in this phase of his journey, he has been morally bested by a wild beast.

THE PIOUS ANIMAL

In the legends of saints, especially martyrs, we frequently come across animals who show obedience or helpfulness toward the legends' heroes: unlike humans, these animals are able to recognize the saintliness of the saint. A biblical model was provided by the story of Daniel in the lion's den (Daniel 6:16ff); early imitations can be found in the legends of the Apostle Paul and of Saint Thekla.[12] In his *Dialogues* (written around AD 404), Sulpicius

Severus recounts that when Saint Martin saw a snake approaching
the riverbank where he had gathered his friends, he invoked God's
name and commanded it to retreat.[13] The "wicked animal" (*mala
bestia*) instantly turns away and swims back to the far bank. With a
sigh, Martin observes, "I am heeded by snakes, but not by men"
(*serpentes me audiunt, et homines non audiunt*). Here we see that
serpents, symbolic of evil though they may be, "show more
obedience to saints and thus to God than do human beings."[14]

The unexpected intelligence, morality, and piety shown by
animals in these stories are meant to inspire humans to show the
intelligence, morality, and piety that befit humankind. In order to
serve as a positive example, the animals are depicted as more human
than humans often manage to be. In the process the philosophical
ordering of nature seems to be turned on its head. Yet these literary
examples do not really depart from the assumptions about animals
that we find in philosophical discourse. On the contrary, the
literary motif of the exemplary animal is premised on the
assumption that animals are inferior to humans. Walther's insect,
Yvain's lion, and Martin's serpent can serve as more persuasive
models precisely because they are usually seen as lacking humanity:
if animals can act as humans, all the more should humans do so.[15]
So it is not a matter of reversing the natural order, or even of
anthropomorphization: the motif of the intelligent animal works
only when we admit that here an animal behaves better than a
human, yet still as an animal.[16]

One might see a counterexample in the work of another poet,
Reinmar von Zweter (thirteenth century),[17] who presents the "ideal
human" as combining the best features of seven sorts of animal:
the eyes of an ostrich (*strûzes ougen*, 99:4), in order to look
affectionately on his familiars (100:2); the neck of a crane (*eines
cranches hals*) with polished tongue (99:5), that he may speak with
due consideration (100:3–5); pig's ears (*zwei swînes ôren*, 99:6),

enabling him to hear well whether in battle he should stand or take flight, and a lion's heart (*lewen herze*, 99:6), with which to fight bravely (100:7). Furthermore his two hands have the characters of the eagle (99:7–8), representing generosity (100:6–7), and of the griffin (99:9), which means avoiding prodigality (100:9), while his feet are those of the bear (99:10), so that he may conquer anger (100:10).[18]

It is, however, no coincidence that the features named by Reinmar are the very features of humankind that are shared with other species. Animals are admitted to be our superiors, but only in respect of the features that belong to our animality: physical constitution, social behavior, and the acuity of sense-perception.[19] By using these features as part of his allegory, Reinmar converts them to human "virtues."

Medieval literary texts may sometimes seem to forge a different path by portraying animals as our betters, but in fact they adhere to the conception of animals typically found in medieval philosophy.

Reflection

SUBVERSIVE LAUGHTER IN *REYNARD THE FOX*

James Simpson, Harvard University

Medieval literature abounds in stories about animals, of which
there are two main, easily distinguished, varieties: animal fables and
beast epic.[1] Animal fables claim Aesop as their source. They are
small narratives in which animals act and speak, with even smaller
morals tacked on at the end of the little stories. They involve many
animals (e.g., mice, lambs, cocks, foxes, birds, wolves, lions, and
frogs). Such stories were used to teach schoolboys both Latin and
some commonsense morality into the bargain (e.g., do not overeat;
do not overreach; save up for the hard times; justice can be rough
and ready, so keep clear of the predators). Beast epic, by contrast, is
a group of interconnected narratives, set in the court of the lion; its
single (anti-)hero is Reynard the Fox. Beast epic presents narratives
of dark but vital humor that repeat the same narrative with many
variations: its rhetorically brilliant fox, Reynard, outwits all comers
by manipulating their bottomless greed. No matter how tight the
corner into which Reynard has been backed, we know he will
escape. He escapes through brilliant narrative control and intimate,
intuitive knowledge of his enemies' weaknesses. He exposes the
arrogance of the greedy but even more damagingly the hypocrisy
of the "civilized" order. We learn a fundamental truth from these
stories: both animals and humans are predatory and self-interested

and will, if necessary, exercise cunning in order to serve their own ends.

The Reynardian stories derive from the much older Aesopian tradition: one of its central stories, the tale of the sick lion, in which the fox tricks the wolf, appears in Aesop. The continuous narrative characteristic of the Reynard material begins, however, with *The Escape of the Captive* (or *Ecbasis Captivi*, mid-eleventh century) and is greatly developed in the *Ysengrimus* (1148–49)—an important source for the earliest branches of the French *Roman de Renart*.[2] The so-called branches of the *Roman de Renart* are short narrative sequences in French, composed probably between the 1170s and the middle of the thirteenth century.[3] These stories ultimately inspired many more adaptions in other Western European languages for the next 250 years and beyond, including William Caxton's *History of Reynard the Fox* (1481).[4]

Like earlier medieval animal fables, *Reynard* contributes to the tradition of narrativized ethics but in a way that threatens to undo that tradition altogether, by giving a very different meaning to Aristotle's claim that man is a political animal. Aristotelian ethics requires imaginative recognition of pleasure, pain, and desire in the other—a recognition that is itself dependent on identifying one's own pleasure, pain, and desire with the experience of someone else. *Reynard*, by contrast, challenges the notion that we can ever see beyond our own desire through a central figure whose all-powerful imagination serves nothing but his own relentless self-interest. In the process, we learn how easily desire can rule the imagination. This is not to say that Reynard is simply amoral, as is his rival Ysengrimus the wolf. He is something more interesting: a character who subverts ethics, for instance by provoking such sentiments as pity but exploiting them to wholly unethical (pitiless) ends. This may explain why *Reynard* is so funny; it allows us to laugh at the pretensions of the ethical by observing the operations of ethical sympathy so closely. We do not laugh at Ysengrim.

The arc of Caxton's brilliantly coherent narrative is very clear: Reynard starts off as an outlaw to the court and ends up as the king's most prized counselor. By contrast, his enemy, Ysengrimus the wolf, starts off as the king's trusty messenger and ends up as the humiliated and physically damaged victim in court. Reynard's progress from outlaw to royal counselor is by no means smooth. On the contrary, the fascination of watching Reynard at work is to see him move into ever more dangerous situations and to escape each time. He plays for extremely high stakes, which get higher each time, with more opponents and more evidence clearly stacked up against him. Each time, however, he escapes through the imaginative exercise of rhetorically shaped narrative. From easy victims like the bear, Reynard moves on to slightly more challenging opponents like the cat and then to the assembled court, ruled over by the lion, who, as king, has at his disposal the full violence of the state. But Reynard has something more powerful still: the rhetorical skill that allows him to be the author of his own story.

This is highlighted as soon as Reynard arrives in court, when he announces that no matter how strong the king's council and his enemies, "As long as I can speak, I'll come as high in court as they would have me on the gallows. I've got so many tricks up my sleeve!" (chapter 15). Condemned to death, Reynard begs first to confess his sins before execution. This chance is granted to him out of pity, and, once granted, he exploits it to the full, so as not only to exculpate himself but to go on the offensive by incriminating his rivals as traitors and by fooling the king with the promise of much (wholly invented) gold and silver (chapters 16–17). He invents a narrative of treacherous conspiracy involving his own father, Ysengrym, and all his other enemies at court, along with one or two friends by way of authenticating the story. Reynard concocts the following tale: Reynard's father, said to have found an immense store of gold, convenes a conspiracy to assassinate the king. When

drunk, one of the conspirators tells his wife, and she tells it to
Reynard's wife, who tells it to a shocked Reynard. In fear for the
king's life, Reynard keeps a watch out for his wily father until he
finally spies the whereabouts of the hidden gold. Reynard removes
it, working night and day to carry it to safety and thereby to protect
the lion from treachery—for the 1, 200 kin of Ysengrym and his
fellows have agreed to rebel, but only on condition that they are
paid in advance. Once the funds are found to be missing, the
conspiracy fails, and Reynard's father hangs himself in despair.

The lion swallows the whole cock-and-bull fiction, and well he
might, since Reynard forestalls any rational objection while
appealing to his listener's greed and pity. Ironically, Reynard builds
his tale around a wily fox—namely his own father—and surely, he
would not make such an accusation unless it was true. Reynard also
exploits the audience's distrust of foxes, displacing that distrust
from himself onto his father. He furthermore insists that he is
making his final confession: slated for execution in any case, he no
longer has any interest in lying. Obviously, his allusion to a store of
gold plays on his audience's greed, but he also provokes pity by
presenting himself as an orphaned child, unjustly condemned by
the very king whose life he had saved. All this manipulation permits
Reynard to get the better of his enemies while mocking the
ideology of the court itself, for which he has nothing but contempt.

Violence follows directly on from the pity-inducing, beautifully
constructed narrative. The lion asks Reynard to show him the gold,
but Reynard says he cannot do so because he must go on pilgrimage
to Rome to confess his sins. He requests some shoes and a pouch
for the journey, which is given to him by tearing off the footpads of
the wolf; the euphemistic metaphor of "shoes" permits the violence
of stripping the wolf's flesh (chapter 19). Reynard also asks for the
ram and the hare as companions. Needless to say, he does not in
fact go on pilgrimage. Instead, he eats the hare in his own home and
sends the ram back with the pouch made of the wolf's skin,

ordering the ram to say that it contains a "letter" for the king
composed by the ram. Of course, the stupid ram obliges—but this
"letter" is the head of the hare (chapters 20–21).

The humor, if we find any, comes from Reynard's endless
resourcefulness under fire and his ability to find a way out of any
situation; it also comes from his being always on the offensive, and
never giving in to pity. In addition, there is amusement in Reynard's
evident enjoyment in his work—he revels in using his skill, in ways
that are often gratuitous. He understands ethical sentiments and
rational suspicion so perfectly that he can manipulate both with
consummate ease. But is this comedy subversive? If Reynard is a
consummate trickster, is he anything more than a trickster? Does
his trickery reveal anything about the institutions in which he
operates, and the practices he manipulates?

I think the answer to these questions is unquestionably yes.
Consider the way that the narrative undermines the political order
in this animal "kingdom." The lion is just as much a gull for
Reynard's flattery and appeals to greed as any other animal. By the
time Reynard sends the hare's head as a letter to the king who has
forgiven him, the pretentions of the court are exposed as easily
vulnerable. Reynard's wholly invented stories about the treason of
his enemies include a little vignette of the alternative political
order. The treasonous animals want to displace the lion but only
end up with a tyrant in the lion's place. Reynard adds a parallel
story of frogs who appointed a stork to rule over them, only to
discover that the tyrannical stork eats frogs, in bulk (chapter 17).
This inset narrative offers a revealing image of the political order as
an order of consumption by the powerful. It is posed, of course, as
the alternative, *undesired* order, but in fact it exposes the order
governed by the lion, the most predatory and hungry animal of all.

What difference does it make that these subversive ideas are put
into the mouth of an animal? The *Reynard* narrative is governed by
a tripartite, sequential logic of likeness, difference, and likeness

again. The reader at first has to concede a *likeness*: the whole genre depends on the premise that animals are like humans. Faced with the relentless brutality of the animal world, however, the reader is invited to insist on a *difference*: "they're animals, after all," we want to say. The capacity to hold the animal world at bay progressively diminishes, however, as Reynard exploits fundamentally human practices. Finally, the text insists, we are back in the land of likeness—though this time the likeness is the other way around, as humans are revealed to be like animals. This tripartite sequence of responses accounts for both the comedy (animals are like humans) and the shocking violence (humans are like animals) of *Reynard* narratives. Anthropomorphism is under siege in the narrative; it finally cedes to zoomorphism. Human rulers are like lions, and the political order is fundamentally predatory and self-interested. Along with this comes the correlative exposure of the textual instruments of political culture as empty of ethical content, even as Reynard engages in what appear to be precisely calibrated ethical practices. *Reynard* is thus a subversion of both the political order and the discourse that underlies that order. The laughter bites very deep, into both politics and ethics.

CHAPTER SIX

Animals in the Renaissance*

YOU EAT WHAT YOU ARE

Cecilia Muratori

Not very far from that island there were some islands of those most cruel men who eat human meat...They castrate the boys they catch, just like we castrate animals to make them grow fatter in order to kill them, and they kill on the spot and eat the adult men they catch, and eat their intestines fresh and the extremities of the body. They cure the rest and preserve it for future times, as we do.[1]

With vivid imagery, this passage reports one the most famous episodes of the Spanish expedition led by Columbus: the encounter with the American cannibals. Or at least it reports what the sailors believed they understood from a conversation with peaceful indigenous people, who confided to them their fear of their savage, man-eating neighbors, who would occasionally come and attack them—the cannibals.[2] Indeed the author of this vernacular report, which is entitled *Libretto de tutta la navigatione de Re de Spagna de le isole et terreni nouamente trouati* (*Brief Account of the Entire Navigation of the King of Spain to the Newly Discovered Islands and Territories*), and based on Pietro Martire D'Anghiera *On the New World* (*De orbe novo*),[3] even remarks that the inhabitants of the island initially ran away at the sight of the ships approaching, mistaking the civilized and peaceful Europeans for the dangerous cannibals. In this respect the report is more revealing about the

European mindset in approaching the New World than as a factual description of that world.

The discourse about the cruelty of the cannibals is constructed on the constant parallel between the Europeans' use of animals and the cannibals' use of humans:[4] what we (legitimately, it is implied) do to animals, such as preparing sausages and ham, they illegitimately do to humans as well, preparing human sausages.[5] The brutality of their behavior thus consists in inverting this order: in the New World, humans are eaten in the place of animals. By relating the perverted preparation of human meat to the standard practice of slaughtering animals, the passage places food as the nodal point. The focus on dietary practice is used to differentiate between groups of humans: those who eat members of their own species and those who do not. Furthermore it serves as the basis for defining the approach of humans to certain animals that are commonly eaten, thus implicitly drawing a line between animals that may be eaten and those that are taboo.

Food acts here as a filter through which the New World is perceived. The passage from the *Libretto* implies a series of questions, which pivot on the problem of distinguishing human from animal. First of all, are those men eating human meat still human, or does their animal behavior make them as brutal as the most savage of creatures, like wolves and lions? How does their dietary practice compromise their membership in the same group as the Europeans, who are appalled at (hearing about) their cannibalistic practices? At the bottom of this problem lies the question as to the proper food for each group of living beings: what should humans eat, and what should animals eat? Conversely, can diet have an effect on a living being's inclusion in or exclusion from the group of animals or that of humans?

In this chapter I will argue through an investigation of comments on food that Renaissance philosophical discourses often treated the borders dividing different classes of beings, and especially humans from animals, as in some respect permeable. Food, I suggest, is a focal point that reflects the sense of crisis characterizing Renaissance stances on animals.[6] Renaissance authors challenge the traditional conception of a clear hierarchy of living beings by directing attention to the practical issue of eating, the choice of food, and the observation of the variety of dietary habits. Examining the views of a range of philosophers on these topics will enable us to locate differences with traditional, medieval debates on animals and the distinction between animal and human nature. It is particularly important to recover Renaissance discourses on animals since these have long been neglected in favor of a concentration on Descartes and his thesis that animals are radically different from humans. In fact well before Descartes the question of whether there is a radical differentiation or elements of continuity between humans and animals was a topic of debate among Renaissance thinkers.[7] This, it is argued, becomes most apparent by bringing attention to Renaissance discussions of food, whether animals are the subjects or the objects of eating.[8]

EATING HUMAN ANIMALS, OR: BODIES AGAINST SOULS

Comments on the dietary habits of other people had played an important role in defining humanity well before the Renaissance discovery of the New World. For instance, a report of the travels of Marco Polo (1254–1324) narrates how the people of Zipangu (probably to be identified with Japan[9]) divided humans into two main categories—friends and enemies—and claims that this differentiation had a direct impact on their dietary habits as well:

When they catch a man who is not their friend and cannot be bought, they invite all their relatives and friends to their place, and they let the prisoner be killed and cooked, and they eat him together joyfully, saying that human flesh is the best and tastiest that you can find in the whole world.[10]

Enemies are human beings that can be eaten; friends are human beings who gather to eat together the bodies of the enemies: the practice of anthropophagy marks the border between the two groups of humans.

With the discovery of the Americas comes a reassessment of humanity's position in the world and of its relationship with nature. Descriptions such as those of the inhabitants of the islands at the center of the *Libretto* do not merely broaden the Europeans' knowledge of the variety of human behavior; they deeply challenge the belief in the uniformity of human nature. The question of how to identify the borders dividing humans from other animals becomes compelling.

The emphasis on the practical aspect of diet, not only in Renaissance travel reports but also in medical and philosophical literature, is not surprising given that the expansion of the limits of the known world involved European encounters both with other human populations and with a variety of different animal species.[11] Indeed descriptions of the territories newly discovered often linger on the availability of certain plants or animals and on their use as foods.[12] One of the letters attributed to Amerigo Vespucci, for instance, describes the New World as a fertile land in which vegetation thrives, almost as if it were a paradise on earth:

> This land is very agreeable and full of uncountable and huge green trees, which never lose their leaves, and all have the most pleasant and fragrant smells, and bear an enormous variety and quantity of fruits, many of them tasty and healthy for the body. And the fields produce many herbs, flowers, roots, which are very agreeable and tasty, and sometimes I was so amazed by the pleasant smells of the herbs and flowers and by the tastes of those fruits and roots, that I wondered to myself whether I was in an earthly paradise. Finding myself among such foods I would have thought so.[13]

Remarks on dietary habits and on the tastes of the New World show that Renaissance travel reports played a significant role in organizing freshly acquired information into traditional discourses about how to classify living beings, but at the same time these reports prompted questions that challenged previous categorizations and taxonomies. This is the background to the comparison in the *Libretto* of the practices of those brutal humans to the European use of animals: they treat members of their own species in a way that we confine exclusively to other species. The precision with which the text describes this overturning makes clear that this is not just an (imaginative) account of exotic habits, in line with medieval travel writings; it is rather a reflection on how categories such as "human" and "animal" shift as a result of the geographic discoveries.

Giovanni Battista Ramusio (1485–1557), editor of an influential multivolume collection of travel reports, *Navigazioni e viaggi* (*Navigations and Journeys*), writes to the humanist Girolamo Fracastoro (1476/78), in the dedicatory letter of the third volume, that the discovery of the New World has shown that the design of the terrestrial globe is suited to foster life on its entire surface. The encounter with human and animal creatures in the Americas has thus proven the validity of philosophical theories for which there was previously no evidence: the existence of people "on the other side" of the earth, which had long been an object of speculation, was finally directly verified.[14] Ramusio writes that Plato had already remarked that it would be illogical to assume that the sun, in its course, would shine on deserted spaces with no animals. He adds that the new discoveries have demonstrated that "the inhabitants of that part do not live buried in the earth like moles but they receive light like all other creatures on the terrestrial globe."[15] Yet even if their lives are sustained by the light of the sun, as with the creatures on the rest of the globe, these newly discovered inhabitants of the earth appear to be radically different from anything the Europeans had seen before. It is not simply the appearances that are new and different, as in the case of the encounter with autochthonous animal species never seen in Europe, but also the behavior that, from a European perspective, served as an anchor to differentiate between humans and animals.

Reports on the encounters with the creatures of the New World both presupposed and interacted with ongoing philosophical debates on the hierarchy of living beings, in particular with regard to the distinction between animals and humans founded on the faculties ascribed to their souls. In the aftermath of the reception of Aristotle,[16] it was especially the conception of human rationality that was identified as the main point of difference.[17] Of course such a definition depends entirely on the meaning attributed to rationality—a complex concept even from a terminological point of view, as the Greek vocabulary used to define it (*nous, to noētikon, logos*) was translated into Latin (*ratio, intellectus, anima rationalis*, etc.), adding features to an already complex debate.[18] If Aristotle's *On the Soul* is taken as the starting point,[19] and rationality is understood accordingly as a capability of the human soul which animals lack, due to the fact that their souls possess the capacity for growth and nourishment and for sense-perception but not for thinking, then this can be considered the root of the Aristotelian position on the uniqueness of the human soul.

Yet a close examination of this well-known differentiation between thought (as properly human) and sense-perception or the passions (as shared with animals) shows that food was already, in Antiquity, one major root of the controversy over humanity's uniqueness. Ancient medical discourses clearly register the uncomfortable dual role of food: on the one hand food nourishes the body, and on the other it also supports the activity of the brain, and thus can have a direct influence on a living being's ability to think. As James Longrigg has shown, this duality is evident already in Empedocles's understanding of nutrition and in the influential medical and philosophical legacy of this theory. Nutrition takes place thanks to the blood, which by flowing through the body reaches and nourishes the brain as well: from this perspective, blood is the fuel that enables the activity of thinking.[20] By attributing to blood, and thus to food, this dual effect, Empedocles set the basis for a debate that reached one of its points of highest intensity in the Renaissance: that of the qualitative or merely quantitative differentiation between animals and humans.[21] If food is held to be able to fuel not only the bodily functions but also the less corporeal activity of thinking, this leads to asking both how different types of food best support thinking and even whether thinking itself may be simply a bodily activity that certain living creatures perform better than others (perhaps on account of the better functioning of their bodily organs). From this perspective, food appears as the cornerstone of the long-lasting philosophical debate about how to distinguish between animals and humans: if even the activity of thinking boils down to nutrition, then food is a vital part of the well-known tradition of defining animals and humans with reference to the functions of their souls.

Indeed the echo of this problematic connection between thought and nutrition is clearly evident in sixteenth-century travel reports, where reflections on the cannibals' diet are linked to "observations" of their behavior and consequent assumptions regarding their ability to think. The sense of bewilderment that characterizes texts such as the *Libretto* is created by the fact that at least some of the human beings living on the American islands seem not to behave in a reasonable way, also implying the question of what role behavior plays in judging whether or not a creature is rational. As another famous travel report, a group of letters attributed to Amerigo Vespucci, puts it, the "rational animals" living in the New World display a range of behaviors that, for the European travelers, are very difficult to understand and interpret, even after spending several days with them.[22] These people do not wear clothes, seem not to form societies based on the acceptance of laws, lack the basic beliefs on which (European) humanity is constructed—and also have deviant diets. The author emphasizes the dietetic aspect by stating that he ate with this population for as long as twenty-seven days. Observations about diet thus become an integral and crucial part of a broader picture, which includes assumptions regarding the theory of the soul and is founded both on a comparison between European humans and American humans, as well as between the behavior of animals and that of humans:

They have neither law nor faith. They live according to nature. They do not know about the immortality of the soul. They do not have possessions, because everything is in common... They eat sitting on the ground. Their foods are many vegetable roots and delicious fruits, huge amounts of fish... The meat they eat, especially the one eaten commonly, is human flesh.[23]

Some of these characteristics appear to be common denominators in various reports dealing with "intercultural" encounters: the fact that these indigenous people supposedly speak no meaningful language, for instance, is another stumbling block in identifying them as animals endowed with rationality, like the European members of the same species. (And this, of course, is a crucial element if the idea of converting such natives to Christianity is to be contemplated.)[24] All in all, they seem to be uncomfortably similar to animals; even if they have human bodies, they behave like animals in that their ferocity leads them to break the taboo of not eating members of one's own species.

Of course the cannibals are only a specific type of indigenous people, to be differentiated, for instance, from those people whom the Europeans first encounter upon arrival, according to the *Libretto*.[25] But focusing on the "special case" of the cannibals brings to light the need to reassess the foundation of underlying conceptions of animality and humanity. Their voracious bodies speak for an inclusion in the group of animals, while their mouths do not utter meaningful words: it is their behavior, therefore, that problematizes the inclusion of these speech-less and man-eating humans in the same group with the rational conquerors. Practical aspects of these humans' lives seem to undermine the clear division between humans and animals.

As Karen Raber has argued, bodies in general tend to provide material with which to observe the similarities rather than the differences between "rational" humans and "irrational" brutes; on the other hand, it was upon the assertion of a faculty not present in the animal soul that the border supposedly separating animals from humans depended. The similarities of the bodies fit badly with any theory committed to a radical differentiation between souls. As Raber puts it, "anatomical and physiological sameness is at the root of many modern assaults on the supposedly firm boundary efforts to establish human exceptionalism. If, after all, we sleep, eat, breathe, procreate, communicate with others of all species, avoid dangers, and pursue pleasures through the same instrument, the body, how is it that these activities come to mean different things if they are performed by a 'human,' rather than an 'animal'?"[26]

Raber's observation that bodies tend to flatten out points of radical differentiation becomes more radical if everyday activities and forms of behavior do not stop at revealing similarities between animal and human life, but even produce division within the human group itself, eroding the secure foundation of practices shared at least by the members of the human group. In this sense the cannibals embody the disbelief in human exceptionality: man truly becomes an animal like any other when he finds himself on someone else's menu. The man-eater is a liminal figure, constructed (at least in the European imagination) on the border between humanity and animality,[27] ultimately showing the weakness of such a classification itself, and emptying both categories— that of animal and that of human—of their desired meaning. The bodies of the cannibals, and the bodies they eat, unsettle the hierarchy based on the faculties of the soul. Indeed Pietro D'Anghiera calls the cannibals "feri homines," bestial men, an expression that indicates their puzzling hybridity.[28] In Vespucci's *New World*, the man-eaters are "similar to the beasts": clear signs of their dangerous proximity to the animal world are their eating habits but also the fact that they do not use clothing to cover their nudity.[29]

Referring to the cannibal as a figure in which the human-animal border is brought to a crisis, Leonardo da Vinci (1452–1519) recalls in his *Quaderni di Anatomia* (*Notebooks on Anatomy*) the very same scene of the curing of human meat in the *Libretto*. Using the example of the cannibals as a starting point, Leonardo broadens the perspective by drawing out the consequences of this act of eating with regard to the general question of humanity's inclusion in the group of animals.

In this case, too, reflecting on the detail of nutrition opens the path for a broader assessment of humanity's relation to the worlds of animals. Leonardo argues that the existence of cannibalistic behavior proves that humans are not animals after all, since no animal would eat members of its own species unless it had lost its mind (note the implication that animals have a mind to lose):

> Among these [i.e., the animals of the earth] there are no animals which eat their own species except from want of brains (as there are fools among them as among humans, although they are not in so great number); and this is not the case, except among the beasts of prey, as in the species lion and leopards, panthers, lynxes, cats and the like, which sometimes eat their young ones; but you eat, besides the young ones, the father, the mother, the brothers and friends, and this is not enough to you, as you go hunting in foreign islands, catching other humans; and these, mutilating their *membrum virile* and their testicles, you fatten and force them down your gullet.[30]

Cannibalism represents for Leonardo the ultimate form of human violence, and he consciously mixes the perspective of the indigenous cannibals, at the center of the *Libretto* and of Vespucci's reports, with that of the European conquerors and of humanity in general. Stressing the violence of eating members of one's own kin allows Leonardo to suggest that the group to which humans truly belong is a very specific one within the category of animals, namely that of the beasts of prey. Yet even they kill their young ones only in an unsound state of mind. The cannibals are here invoked as a radical example of a violent attitude that, instead of setting those deviant humans apart from the rest of civilized humanity, distinguishes humans from the majority of animals, since not all animals are predators, and moreover only crazy ones display "cannibalistic" behavior. Leonardo bitterly remarks that man is not "the king of the animals," as he likes to portray himself, but rather "the king of the beasts" because he is "the greatest" beast of all, even compared to the most ferocious ones.[31] Behind this line of reasoning is the idea that the violence of humanity extends far beyond actual episodes of cannibalistic eating, thus paving the way for a subversion of the contrast between the civilized Europeans and the brutal American cannibals.

With a similar twist Michel de Montaigne (1533–92) challenges a uniform conception of humanity in the essay "On the Cannibals," which opens with a quotation from Plutarch about a journey to Italy rather than to the Americas. Upon arrival Pyrrhus is supposed to have commented on the barbarity of the Romans, just as the Europeans will comment in sixteenth-century travel reports on the bestiality of the cannibals. He is supposed to have asked, "What kind of barbarians are these?"[32] Yet it is relevant that Montaigne employs the word *cannibal* rather than the more general *barbarian* in the title: the starting point of the essay is the fact that the cannibal is a special kind of barbarian, a human being who places himself at the very limits of humanity by consuming human flesh.[33] Just like the word itself, which was created in the aftermath of the first explorations of the Americas and is thus in all respects a Renaissance term,[34] the figure of the cannibal embodies a new and particularly radical kind of barbarity. Montaigne uses it to get to the heart of what Europeans believe to be properly human: civilization. Yet the essay makes clear that civilization is simply the known state of things, questioned against the new and unknown. With an ironic touch, Montaigne even underlines that the extent of the unknown is great, since portrayals of the cannibals might be flawed due to poor communication and inadequate translations.

The case of the cannibals becomes iconic for the fragmentation of the uniformity of humanity, creating a hybrid level in which animal and human characteristics are confounded. By eating like the animals, a human being slides into animality; food thus contributes to define the nature of the eater. But this means that food can also turn into an element of distinction between humans and animals if one asks directly a question that was already implicit in the dual conception of food as nutrition for the body and as food for thought: What is the best and most appropriate nutrition for each type of creature?

EATING BRUTE ANIMALS, OR: BECOMING WHAT YOU EAT

It might come as a surprise that in Renaissance discussions on the best diet for human beings, human meat is one of the most controversial foods that are debated, and this even before the encounter with the American cannibals. The background for the discussion of the nutritional role of human meat is the medical theory, already to be found in Hippocrates, according to which "like nourishes like."[35]

In Girolamo Manfredi's Renaissance best-seller, *On the Human Being* (*Liber de homine*, 1474; also known as *Il Perché*), we find a formulation of the consequences to be drawn from this simple principle, a formulation that is as clear as it is astonishing: "There is nothing and no food which would be more appropriate to human nutrition than human meat, were it not for the aversion that nature has against it."[36] Manfredi (ca. 1430–93) reasons purely from the point of view of the physiology of nutrition, phrasing in a particularly direct and detached manner a well-known medical theory about identifying the best food for each type of creature. According to the principle that the best food for each body—whether of a plant, an animal, or a human—must resemble that same body, then the most similar food of all should also be the best from the point of view of medical physiology. In the case of humans this implies that human meat should be the best, most nourishing food. Therefore the cannibals, who are different from other human beings only in that they lack the sense of disgust at ingesting bodies of their fellow humans, make use of a food that, from the point of view of medicine, is not only legitimately to be included on the menu but is even an excellent nutritional option.

What is more, the theory that "like nourishes like" shows once again why food is integral to the question about the nature of humans and animals: it is necessary to know what kind of creatures are similar to each other in order to assess their nutritional value for each other. With regard to human nutrition, if humans refrain from the best food—human meat—out of disgust, then one must decide what other living beings provide the next best option. This means that dietary choice ultimately leads to the construction of a hierarchy, in which the borders between humans and (certain) animals are drawn by observing the aspects of similarity from a very practical point of view rather than speculating on the faculties of the souls.[37]

Elaborating on the nutritional principle of likeness, Galen (ca. AD 129–ca. 216) explained that the animal closest to humans is the pig, which thus provides the best kind of flesh for human nutrition: "The similarity between the flesh of man and pig in taste and smell has been observed when certain people have eaten unawares human meat instead of pork." He had then concluded, "Of all foods, therefore, pork is the most nutritious," and for certain humans who need to strengthen their bodies pork is even an essential aliment.[38] The resemblance between the body of the pig and the human body had also functioned as a theoretical basis for another practical application, namely vivisection; at least since Galen, the pig had been one of the main animals on which vivisection was performed with the intention of drawing conclusions for the functioning of the human body as well.[39]

Yet despite a certain similarity with regard to the general structure of the body, as well as the specific texture of the flesh, notable differences between pigs and humans emerge in light of the twofold role of food, as nutriment for the body and for what we could call the "mental capabilities." How far does the similarity stretch between animals with similar bodies, given the effect that food has on the nature of the eater?

In On Life (De vita), Marsilio Ficino (1433–99) recalls Galen's recommendation about the properties of pork,[40] but adds a specification whose importance emerges only if we bear in mind this last question: "Nevertheless the ancient physicians, especially Galen, strongly recommend the meat and blood of a pig because of a certain similarity with our body. Pork is best, therefore, for bodies which are pig-like, as are those of rustics and hardy men and those which get a lot of physical exercise."[41] Galen considered pork a very fortifying aliment, but Ficino here stresses another aspect of human-pig similarity: not only do pigs bear a general similarity to all humans, but there are also certain humans who bear a particularly strong resemblance to pigs. Seen from this angle, pork is not the best aliment for *all* humans but rather for those whose constitution is pig-like, robust in body but, as this passage suggests, lacking in mental agility.

Desiderius Erasmus (ca. 1466–1536) had already pointed to the ridiculously extreme implications of such a view of food in unsettling the human-animal boundary. In one of the dialogues included in his *Colloquies*, Erasmus staged a conversation in which the two characters—a soldier and a monk belonging to the order of the Carthusians—discuss specifically the effect of foods. The starting point for the discussion is the fact that diet played an important role in the life of the Carthusian monks, who refrained from eating the flesh of animals, with the exception of fish.[42] The soldier ironically asks whether the Carthusians will not turn into fish because of their diet: "There's the tonsure, the unnatural dress, the solitude, the constant diet of fish; I marvel you're not turned into a fish." But the monk himself replies that if food had such an effect, then humans should turn into pigs, given the abundance of pork especially on the table of soldiers, who belong to those exercising the body and thus traditionally needing pork as the most nutritious food. "If humans turned into everything they ate," the monk rebukes, "your fondness for pork would have made you a pig long ago."[43]

The joke about turning into pigs originates from the question regarding the extent to which food influences a person's nature by mingling human with animal characteristics. Indeed while the distinction between humans and pigs, in particular, is undermined by the theory about the pig's resemblance to humans, eating any animal might seem potentially to bring humans closer to the nature of that particular animal. Galen had already envisioned such a set of possibilities:

The horse and the ass would only be consumed by someone who was himself an ass; and to eat leopards, bears, or lions you would have to be a wild beast…But there are apparently many parts of the world where [dogs and foxes] are eaten, and my conjecture would be that their effects would be similar to those of the hare; for hare, dog, and fox are equally dry.[44]

The passage begins with a reference to the principle of the likeness between food and consumer, continues with a remark on the flexibility of dietary habits, and proceeds to speculating about the character of exotic foods (such as dog) by comparison with common ones such as hare. It thus reveals the connection between the choice of food and the nature of the eater by going beyond a simple classification into classes of beings. This is expressed most clearly by the example that eating wild animals would literally transform a human being into one of them. In fact the action of eating food could be seen as akin to entering a battlefield: in eating a certain food, the eater faces and tries to absorb, or digest, the nature itself of what he ingests.[45]

In the chapter on human nature in his encyclopedic work *On the Variety of Things* (*De rerum varietate*) (1557), Girolamo Cardano (1501–76) reasons along these lines when he states that "foods can change human beings into every nature, just like dogs, as is said elsewhere about the causes of rabies. Therefore it is to be studied diligently who makes use of which food."[46] The transformation into a beast to which Cardano here alludes is abnormal, pathological, since the starting point is the effect that rabies has on dogs. Nevertheless the principle Cardano draws from this example of the causes of rabies—that is to say, that food has a clear impact on the very nature of the eater—still stands. In *On Subtlety* (*De subtilitate*) Cardano explains in more detail how food affects the body: the nature of what is eaten penetrates deeply into the flesh of the eater, setting in motion a whole series of changes, which tend to align the habits of the consumer with that which has been eaten.[47] Furthermore Cardano sketches a gradation in the intensity with which a creature responds to this mutation of its nature through food: plants are the most sensitive to this because, apart from nutrition, they are not subject to many other factors that affect their nature; then follow animals, and finally humans, whose complexity, including their use of mental faculties as well as cultural elements, resists, so to speak, too quick and radical a transformation.[48]

Without losing sight of this gradation, Cardano thus argues that care must be put into studying which animals are a suitable food because the consumption of flesh also involves incorporating the whole nature of a creature. Eating is not simply a matter of flesh feeding flesh;[49] it also creates a link and a commixture between human and animal natures. Cardano, like Galen, appears particularly fascinated by the example of eating dogs, an animal not usually considered to be food but rather a companion or a support to man, so that for a human to acquire its nature would represent a particularly powerful crossing over of the human-animal border. Reports about the population of Corsica provide the material for speculating about the brutalizing effect that dog flesh has on humans: "Since the inhabitants of the island of Corsica feed on puppies, not just tame ones but also wild ones, they are ill-tempered, cruel, treacherous, daring, responsive, nimble, strong—that is the nature of dogs."[50] Clearly the food has affected their bodies, making them as strong as those of dogs, and also their character, as shown by the tendency toward cruel behavior. Just how deep this transformation is, depends on a number of factors; what is not in doubt is that humans can slide into animality, and indeed into different types of animality depending on the peculiar characteristics of the animal consumed.

The role of food in creating a resemblance between certain humans and certain animals is thematized very clearly in Giovan Battista Della Porta's principal work on human physiognomics: *De humana physiognomia*.[51] Della Porta (ca. 1535–1615) too discusses the beastly behavior of the inhabitants of Corsica, explaining that foods can mold the character of a creature because they have an impact on the soul, not only on the body, a theory he traces back mainly to Plato and Hippocrates: "Plato in the book on *Laws* says that the habits of humans can be better or worse depending on the water they drink, [and] the foods they eat, produced by that soil; and that they [the foods] not only alter the body but also penetrate into the soul."[52] Reasoning on the basis of this conception of the profound effect of food, Della Porta claims that the human beings living on that island not only look like beasts but even behave more cruelly than the beasts themselves. This is thus an instance of transformation from human to animal nature: the borders dividing categories of beings in a hierarchy, following the example of Aristotelian psychology, have become permeable. Elsewhere in the same work Della Porta remarks on the fact that humanity's choice of food reveals what seems to be a uniquely human characteristic: the endless possibilities of the human diet. While animals always spontaneously turn to one specific type of food—carnivores to meat, and herbivores to plants—humans can eat potentially anything. This flexibility of human diet also means that food can turn into a powerful means to trigger processes of human-animal crossover, since human behavior with regard to food can be civilized or beastly:

> Brute animals [*animali bruti*] eat only one type of food, some eat grass, some roots, some fruits, some meat, but each of them has only one [dietary] habit. Only man enjoys and wants to help himself to all of them, so that it is still unclear which is his own and proper food beyond bread and water; and yet he has various habits, pleasant, savage, indulgent, beastly [*ferini*].[53]

While Della Porta seems to have in mind mainly instances of humans turning into animals by beastly food choices, Cardano envisaged the possibility that the opposite might happen as well, namely that an animal eating human flesh might acquire certain human characteristics—and the supposed nature of these characteristics again raises the issue of drawing borders around the definitions of animal and human.

Cardano mentions a particular iconic case, taken from Gonzalo Férnandez de Oviedo's *General and Natural History of the Indies* (*Historia general y natural de las Indias*) (first part published in 1535), one of several sources about the inhabitants of the New World from which Cardano draws information regarding the link between the nature of a creature and its food. Cardano writes in his autobiography, "Among the extraordinary, though quite natural circumstances of my life, the first and most unusual is that I was born in this century in which the whole world became known."[54] It is therefore not by chance that he appears to be particularly fascinated by the story of a shrewd and cruel dog as narrated by Oviedo. Cardano reports that the Spanish conquerors had trained a dog to distinguish Spanish people from indigenous people and, if required, tear the latter apart. He could do this because his senses were remarkably sharp, and, in turn, this was due to the fact that he ate human meat.[55] Human flesh could thus be a possible explanation for this animal's incredible capabilities; Cardano remarks that dogs have a dangerously active wit (*ingenium*), and therefore it might be that feeding on human meat sharpened this particular dog's shrewdness even more, bringing to the fore the similarity with human acuity, while at the same time giving it a tendency toward cruelty. This effect is particularly noteworthy if we consider the fact that, in the case of the cannibals, eating human meat also appears to intensify cruelty, which provoked Leonardo's comparison with certain ferocious animals that on occasion also eat members of their own species. The paradox thus seems to be that humans eating humans are viewed as behaving like beasts, while animals eating humans display a higher degree of what has been traditionally considered to be properly human, a characteristic that could be loosely labeled intelligence— even if a type of intelligence coupled with brutal cruelty.

The notion that certain foods intensify the cruelty of a creature is a principal topic throughout Renaissance philosophical texts in which the encounter with animals—as food, as exotic wild animals in faraway countries, or as human animals, as in the case of the cannibals—is problematized. Cardano believes that the key to the cannibals' behavior is their animosity: the origin of their practice is to be found in hatred.[56] Meat is, in general, a powerful aliment for Cardano: the flesh of animals nourishes more deeply than plants, for instance, because it is made of the elements already split into their smallest parts, a theory that ultimately is based on the idea that meat nourishes meat.[57] It is thus understandable that the flesh of different animals will have different kinds of influence on the human body, according to a process of assimilation. All meat-eaters, for Cardano, are irascible, deceitful, cruel, and proud;[58] those eating human meat are thus simply even more ferocious than other carnivores. So certain human populations (and not only the cannibals) can be more brutal than others, as is the case with the inhabitants of Corsica, or the Lithuanians, who are described as highly voracious.[59] Such an interpretation of the influence of meat leads to an emphasis on the idea that, depending upon their behavior and dietary choices, humans can be more or less close to the kingdom of animals—and further, that they can be closer to certain animals (in particular cruel, wild beasts) than others.

The possibility that food might play a crucial role in upsetting this human-animal border is clearly, and ironically, presented in a text that makes use of Cardano's works (often without declaring the source): *On the Marvelous Secrets of Nature, the Queen and Goddess of Humans* (*De admirandis naturae reginae deaeque mortalium arcanis*; 1616) by Giulio Cesare Vanini (1585–1619). In the dialogue, the character Julius Caesar explains that the most vile and depraved among human beings eat foods that are high in fat; as a consequence their mind (*mens*) also becomes thick (*ingrassata*), and this is ultimately the reason they have no reverence for religion. Another example of the far-reaching effect of food is the population of the Tartars, whose notorious cruelty is due to their habit of drinking horse blood (while British people have a mild character because of their consumption of beer). Vanini thus uses the ambiguity about the effect of food on the dual level of the body and the mind to expose the weakness in the conception of humans as a special kind of animal. As a finishing touch, he lets Julius Caesar assert that despite such radical effects of food on the human constitution, it is not worth spending time dealing with these silly matters, because only religion functions as an antidote to human cruelty—a cruelty that makes humans beastly and that is brought about by certain dietary habits.[60] The impression the dialogue arouses is of course exactly the opposite: humans and animals are connected at a very basic level, that of bodily nourishment, and this level remains crucial despite the attempts of religion to elevate humanity. In fact the text implies that heavy, fatty foods are very effective in weighing humans down, binding them to the body and to life on earth and making the (imagined?) heights of religion unreachable. Once again food appears as a powerful agent in unsettling the hierarchy between animals and humans.

Conclusion: Defining Humanity through Food

In contrast to animals, humans can choose to change their dietary habits radically as a result of reflection on the benefits or disadvantages of certain foods, but also in response to the way human societies prescribe rejection or acceptance of certain aliments. All these elements are essential, and yet often overlooked, aspects of Renaissance debates on the distinction between humans and animals. These debates involve radical questions that inevitably complicate the picture of a clear division into classes of beings: What is the effect of eating certain animals, and why is it not not acceptable to eat human beings? Furthermore why does eating meat, and human meat in particular, transform man into a brute himself?

But the last question to be asked is whether there still remains any aspect of humanity that resists this process of transformation: Is it possible to identify a strictly human characteristic that survives entanglement in the troubling materiality of becoming the beasts we eat? Being a beast is not the same as behaving like a beast, and in the above examples transformation through diet seems to correspond more to the latter than the former. Eating wild animals can make humans beastly, and vice versa: eating human meat can make dogs more like humans, yet still they remain dogs.

One answer to this problem might be that, despite certain notable similarities between human and animal physiology (similarities that are the foundation of the explanation for the effects of food on humans and animals), humans are not like other animals after all. The Franciscan Francesco Zorzi (1466–1540) remarked that the variety and flexibility of human diet is a clear sign that man is a microcosm, in which everything existing in the macrocosm of the world is present and converges. In his *Elegant Poem* (*Elegante Poema*) he writes that "among birds, some eat wheat, but not meat; and the birds of prey eat meat, but not wheat. And wild beasts [*fiere*] eat meat, and not wheat. And dogs eat bread and meat, but not grass. Truly man, who contains everything, eats all foods, meat, fish, wheat and grass."[61] Zorzi, whose philosophy is influenced by Platonic as well as cabalistic sources, applies the idea of the relationship between micro- and macrocosm to the interpretation of human diet. From this perspective the fact that humans do not turn to only one type of food thus becomes a sign of God's design: the "universality of foods eaten by humans" comes to signify human dominion over all other creatures—both practically, because humans can eat them, and metaphorically, because the animals can represent the passions, which must be "eaten up," that is to say destroyed by higher mental faculties, which are the prerogative of human beings.

Using a different argumentative strategy, Tommaso Campanella (1568–1639) also elevates man to the condition of a special creature. Campanella was well aware of the effects of different foods, which he discusses in his *Medicinalia*. He writes that the flesh of young animals, for instance, is more appropriate to young people, and that of old animals more suitable for the elderly. But foods, and meat in particular, also influence the habits, and that is the reason the flesh of libidinous animals, such as doves and pigs, should be consumed in moderation, because their lust will be transferred to the eater, just as the slyness of the fox or the timidity of the rabbit will also affect the character of people who eat these animals.[62] Yet Campanella's medical approach in this work is not maintained in other writings, where instead he shifts the attention from the body to the soul, thus safeguarding humanity's uniqueness. According to Campanella, even if from the point of view of anatomy the human body is simply better organized than that of all other animals, the real point of distinction is the human mind: the more complex organization of the "machine" of the human body allows the divinity of the soul to shine through it, and the possession of the mind is the clearest evidence of that divinity.[63] As he states in *On the Sense of Things, and on Magic* (*Del senso delle cose e della magia*), animals have sense-perception and memory, as well as the capability to discern on the basis of their sense-perception, but they are devoid of rationality proper, which derives from the possession of an immaterial and immortal mind. Therefore even if they might have better organs, which give them sharper sense-perceptions, they lack the essential requirement that marks humans out as the only rational creatures: the mind.[64]

But can the idea of human uniqueness be justified in terms of physical processes, as opposed to psychological differentiations? Are any specifically human features still detectable *within* the process of transformation into a beast that takes place through the assimilation of animality via food? A possible answer is provided by Anton Francesco Doni (1513–74) in a passage from his collection of pieces on several imaginative worlds titled *Worlds* (*Mondi*), which shares some stylistic traits with Renaissance utopian literature while also using a caustically ironic tone. In a passage in which the god Momus speaks, we read that humanity ultimately consists in the following:

One needs to be able to play a certain card game, to be a sycophant, to be able to fake, to be double-faced, to be a clown, to boast with big words and act aggressively, to want to cut, slaughter, trash, break, and ruin the world: otherwise everyone would remain a beast.[65]

According to this passage, it is the intensity of human violence that marks the real point of difference from the animals. This resonates with accounts about the extreme brutality of cannibals. As Leonardo remarked, only wild beasts that have lost their minds eat members of their own species. And indeed the human mind is also lost in the process whenever the powerful effect of food is allowed to unfold in its radical consequences: the specific brutality of humanity stands in the way of arguing in favor of human rationality as a shared feature across different human populations, and even sets humans apart from the world of animals. In this context the instances of human-animal proximity discussed, for instance, by Della Porta, rather than simply showing that humans can resemble animals, ultimately seem to prove humanity's difficulty in escaping a kind of animality that is properly human. If the points of departure and arrival of the discussion remain the observation of the body, human uniqueness crystallizes within the animal world.

Following this thread thus offers an alternative history of the engagement of Renaissance philosophers with the topic of animality. It shows that more traditional views of the hierarchy of beings, based primarily on radical distinctions on the level of psychology, were accompanied and continuously challenged by approaches that favored observation and comparison of human and animal behavior. Instead of marking a precise line of distinction at the presence (in humans) or lack (in animals) of certain faculties of the soul, this perspective emphasizes the similarities rather than substantial differences. The two levels of the discourse might even intertwine, as in the case of Campanella, who endorses a psychological view favoring the human-animal discontinuity, while acknowledging the fact that humans often behave like animals—and that animals, in turn, can appear to behave like humans.[66] If the focus falls on bodies, the distance tends to shorten; on the other hand, proceeding from the identification of different faculties of the soul tends to widen the gap.

The conflict between these two poles emerges clearly when dealing with a process that links together the body and the soul: ingesting food. At the same time the Old World of Europe and the New World of America are also linked through reflection on dietary comparison, especially when Renaissance philosophers focus on the liminal figure of the cannibal. Between harmonizing elements of continuity and managing the conflict, a radical solution also emerges, exemplified in Leonardo's notes as well as in Doni's *Mondi*: that human uniqueness might not consist in the possession of the mind but in the exceptional behavior of humans within the animal world. From this point of view the essence of cannibalism is the essence of humanity itself; as Leonardo puts it, no other animal is so brutal in using violence against all other creatures, including other humans. The cannibal thus becomes the emblem of humanity's ferocious hunger, which transforms human stomachs into sepulchers of other living beings, human and animal.[67] Humans are indeed special animals, but only because of their violent, unstoppable voraciousness.

CHAPTER SEVEN

Animal Souls and Beast Machines

DESCARTES'S MECHANICAL BIOLOGY

Deborah J. Brown

I desire, say I, that you would consider that these functions all follow naturally in this machine solely from the disposition of its organs, neither more nor less than the movements of a clock or other automaton [follow] from those of its counterweights and wheels, with the result that it is not at all necessary to conceive for their operation any other vegetative or sensitive soul in it or any other principle of movement and life than its blood and spirits, agitated by the heat of the fire which burns continuously in its heart and is in no way of another nature than all the fires that are in inanimate bodies. (*Oeuvres de Descartes* 11:202)[1]

In the Aristotelian tradition, the soul—principle of life in an organized (*organikos*) body, as Aristotle defines it[2]—marked a definitive boundary between the living and the nonliving. It is because of its soul that the matter of an organism develops in a regular fashion, "always or for the most part," for the sake of perfecting and reproducing its form.[3] Against this well-worn way of thinking that organic nature demands a distinct principle of nature, René Descartes stands out in the seventeenth century as an uncompromising critic, accepting neither the distinction between *essential* parts—soul and matter—nor the idea that nature unfolds for a reason, at least not one discernible by the human mind. His confidence that all of animate nature will be explained solely in terms of the divisibility and law-governed movement of *integral* parts—the microscopic "corpuscles" of matter of which all bodies are composed—without doubt exceeded the limitations of what was actually known at the time of the mechanisms of organic development, but so rich with promise was the new physics that, in Descartes's eyes at least, it had already overshadowed the Aristotelian framework.

The doctrine of animal automatism—that animals are just complex, self-moving machines, no different in nature from clocks or other automata—met with swift and widespread rebuke. Descartes advanced the doctrine at an early stage of his philosophical development, beginning around 1619, and at various times experimented with creating automata using magnets: a flying bird, a pheasant chased by a spaniel, and even a humanoid automaton, whom he allegedly named Francine.[4] His last letters to Henry More in 1649 show him still engaged in defending the doctrine. That his infamy was to a significant extent tied to his defense of the doctrine of animal automatism is clear from one salient fact to which Leonora Cohen Rosenfield draws our attention, namely, that every set of *Objections* to the *Meditations* contains some rant or other against the doctrine, even though it nowhere appears within the *Meditations* itself.[5] What was it about the idea of the *bête-machine* that was so provocative?

Clearly something significant was going on, although exactly what the perceived threat was is unclear. While Descartes's critics were championing the intelligence and prudence of animals, a tragicomedy involving our relations to animals of ludicrous proportions was, as we shall see, playing out in the background. Unsurprisingly Descartes finds nothing but confusion and inconsistency in the objections to his doctrine, declaring that philosophers would be hard-pressed to hold that in all of nature only the human soul has any claim to immortality while denying a sharp distinction between it and whatever it is that accounts for the organization of parts of matter within an animal body. Far better, he advises, to admit that "worms, flies, caterpillars and other animals move like machines than that they all have immortal souls" (*Oeuvres* 5:277; cf. *Oeuvres* 4:576). But this theological consequence was only one concern among many for Descartes's critics. More often than not the responses have an air of incredulity. Could all that regularity and order, all that *perfection* in animal development and behavior be just the product of brute physical forces?

It is this question that makes the status of animals in seventeenth-century philosophy particularly fascinating. Animals and organic bodies generally were the test case for the new science, and many philosophers, from the Cambridge Platonists to Harvey to Leibniz, simply could not let go of all the occult elements of Scholastic philosophy while mechanism was perceived as dealing with essentially "dead" matter and "life" remained elusive.[6] Descartes is the most radical champion of the doctrine of animal automatism and will therefore be the focus of this chapter, but others, including Hobbes and Digby, are engaged in similar projects, attempting to understand how the emergence of life is continuous with the emergence of crystals and other complex inanimate structures and yet importantly different from them as well.[7]

It is with this last point of difference that this chapter is primarily concerned. What is the status of animal bodies according to a mechanist like Descartes? Are we, in his eyes, permitted to make categorical distinctions between the organs—the functional parts—of animals, and what follows for his mechanical philosophy if we are? What grounds are there for Descartes's postulating a radical difference in nature between humans and animals? And how, with the hindsight of history, are we to evaluate his contribution to our thinking about animals and about our relationship to them?

"Wisdom Gone Astray": The Historical Backdrop

The subject of animals provided philosophers of the early modern period with the opportunity to reflect on nature, on human nature, on the creative power of God, and, perhaps most important for Descartes, on the distinctive character of reason. Where Descartes differs most from his critics is on the question of whether or not animals have any claim to intelligence. But there was much confusion in this debate, and whether or not we are sympathetic to Descartes's conclusions, we have to admire the intellectual clarity that he brought to the debate.

Consider, for example, a typical set of remarks defending the idea of animal intelligence. "What is there," Montaigne asks in the *Apology of Raimond de Sebonde*, "in our intelligence that we do not see in the operations of animals? Is there a polity better ordered, the offices better distributed, and more inviolably observed and maintained, than that of bees? Can we imagine that such and so regular a distribution of employments can be carried on without reason and prudence?"[8] Here Montaigne is surely wrong, for if order and perfection are the mark of reason and prudence, then the very disorder of human polities and the perfection of animal societies would suggest that animals surpass us in reason and prudence, which is not what Montaigne intends to suggest. The capacity for reason and prudence entails the capacity for irrationality and imprudence, and the difficulty we have attributing these defects to animals, however unproductive their behavior may be for them, is a sign that they lack reason and prudence rather than possess them. That dogs and cats scratch the earth in a vain attempt to bury their excrement—a favorite example of Descartes's is not a sign of reason operating defectively but instinct operating invariably (*Oeuvres* 4:575). As Descartes observes, "From the very perfection of the actions of animals, we suspect that they do not have free will."[9]

Montaigne is not alone in attributing to animals the capacity for reason and prudence but represents rather one side of a debate about what animals are and how they should be treated. This was by no means an idle intellectual dispute but one that shaped a range of practices that blurred the boundaries between humans and animals. A question much debated in antiquity was whether, if animals possess reason, albeit of a lesser form—an intellect "feeble and turbid, like a dim and clouded eye," as Plutarch describes it[10]—they too should be bound by principles of justice. A positive answer to this question would constrain not only our own unjust behavior toward animals but *mutatis mutandis* theirs toward us.

Settling this question depended on answering others—e.g., whether animals were capable of a form of consent and of entering, therefore, into contracts with humans. Lucretius, for example, held that at least some relationships (e.g., those with animals used in warfare or domestic arrangements) were contractual.[11] The widespread practice of trying animals in courts for crimes committed against humans or their property, which occurred in various jurisdictions in continental Europe between the thirteenth and eighteenth centuries, represents one extreme in this debate. The presumption underlying such practices was that animals (and not simply their owners) could be held morally and legally responsible for any harms they commit. Opposed to this practice was English deodand law, which placed animals in the same category as inanimate objects, allowing recourse to those injured by animals not by prosecution of the animals themselves but only of their negligent owners. Being attacked by your neighbor's cow was, under English law, no different from being accidentally struck by one of your neighbor's roof tiles. But in those jurisdictions in which animals could be tried, things were very different. Homicidal pigs, horses, oxen, dogs, and cows were tried in secular courts, and pestilent rats, mice, and other vermin in ecclesiastical courts, in "observance of legal custom and proper judicial procedure."[12] Lawyers were appointed to defend animals,[13] and those found guilty were sentenced to the same forms of punishment as human perpetrators—being sometimes dressed in human clothing and dragged, hanged, exiled, or excommunicated as befitting their crimes.[14]

The history of animal trials is a salient reminder of the extent to which the boundary between animals and humans was perceived as much more fluid than it is today. Further evidence of this fluidity lies in philosophical discussions about monstrous births. The term "monster" (Latin *monstrum, monstra*) is etymologically linked to the verbs "to demonstrate or show" (*monstrare*) and "to warn or advise" (*monere*). Monstrous births were considered demonstrations of the sins of the parents—more often than not, the mother's—and portents of the power of divine retribution. The plethora of broadsheets announcing the birth of a monster is testimony to the level of hysteria and perverse fascination in the period for deviations from what was perceived as normal.

Philosophically these reactions to monstrous births are incoherent. Scholastics who followed Aristotle in holding that the development of every organism was governed by a substantial form that arranged matter for the sake of the perfection and reproduction of the form, and who also followed Aristotle in holding that matter was nothing apart from form, were hard-pressed to explain how such deviations from what was normal could occur. Aristotle himself unconvincingly describes monsters as "failures in the purposive effort"[15]—unconvincing because if the substantial form is operative, as it must be to produce any structure at all, and if matter has no forms of its own that could interfere with the operation of the substantial form, monsters ought not to be possible. For Christians, the idea of natural "failures" raised the specter of a not wholly benevolent God, or at least one with His hand off the wheel—God's "wisdom gone astray," as Augustine portends—and so an inevitable tension between the two views ensued.[16]

For the monsters themselves, such theological and philosophical perplexities were the least of their troubles. They were generally feared, maligned, and often treated like animals. Erica Fudge describes a legal case from the sixteenth century of a boy so deformed he resembled a satyr, defending his right to inheritance on the grounds that "albeit he had his visage and some parts of his body in some sort deformed: yet that was no reason that he should be held and reputed as a monster, seeing he had the use of reason and humane discourse."[17] Being articulate was this monster's saving grace, as the court upheld his defense.

The legacy of Hellenistic debates focused thinking about animals on two questions: whether the capacity for sensation, which no one denied of animals, presupposes intelligence, and whether animals are capable of language, the definitive sign of reason.[18] Where Aristotle had argued in *De Anima* that there could be no understanding without sensation, Hellenistic defenders of animal intelligence argued that this dependence was reciprocal. Where Aristotle himself seemed to vacillate on the question of animal intelligence,[19] Plutarch and his followers are clear. Citing an argument of Strato's, Plutarch remarks, "If we are so constituted that to have sensation we must have understanding, then it must follow that all creatures which have sensation can also understand."[20] Prominent medieval philosophers, such as Avicenna and Aquinas, accepted the idea of a connection between sensation and judgment but denied the inference that animals thereby possessed reason.[21] As animals were seen as capable of making evaluative judgments of some sort and thus to have moral or quasi-moral interests, the question naturally arose as to what sort of moral obligations, if any, we have toward them. To this Aquinas offers only the instrumentalist answer that cruelty toward animals disposes humans to brutality against each other and is for this reason wrong.[22] But this argument begs the crucial metaphysical question, for why should beating animals incline us to brutality against each other any more than, say, beating tin, unless in being cruel to animals we recognize an essential continuity between ourselves and animals that is lacking from our relationship to base metals?

Where does Descartes sit in relation to this protracted debate about animals? The two issues that dominated Hellenistic debates are very much at the forefront of his thinking. One can see the mechanistic account of unconscious sensory processing developed in the *Optics* and other physiological texts as a response to the challenge that all sensation presupposes cognition. Descartes envisages being able to construct a machine that "senses" in the way animals do. If you were to touch the machine in one spot, he says, it would ask what you want, and if in another, cry out that you are hurting it, but none of this would convince us that the machine really feels pain or is communicating its wants (*Oeuvres* 7:56). If we could construct such a machine with neither genuine feeling nor consciousness, why suppose that the responses of animals are indicative of genuine feeling or awareness? In Descartes's technical language, machine sensation corresponds to the "first grade" of sensory response in humans. The stimulation of the nervous system (first grade) is a necessary condition for the feeling (second grade) and judgment (third grade) associated with sensation in humans, but only the second and third grades presuppose consciousness or cognition (*Oeuvres* 7:436–38; *Philosophical Writings* 2: 294–95).

On the question of whether animals possess the capacity for speech, Descartes's view aligns with those of the Stoics.[23] He dismisses the view, attributed to Montaigne and Charron, that there is a greater difference between one human being and another than between a human being and an animal on the grounds that there is no human so imperfect as to be incapable of communicating thought, as deaf mutes show when they invent sign language, whereas no animal has succeeded in demonstrating the power of language (*Oeuvres* 4:575). The argumentative strategy is clear: if it is not necessary to assume that animals possess reason in order to explain their behavior, then we are under no obligation to do so (*Oeuvres* 4:574). Let us look at this strategy in more detail.

The "Universal Instrument"

Part of what is at stake in the ancient and medieval debates about animal intelligence is just what reason is. Given Descartes's general antipathy to thinking that reason is a property of matter, it is not surprising to see him amassing arguments against the intelligence of animals. Given the identification between animals and machines, his arguments against animal intelligence are tantamount to arguments against machine intelligence.

The analogy between animals and clocks and other artificial automata is ubiquitous throughout Descartes's physiological texts. The *Treatise on Man* offers a detailed description of the fountain automata of the royal gardens: a bathing Diana who hides in the reeds when approached, Neptune brandishing his trident, and a sea monster that sprays water in the faces of passersby (*Oeuvres* 11:131).[24] As these animated movements are all explained by the operations of devices and springs, storage tanks and the sudden flow of water through pipes produced by visitors stepping on tiles, so too Descartes explains the behavior of animals according to hydrodynamic principles. Indeed, given the high degree of fluidity in animal bodies, including our own, hydraulic automata serve as the perfect model for understanding animal bodies:

> Indeed, one may compare the nerves of the machine I am describing with the pipes in the works of these fountains, its muscles and tendons with the various devices and springs which serve to set them in motion, its animal spirits with the water which drives them, the heart with the source of water, and the cavities of the brain with the storage tanks. (*Oeuvres* 11:131)

He proceeds to explain "how the external objects which strike the sense organs can prompt this machine to move its limbs in numerous different ways" in terms of how the innermost parts of the brain are pulled by the contracting fibers that connect the brain to the sense organ when an external object comes into contact with that particular sense. When these fibers are tugged, tiny pores on the surface of the brain open, and the "animal spirits" (highly rarified bits of matter) pour from the brain into the nerves that link to the muscles, resulting in animal movement (*Oeuvres* 11:141; *Philosophical Writings* 1:101).

In responding to an environmental stimulus, the *bête-machine* uses "images"—figures impressed on the back of the eye and on the internal surface of the brain by rays of light bouncing off the external object (*Oeuvres* 11:175; *Philosophical Writings* 1:105). These images play a role in explaining the functions of *imagination* (a short-term image storage and combination facility), *common sense* (where images from diverse sources are combined into a unified image of the object), and *memory* (a long-term storage facility), each of which has its "seat" in the brain (*Oeuvres* 11:176–80).[25] The nature and function of these images is described in thoroughly mechanical terms, with no hint that there might be anything consciously aware of the external objects causing changes in the animal's movements, no "interpreter" required to understand how they achieve their effects. They are capable of eliciting the right response from the animal wholly through their physical properties.

But why is Descartes so confident that we do not need anything but this mechanical explanation to explain all types of animal behavior? In the *Discourse* he proposes two behavioral tests for intelligence. Following Gunderson,[26] I refer to these as the *action test* and the *language test*. According to the action test, for a creature to count as intelligent, it must demonstrate sufficient flexibility and creativity in its actions to suit "all the contingencies of life" (*Oeuvres* 6:57–58). According to the language test, only a creature capable of demonstrating an understanding of signs (through speech or gestures) counts as intelligent. The language test imposes two conditions on a creature for intelligence: that it exhibits a *productive* capacity, the capacity to "arrange words so as to be understood" and that its utterances convey meaning or *refer* to things, of which even "madmen are capable although their thoughts do not follow reason" (*Oeuvres* 6:57, 4:574). Descartes connects the productivity of language to its compositional structure—the fact that words can be arranged and rearranged to convey new meanings. Mere mimicry, which is as close as animals come to demonstrating the capacity for language, fails both aspects of the language test: "We see that magpies and parrots can utter words as we do, and yet they cannot speak as we do: that is, show that they are thinking what they are saying" (*Oeuvres* 6:57).

In arguing that animals fail the language test, Descartes is, however, making certain assumptions about the impossibility of automated language use. To a modern critic, productivity seems less a problem in light of the many achievements of computational linguistics. If a Universal Turing Machine is, by definition, a machine capable of computing any computable function, then whether a machine is capable of exhibiting the productivity of a natural language depends on the extent to which natural languages consist of computable functions. On this question the jury is still out, but even if a machine were capable of passing the productivity test to the satisfaction of a human interlocutor (as the Turing test demands), Descartes would not likely be convinced.[27] Being able to manipulate symbols in rule-governed ways is not the same as "showing that you are thinking what you are saying." At the very least, understanding requires a grasp of the *semantics* of the language. Descartes's meaning requirement, which foreshadows John Searle's "Chinese Room" argument,[28] is the more exacting component of the language test.

The suggestion behind the denial that animals pass the action test, meanwhile, is that their responses are all hardwired. Behaviors we share with animals are supposedly all automatic—startle reflexes, pain responses, convulsions, and actions performed while distracted or sleepwalking—which do not in any way presuppose conscious thought (*Oeuvres* 4:573, 5:277). As Descartes writes to the Marquess of Newcastle, the work of honeybees, the discipline of cranes in flight or apes fighting, the cunning of foxes, the way animals express their passions are all performed as mechanically as the movements of a clock (*Oeuvres* 4:575–56). By contrast, reason is a "universal instrument," and thus are the organs of human beings disposed to a greater variety of movement:

For whereas reason is a universal instrument which can be used in all kinds of situations, these organs [of animals] need some particular disposition for each particular action; hence it is morally impossible for a machine to have enough different organs to make it act in all the contingencies of life in the way in which our reason makes us act. (*Oeuvres* 6:57)[29]

Are human actions radically different from those of animals, and if so, what does this tell us about the prospects for animal or machine intelligence? The passage just quoted suggests that animal bodies are deficient relative to human ones—they do not have "enough organs" to vary their movements—suggesting some kind of engineering constraint. If each movement of a machine required a dedicated mechanism, there would be an upper bound on how many mechanisms the machine could support. This was certainly true of seventeenth-century gear-based automata, in which each movement is governed by a separate gear train and the number of gears a machine could house was thus restricted. The question arises, however, why our bodies are not as con-strained as the bodies of animals. There are, after all, many adaptive behaviors animals can perform that humans cannot and many at which animals clearly surpass us in skill, as Descartes is well aware (*Oeuvres* 6:58; *Philosophical Writings* 1:141).[30] The suggestion is rather that whatever animals do, their responses are always fixed. They cannot vary what they do in one context to suit what might be appropriate in an-other, the way human reason lets us do.

Other passages, however, acknowledge that the variety of movements of which the human body is capable is due to its inherent *plasticity*, a feature connected to its high degree of fluidity. Because the particles of hard bodies are more at rest relative to each other, the more fluid the structure of a body is, the greater its capacity for varying its movements.[31] Plasticity is a feature shared by *both* human and animal bodies, as Descartes explains to Arnauld in the *Fourth Replies*:

> Both in our bodies and those of brutes, no movements can occur without the presence of all the organs and instruments which would enable the same movements to be produced in a machine. So even in our own case the mind does not directly move the external limbs, but simply controls the animal spirits which flow from the heart via the brain into the muscles, and sets up certain motions in them; *for the spirits are by their nature (ex se) adapted with equal facility to many diverse actions.* (*Oeuvres* 7:229; *Philosophical Writings* 2:161, translation modified, my emphasis)

This diversity of animal movements is connected to the capacity for learning. In several passages Descartes appears to acknowledge what we would now refer to as *learned adaptive behaviors*.[32] Dogs can be taught against their natural inclination to fear sticks or stop at the sound of gunshot and retrieve birds (*Oeuvres* 1:134, 11: 369–70), and some animals are said to learn better than others because of their stronger constitutions (*Oeuvres* 5:278). There is no analog of learned or flexible responses in the artificial automata of Descartes's time, which is why a seventeenth-century clock would continue to exhibit the same time when moved between time regions.

Descartes may have exaggerated the analogy between animals and artificial automata, but it is not clear that he is being inconsistent. The question remains: Does the capacity for learning or the "facility for many diverse actions" presuppose cognitive capacities as well? Descartes would say no. If an animal learns to respond differently to a given stimulus, it is solely because new connections have been forged between the parts of its brain that receive the stimulus and those that initiate a particular action. No intervening deliberation or decision-making is required (*Oeuvres* 6:54–56).

If we take Descartes at his word about the power of reason over action, then it follows that the difference between animal and human bodies is not primarily a mechanical difference. This stands to reason given the thought experiment of the *Treatise on Man*. This animal body—a human body minus a soul—surely has "enough organs" to make it act in all the ways in which human bodies act, but still it must not be able to do everything a real human body can do (*Oeuvres* 4:576). It would, presumably, be incapable of speech or any action that depends on the activity of reason. Any action reliant on intellectual discriminations that could not be captured imagistically would, for example, be prohibited.[33]

Still, it may seem that Descartes cannot rule out that human actions are more automatic than we think, and cannot say, by applying the action test alone, whether or not animals think. The human mind cannot, as he concedes to More (February 5, 1649; *Oeuvres* 5:276; *Philosophical Writings* 365), "reach into the hearts" of animals, and hence there may seem to be no conclusive proof that animals do not think. On the other hand, those who think they are "present in the animals' hearts" and surmise what animals know when they are running or what they dream when they bark in their sleep "are simply saying something without proving it" (*Oeuvres* 7:426; *Philosophical Writings* 2:288). This concession to More suggests that as Descartes's thinking about animals matured, the action test ceased to be regarded as definitive. What is "more probable" is that of the two principles that cause all our movements—one, mechanical and corporeal, and the other, incorporeal or thinking—only the former is necessary to understand animal behavior. Descartes never, however, draws a merely probabilistic conclusion from the language test. So long as animals fail to communicate through speech or gestures, we can know for certain that they are not intelligent.

THE STATUS OF ANIMALS

As the apparent deliberate, conscious behavior of animals is explained away without postulating an animal soul, so too are the very formation, structure, and functions of animal bodies. "Life" has no privileged status in the mechanical framework. There is no difference "in nature" between living and dead bodies—the "living" are simply those whose internal organs enable them to be self-moving and self-regulating, but they do this blindly, without intention or purpose. The difference between a living thing and a nonliving thing is no different from that between a clock wound up and functioning and one that has wound down, a difference wholly accounted for in mechanical terms (*Oeuvres* 11:330–31; *Philosophical Writings* 1:329).

In light of the collapse between animate and inanimate nature, what are we to make of our folk biological categorizations? There has been a tendency to think of Descartes as having *eliminated* all categorical distinctions between kinds of organisms and between organic and nonorganic things, rendering whatever distinctions we make mere projections of the imagination onto an utterly homogeneous material nature.[34] Mechanical explanations subsume all interactions among bodies directly under the laws of mechanics and collision rules, for which it is only physical properties—relative mass, shape, surface area, and speed—that count. How well suited is this mode of explanation to understanding all the nuances of animal behavior? If Betsy the cow falls off the roof and lands on the chicken coop, all that is relevant to understanding the effect on the coop is her mass, shape, surface area, and speed relative to the mass, shape, surface area, and resistance of the coop, but if she chews her cud, moans for her calf, or scoots out of the path of an oncoming tractor, then the relationship between her behavior and the laws of mechanics begins to look substantially more remote. (And what was she doing on that roof in the first place?) It is such apparently intentional or goal-directed behaviors that have convinced philosophers for centuries that something more than the laws of motion and impact are operative. But this, Descartes seems to want to claim, is all an illusion.

Several observations support the conclusion that Descartes is attempting to eliminate biological distinctions. First, animal bodies are not substances, and "substance" is the official category for distinguishing between kinds of things. Not even the human body is a substance, for it naturally perishes, and substances are not corruptible except through an act of God (*Oeuvres* 7:14; *Philosophical Writings* 2:10). Human bodies enjoy a special kind of unity over time by virtue of their relationship to the human soul, the identity of which persists unchanged throughout all the changes in the body. Since animals do not possess souls, their unity cannot be explained in this way:

This is confirmed by the example of the soul, which is the true substantial form of man. For the soul is thought to be immediately created by God for no other reason than that it is a substance. Hence

since the other "forms" are not thought to be created in this way, but
merely to emerge from the potentiality of matter, they should not be
regarded as substances. (*Oeuvres* 3:505; *Philosophical Writings* 3:208)[35]

Does it follow then that animals lack an identity altogether in
Descartes's universe?

Dennis Des Chene has identified four senses of "unity" at work in
Descartes's corpus, of which "substantial unity"—the kind of unity
that applies to bodies when united to a substantial form—is only one.[36]
Any part of matter can be considered a substance—"body in general"
(*corps en general*) or a "determinate part of matter." According to
this first criterion of unity, a body just is a collection (*ensemble*) or
quantity of matter, any change in which signals a change in the substance.[37] A second criterion, "physical unity," refers to a determinate
part of matter that moves together.[38] Since organisms undergo continual replacement of parts, they do not constitute physical unities either.
A third criterion, "dispositional unity," refers to what is more or less the
same arrangement of matter over time. Arrangements can tolerate
small changes in quantity or size and shape (*Oeuvres* 11:251). A drop of
oil or blood can thus be said to have a dispositional unity even if small
bits of it are shed as it moves. While this may seem a promising notion
of unity to apply to animals, Des Chene objects that it is arbitrary to
carve out from nature one arrangement or one activity as constituting
a single organism, unless we presuppose the purposes for which God
arranged matter in that way—but Descartes denies that we can make
suppositions about God's intentions.[39] The final criterion, "functional
unity," by which the boundaries of an arrangement of matter are drawn
according to what is needed to fulfill a certain function, also requires
making assumptions about God's design. Identifying an arrangement
of matter as a *heart* is possible only by reference to the function of heating and circulating the blood, but in the absence of specifying what
purpose the heart was created to serve, it is impossible to specify its
proper function.[40]

Although animals do not have a unity bestowed upon them by being united to a soul (substantial unity), they nonetheless have features that distinguish them from other arrangements of matter and unique modes of explanation:

(i) Animals have a special status as "natural automata" or "self-moving machines" (*Oeuvres* 11:120, 6:55–56, 5:277).

(ii) Animals have a "unity of composition," in contrast with the "unity of nature" (essence) that a substance possesses (7:423–24).

(iii) Animal bodies (particularly those of the higher mammals) and human bodies have very similar organs (11:200).

(iv) Animals have "life," attributed to the heat of the heart (6:46; 11:202) or the blood and spirits (11:202). There is "absolutely no principle of movement in animals apart from the disposition (arrangement) of their organs and the continual flow of spirits which are produced by the heat of the heart as it rarefies the blood" (7:230).

(v) Animals "sense," at least according to the "first grade of sensation" (4:576, 5:276).

(vi) Animals may be said to have a "corporeal or animal soul," which "depends solely on the force of the spirits and structure of [the] organs" (5:276).

In all these respects, animals are treated differently from bodies in the sense of physics. Is Descartes simply being inconsistent, or is there room within his ontology for different categories of extended things?

Although animals are not substances, they are said to have "natures," even if those natures are "not transparently clear" to us (*Oeuvres* 7:117–18). This is an odd use of "nature" because it represents a collapse of Aristotle's distinction between nature and art—and on the side of art! If an artificial automaton were engineered to act in ways wholly indiscernible from that of an animal—say, a monkey—we would, he writes, have no grounds for concluding that they were "not of the same nature" (*Oeuvres* 6:56). Such assertions make no sense if "nature" is being used in the same way that it is used when referring to the essence of a substance, for no one would find it contentious to think that the nature of an artifact and an animal was extension in both cases. The idea is rather that within extension there is a plurality of natures, some of which emerge solely "from the potentiality of matter," and some with the assistance of human ingenuity.

But when exactly does a collection of matter constitute a distinguishable nature? Not just any aggregate or arrangement of matter is going to count as having a nature distinct from other arrangements. A larger pile of rocks does not have a distinct nature from a smaller pile. Descartes only distinguishes between natures when dealing with specific kinds of composite things, composites that cannot be analyzed in terms of the sum of natures belonging to their parts. One category of irreducible composite natures is included in the category of "true and immutable natures" (*Oeuvres* 7:64; *Philosophical Writings* 2:44–45). The natures of simple substances do not change when aggregated unless their arrangement generates properties that cannot be accounted for in terms of the properties of the parts. If new properties are generated, then we must suppose that the nature of the composite is different. The whole human being, for example, has a "nature" of its own on account of the fact that sensibility emerges only when the mind exists in a "substantial union" with the body (*Oeuvres* 7:227–28; *Philosophical Writings* 2:160). The proper term for this kind of composite is a "nature"; Descartes nowhere refers to this union as a substance.

Animals are natural automata, and automata of all kinds have what Descartes calls "objective perfection" (*perfectio objective*) (*Oeuvres* 8A:11). What this appears to mean is that the more complex a machine, the more reality is present in our idea of it, and the more sophisticated must be its cause. If this is so, then an automaton, and especially a highly intricate automaton like an animal, has more objective reality than does the bare matter of which it is constituted. Thus while an animal is nothing other than bits of matter suitably arranged, the arrangement is not reducible to the properties of the component material bits. This is the analog for animals of being united to the same mind.

One example that Descartes gives of a composite arrangement that does not have a true and immutable nature is that of a chimaera, which, according to one legend, has the tail of a serpent, the head of a lion, and the body of a goat. The implication is that while the composite does not have a true and immutable nature, the animals from whose parts it is composed do (*Oeuvres* 7:118). Applying the objective perfection test, the idea of a chimera must fail to have more objective perfection than the sum of its animal parts. But why exactly does the chimaera fail to pass the test for having a distinct true and immutable nature? One way of answering this question would be to consider whether the explanation of such a creature could exceed what we already know about lions, serpents, and goats. The answer seems to be no. We can imagine what we like, but whether we could truly conceive of such a creature is far from obvious. What would it be, for example, for there to be a creature composed of warm- and cold-blooded parts?

The "unity of composition," which animals enjoy and which is lacking in a chimaera, appears to cut across Des Chene's dispositional and functional senses of unity. The parts of an animal have the same essence (extension) or "unity of nature" but differ in their relations to the whole animal:

Notice that if we have different ideas of two things, there are two ways in which they may be taken to be one and the same thing: either in virtue of the unity and identity of nature, or else merely in respect of the unity of composition. For example, the ideas which we have of shape and of motion are not the same, nor are our ideas of understanding or volition, nor are those of bones and flesh, nor are those of thought and of an extended thing. But our perception is different in the case of the thing that we consider under the form of bone and that which we consider under the form of flesh; and hence

we cannot take them as one and the same thing in virtue of a unity
of nature but can regard them as the same only in respect of unity of
composition—i.e. only in so far as it is one and the same animal
which has bones and flesh. (*Oeuvres* 7:423–24; *Philosophical Writings*
2:285–86)

The categories of bones and flesh are functional, and their being defined in terms of their relationship to the whole animal suggests that
the unity of composition is a functional unity. But what are we to say
in response to Des Chene's objection that selecting arrangements by
reference to functions presupposes ends or purposes, which Descartes
denies have any place in natural philosophy?

Descartes's use of functional terminology—"function" (*fonction*)
and "use" (*l'usage*; *utilius*)—does not signal a reliance on assumptions
about purpose or design but represents instead a shift toward thinking
of functional relationships as a special class of (brute) causal relationships.[41] Not just any causal relationship, which, for Descartes, always
involves the *dependence* of one thing or event upon another, suffices for
a functional relationship. The sun causes plants to grow, but the sun
does not have this effect as its function (or any other function either).
Functional explanations apply only in contexts where the effects of various parts of matter are *mutually dependent* on one another. Where
there is a composite that constitutes a distinct nature, where it exhibits
unique properties, activities, or movements, and where its parts are so
interconnected and hierarchically arranged that their activities are mutually sustaining, there Descartes is apt to apply the tools of a functional analysis. We see functional analyses put to work most clearly in
those texts devoted to explaining how an animal body forms (embryo-
genesis) and how its parts work collaboratively to explain its life-
sustaining, self-regulatory behavior. The formation of all the organs of
an animal body depends upon the initial formation of the heart, but
the heart in turn depends for its continued functioning on the formation and effects of the brain, the lungs, and other organs. Similarly, the

conducive behavior of an organism (e.g., pulling its foot away from a fire) is understood in terms of the coordinated activities of the parts. The process begins with the agitation of the nerve endings, followed by the rapid flow of animal spirits to the brain and blood flowing to the heart, and then by signals returning to the muscles, and, finally, the contraction of the relevant muscles (*Oeuvres* 11:141–42). There is nothing analogous to these interdependent causal processes in nonorganic contexts even where one phenomenon depends for its existence upon another. The dependence of the tides on the gravitational effects of the moon, the dependence of plants on the sunlight—neither of these warrants a functional description. The moon is not *for* the tides or the sun *for* the plants, for there is nothing to suggest that the dependence of the one upon the other is reciprocated.[42]

What, then, is the relationship between Descartes's functional mode of explanation and the micromechanical, to which all material phenomena must, in Descartes's physics, succumb? Whereas the behavior of corpuscles in collisions is directly subsumed under the laws and rules of nature, the formation and behavior of an animal is subjected first to a functional analysis of its macroscopic organs and parts and only then to an analysis in terms of underlying mechanical processes. Descartes's *Traité de l'Homme* is a paradigm example of this analytic strategy in operation. Such a body would have within it "all the parts required to make it walk, eat, respire, and finally… all of our functions which can be imagined to proceed from matter and to depend only on the disposition of the organs" (*Oeuvres* 11:120). We are then asked to conceive of this body as having the "bones, nerves, muscles, veins, arteries, stomach, liver, spleen, heart, brain and various other parts from which it must be composed," and then to consider "the parts which are too small to be seen" about which we can learn enough if we know "the movements which depend on them" (*Oeuvres* 11:120–21). This two-step method of explanation exhausts what we need to know about the development and operation of animal bodies, but there is no suggestion that the first—the functional analysis—is either dispensable or does not describe what are real categorical modes of nature. On the contrary: "I need only explain these movements in order [and] tell you by the same method which of our functions they represent" (*Oeuvres* 11:121).

Finally, there is nothing in Descartes's description of functional interrelationships that presupposes the governing effects of purposes or final causes. The formation of an animal is described in wholly mechanical terms—the circulation of matter in the fetus obeying the laws of inertia, rectilinear motion, and conservation, heating and moving, cooling and compacting the matter that forms the major organs of the body. And while this development tends to follow a regular pattern, irregularities are as much the effect of nature at work as the regular forms we observe and on the basis of which we form ideas of what is "normal." There is no implied failure in the existence of a monster, which Descartes regards as equally a product of the laws operating on matter as any other natural phenomenon. Should we be inclined to think otherwise, he warns, we must attribute such failures either to God, which is heresy, or to the "wisdom of nature," which Descartes asserts is nothing but a "folly of human thought" (*Oeuvres* 11:524). We see, therefore, in Descartes the very beginning of secular approaches to biology as we understand them today—divorced from considerations of deliberate design or universal intelligence, but defended as *more* consistent with the teachings of the Church than the official, Aristotelian modes of explanation that were at the time theologically sanctioned.

CONCLUSION

To dismiss Descartes as either a chauvinist or an eliminativist about animals is, as I hope to have shown, too crude. He was above all else a scientist, and whatever categorical differences there are between animate and inanimate natures can be understood without invoking souls, divine purposes, or the wisdom of nature. To his mind, the best science would tell us that animal cognition and sensibility are only apparent—anthropomorphic projections of the kinds of explanations we use to understand each other. We may be inclined to think that here his pronouncements exceeded what could actually be known at the time about animal thought and feeling, but in questioning what was commonly accepted and the inconsistent attitudes and practices with respect to animals in which humans indulged, he forced the debate to a new level of complexity. Moreover, he forced his interlocutors to accept the role of science in settling questions about which things have souls, which things think, and which act in deliberate, intentional ways—a move he could not have anticipated would open the door to the kind of naturalistic psychology developed by Hume and the undoing of his own dualistic conception of the human being.

Did Descartes contribute to undermining our respect for animals? The answer to that is not at all clear, for with the exception of a few Hellenistic sects, few defenders of animal intelligence have been willing to practice what they preach and abstain from eating animals or using them for human purposes. What Descartes did contribute to debates about animal welfare is the observation that it is sheer hubris to think of animals as creatures of God, possessing reason or intelligence, capable of feeling and intention, while using them for human purposes and excluding them from the kingdom of heaven. As we subject Descartes to the judgment of history, we should bear in mind that for him the admiration we bear toward an animal is not in any way diminished by the recognition that it does not possess a soul. The craftsmanship involved in producing such an intricate machine is cause not for less wonder at the power and ingenuity of God but for more.[43]

CHAPTER EIGHT

Kant on Animals

Patrick Kain

The eighteenth-century German philosopher Immanuel Kant (1724–1804) developed a sophisticated account of the nature of animals and, based on this account and his distinctive moral philosophy, argued that human beings do not have "duties to" nonhuman animals but do have significant "duties *with regard* to" these animals (*Metaphysics of Morals*, 6:443). In the first section I describe in some detail Kant's account of the nature of animals and the distinction between humans and nonhuman animals.[1] With this account in hand, I turn in the second section to explaining Kant's account of the nature of moral obligation and his complex and oft-misunderstood contention that we have duties regarding nonhuman animals that are grounded in their nature.[2] In the third section I consider Kant's position in relation to that of another important eighteenth-century moral theorist, Francis Hutcheson (1694–1746).

The Nature of Animals

Kant made significant and influential contributions to eighteenth-century debates in biology and psychology, and he was a pioneer in the emerging disciplines he called anthropology and physical geography.[3] An appreciation of Kant's account of the nature of and distinction between humans and nonhuman animals emerges from a survey of his commitments in these various contexts.

Kant articulated a naturalistic framework for systematic biological and psychological investigations.[4] He insisted that, in natural science, we must seek to identify a system of efficient or "mechanical" causal laws responsible for observable regularities, though there are phenomena that resist such an understanding (*Power of Judgment*, 5:387–88, 372–76, 401–4). To bring such regularities "under laws," a set of teleological concepts are needed, including the concept of an *organism*, a "natural end" that is a teleologically organized and self-organizing whole, organized for life and reproduction (VR 2:429,[5] *Power of Judgment*, 5:376). When using such concepts, we must still observe the maxim that "in a natural science everything must be explained *naturally*" (GtP 8:178,[6] cf. *Critique of Pure Reason*, A544/B572, A773/B801). One should seek a systematic and parsimonious account that relies upon analogies to observed powers and eschews both unnecessary and unhelpful complexity and direct appeals to divine intervention.

To explain a number of important apparent regularities of organic reproduction and development, Kant was a prominent advocate of an epigenetic theory of the reproduction of organisms, a conception of real species, and a doctrine of original predispositions. On Kant's moderate version of "epigenesis," or merely "generic preformationism," adult organisms produce a new organism endowed with the parents' specific organization rather than simply unfolding a preformed body contained in one of the parents' bodies (*Power of Judgment*, 5:423). The specific organizing form of the offspring is present in both parents in advance, and the particular organizing form that a given individual begins with is a result of its parents' activity, a result of their "mixing," rather than the sole contribution of either parent. Kant insisted that, if we are to trace "the present properties of things" back to their causes as far as we can go by analogy with observed powers, natural science should focus on identifying the "real kinship" relationships between organisms, a kinship revealed by individuals' reproductive origins and their capacity to produce fertile offspring with one another.[7] Kant argued that this "historical" criterion of kinship, grounded as it is in the conception of the epigenetic reproductive power that we can observe, is the key to a naturalistic account of "real" or "natural species" of organisms and of the variations and developments within species (BBM 8:102[8]; GtP 8:178).[9] His proposal is that the characteristic features and capacities of the members of each species be understood in terms of an underlying common specific nature, a set of "predispositions" (*Anlagen*) and "germs" or "seeds" (*Keime*), originally implanted in the species and then epigenetically imparted to each of its members via the reproductive power of their parents (GtP 8:179; *Power of Judgment*, 5:423).

In psychology Kant extended his naturalistic biological framework and offered an account of animals or "living" organisms, those organisms endowed with "sensation and choice" (*Metaphysics of Morals*, 6:442). He advocated a tripartite psychology, which he applied to both humans and animals: the "faculty of desire" (the capacity "to be, by means of one's representations, the cause of the objects of these representations") is linked with a "faculty of cognition" or "intuition," which gives rise to representations (via the senses, but also via reproductive and anticipatory imagination), and to a "faculty of feeling pleasure or displeasure" in conjunction with a representation (*Metaphysics of Morals*, 6:211).[10] The predispositions and propensities of an animal species, which may underlie or manifest themselves in a variety of instincts, acquired inclinations, and habits, serve as causal grounds for the occurrence of certain thoughts, feelings, desires, and behaviors.[11] We humans can be "immediately aware" of our own representations, especially those representations upon which we act. Since animals can perceive and respond to changes in their immediate environment in ways that (most) plants cannot, and because of observable similarities between our actions and the behavior of nonhuman animals (such as dam-building beavers), we infer that animal behavior is a product of inner principles (even if less than fully conscious or self-conscious ones). They have some capacities, analogous to, if yet specifically different from, our capacity to reason and our capacity to act from reason (*Power of Judgment*, 5:464n). Animal behavior suggests that animals can represent, perceive, and be acquainted with objects through their representations and are capable of subtle differentiations among objects.[12] Some animals have more refined external senses than we humans (*Lectures on Metaphysics*, 28:277). Animals can move themselves according to the power of choice (*Willkür*; *Metaphysics of Morals*, 6:442), that is, in virtue of their representations, and, in some cases, it seems "the acts of animals arise out of the same principle (*principium*) from which human actions spring, and the animal actions are analogues of this" (*Lectures on Ethics*, 27:459).

Kant argued that mental representations can, in general, be cognized and explained naturalistically, but he insisted they cannot be fully explained "materialistically." The mental representations that are essential constituents of the genuine psychological regularities we observe, Kant argued, must be regarded as states of an immaterial *soul* (though not necessarily of a simple, substantial, or immortal soul; *Critique of Pure Reason*, B419–20; *Power of Judgment*, 5:460).[13] Thus Kant insisted, against Descartes and Malebranche, that animals are not "mere machines" but have minds or souls with a locomotive power (*vis locomotiva*) because the mental representations that guide their behavior cannot be realized in matter (*Power of Judgment*, 5:457, 464n).[14]

We have no access through our own introspection, however, to evidence that nonhuman animals have inner sense, concepts, or cognition that we encounter in our own case. Kant noted that animals do not possess a capacity for language use—which would indicate concepts and higher cognition—much less a first-person pronoun. As for the "artistry" of beavers, Kant endorsed Bonnet's contention that beavers always build dams according to a single model or plan, an indication that whatever their artistry and the complex form of social cooperation they employ, they lack the ability to reflect upon, modify, and improve their craft or inhibit their instincts.[15] Generally speaking, Kant saw animals' behavior as guided by rather determinate and pervasive instincts; they are incapable of impulse control, and many are easily duped; their behavior does not progress cumulatively over the course of generations. Parsimony counsels not ascribing more sophisticated mental capacities than necessary to explain the phenomena, so Kant concluded that nothing in their behavior required positing full-blown "consciousness," a capacity for "inner sense" or for second-order representations, including representations of oneself or one's entire condition: animals lack concepts, judgment, apperception, and self-consciousness, and thus genuine cognition of objects. Unable "to represent to themselves the ground of their movement (*Beweggründe*)," they cannot reflect upon their desires or have "a desire within a desire" (*Lectures on Metaphysics*, 28:99). Unable to conceive of "what is useful or injurious" or "desirable in regard to [their] condition as a whole," animals are unable to pursue or experience happiness as such. Perhaps most important for moral purposes, absent the capacity to represent what is "unconditionally good," animals must lack the capacity to act upon (or against) the representation of such an unconditional law (*Critique of Pure Reason*, A802/B830).

In contrast, we human beings have language, "inner sense," and second-order representations, concepts, apperception, self-consciousness, cognition, and capacities for reflection and inhibition in light of general representations. In his *Anthropology* text, Kant claimed that each of humans' three practical predispositions, the "technical, pragmatic and moral" predispositions, distinguish human beings from all other terrestrial animals. The profound flexibility of our instincts and skills and the connection between our "consciousness" and our technical skill at manipulating things (especially with our hands) distinguish us from all other animals with which we are familiar; our capacity to use other humans in pursuit of happiness and culture and to govern ourselves according to rational principles distinguish human beings yet further (*Anthropology*[16], 7:321ff.).[17]

This creates an opening, in the human case, for Kant to contend that we also have a capacity for a rational will, a moral predisposition for "freedom under moral laws." Kant famously argued that neither "theoretical" philosophy nor empirical investigation can establish that there is *any* such absolute freedom. "Experience lets us cognize only the law of appearances and hence the mechanism of nature, the direct opposite of freedom" (*Critique of Practical Reason* [KgS 5], 5:29). Kant came to insist that the reality of absolute freedom, or freedom under moral laws, can be established, but established only in practical philosophy, by the "fact of reason."[18] We are each "immediately conscious (as soon as we draw up maxims of the will for ourselves)" of the moral law; the moral law is given to us as "the sole fact of pure reason," and this fact leads us to the concept of freedom and the postulation of its reality in us (*Critique of Practical Reason*, 5:29–31). "The categorical imperative proves for morally practical purposes" that we human beings are free (*Metaphysics of Morals*, 6:280n).

It is seldom recognized that, in addition to his interest in distinguishing human beings, and human behavior and mental capacities, from those of nonhuman animals in general, Kant had a significant interest in animal ethology, comparative morphology, and natural history, as part of a proper "pragmatic" knowledge of the world. Freshly transcribed and edited notes from his lecture course "Physical Geography" show Kant synthesizing the observations of leading biologists and travelers into characterizations of nonhuman animals that go beyond the occasional comments in his published works (including the *Physical Geography* text he allowed to be published in 1802).[19]

On the basis of Kant's comments in the *Anthropology* and the obvious morphological similarities between humans and monkeys (particularly

in the hand, so emphasized by Linnaeus and Buffon), we might expect
him to have had particular interest in monkeys.[20] While impressed by
their manual dexterity and their deployment of it to catch mussels, make
a bed, and put on clothes, for example, Kant was less than fully impressed, given reports that they steal produce from field and garden and
band together to slay lions, tigers, or even humans (*Physical Geography*,
9:336–37).[21]

Although the monkeys have an analogue of reason (*analogon rationis*), no analogue of morality (*analogon moralitatis*) will be found in
them, as they are always wicked, spiteful and obstinate, and everywhere they go, they wreak havoc.[22]

Wickedness is [the monkey's] primary attribute; it is never capable of complete trust; with respect to its mental powers, so to speak,
the dog and elephant are much to be preferred.[23]

Indeed

[dogs] seem to be the most perfect animal, and to manifest most
strongly the *analogue of rationality*. … They carefully look after their
responsibilities, remain with their master; if they've done something
wicked they become disturbed; and if they see their master angry,
try to win him over with a submissive posture.[24]

While dogs may be Kant's prime example of brutes' necessitation by
external stimulus and the lack of impulse control—"a dog must eat if
he is hungry and has something in front of him" (*Lectures on Ethics*,
27:267)—he notes that dogs learn to howl or open a gate and that with
practice they can learn a rabbit's tricks and outwit a rabbit. Their instinct, by repetition of similar cases, "forms an experience which serves
the dog as a guiding thread," despite its lack of concepts.[25]

Kant's greatest sense of wonder, though, is reserved for elephants:
"When one observes their strength and their similarity to man, [an

elephant] is an animal worthy of admiration [*ein bewunderungswürdiges Thier*]."²⁶ The elephant's trunk is "the most noble tool," comparable to a hand in its dexterity and sensitivity, and with a wider range of uses as well; an elephant can use its powers more generally than any other animal.²⁷ Elephants are very useful because of their strength and speed on land and in water and because they are teachable (*gelehrig*) and prudent (*klug*). "Unprovoked, an elephant does no one harm" (cf. *Physical Geography*, 9:329); "it is often so gentle that one can break coconuts open on its head, although it must be given some or it will avenge itself with its trunk." They can be not only tamed but also "disciplined" (perhaps the only animal that is capable of discipline). Kant notes that people in Surinam use an elephant in place of a servant, a role elephants carry out well and patiently.²⁸ In one set of notes, Kant is reported to have concluded his comments on elephants thus: "An elephant is a gentle animal, and seems to be an analogue of morality. It understands jokes, but cannot be duped."²⁹ Unfortunately neither the precise basis of such remarks nor their implications is further elaborated. Clearly reports about elephant behavior (or at least the parts that Kant found credible or worth collecting and remarking upon) made an impression upon him. Rather than emphasize differences between or the distance between elephants and humans, he attributes significant mental sophistication to elephants and uses words with significant positive ethical overtones ("prudence," "good-natured," "patience," "discipline") without reservation.³⁰

This survey of some elements of Kant's systematic, "naturalistic," and empirical biology, empirical psychology, and pragmatic anthropology and "physical geography" establishes that he had a sophisticated account of the nature of animals. He concluded that human beings have *rational* souls and that, as a contingent empirical matter, no other animals with which we are familiar do.³¹ While many of the details and assumptions of Kant's account have been superseded by subsequent scientific and philosophical developments, it is not clear that his primary conclusions have been.³² This is the account to which his *Lectures on Ethics* makes reference.

MORAL OBLIGATION

Moral Obligation and the Dignity of Rational Beings

Kant is well known for his distinctive *Lectures on Ethics*. In his *Groundwork of the Metaphysics of Morals* (1785), he analyzed the concept of obligation and concluded:

> The practical necessity of acting in accordance with this principle [of morality], that is, duty, does not rest at all on feelings, impulses, and inclinations, but merely on the relation of rational beings to one another, in which the will of a rational being must always be regarded as at the same time *lawgiving*, since otherwise it could not be thought as an *end in itself*. Reason accordingly refers every maxim of the will as giving universal law to every other will and also to every action toward oneself, and does so... from the idea of the *dignity* of a rational being, who obeys no law other than that which he himself at the same time gives. (*Groundwork*, 4:434)

Kant's *Lectures on Ethics* draws a sharp distinction between beings with *dignity* (*Würde*) and those with mere *price* (*Preis*). Price is a kind of relative value, a value something has if it is related in the correct way to something else, in particular to the needs or desires of human beings. By contrast, dignity is a kind of absolute and intrinsic value; something with dignity "is raised above all price and therefore admits of no equivalent"; it cannot "be replaced by something else" (*Groundwork*, 4:434).[33] Kant claims that what gives a being dignity and marks it out as an "end in itself" is its innate rational capacity (*Fähigkeit*) for autonomy, a predisposition (*Anlage*) to "personality," the capacity to "legislate" the moral law and to act out of respect for the moral law, or having "freedom... under moral laws" (*Metaphysics of Morals*, 6:223, 418, 434–35; *Groundwork*, 4:428, 435–36; RGV[34] 6:27).[35] Moral obligation itself must be, fundamentally, a necessary relation of a rational being to itself and to other rational beings.[36] Kant also argued that concrete moral obligations can be articulated in terms of the demand to respect the dignity and autonomy of every rational being (*Groundwork*, 4:428–36). Thus his second formula of the categorical imperative famously demands, "So act that you use humanity, whether in your own person or in the person of any other, always at the same time as an end, never merely as a means" (*Groundwork*, 4:429).[37]

In Kant's theory only rational beings are capable of "passive" or "active obligation": only rational beings can be obligated or obligate others. "Duty to any subject is moral constraint by that subject's will" (*Metaphysics of Morals*, 6:442). So an obligator (a being *to whom* one can have a duty, a being capable of "active obligation") must have a will that can impose a moral constraint upon the obligated, and the obligated (one capable of "passive obligation") must have a will that can be constrained by the obligator (*Metaphysics of Morals*, 6:442). Kant isolated two necessary conditions for fundamental moral status: we can be obligated only to a being that is both (i) a "person," a being with a free will "standing under the moral law" and (ii) "given as an object of experience," so that we can recognize that it can obligate us and so that we can, through our actions, have some bearing upon it or its ends (*Metaphysics of Morals*, 6:442). This insistence that we can have obligations only to persons who are "given as an object of experience" suggests that experience—and the biological, psychological, and anthropological theories, concepts, and judgments through which we make systematic sense of the objects we are given in experience— must play a significant role in helping to determine, in a naturalistically respectable way, which objects of experience we should consider to be endowed with the relevant predispositions. This suggestion is confirmed by Kant's appeal to "experience" and his employment of biological and psychological terminology in his discussion of our duties regarding nonhuman animals (and of the moral relationship between human parents and the children they conceive) (*Metaphysics of Morals*, 6:280, 442).[38]

Kant's Rejection of Duties "to" Animals

Given the foundations of Kant's moral philosophy, it is crucial to consider whether careful attention to the nature and behavior of any nonhuman animal provides evidence that it, and by extension the other members of its species, possess the predisposition to "personality," the capacity for morality. Kant's conclusion was that it does not. Indeed his judgment was that there is insufficient evidence even to ascribe to nonhuman animals many of the predispositions and capacities that are necessary components of the predisposition to personality: they lack the capacity for concepts, self-consciousness, judgment, and so forth. While it is not clear precisely why he interpreted the behavior of monkeys, dogs, and elephants as he did, absent the manifestation by some of those animals of rather full-blown "Kantian" moral consciousness, or at least the manifestation that such consciousness was developing, this judgment is hardly arbitrary. Animals are "endowed with sensation and choice" yet are "non-rational"; they are incapable of rational cognition, and most important, they lack a free rational will (*Metaphysics of Morals*, 6:442–43). Love, fear, admiration, and amazement are proper for a variety of objects and are especially proper to have for animals, but the "proper object of respect" is the moral law and those beings with dignity, ourselves and other human beings, with the capacity to "legislate" the law and to hold it before us (*Critique of Practical Reason*, 5:76–78; *Metaphysics of Morals*, 6:443; *Groundwork*, 4:435–36, 440).[39] This is why Kant concludes that "a human being can therefore have no duty to any beings other than human beings" (*Metaphysics of Morals*, 6:442). "Since all animals exist only as means, and not for their own sakes, in that they have no self-consciousness... it follows that we have no immediate duties to animals; our duties toward them are indirect duties to humanity" (*Lectures on Ethics*, 27:458–59).

Perhaps what strikes many readers as fundamentally objectionable about Kant's denial of duties *to* animals is the apparent implication that they are completely devoid of moral significance and liable to arbitrary treatment and disposal as mere "things" at best only accidentally distinguishable from any arbitrary hunk of matter. But before jumping to such a conclusion, careful attention must be paid to Kant's positive account of the place of animals in the moral life.

Kant's Account of Duties "regarding" Animals

In the *Metaphysics of Morals* and in notes from his "Lectures on Ethics," Kant identifies a general duty to oneself to refrain from unjustified "violent and cruel treatment of animals," as well as a number of examples of more particular moral requirements regarding our behavior toward certain animals. After laying out in some detail his core argument for this general duty regarding animals, we will consider some of the additional, particular duties he mentions.[40]

Casual readers of Kant's *Groundwork* may expect that his system of ethical duties is constructed by examining a series of particular action "maxims" with the "Formula of Universal Law"—viz. "act only in accordance with that maxim through which you can at the same time will that it become a universal law" (4:421). However, the method and the general system of ethical duties that Kant sketches in his lectures and elaborates in the *Metaphysics of Morals* takes a somewhat different form. In the *Metaphysics of Morals*, he argues that there are two universalizable ends—"one's own perfection" and "the happiness of others"— which we ought to make our ends (6:385). These obligatory ends are the basis of a system of ethical duties, to oneself and to others (other human beings). Duties to oneself are tied to the requirement to have "one's own perfection"—one's own natural perfection and moral perfection—as an end (*Metaphysics of Morals*, 6:385–87, 391–92). There are two different kinds of ethical duty. The perfect or limiting or "negative duties [to oneself] forbid a human being to act contrary to the end of his nature and so have to do merely with his moral self-preservation." In contrast, positive, widening, or imperfect duties to oneself "command him to make a certain object of choice his end, concern his *perfecting* of himself.... They belong to his *cultivation* (active perfecting) of himself" (*Metaphysics of Morals*, 6:419). Suicide, for example, is contrary to one's perfect duty to oneself because of the way it conflicts with the agent's natural inclination to self-preservation; it involves "renouncing his personality" and "debasing humanity in [his] person" (*Metaphysics of Morals*, 6:420, 422–23). Because of what the agent expresses and manifests about his nature when he violates a perfect duty to himself, such actions are particularly dishonorable.[41]

Kant's discussion of duties regarding animals comes at the conclusion of his discussion of *perfect duties to oneself*, before he proceeds to his detailed examination of imperfect duties to oneself or any duties to others, as Baranzke has emphasized.[42] "With regard to the animate but non-rational part of creation," Kant insists that "violent and cruel treatment of animals" is quite "intimately opposed to a human being's duty to himself, and he has a duty to refrain from this" (*Metaphysics of Morals*, 6:443). The "violent and cruel treatment of animals" violates a perfect duty to oneself. But why does Kant consider such behavior regarding animals to be contrary to the end of human nature and to a human being's moral self-preservation? As Denis has explained, Kant insists that "the ways that we treat animals reflect and affect morally important attitudes and feelings."[43] To understand Kant's position, we need to recognize two important points: one about the moral significance of certain of our feelings, the other about the nature of animals and how, given that nature and our own, animals properly engage these feelings.

First, Kant argues that "certain emotional predispositions are extremely useful natural tools for us as moral beings," useful both motivationally and epistemically, and they "may also reflect certain moral commitments" insofar as they "can be shaped" by our choices.[44] In particular Kant singles out the "disposition of sensibility... to love something... even apart from any intention to use it" and, especially, the "natural predisposition" to the "shared feeling of [other's] suffering" as feelings that may "promote morality or at least prepare the way for it" and are "very serviceable to morality in one's relations with other people" (*Metaphysics of Morals*, 6:443). Moreover Kant insists that some "feelings," namely "moral feeling, conscience, love of one's neighbor [*die Liebe des Nächsten, Menschenliebe*], and respect for oneself (self-esteem)," are "moral endowments" that "lie at the basis of morality, as subjective conditions of receptiveness to the concept of duty" (*Metaphysics of Morals*, 6:399). These are feelings that ought to be cultivated, and more important in the context of this perfect duty to oneself, they ought not be degraded, demeaned, or devalued. The two feelings to which Kant directly appeals in his discussion of duties regarding animals and inanimate nature, i.e., love and sympathy, are "intimately" connected with the feelings on this list of moral endowments. At least for "animals endowed with reason," such as ourselves, love and sympathetic feeling are a necessary precondition for moral obligation.[45] These feelings of love and sympathy are not simply morally useful, as one means among others, or merely useful because of some highly contingent facts about human psychology; they may be "an essential part of the fulfillment of duty itself," at least for beings much like us.[46] They are feelings that we have a perfect duty to ourselves to preserve and neither denigrate nor demean, in addition to being feelings that we have an imperfect duty to ourselves to cultivate.

The second crucial point in Kant's case for this perfect duty to ourselves regarding animal cruelty is that, on Kant's account of the nature of animals, *animals by their nature properly engage our morally significant feelings*. An animal is not only a beautiful and teleologically organized creature but also a creature that can feel pleasure and pain, represent the world, have desires (including desires conducive to its self-preservation, reproduction, and enjoyment), and act upon those desires and "principles" analogous to ours. Such a creature is a psychologically proper object of our love and sympathy in ways that plants, machines, and crystal formations are not.[47] As Denis says, "many of our morally important sentiments do not discriminate between animals and humans," and, we might add, this is no accident or psychological quirk.[48] It is because of these genuine analogies between human and animal nature that "the ways that we treat animals reflect and affect morally important attitudes and feelings."[49] It is love and/or sympathy that we feel, or at least have a predisposition to feel, toward animals as well as human beings, and in many cases such feelings may be based upon the presence of some of the same, or closely analogous, features present in animals and humans. Animals, as well as humans, are properly the direct objects of these feelings. Unjustifiable cruelty to an animal, then, is a failure of love and sympathy to that animal; it is "hard-heartedness" and "small mindedness" (*Lectures on Ethics* 27: 460; *Lectures on Ethics* 27:710). [50]

Yet, on Kant's theory, failures of feeling—even failures of a morally significant feeling—toward an animal do not amount to the violation of any obligation *to* that animal.[51] Nor does the presence (or the propriety) of feelings of love or sympathy for animals, all by itself, provide a rule for action. No feeling, not even "moral feeling" itself, plays such a role in Kant's theory, and feelings of sympathetic love, even when directed at other humans, are neither an infallible guide to other's needs nor by themselves a rule for action (*Metaphysics of Morals*, 6:400; *Groundwork*, 4:398). So how does appeal to these morally significant feelings help to reveal a perfect duty to oneself regarding that animal? How exactly is this "hard-heartedness towards animals...not in accordance with the laws of reason"? (*Lectures on Ethics* 27:710) Kant says that "any action whereby we may torment animals, or let them suffer distress, or otherwise treat them without love, is demeaning to ourselves," (*Lectures on Ethics* 27:710). The violent or cruel treatment of animals (at least when unjustified) is incompatible with respect for ourselves, on his view, because it essentially involves the disregard, denial, or demeaning of these predispositions, feelings, and bonds that are integral to our own nature as moral animals. Choices that deny, avoid, trivialize, or cavalierly violate such bonds of love or sympathy (or the predispositions to such bonds) for animals express disrespect for ourselves. Animals ought not to be harmed or destroyed "without reason" (*Lectures on Ethics*, 27:459).

It is important to note how this core argument for duties regarding animals differs from the argument often attributed to Kant. It is often thought that Kant's only objection to animal cruelty focuses exclusively on the putative psychological effects of violence and cruelty toward animals: the effects on the human agent that perpetrates it, and especially the effects on other humans whom the agent may subsequently encounter and be more likely to mistreat.[52] Certainly Kant does endorse plausible empirical hypotheses about the harmful long-term effects of animal cruelty on the perpetrator and his fellow humans. Yet the "intimate opposition" of animal cruelty to one's duties to self is not reducible to the "brutalization argument," namely that those who are in the habit of treating animals cruelly will inevitably tend to treat humans cruelly. The long-term effects of animal cruelty, Kant believes, help to confirm both the range of objects of sympathy and love (including animals) and the general moral significance of those feelings, two of the crucial elements in the argument that we have a perfect duty to ourselves regarding animal cruelty. Of course the effects of cruelty do also suggest the more indirect "brutalization argument," which is vulnerable to two familiar objections—namely, that a single act of gratuitous cruelty may fail to have a discernable long-term impact and that the argument turns on merely contingent features of human psychology and so cannot ground a truly moral prohibition against animal cruelty. But Kant's core argument evades both of these objections: his focus is upon the immediate disregard for one's morally significant feelings and predispositions that is integral to the mistreatment of animals, even in isolated instances, and this element is independent of many human psychological contingencies.[53] Kant's deepest moral objection to animal cruelty is not simply that it increases the likelihood of other behavior that would be genuinely morally wrong.[54]

With respect to certain kinds of animals and to particular relationships to individual animals, Kant suggests a few additional conclusions. An animal's specific capacities, not just for experiencing pain but for excessive strain or for loyalty, may come into play, as may its individual history. The kinds of work to which an animal may permissibly be put should accord with its capacities; animals "should not be strained beyond their capacities" (*Metaphysics of Morals*, 6:443). Horses and dogs may provide service over many years, and dogs in particular may do so with particular loyalty and attachment to their master, as we have seen. Having done so, they must be rewarded with gratitude, "just as if they were members of the household"; "once the dog can serve no longer, [we] must look after him to the end" rather than "turn him out," starve him, or have him shot. Failure to do so reveals "a very small mind" and is contrary to one's humane or sympathetic feelings (*Metaphysics of Morals*, 6:443; *Lectures on Ethics*, 27:459, 27:710). A dog's capacities for particular kinds of feelings, desires, and attachments make it the proper object of greater love and sympathy than is appropriate to feel for a grub, and one's own dog's particular devotion makes its especially apt for a significant measure of one's love, sympathy, and gratitude.[55] One can imagine how Kant's analysis would entail similar, indeed stricter requirements for the treatment of elephants, given his understanding of their nature, especially their "analogy of morality."

Kant explicitly allows the killing of some animals "quickly (without pain)" and even some "agonizing physical experiments" for important human ends, though not for sport or pure speculation (*Metaphysics of Morals*, 6:443; *Lectures on Ethics*, 27:460). As with other perfect duties, what needs to be determined in each context is which courses of action or, better, which maxims of action are incompatible with respect for one's rational nature, in this case incompatible with one's moral self-preservation. Just as the permissible assumption of some risks to our own life and bodily integrity is compatible with the prohibition on suicide (and with proper regard for the inclination to self-preservation), so may some use, some killing, even some cruel treatment of animals for important human ends be permissible or even required.[56] In *The Metaphysics of Morals*, Kant intends to outline some first principles that provide a basic framework for such deliberations and determinations rather than to provide an algorithm or exhaustive treatment of examples. His principles may raise significant questions about a wide range of human conduct that affects nonhuman animals, from animal research to our eating and farming practices and some of our leisure activities; not just any human interest may justify the killing of or cruelty to an animal.[57] There are both general protections for all sentient creatures and various particular requirements regarding specific kinds of animals and specific kinds of human-animal relationships, requirements that depend significantly upon the nature of the animals in question.

An Eighteenth-Century Alternative

It is beyond the scope of this chapter to assess completely the philosophical adequacy of Kant's account of duties regarding animals, but consideration of an eighteenth-century alternative may shed additional light on his account.[58] Francis Hutcheson (1694–1746) was another important eighteenth-century philosopher who condemned animal cruelty. Hutcheson insisted, "These creatures [inferior animals] are capable of some happiness and misery; their sufferings naturally move our compassion; we approve relieving them in many cases, and must condemn all unnecessary cruelty toward them as shewing an inhuman temper" (*System*, II.vi, 311).[59]

Since Kant was quite familiar with Hutcheson's influential moral theory and was likely aware of some of Hutcheson's views about cruelty to animals, a brief comparison of their positions seems appropriate.[60]

Several points of similarity emerge quickly. Hutcheson and Kant agreed that animals can feel enjoyment and suffering. They also agreed that humans naturally and properly feel compassion and pity and other affections toward animals because of animals' capacity for enjoyment and suffering. (While neither provided an exhaustive account of the distinctive ways in which animals properly engage these feelings,

Hutcheson certainly theorized more about the human affections than did Kant.) Both also argued that our natural and proper affections toward nonhuman animals suggest an ethical prohibition on unnecessary cruelty to animals, a prohibition they agreed could be systematically defended. One thing about which Hutcheson and Kant disagreed was the nature of that defense.

Hutcheson famously argued that humans have a natural "moral sense" that approves of a range of benevolent affections, including our benevolent affections toward nonhuman animals.[61] In Hutcheson's ethical system, we do not properly judge actions or characters solely by the immediate outputs of our moral sense. Rather the moral sense leads us to judge in terms of a relation to the "general good" or the "common good" of the "well-ordered complex system" of creatures (*System* II.iii; II.vi). The most approved of affection is a "universal good-will to all" rather than any more narrow or "limited affections" toward particular individuals or groups (*System* I.iv.x). On Hutcheson's proto-Utilitarian version of natural law theory, "the grand aim of the law of nature is the general good of all."[62] "That action is best, which procures the greatest happiness for the greatest numbers; and that worst, which, in like manner, occasions misery" (*Inquiry* II.III.viii[63]). Since animals can suffer, Hutcheson contends, animals have interests, interests that are a part of the "common interest" within the system of creatures, and our reflection should help us to regulate our behavior regarding animals as part of the well-ordered complex system aimed at the common interest or greatest happiness. On Hutcheson's account, unnecessary cruel acts are wrong because they occasion misery that is unnecessary for and detracts from the general good; an "inhuman temper" disposed to such unnecessary cruel acts is condemned because of its opposition to the well-ordered system and its opposition to the benevolent affections that support that system. Of course several features of this account reflect an underlying approach to moral philosophy that Kant sharply criticized.[64] While adjudication of such deep disagreements in ethical theory between Hutcheson and Kant is beyond the scope of this chapter, we may still consider and evaluate three apparent differences between their competing accounts of the ethical treatment of animals.

First, Hutcheson famously claimed that, in virtue of their capacity to suffer, animals may have some rights:

> Brutes may very justly be said to have a right that no useless pain or misery should be inflicted on them. Men have intimations of this right, and of their own corresponding obligation, by their sense of pity. 'Tis plainly inhuman and immoral to create to brutes any useless torment, or to deprive them of any such natural enjoyments as do not interfere with the interests of men. (*System* II.vi.iii, 314)[65]

Hutcheson's assertion of animal rights may seem significantly more robust and more demanding than anything found in Kant's account, but this appearance deserves careful examination. On Hutcheson's account, rights result from relations of rightness and wrongness, understood in terms of the general good. One has a right if one would be (the) one who would suffer when something wrong is done, i.e., something that does not conduce to the greatest happiness of the greatest number. "Whatever one so possesses and enjoys in certain circumstances, that we would deem it a wrong action in any other to disturb or interrupt his possession, we say 'tis his right, or he has a right to enjoy and possess it" (*System* III.iii).[66] On this account of rights, a right to be free of useless torment will quickly follow, since animals have a capacity to suffer and some actions that cause animal suffering are not necessary for the "general good." This result, however, is primarily a function of Hutcheson's broad conception of rights rather than an indication of particularly robust claims about animals or heightened scrutiny of our treatment of them.[67]

Second, Hutcheson's assertion of animal rights may seem to suggest that his condemnation of cruelty to animals involves humans having obligations *to* animals, in the sense Kant himself rejected; but this is far from clear. Hutcheson's account of obligation in general, and of obligations regarding animals in particular, provides little support for such a contention. He had a very broad conception of obligation (just about any motive for a right action might establish an obligation; *Inquiry* II.vii.v; *System* II.iii.vi), and he had little interest, in general, in tying obligations or rights to some individual obligator or beneficiary for whose sake the obligation exists (*System* II.iv.iii).[68] More substantively, on Hutcheson's account, the right treatment of animals is ultimately dependent upon the overall "general good" rather than on the good of any particular animal or of animals in general; the well-being of particular animals, or of animals in general, is simply one, relatively minor component of the "general good."[69] While pity, including pity for animal suffering, is admirable and approved, the "most extensive" benevolence concerned with the general good is a higher motive that should regulate and take precedence over pity. So when it comes to behavior affecting animals, Hutcheson's virtuous agent performing obligatory actions may or may not have certain beneficiaries in view, and her sentiments, deserving of approbation, may range widely from the most approved "universal good-will to all" to the more narrow or "limited affections" toward particular individuals (*System* I.iv.x). It is not clear how this would amount to a duty to animals rather than a duty regarding animals.

Third, and perhaps most interesting, we might consider whether or how Hutcheson and Kant disagree about our proper attitude toward nonhuman animals. The idea that animals are the proper direct object of our love and sympathy is at least as central to Kant's account as it is to Hutcheson's. Kant insists that a self-respecting human being is directly concerned with the fate of animals: she takes animals as proper direct objects of her love and sympathy, and she acts in ways that preserve her own disposition to such love and sympathy. As we have seen, Hutcheson's virtuous agent may or may not have, or cultivate, certain "narrower" loves or sympathies, such as those toward animals in particular. Of course Kant does maintain that in addition to love or sympathy—which again, given the nature of animals, is properly directed at animals as well as human beings—there is also something more required by reason, namely *respect*, respect for rational beings. Kant denies that concern for nonhuman animals should take the form of respect for such animals. Yet it is not clear that respect, as Kant conceives of it, is a form of regard that Hutcheson requires of us toward anyone, much less toward animals. So this may not indicate a significant difference between Kant and Hutcheson about our proper attitudes toward animals.

While Kant avoided talk of animal rights, which can be found in Hutcheson, and while he denied that we have duties to animals, his account of our duties regarding animals, rooted in animals' natures and our proper feelings toward them, may be a worthy rival to Hutcheson's account.[70]

Reflection

THE GAZE OF THE APE: GABRIEL VON MAX'S *AFFENMALEREI* AND THE "QUESTION OF ALL QUESTIONS"

Cecilia Muratori

Why is it at all pleasurable to be in the company of animals such as dogs, monkeys, and cats? According to Schopenhauer, it is because of their "complete naïveté" that we find these creatures so amusing.[1] But the company of apes, in particular, must have been especially fascinating to Schopenhauer. He longed to see a living specimen of the great ape, and finally succeeded when a young orangutan was put on display at the 1856 autumn fair in Frankfurt am Main. Upon hearing that the same animal had then been sold and transferred to Leipzig, Schopenhauer was indignant to find out that an acquaintance of his had not seized on this chance to go and see the creature himself. "You must believe me, the orangutan recognizes in man his nobler brotherly relative," Schopenhauer is supposed to have exclaimed.[2] For Schopenhauer, it is in the eyes of the great ape that humankind finds its place in the order of nature: man recognizes his own humanity when the gaze of the great ape is directed at him, and therefore nothing can substitute for a real encounter with a living specimen.[3] More than in the case of any other animal, the company of apes is thus not only amusing but a truly eye-opening experience of philosophical and scientific depth.

The painter Gabriel von Max (1840–1915) shared Schopenhauer's fascination for apes, grounded at the intersection of philosophical speculation and scientific curiosity. Known as "the philosopher among painters,"[4] Max was interested in anatomy as well as in "spiritism" and mysticism. The subjects of his paintings testify to his continuous research in these areas, and they tend to intertwine especially when Max represents death scenes on his canvases: from the famous painting of Saint Julia on the cross (*Märtyrerin am Kreuz*, presented at the 1867 *exposition universelle* in Paris), to *The Anatomist* (*Der Anatom*), wherein an old scientist glances at the corpse of a young woman, whose white, luminous skin signals the fact that she has already transcended the realm of earthly life.

Both approaches—that of the natural sciences and that of "psychology" (a broad term encompassing the study of whatever transcends measurable phenomena)[5]—are, for Max, essential in order to answer the "question of all questions":[6] where man came from and where he is going.[7] His private collection was devoted to researching the origin of humankind through ethnography and anthropology. In fact it was so rich that a contemporary biographer wrote, "In his fine home in Munich he has everything he requires, and therefore he does not need to go out; only he is rarely absent from local classical concerts or where there is something new to hear or to see in the areas of physiology, psychology, as well as the natural sciences and ethnography."[8] Yet until the late 1860s something essential was missing from the painter's home: real, living apes.

For Max, understanding humanity and capturing it on canvas appears an impossible task without observing apes. Stuffed animals or bodies to dissect (which he had delivered for his anatomical studies) were no substitute for the encounter with live animals, and so for a few years in the early 1870s Max kept various ape specimens at home. The experiment proved particularly difficult, as observing animals required in the first instance learning how to care for them in a climate that was inhospitable to them. Observing the animals'

lives often gave way rather suddenly to witnessing their premature
deaths. Max's report on the death of a young capuchin monkey in
1871 displays a scientist's attention to detail together with the
doubts and sentiments arising from having lost an animal that
could almost be called a pet: the animal had been in good health
when Max brought him to Munich from Prague and had been keen
on playing "with anything, like a child." The cause of death might
have been the cold—and maybe feeding him too much milk?[9]

Max's changing relationship with apes is captured in
photographs that reveal the whole spectrum of the painter's
interests, mapping the story of his attempts at approaching these
animals, so mysteriously similar to humans. When the animals
died, he took photographs of the bodies and dissected them to
further his understanding.[10] Yet when after 1893 he moved to
Ambach with his second wife, Ernestine, they shared their home
with only a few monkeys—and, significantly, this time a few were
given names. A series of photographs portray him and his wife in
this private, homely setting with the capuchin monkey Pali: in the
garden, looking out of a window, eating together at the table.

Among Max's paintings the series of portraits of apes (so-called
Affenmalerei) plays a prominent role in his quest for an answer to
the "question of all questions" regarding the origin and future of
humanity, showing not only that animals are pivotal in this project
but that Max developed through painting his own original
approach. The anatomically accurate representation of the animals
contrasts with the ironic settings and titles of the compositions. For
example, one portrait of two monkeys tenderly embracing is titled
Abelard and Heloise. In contrast with the tragic love story of the
philosopher Abelard (1079–1142) and his student Heloise, Max's
two apes are united in a calm and secure embrace. But is the gaze
of the ape "Heloise" a statement about the love between the two
animals, like the paw of "Abelard" on her back, or is it simply a
contented look, whose motives remain inscrutable? Another

painting shows two monkeys looking inquisitively at what appears
to be a canvas, turned away from the curious observer, and bears the
title *The Art Critics: Two Monkeys Contemplate a Painting*. But are
they really assessing the quality of the painting or merely staring
at a piece of wood? Maybe they are interested in something
completely different, which the observer cannot even imagine. In
both cases the titles deliberately invite very specific interpretations,
painting the apes as if "in the place of humans."

The ironic setting brings into focus the originality of Max's
approach to understanding humanity in its relation to animals.
Irony is used as a powerful instrument to measure the distance
of humans from apes, considered from an evolutionary perspective
humanity's closest relative in the animal world,[11] but also
traditionally represented as the most ridiculous animal, mimicking
humans without understanding the meaning of the actions
performed.[12] The portraits of apes become Max's personal way of
filtering naturalistic observation through the lens of his personal
encounters with the animals.

This approach is illustrated very clearly in a painting entitled
Anthropological Lesson (1900), in which a young monkey stares up
at an adult one (the mother?) while keeping his paw on the leg of a
doll, which reclines between the legs of the adult (Fig. 8R1 in the
art insert). The title prompts a superficial interpretation: we see
two monkeys *as if* the older one were lecturing the younger
about human anatomy. Yet the fact that they are handling a doll
immediately suggests that, in fact, the animals are completely
unaware of anatomy and are possibly just entertaining themselves;
hence the irony of the title. The gaze of the adult monkey seems to
indicate that the animal is actually more concentrated on the action
it is performing with its free hand, namely scratching its own back.
The irony of the scene consists in this reversal: instead of humans
contemplating a monkey—a stuffed specimen or a skeleton—the
painting stages two monkeys holding a doll that represents the

human. The title raises a smile, until one discovers, at the left side of the painting, part of a chain that appears to be attached to the adult monkey (almost reminiscent of Pieter Bruegel's famous *Two Monkeys in Chains*). The animals could be prisoners after all, maybe kept by an eager scientist interested in comparative anatomy. The viewer thus becomes aware that the subject of the scene keeps sliding out of reach and is left at a loss about what it truly represents: animals playing mindlessly or a setting carefully designed by a human viewer, in which the animals are played with as puppets? The monkeys in the painting do not look at the viewer, and the ironic title points to an unbridgeable gap dividing the human viewer from the animal subject.

Max's portraits of apes deploy irony as a medium for staging the challenges of bringing together Darwinism and practical anatomical study with investigations into the territories of philosophy and psychology and, most important, with personal experiences of life with animals. Ultimately it is not the apes' knowledge of anatomy that is revealed to be limited but rather the human view of the world of animals, unmasking the humans' inability even to imagine what it is like to be an ape, despite scientific progress in biology and zoology. From this perspective, the paintings themselves track the artist's own attempts at penetrating the life of the apes, both as dead objects of study and as living creatures that shared with him the intimate space of a home.

Just like Schopenhauer, Max looked to the ape in order to see humanity's own nature, but in his case the ape does not seem to look back: the gazes do not meet, and man is left without that which Schopenhauer considered the most important experience in meeting the ape: the gaze of the ape upon him. A self-portrait from 1910 shows Max himself holding a small monkey in his arms: they both look away from the viewer and appear close to each other, the hand of the painter affectionately placed on the animal's back (Fig. 8R2 in the art insert).

CHAPTER NINE

The Emergence of the Drive Concept and the Collapse of the Animal/ Human Divide

Paul Katsafanas

In the late eighteenth and early nineteenth centuries, Kant, Hegel, and other philosophers draw a sharp distinction between the human and the animal. The human is self-conscious, the animal is not; the human has moral worth, the animal does not. By the mid- to late nineteenth century, these claims are widely rejected. As scientific and philosophical work on the cognitive and motivational capacities of animals increases in sophistication, many philosophers become suspicious of the idea that there is any divide between human beings and other animals. As Ludwig Büchner puts it in his 1855 best-seller *Force and Matter*, "The plant passes imperceptibly into the animal, the animal into man."[1] In this chapter I'll trace these transitions in eighteenth- and nineteenth-century thought about animals.

My focal point will be the notion of drive or instinct (*Trieb, Instinkt*). The term *Trieb*, and its cognate *Instinkt*, originally refers to any physical, biological, or psychological force that initiates motion. Thus, when it originates in the thirteenth century, the term *Trieb* can be used equally well to pick out the forces driving a herd of animals over a hill or the energy needed to begin the turning of a windmill. Although initially restricted to nonhuman animals and physical processes, by the sixteenth century drive is applied to forces that operate in human beings; Leibniz, for example, refers to the "flames of the divine will which give us a drive [*Trieb*] to do good."[2]

Although in sporadic usage during these centuries, the drive concept explodes in the eighteenth and nineteenth centuries. It begins playing central roles in three distinct areas: embryology, ethology, and metaphysics. In embryology drive describes a force, inaccessible in itself but whose results are visible and susceptible to scientific and philosophical study, governing organic development. In ethology drives are the sources of seemingly deliberate, highly articulated, yet nonconscious activities, which are directed at ends of which the animal is ignorant. In metaphysics drive describes the human essence.

Clearly the concept *Trieb* has a tangled history; it is initially astonishing that a single concept would play a role in each of these debates. It becomes still more surprising when we see how these debates influenced one another. The first three sections treat these three areas of thought in turn. I focus on the way the emergence of the drive concept in each of these three domains undermines the idea that there is any sharp distinction between the human and the animal. The fourth section considers how, in light the collapse of the human/animal divide, ethical theories are reshaped.

EMBRYOLOGY AND THE *BILDUNGSTRIEB*

During the eighteenth century a number of scientists, philosophers, and theologians engaged in a spirited debate over fetal development. The puzzle was this: animal fetuses seem to start out as largely undifferentiated masses which, in the course of development, gradually become ever more articulated. At the earliest stages we see merely a clump of cells; a bit later limbs seem to develop; later still we see the traces of organs; until at birth the organism is present in all its complexity. There are two ways this development might take place. First, the earliest stages of the fetus might lack various parts: the fetus might be an originally undifferentiated mass that is gradually articulated into organs and other parts. This option is termed *epigenesis*. Second, the earliest stages of the fetus might already contain, in miniature, all the organs and differentiation of the adult organism. We may not be able to see the organs, limbs, etc., but they are there. Gestation would then involve nothing more than growth. This option is called *preformationism*.

Although we now know that the first possibility, epigenesis, is the correct one, thinkers of the time hotly debated the two possibilities. They deployed not only empirical observations but also theological and philosophical considerations. One can see why epigenesis looks mysterious and engenders philosophical puzzles. How could a formless mass differentiate itself into a system of mutually interacting organs and tissues? Attempts to answer this question with the resources of eighteenth- and nineteenth-century science were far from convincing. For example, in *Theoria generationis* (1759), Caspar Friedrich Wolff argued in favor of epigenesis by positing a *vis essentialis*, an essential force, that drove the process. But this looks circular: it seems that he is simply stating that differentiation occurs because there is some unknown force that drives differentiation. The alternative possibility, that all the interacting and mutually dependent parts are already present in miniature, seemed to many a more sensible hypothesis.

This debate raged on for generations. I will focus on one moment: Johann Friedrich Blumenbach's (1752–1840) publication of *Über den Bildungstrieb* in 1781. This tract defends a version of epigenesis. In particular Blumenbach draws on empirical observations to defend the following conclusion:

There exists in all living creatures, from men to maggots and from cedar trees to mold, a particular inborn, life-long active drive. This drive initially bestows on creatures their form, and then preserves it, and, if they become injured, where possible restores their form. This is a drive... that is completely different from the other special forces of organized bodies in particular. It shows itself to be one of the first causes of all generation, nutrition, and reproduction.... I give it the name of *Bildungstrieb* (*Nisus formativus*).[3]

Blumenbach is positing a force that drives not just embryo development but the maintenance of animal form in general. For Blumenbach, paradigmatic instances of this self-maintenance include the hydra's ability to regenerate parts of its body and the human body's ability to heal wounds. The idea here is that animals have an observable tendency to generate and regenerate their bodies according to some "form" or blueprint of the animal.

Blumenbach calls this force the *Bildungstrieb*. It is a force that operates on originally undifferentiated material, endowing it with a form, and is likewise at home in developed animals, preserving and maintaining their forms. Note the connotations of the term: it is a *Trieb*, a force, and it is a force of *Bildung*—that notorious German word that can mean development or formation or education or cultivation. (The resonances of this word will be important in the *Bildungstrieb*'s reception by Goethe and others.)

Blumenbach is careful to emphasize the epistemic status of the *Bildungstrieb*. He claims that it is a force *whose cause is unknown but whose effects are perceptible*. He models it on Newtonian accounts of gravity: we can see *that* there is a force at work in the universe; we can name it "gravity"; and we can specify its effects. But we (at the time) cannot say what *causes* this force to be manifest. Just so, Blumenbach suggests, with the *Bildungstrieb*:

I hope it will be superfluous to remind most readers that the word *Bildungstrieb*, like the words attraction, gravity, etc., should serve, no more and no less, to signify a power whose constant effect is recognized from experience and whose cause, like the causes of the aforementioned and commonly recognized powers, is for us an occult quality. What Ovid said pertains to all of these forces—the cause is hidden, the force is well recognized.[4]

In sum, Blumenbach postulates a force, known by its effects, that gives rise to differentiation, development, and maintenance of form.

It is of tremendous consequence for philosophy that Kant was impressed by Blumenbach's work. He sends Blumenbach a letter praising his "excellent work on the *Bildungstrieb*," saying that through it he has seen how "you unite two principles—the physical-mechanical and the sheerly teleological mode of explanation of organized nature. These are modes which one would not have thought capable of being united."[5] Kant's thought is that nature must be understood mechanistically but that biology demands teleological explanations. Kant interprets Blumenbach's *Bildungstrieb* as a way of reconciling this conflict: we see that there is some causal principle at work in nature, a principle that generates what look to us like teleologically structured biological phenomena. We assume that these telic phenomena have some mechanistic ground, but we cannot understand what that ground is. Thus we use the *Bildungstrieb* as a regulative ideal. In other words, Kant suggests that we conduct biological explanations by positing, as a regulative idea, purposes in nature. (This differs from the way Blumenbach himself sees the *Bildungstrieb*; he treats it as a real force in nature, not simply a regulative ideal.)

From Kant the concept makes its way into the philosophical lexicon. Two features come to be emphasized. The first is the general idea that there are observable psychological or biological forces whose causes are unknown. The second is that there is some way of bridging the apparent divide between efficient causes and final causes. This second point seizes the philosophical imagination: we soon find philosophers who go beyond these points about efficient and final causes, claiming, more radically, that the drive concept unites necessity and

freedom. Witness Schelling, who writes, "For this unification of freedom and lawfulness we have no other concept than the concept of a
drive."[6] But that is to step ahead; let me dwell, for a moment, on another strand in the emergence of the drive concept.

Accounts of Animal and Human Behavior

The Traditional View

A separate debate, though again occupying a central role in philosophical, scientific, and theological thought: What happens when a nonhuman animal acts? In the eighteenth and early nineteenth centuries it is
common for philosophers and other thinkers to draw a sharp distinction
between free, rational human activity and necessitated, mechanistic
animal behavior. According to this picture, human beings are capable
of determining their actions via episodes of reflective, self-conscious
choice. Motives do not determine these choices: we have the capacity
to survey our motives, check them, and decide, freely and rationally,
which ones to act upon. This is how we differ from the other, less cognitively sophisticated animals: while "the brutes," as philosophers used
to call them, are directly actuated by stimuli, self-conscious creatures
can rise above their motives, reflect on them, and decide which ones to
act upon.

This is a model of agency with a very long history: we can see traces
of it in Plato's claim that reason can exert a controlling influence on
appetite and spirit (*Republic*); in Augustine's attempt to locate moral
responsibility in the will (*De Libero Arbitrio*); and in Aquinas's claim
that human beings have a capacity for "rational judgment," which
enables them to reflect upon and determine their own judgments,
whereas the other animals merely have "natural judgment," which is
determined by external factors (*De Veritate* 24.2). But it culminates,
perhaps, in Kant, who tells us that the will "can indeed be *affected* but
not *determined* by impulses. ... *Freedom* of choice is this independence

from being determined by sensible impulses" (*Metaphysics of Morals*, 6:213–14).[7] Elsewhere Kant writes that the will is "a faculty of determining oneself from oneself, independently of necessitation by sensible impulses" (*Critique of Pure Reason*, A534/B562),[8] and that "an incentive [or desire] can determine the will to its action *only insofar as the individual has taken it up into his maxim*" (*Religion within the Boundaries of Mere Reason*, 6.24).[9] In other words, self-conscious agents are capable of standing back from the workings of desire and choosing in a way that is not determined by any of them.[10]

The brutes, by contrast, are actuated in a far simpler fashion. The *mechanists*, following Descartes, argue that we can understand the animal as a purely mechanical system: animal actions are simply mechanical responses to predetermined stimuli:[11]

Now a very large number of the motions occurring inside us do not depend in any way upon the mind. These include heartbeat, digestion, nutrition, respiration when we are asleep, and also such waking actions as walking, singing, and the like, when these occur without the mind attending to them. When people take a fall and stick out their hands so as to protect their head, it is not reason that instructs them to do this; it is simply that the sign of the impending fall reaches the brain and sends the animal spirits into the nerves in the manner necessary to produce this movement even without any mental volition, just as it would be produced in a machine. And since our own experience reliably informs us that this is so, why should we be so amazed that the light reflected from the body of the wolf on to the eyes of a sheep should be equally capable of arousing the movements of flight in the sheep?...All actions of the brutes resemble only those which occur in us without any assistance from the mind.[12]

In this passage Descartes starts by noting that many human actions, such as the beating of a heart and one's hands flying in front of one's face as one stumbles, are explicable as mere mechanisms that involve no mental activity whatsoever. In the final lines he suggests that all animal actions fall into this camp. And again in the *Treatise on Man*, Descartes writes that, in the animal, functions such as sense-perception, "internal movements of the appetites and passions, and finally the external movements of all the limbs...follow from the mere arrangement of the machine's organs every bit as naturally as the movement of a clock or other automaton follow from the arrangement of its counterweights and wheels."[13]

This Cartesian picture enables a sharp divide between human and animal actions: *our* actions are genuinely goal-directed, and are—or can be—products of self-conscious thought. But the brutes are different: their actions are explicable in terms of efficient causation alone; moreover they experience no genuine thought, no genuine emotion. What appears, in them, to be goal direction is exactly analogous to what happens in the clock: mechanical processes involving nothing more than efficient causation yield fixed behavior with law-like regularity.

Elements of the Cartesian theory are controversial, with many thinkers claiming that animals experience feelings and emotions. For example, Hume claims that animals experience sophisticated emotions such as sympathy (*Treatise*, 2.2.12), and Kant allows that animals have a "faculty of desire" and experience pleasure and displeasure (*Metaphysics of Morals*, 6:211). But the general picture according to which there are two classes of behavior—animal behavior and human behavior, necessitated behavior and free activity, behavior understood in terms of efficient causation alone and behavior understood in terms of final causes—has a long and distinguished history.

It's easy to see why we'd be tempted in this direction. Attributing genuine goal direction and conscious thought to the bird or the fish seems unnecessary in order to account for their behavior. Moreover it's difficult to imagine that the bird or the fish reflectively surveys its actions and decides which one to perform. So if there are only two choices—fully reflective rational deliberation or blind mechanism— we slot the animal actions into the mechanistic camp.[14]

In the nineteenth century this tendency dissipates. It becomes increasingly common to claim that there is no essential difference between human and animal activity. Thus in the *Descent of Man*, Darwin writes:

If no organic being except man had possessed any mental power, or if his powers had been of a wholly different nature from those of the lower animals, then we should never have been able to convince ourselves that our high faculties had been gradually developed. But it can be clearly shown that there is no fundamental difference of this kind. We must admit that there is a much wider interval in mental powers between one of the lowest fishes, as a lamprey or a lancet, and one of the higher apes, than between an ape and man; yet this immense interval is filled with numberless gradations.[15]

How do we get from Descartes's sharp distinction to Darwin gradations? At least part of the path is that made available by the drive concept.

Introduction of a Third Category of Behavior

If there were only two options—if action had to be either purely mechanistic or fully free and self-conscious—then we'd be tempted to put animal activity in the former camp and human activity in the latter. But something interesting happens in the eighteenth and nineteenth centuries. Ethologists introduce a third, intermediary category of behavior: the *instinctive*. This is something that is neither purely mechanical, because it involves thought or sensation and direction toward some definite end, nor purely conscious, because it is performed without awareness of its ultimate end. Once this third category is introduced, it is seen that it is present in humans; then the human/animal divide begins to look less sharp. Let me explain.

Studies of animal behavior in the eighteenth and nineteenth centuries begin to call the traditional picture into question. Set aside simple and immediate cases of action, such as the dog snarling at its enemy or the cat drinking milk. Consider, instead, extended episodes of behavior. What comes to fascinate thinkers of this time is that animals perform some highly complex behaviors that are directed not only at proximate goals but also at distal goals; moreover they often perform these complex behaviors without seeming to have learned how to do so. Simple examples include the spider weaving its web and the caterpillar producing its cocoon. What's common to all of these cases is a complex, unlearned system of behavior directed at an end. Crucially, knowledge of the action's end does not appear to be necessary. Let me give just one example: Henry Lord Brougham discusses a species of solitary wasp that gathers grubs and stores them beside its eggs, then departs before the eggs hatch. The grubs serve as food for the larvae that will hatch from the eggs, but the wasp cannot possibly know this. For "this wasp never saw an egg produce a worm [i.e., a larva]—nor ever saw a worm—nay, is to be dead long before the worm can be in existence—and moreover she never has in any way tasted or used these grubs, or used the hole she made, except for the prospective benefit of the unknown worm she will never see."[16]

These are the sorts of actions that occupy center stage in the eighteenth- and nineteenth-century discussions of ethology. A term is introduced. Call *instinctive* actions those behaviors that are complex, directed at a distal goal, and done without learning. As Darwin writes:

> An action, which we ourselves require experience to enable us to perform, when performed by an animal, more especially by a very young one, without experience, and when performed by many individuals in the same way, without their knowing for what purpose it is performed, is usually said to be instinctive.[17]

How are we to account for instinctive activity, so described? A common view is that we cannot reduce instinctive activity to mechanistic activity, nor can we treat it as conscious activity. We need a third, intermediary category. Thus in an 1885 issue of the *Fortnightly Review* the prominent English biologist St. George Mivart heaps effusive praise on Schelling's "affirmation that the phenomena of instinct are some of the most important of all phenomena, and capable of serving as a very touchstone whereby the value of competing theories of the universe may ultimately be tested."[18] For, the author claims, "the real existence of such a thing as 'instinct' must necessarily be fatal" to mechanistic explanations of the universe. Mivart allows that reflex actions, such as respiration and digestion, are explicable purely mechanically.[19] Instinctive actions, though, "hold a middle place between (1) those which are rational, or truly intelligent, and (2) those in which sensation has no place."[20] They are "neither due to mechanical or chemical causes, nor to intelligence, experience, or will."[21]

I think we can see well enough why mechanistic explanations of instinct seem problematic: it's hard to envision what the mechanistic processes driving complex, temporally extended, goal-directed courses of activity would be. It's also easy to see why instinctive activities can't be treated as fully conscious activities: while we might say that these actions involve awareness of certain proximate goals, the organism has no awareness of the distal goal that is served by these proximate ones. The wasp may know that it is collecting grubs and so on, but it cannot know that it is storing these grubs near its eggs so that the larvae that it will never see will have a nourishing meal. Moreover the entire stretch of activity is unlearned yet performed perfectly the first time it is done. Conscious direction can't be required here.

So what form of awareness and sensation is thought to be present in these instinctive actions? The idea is that instincts involve motivation via sensation or feeling: "Instinct is a certain felt internal stimulus to definite actions which has its foundation in a certain sense of want, but is not a definite feeling of want of the particular end to be attained. Were that recognized, it would not be *instinct*, but *desire*."[22] The animal desires some series of proximate ends without seeing how attainment of these ends serves a distal goal. Consider two examples. William James writes:

We may conclude that, to the animal which obeys it, every impulse and every step of every instinct shines with its own sufficient light.... What voluptuous thrill may not shake a fly, when she at last discovers the one particular leaf, or carrion, or bit of dung, that out of all the world can stimulate her ovipositor to its discharge? Does not the discharge seem to her the only fitting thing? And need she care or know anything about the future maggot and its food?[23]

Or, to choose an earlier and quite influential example: Georg Heinrich Schneider, in *Der Thierische Wille* (1880), writes that "it might easily appear" that the cuckoo "acted with full consciousness of the purpose" when it laid its eggs in another bird's nest. But no, "the cuckoo is simply excited by the perception of quite determinate sorts of nest, which already contain eggs, to drop her own into them, and throw the others out, because this perception is a direct stimulus to these acts. It is impossible that she should have any notion of the other bird coming and sitting on her egg."[24] The fly experiences a voluptuous thrill in the presence of a bit of dung; the cuckoo is excited by the perception of a certain kind of nest. These creatures do not know *why* they are excited or attracted to certain courses of action, but we, the external observers, can see that their attraction to these actions serves some distant goal.

Degrees of Sensation and Thought

Can we be more precise about what types of awareness, affect, and sensation are present in instinctive actions? Early thinkers tend to equate instinctive activity with blind, unthinking movement. Take Thomas Reid: instinct is "a natural blind impulse to certain actions, without having any end in view; without any deliberation and often without any conception of what they do."[25] But this belief fades, and a consensus gradually emerges that instinctive activities involve cognition and affect. Condillac (1714–80) and Erasmus Darwin (1731–1802) endorse this position, arguing that animal and human behavior involved some form of reason and sensation. But the position emerges most clearly in two thinkers who are initially unaware of each other's work: Schneider and Herbert Spencer.

Schneider, whose *Thierische Wille* I mentioned earlier, argues that drive-motivated actions involve some awareness and are performed under the pressure of some feeling or urge; his discussion of the cuckoo's urge to lay eggs in certain nests is meant as an example of this. His book offers a sustained defense of this idea. He proceeds by surveying a wide range of animal actions and offering a systematization of them. For example, he classifies feelings as produced in one of four ways: they are dependent on and activated by either sensation, perception, ideas (i.e., representations of one's sensations or perceptions), or judgments. Impulses or motives can be classified in an analogous fourfold category.[26] Using these distinctions, Schneider argues that instinctive activities always involve feeling, and sometimes involve memory, ideas, and conscious purposes. Humans and animals differ only in what sparks their feelings: in the simplest animals, feelings are simply caused mechanistically, without any mental antecedents; in somewhat more complex animals, perceptual states can lead to motivation; in more complex ones, "ideas" or representations of perceptions can motivate; and in still more complex ones, including perhaps only humans, thoughts can engender motivations. So the Cartesian view that we have either pure mechanism or fully fledged rational thought is rejected: all instinctive actions involve genuinely mental phenomena, though the types of mental phenomena involved do differ across species of animal and types of action.

Spencer defends an analogous account, arguing that instincts in "inferior creatures" are automatic, in the sense that Reid and others describe. However, this automatism ceases to be blind in more complex creatures.[27] He writes, "In its higher forms, Instinct is probably accompanied by a rudimentary consciousness. There cannot be co-ordination of many stimuli without some ganglion through which they are all brought into relation.... The implication is that as fast as Instinct is developed, some kind of consciousness becomes nascent."[28] His claim is that complex instincts involve the coordination of a range of factors, and this requires consciousness:

> Further, the instinctive actions are more removed from the actions of simple bodily life in this, that they answer to external phenomena which are more complex and more special. While the purely physical processes going on throughout the organism respond to those most general relations common to the environment as a whole; while the simple reflex actions respond to some of the general relations common to the individual objects it contains; these compound reflex actions which we class as instincts, respond to those more involved relations which characterize certain orders of objects and actions as distinguished from others. Greater differentiation of the psychical life from the physical life is thus shown in several ways—in the growing distinction between the action of the vegetative and animal systems; in the increasing seriality of the changes in the animal system; in the consequent rise of incipient consciousness; and in the higher speciality of the outer relations to which inner relations are adjusted: which last is indeed the essence of the advance, to which the others are necessary accompaniments.[29]

When he claims that purely physical actions respond to the "most general" relations, Spencer has in mind tropisms, such as the plant's turning toward the sun. Reflex actions respond to somewhat less general relations: Spencer mentions polyps that withdraw or contract when they receive any tactile sensation.[30] He then asks us to consider polyps that withdraw to different degrees when a different tactile or visual sensation occurs, and then motile aquatic organisms, which respond in more complex ways to different visual and tactile sensations. Spencer interprets these instincts as responsive to less general, more particular occurrences. Crudely put, the polyp responds to all movements in the same way; the fish responds differently to movements of different types, movements in different directions, movements of different speeds, and so on.[31] As the organism becomes responsive to more particular and complex characteristics, Spencer reasons, it will need increasingly sophisticated forms of consciousness.

There are two reasons why increasing complexity puts increasing demands upon consciousness. First, the organism will need some way of processing an increasing number of variables. Consider the difference between a simple physiological process such as contracting in the same way when any tactile stimulation occurs and more complex processes that require tracking and coordinating data from distinct sensory modalities. Second, as the characteristics tracked by instinctive actions become more complex, Spencer argues that the connection between the characteristics and the actions will loosen:

> If, as the instincts rise higher and higher, they come to include psychical changes that are less and less coherent with their fundamental ones; there must arrive a time when the co-ordination is no longer perfectly regular. If these compound reflex actions, as they grow more compound, also become less decided; it follows that they will eventually become comparatively undecided. They will begin to lose their distinctly automatic character. That which we call Instinct will merge into something higher.[32]

His idea is something like this: If instinctive action A arises from a conjunction of stimuli B, C, D, E, F, G, then these stimuli will occur together less frequently, and when they do occur they may be mixed with stimuli that initiate alternative actions. Thus action A will follow less directly from the presence of the stimuli; the action will become less automatic. When the instinctive action becomes highly complex, rational action arises: "rational action arises out of instinctive action when this grows too complex to be perfectly automatic."[33] The complex sets of stimuli no longer pick out just one action. So some further factor is needed to determine the animal's action. In these cases memory and reason will be deployed: an executive faculty will play a role in determining which action is performed, and it will base its decisions in part on accumulated past experiences. Thus "that progressive complication of the instincts, which, as we have found, involves a progressive diminution of their purely automatic character, likewise involves a simultaneous commencement of Memory and Reason."[34]

Though the details need not detain us, we can see that Spencer is making several claims. First, there is a continuum from purely physical or mechanical processes to reflexes to instincts to rational action. Second, as we progress across this continuum, the complexity of the stimuli increases, and with it the demands placed upon cognition and memory; so too, as we progress across this spectrum, the connection between the occurrence of the stimuli and the performance of the action weakens. What looked like a sharp divide between the mechanistically explicable, fully determinate actions of animals and the reflective, reasoned actions of human beings has collapsed. As Spencer puts it, "The commonly-assumed hiatus between Reason and Instinct has no existence.... The highest forms of psychical activity arise little by little out of the lowest, and cannot be definitely separated from them."[35]

In sum, Spencer, Schneider, and other thinkers put a great deal of pressure on the metaphysical and psychological distinctions between human and animal.[36] To be sure, some thinkers do try to preserve the old regime, treating instinctive actions as explicable in purely mechanistic terms and human actions as involving something more. However, the dominant view has shifted. As Büchner puts it, "The animal also possesses an *ego* and self-consciousness; but nobody is inclined to consider this consciousness as something absolute or divine."[37] What was, in Kant's day, good common sense has fallen into disrepute.

Drives and the Obscurity of Human Action

To summarize: The venerable dichotomy between necessitated, mechanistic animal behavior and free, conscious human behavior is complicated by the introduction of a third, apparently intermediary category, instinctive behavior. Instinctive actions share features with each of the others: like mechanical actions, they do not involve conscious direction; like conscious actions, they involve some awareness, sensation, and thought.

These debates on drives are interesting in their own right, for they begin to collapse the human/animal distinction as well as the self-conscious/non-self-conscious distinction. In addition they bring to the fore a neglected possibility for human action: for humans and animals alike, there can be highly complex behavior that requires affective and cognitive monitoring of unfolding patterns of activity yet does not require that the agent be aware of the end toward which this behavior is directed. This is different from the stock examples of, e.g., submerged selfishness that have occupied philosophers since antiquity. It's easy to see how human behavior might present itself as selfless while actually being selfish. It's harder to imagine the agent's many particular goals as subserving some larger end of which he is ignorant. But this is just the possibility for which thinkers of the time emphatically argue. Schneider, for example, argues that every case of human action is instinctive, in the sense that instincts prompt us to act without representing the ultimate goal of our action. In particular Schneider claims that the one end common to every human action is preservation of the species. However, we rarely represent this goal within consciousness.

Schopenhauer makes a similar point, arguing that drives operate by generating illusions or delusions that tempt the agent to pursue their ends. Schopenhauer thinks that sexual love is among the strongest and most pervasive of our drives: "It is the ultimate goal of almost all human effort."[38] However, he claims that we misunderstand the nature of this drive. The drive that is responsible for our experience of love does not aim at love but rather at sexual or reproductive activity. As he puts it, "The true end of the whole love-story, though the parties concerned are unaware of it, is that this particular child may be begotten."[39] Of course we do not experience love as geared solely toward reproduction. Indeed many individuals who are in love, and who engage in sexual activity, desire not to reproduce. As Schopenhauer puts it, these individuals "abhor... and would like to prevent the end, procreation, which alone guides" the drive.[40] Schopenhauer explains that the drive operates by occluding its aim: "The sexual impulse, though in itself a subjective need, knows how to assume very skillfully the mask of objective admiration, and thus to deceive consciousness; for nature requires this stratagem in order to attain her ends."[41] In other words, the reproductive drive *disguises* its true aim. "However objective and touched with the sublime that admiration may appear to be,"[42] what is really aimed at is reproduction. This is a general feature of drives: they operate by structuring the organism's thought, emotion, and perception so that the organism is motivated to pursue the drive's aim, all the while failing to see exactly what that aim is. "Here, then, as in the case of all drive, truth assumes the form of a delusion, in order to act on the will."[43]

Just as many animals are aware of proximate goals without seeing that they serve distal goals, so too with human beings. And this leads us into another area in which the drive concept upsets traditional debates. Below I'll consider how the drive concept disrupts the idea that consciousness is an essential aspect of human nature. If something like Schopenhauer's view is right, we have grounds for thinking that consciousness is not our essential nature, and thus that the thing which seemed to mark us off most clearly from other animals is, in fact, less important than we thought. Indeed we find thinkers—including Schopenhauer, Nietzsche, and Hartmann—arguing that rather than being our essence, consciousness is something that corrupts us, that brings us further from our animal nature.

METAPHYSICAL CLAIMS ABOUT HUMAN AND ANIMAL ESSENCE

In embryology the drive is the life force, the mysterious but observable force powering organic development and self-maintenance; in ethology the drive is the source of instinctive action, action that is directed toward goals the organism may never know, action that arises from teleologically organized patterns of affect and sensation. These ideas are philosophically redolent, and it is not long before they are explored and extended.

The emergence of the drive concept allows us to see animal and human action as different in degree rather than kind: animals too are directed toward ends, experience sensations and feelings, and, more generally, differ from mere mechanisms like clocks and bells. But just as the animal is thereby being brought closer to the human, the human is being brought closer to the animal. For another, closely related debate centers on animal and human essence.

Traditional Views of the Human Essence

Consider, again, a traditional view: the essence of the human being is consciousness or conscious activity. Descartes, who claims that there cannot "be any thought in us of which...we are not conscious," argues that conscious thinking is our "whole essence or nature."[44] Analogously Locke claims that consciousness determines our identity: "Consciousness always accompanies thinking, and it is that which makes every one to be what he calls self, and thereby distinguishes himself from all other things."[45] Others go still further. Kant treats consciousness not only as an essential attribute of human beings but also as conferring a special status on us:

> The fact that the human being can have the "I" in his representations [i.e., is self-conscious] raises him infinitely above all other living beings on earth. Because of this he is a *person*...i.e., through rank and dignity an entirely different being from *things*, such as irrational animals, with which one can do as one likes.[46]

And Hegel gives consciousness a still grander role: "The whole history of the world...seems to have reached its goal, when this absolute self-consciousness, which it had the work of representing, ceased to be

alien, and when spirit accordingly is realized as spirit."[47] World history
reaches its apogee with the emergence of self-conscious creatures who
self-consciously recognize the nature of self-consciousness. And, in
many of these thinkers, this metaphysical distinction underwrites a
moral distinction:

> Beings the existence of which rests not on our will but on nature, if
> they are beings without reason, have only a relative worth, as means,
> and are therefore called things, whereas rational beings are called
> persons because their nature already marks them out as an end in
> itself, that is, as something that may not be used merely as a means.[48]

Animals, lacking self-consciousness, are distinct from us, and this distinction makes a moral difference: animals can be treated as mere
means. But can this distinction be maintained?

Drive as Our Essence

With the emergence of the drive concept, thinkers begin denying that
self-consciousness is our essential nature. I'll focus on Fichte and
Schiller. These thinkers treat drive as a simple, essential force giving
rise to all human activity and as the locus of our essential self. Understanding drives is the key to understanding human nature and living
authentically.

By the turn of the nineteenth century, *Trieb* has begun to refer to an
internal force that organizes mental and physical processes. It is something that is inaccessible to us: as Blumenbach emphasized, we can see
the effects but not the cause. This idea is taken further by Fichte, who
at once associates the drive with our true self and simultaneously questions whether this self is comprehensible: "My nature is drive. How is
it even possible to comprehend a drive as such? That is to say, what
mediates such an act of thinking of a drive in beings such as we are,

beings who think only discursively and by means of mediation?"⁴⁹
Fichte's concern is not just, with Blumenbach, that we can see the effects but haven't yet discovered the cause. His worry is deeper:

> The kind of thinking that is at issue here can be made very clear by
> contrasting it with the opposite kind of thinking. Anything that
> lies in a series of causes and effects is something I can easily compre-
> hend in accordance with the law of the mechanism of nature. Every
> member of such a series has its activity communicated to it by an-
> other member outside itself, and it directs its activity to a third
> member outside itself. In such a series a quantum of force is simply
> transferred from one member to the next and proceeds, as it were,
> through the entire series. One never learns where this force comes
> from, since one is forced to ascend further with every member of
> the series and never arrives at an original force. The activity and the
> passivity of each member in this series is thought by means of this
> force that runs through the [entire] series.—A drive cannot be
> comprehended in this manner, and thus it cannot by any means be
> thought of as a member of such a series. If one assumes that some
> external cause acts on the substrate of the drive, then there would
> also arise an efficacious action, directed to some third thing, lying
> outside [this substrate, i.e., lying outside the I]. Or if the cause in
> question does not have any power over the substrate of the drive,
> then nothing at all would come about. A drive, therefore, is some-
> thing that neither comes from outside nor is directed outside; it is
> an inner force of the substrate, directed upon itself. The concept by
> means of which the drive can be thought is the concept of self-
> determination.⁵⁰

So a drive is a force, whose origins cannot be understood by positing
further causes. A drive cannot be thought through the concept of cause
and effect; it demands to be thought of as freedom or self-determination.

It is sheer activity, inexplicable in causal terms. And this activity is also my essential nature:

> My nature, therefore, insofar as it is supposed to consist in a drive, is thought of as determining itself through itself, for this is the only way that a drive can be comprehended. From the viewpoint of the ordinary understanding, however, the very existence of a drive is nothing more than a fact of consciousness, and ordinary understanding does not extend beyond the facts of consciousness. Only the transcendental philosopher goes beyond this fact, and he does so in order to specify the ground on this fact.[51]

Drives are the most basic or fundamental *sources of activity*. As Fichte puts it in another passage, "The being of the I is absolute activity and nothing but activity; but activity, taken objectively, is *drive*."[52]

Drive is pure activity or freedom. But the philosophical work on drives does not end there: many of the early Romantics associate drives with *Bildung*—that is, with self-formation or self-cultivation. I'll focus on Schiller.

His model of human agency begins by accepting the Kantian distinction between reason and sensibility. In Schiller's terminology, we are moved by two apparently opposed drives: the sense drive and the form drive. The sense drive

> issues from the physical existence of man, or from sensuous nature; and it is this drive which tends to enclose him in the limits of time, and to make of him a material being.... This drive extends its domains over the entire sphere of the finite in man, and as form is only revealed in matter.... It binds down to the world of sense by indestructible ties the spirit that tends higher, and it calls back to the limits of the present, abstraction which had its free development in the sphere of the infinite. No doubt, thought can escape it for a moment, and a firm will victoriously resist its exigencies: but soon compressed nature resumes

her rights to give an imperious reality to our existence, to give it contents, substance, knowledge, and an aim for our activity.[53]

The sense drive disposes us toward the physical, the sensory, the particular, and the limited. The form drive, by contrast, arises "from [human beings'] rational nature, and tends to set free, and bring harmony into the diversity of its manifestations, and to maintain personality notwithstanding all the changes of state."[54] It is concerned with the universal and timeless, and thus

it suppresses time and change. It wishes the real to be necessary and eternal, and it wishes the eternal and the necessary to be real; in other terms, it tends to truth and justice. If the sensuous instinct only produces accidents, the formal instinct gives laws, laws for every judgment when it is a question of knowledge, laws for every will when it is a question of action.[55]

Setting aside many complexities, we can say that the form drive motivates the rational appreciation of universals, whereas the sense drive motivates the engagement with particulars. These drives jointly constitute our essence: they are the most fundamental sources of human activity. And it appears to be an essence in conflict with itself, riven by two opposed drives. As Schiller puts it:

One [drive] having for its object change, the other immutability, and yet it is these two notions that exhaust the notion of humanity, and a third fundamental impulsion, holding a medium between them, is quite inconceivable. How then shall we re-establish the unity of human nature, a unity that appears completely destroyed by this primitive and radical opposition?[56]

His answer is *Bildung:* we seek a form of sublimation, which is to be achieved through culture. Suppose the drives could be combined in a harmonious project, each enjoying its full expression through the other:

> We have been brought to the idea of such a correlation between the two drives that the action of the one establishes and limits at the same time the action of the other, and that each of them, taken in isolation, does arrive at its highest manifestation just because the other is active.... But if there were cases in which he could have at once this twofold experience in which he would have the consciousness of his freedom and the feeling of his existence together, in which he would simultaneously feel as matter and know himself as spirit, in such cases, and in such only, would he have a complete intuition of his humanity, and the object that would procure him this intuition would be a symbol of his accomplished destiny and consequently serve to express the infinite to him—since this destination can only be fulfilled in the fulness of time. Presuming that cases of this kind could present themselves in experience, they would awake in him a new drive, which, precisely because the other two drives would co-operate in it, would be opposed to each of them taken in isolation, and might, with good grounds, be taken for a new drive.[57]

The individual can aspire to perform actions that combine the highest manifestations of the two drives: each drive feels itself at once redirected and given fullest expression by the other. And by doing so the agent would be creating or awakening a new drive, the play drive: "The sensuous drive wishes to be determined, it wishes to receive an object; the formal drive wishes to determine itself, it wishes to produce an object. Therefore the drive of play (*Spieltrieb*) will endeavor to receive as it would itself have produced, and to produce as it aspires to receive."[58] Though Schiller's reflections on play are at once nuanced and obscure, the core idea is easily articulated: in free play we combine spontaneous conformity to rules or laws with sensuous engagement with particulars. We are constrained but see this constraint as wholly self-imposed. We have, in Schiller's nice description, both grace and dignity (*Anmut und Würde*).

But how is this union between the drives to be attained? Through *culture*:

> The office of culture is to watch over them [the sense and form drives] and to secure to each one its proper limits; therefore culture has to give equal justice to both, and to defend not only the rational drive against the sensuous, but also the latter against the former. Hence she has to act a twofold part: first, to protect sense against the attacks of freedom; secondly, to secure personality against the power of sensations. One of these ends is attained by the cultivation of the sensuous, the other by that of reason.[59]

The conflict of the drives motivates sublimation, which is attained through culture. If this sublimation could be attained, we would enjoy an authentic experience of ourselves, having a "complete intuition of [our] humanity." Understanding and redirecting the drives becomes the key to fully expressing human nature.

DRIVES AND ETHICS

The drive concept, as it emerges from discussions of embryology and ethology, and as it is complicated by Fichte and the Romantics, becomes oddly multivalent. Consider the meanings the term has acquired in the course of two centuries. In its humble beginnings drive is simply the energy producing some mechanical effect, as in windmills. Not so by the end of the nineteenth century. We have, first, the idea that there is a force, whose causes are unknown, that manifests itself by driving differentiation and development of organic forms. Second, there are highly complex purposive activities that proceed without conscious direction but involve some form of thought or sensation;

these are described in terms of drives. Moreover we have the idea that there may be a singular source of all activity. Not only that: drive may be inaccessible to us, articulable only in confused or distorting forms. For the drive is sheer activity, which cannot be grasped in familiar causal terms. Nonetheless the drive is our essence. And not just ours: these tendencies are taken to pervade all life. The forces driving us, the forces shaping our essence, are at work throughout the organic kingdom. Thus Goethe, having read Blumenbach, begins using the term *Bildungstrieb* in the mid-1780s. In Goethe the *Bildungstrieb* is a source of all organic activity, but is especially manifest in creative activity; it is inaccessible to or distorted by reflection. As a source of active development, the drive pervades nature, from its depths to its heights.

We've seen numerous ways in which the introduction of the drive concept collapses traditional distinctions between the human and the animal. Before closing, I want to turn, briefly, to the way the undermining of psychological and metaphysical distinctions between the human and the animal leads, in some thinkers, to a reassessment of ethical theories.

First, the idea that animals are fundamentally different from us leads us to think that we can treat them as we see fit. Contrasting Kant and Schopenhauer is a good way of seeing how, once the human/animal divide is abandoned, ethics is rethought. Kant claims that animals "will have no general cognition through reflection, no identity of the representations, also no connections of the representations according to subject and predicate, according to ground and consequence, according to the whole and according to the parts; for these are all consequences of the consciousness which animals lack."[60] In short, animals lack self-consciousness. Kant takes this to entail that we can have no duties to animals: "As far as reason alone can judge, a human being has duties only to human beings (himself and others), since his duty to any subject is moral constraint by that subject's will.... A human being can therefore have no duty to any beings other than human beings."[61] Schopenhauer agrees with Kant that human beings alone enjoy self-consciousness (or, as Schopenhauer puts it, human beings alone have Reason). However, we share a common essence with other living creatures. Our essential nature is not consciousness but *will*: "Consciousness is conditioned by the intellect, and the intellect is a mere *accidens* [accidental property] of our being."[62] He continues, "In all animal beings the *will* is the primary and substantial thing; the *intellect*, on the other hand, is something secondary and additional."[63] But what is the will? It is simply striving, directed at nothing in particular: "The will, considered purely in itself, is devoid of knowledge, and is only a blind, irresistible urge."[64] The will manifests itself in particular drives, such as the sex drive. This is common to both humans and animals.

Given this shared essential nature, Schopenhauer argues that there are no sharp ethical distinctions between treatment of animals and treatment of other human beings. In *On the Basis of Morality* (1840), Schopenhauer strongly condemns Kant for his claim that animals need not be treated as ends: "'There are no duties toward animals' is, frankly, a revolting crudity and barbarism of the West.... It rests on the assumption, despite all evidence to the contrary, of the radical difference between man and beast."[65] Schopenhauer traces this Kantian view to Christian assumptions about humanity's dominion over animals:

> Christian morals has no regard for animals, so in philosophical morals animals are at once fair game, just "things," just *means* to favored ends, thus something for vivisection, for deer-stalking, bullfighting, horse-races, whipping to death as they struggle with heavy quarry carts, etc.—Shame on such a morality...which fails to recognize the eternal essence which exists in every living being and shines forth with inscrutable significance from all eyes that see the sun![66]

Schopenhauer recommends that we alleviate suffering in man and animal alike. He argues that "he who is cruel to animals cannot be a good man,"[67] and writes, "I know of no more beautiful prayer than that with which ancient Indian dramas ended....It was: 'May all living beings be delivered from suffering!'"[68]

Schopenhauer does recognize some reasons for prioritizing humans:

> *Goodness of heart* consists in the deeply felt, universal compassion for all living beings, and especially for man; because responsiveness to suffering keeps in step with increase in intelligence; hence, the countless intellectual and physical sufferings of human beings have a much stronger claim to compassion than the pain of animals, which is only physical, and thus less acute.[69]

Human beings are, supposedly, more susceptible to pain, and hence more in need of compassion. But this is a matter of degree.

So the first point is that if humans and animals have a shared nature, the default ethical assumption shifts: rather than starting with the idea that different ethical demands will apply to humans and animals, we see the ethical claims as applying to both in the same way. There is also a second and more complex point, which I can only sketch here: for Kant and other proponents of the idea that self-consciousness is humanity's essential feature, it's tempting to think that an ethic governing human beings should focus on the operations of self-conscious thought. But if something like Schopenhauer's view is correct—if our essential nature is drive, and if these drives direct us at ends of which we are largely ignorant—then it will seem superficial to focus on conscious phenomena. These conscious phenomena are seen as the product of something deeper: the drives. Thus in Schopenhauer, Nietzsche, and other thinkers ethical theorizing shifts: to put it in the broadest possible way, these thinkers are interested in which configurations of the human mind—including drives, affects, and the social conditions interacting with them—are conducive to flourishing. In neither of these thinkers is flourishing to be achieved principally through conscious activity. Self-consciousness, far from being something distinctive and exalted, comes to play a subsidiary role.

CONCLUSION

I've sketched the development of the drive concept and traced the consequences of its introduction. Originally denoting nothing more than the energies needed to initiate mechanical processes, by the middle of the nineteenth century "drive" can pick out anything from a mysterious but visible force responsible for organic development to a source of purposive activity or a concept of pure activity. Each of these notions puts pressure on the human/animal divide. Freed of the simplistic dichotomy between self-conscious intelligence and mere mechanism, thinkers envision a spectrum of less to more complex mental processes. And, introducing the idea that our deepest aims are concealed from us, our place seems less secure. We are not alone in thoughtful behavior; we are not alone in sensation, affect, and intelligence; and we do not enjoy any privileged knowledge of our ultimate goals. As Büchner writes, "The best authorities in physiology are now pretty much agreed in the view that the soul of animals does not differ in *quality* but merely in *quantity* from that of man."[70]

CHAPTER TEN

Governing Darwin's World

Philip Kitcher

In 1859 Darwin's concern not to arouse unnecessary opposition to his "long argument" for conclusions about the history of life led him to tiptoe around questions about how human beings relate to the rest of the organic world. Late in *The Origin of Species*, he offers one cryptic sentence about our species: "Light will be thrown on the origin of man and his history."[1] By 1870, however, as it became clear that many of the world's most eminent naturalists were persuaded by his case for the interconnectedness of organisms, Darwin was ready to be more forthright.[2] *The Descent of Man*, published in 1871, begins by posing the question of "whether man is the modified descendant of some pre-existing form," and its first six chapters amass the evidence for an affirmative answer. Although part 2 of the book (comprising the bulk of its pages) turns to the different (albeit related) topic of sexual selection, Darwin's interest in defending an uncompromising thesis of the interrelatedness of all animal life is evident.[3] A year later he extended his defense in *The Expression of the Emotions in Man and Other Animals*, a book containing material originally intended for its immediate predecessor.[4]

Darwin is rightly seen as contributing to a radical change in attitudes toward nonhuman animals and, potentially, in our treatment of them.[5] The two books of the early 1870s offer a line of reasoning, which I shall call the "Continuity Argument," and because of the significance of this argument's conclusion, it is all too easy to detach that conclusion and ponder its consequences without attending to other important aspects of Darwin's overall view. Those inspired by Darwin's case for the connectedness of human beings with other animals tend to explore the moral implications of that connectedness without considering the more general picture of the organic world that Darwin painted and without reflecting on the fact that the case for continuity itself depends on an interesting, if embryonic, view about morality.

In what follows I shall defend and explore a pair of theses. First, Darwin posed a new issue for moral and social theory: how is the organic world described in *The Origin of Species* to be governed? Second, in his discussion of morality in the *Descent*, he pointed toward an answer to that question.

THE CONTINUITY ARGUMENT

The *Descent* begins from premises that were easy to defend in 1871 and are even less open to challenge today.[6] Darwin has no trouble in identifying points of close anatomical and physiological similarity between humans and other animals, in noting the organs and structures (like the coccyx) that are residues of ancestral constituents with a far richer suite of functions, and in tracing the similarities of embryos at different stages of development. All this is a straightforward extension of arguments made for connecting species in the *Origin*, and the focus on the human case simply makes explicit what informed readers of the earlier book would already have grasped.

So much is prelude to the crucial work of the Continuity Argument. In *The Origin of Species* Darwin repeatedly asks how to make sense of the organic phenomena he describes from the evolutionary perspective he advocates and from its rival, the "doctrine of special creation." As far as anatomy and physiology go, the links between humans and apes, or humans and primates, or humans and mammals recapitulate in the special instance a compelling general line of argument. What gives comfort to those who yearn for a special status for our species—and provides support for conservative evolutionists like Wallace—is the rich collection of psychological characteristics human beings exhibit. Hence the major step taken in the early parts of the *Descent* consists in explicitly confronting questions of psychological kinship. Darwin aims to show that the "building blocks" of our major psychological capacities are already present in our evolutionary relatives.

His argument has two potential prongs. First, to the extent that he can identify the physiological bases of psychological capacities, Darwin can extrapolate from the relatively straightforward affinities among neural structures to claims about psychological continuity. Second, with respect to those forms of behavior that seem unique to human beings, he can try to show that some nonhuman animals have capacities that, if developed or supplemented, might yield the human performance. Lacking detailed knowledge of the neural bases of the psychological conditions with which he is most concerned, Darwin is forced to emphasize the second prong, offering, again and again, examples of forms of nonhuman animal behavior that can be defended as precursors of our own, more complex activities. Here and there, especially in the later *Expression of the Emotions*, he occasionally attempts to make use of similar physiological responses to emotional states, as for example in the bodily reaction to terror.[7]

Darwin's task is to justify ascribing various kinds of psychological states, processes, and faculties to nonhuman animals, including beliefs and desires, planning, imagination, and memory. His strategy is to offer a series of examples, some of them familiar in everyday experience, others striking and unusual. We are invited to view the mundane examples from the standpoint of the extraordinary cases. So, for example, instead of dismissing the apparently affectionate behavior of dogs toward their owners as the result of a bundle of fixed programs, we should see them in light of the "dog, suffering under vivisection, who licked the hand of the operator" or of Darwin's own (rather unsociable) dog, who "after [his master's] absence of five years and two days," responded to his returning master's voice and resumed his long-suspended routine "exactly as if I had parted with him only half an hour before."[8] The implication is that, even if common types of animal behavior can be dismissed as programmed responses to stimuli, there are others explicable only by attributing genuinely psychological faculties and representational states.

Unlike the *Origin*, where Darwin makes the rival "Special Creation" account explicit and also challenges it to articulate explanations for phenomena he has elaborated within his own framework, the *Descent* offers no extended characterization of an alternative position. It appears as though Darwin does not take seriously the possibility that animal behavior is caused in radically different ways from human conduct.[9] His confidence probably descends in large part from extensive experience in living and working with domestic animals (particularly dogs) of a sort that is rare among contemporary academics who debate animal cognition. Yet even if it were entirely natural for someone with that type of experience to suppose animal mentality to be "manifest," Darwin's selection of instances embodies a tacit argument for the position he seems to take for granted.

That argument emerges most clearly in Darwin's discussion of language, which, as he concedes, "has justly been considered as one of the chief distinctions between man and the lower animals."[10] He emphasizes the modes of communication in various groups (monkeys, frogs, ants, birds).[11] Yet these fall short of human linguistic performance in an important respect: "The lower animals differ from man solely in his almost infinitely larger power of associating together the most diversified sounds and ideas; and this obviously depends on the high development of his mental powers."[12] I suggest that Darwin is implicitly adopting a plausible criterion for distinguishing animals with representational states from those that are mere "bundles of tricks." He sees generativity as the mark of the mental: some animals seem to be able to adapt their behavior to a large (indefinitely large, "almost infinite") range of different situations, and that adaptation seems explicable only on the grounds that they are able to represent commonalities and differences so as to combine their basic programs for action.

Language, Darwin admits, is not an area in which nonhuman animals display generativity.[13] What moves his selection of striking examples, intended to exact our acceptance of the richness of nonhuman psychological life, is, I believe, the tacit thought that, in some other domains, something akin to generativity is present. The unusual cases—the dog licking the surgeon or resuming a routine after a five-year intermission—suggest a whole range of alternative contexts in which animals might exhibit a response, undercutting the skeptical thought that their familiar actions are merely a matter of conditioned responses or of instinctive drives. One such example occurs relatively early in Darwin's discussion in the *Descent*:

> At the Cape of Good Hope an officer had often plagued a certain baboon, and the animal, seeing him approaching one Sunday for parade, poured water into a hole and hastily made some thick mud, which he skillfully dashed over the officer as he passed by, to the amusement of many bystanders. For long afterwards the baboon rejoiced and triumphed whenever he saw his victim.[14]

More recent discussions of animal psychology (and the dangers of anthropomorphism) often focus on similar examples, instances in which a number of behavioral patterns seem to be combined in novel ways to cope with an unprecedented situation, and in which explaining the recombination appears to require ascribing some type of representational states to the animal. One of Frans de Waal's most telling examples of other-directed behavior in chimpanzees describes the action of a young adolescent male who looked on as an older retarded female struggled and failed to remove from a protruding pole a tire in which rainwater had collected. The tire in question was the innermost of six, and, after the female had given up on the endeavor, the young male successively lifted off the first five, carefully carried the water-filled tire to the female, and set it before her.[15] Acting in this way seems to require recruiting behavioral tendencies normally active in very different domains, coordinated on this occasion through representation of the physical environment and of the behavior of another animal. Similarly the many recorded instances of "tactical deception" on the part of animals reveal a rare ability to bring together types of behavior usually employed separately and to coordinate them through representational states—consider, for example, the sneaky subordinate males and their female paramours who contrive a tryst in a place outside the field of vision of a jealous dominant (behind a helpful rock or in a convenient thicket).[16] Such striking examples appear inexplicable without supposing the competence to generate responses across an indefinitely large ("almost infinite") class of situations, thus according with the generativity criterion I have ascribed to Darwin. If this is correct, there is an important continuity between the *Descent* and the arguments deployed in contemporary debates by the friends of animal cognition.

The character of this shared line of reasoning could be probed further, but to do so would divert us from the main business of this chapter. What interests me is that Darwin does not stop with claims about the capacities of nonhuman animals to represent the world. He presses on to morality.

NATURAL HISTORY AND MORALITY

Darwin's motivation for extending the Continuity Argument to the psychological underpinnings of ethical life are evident from the opening of chapter 4 of the *Descent*: "I fully subscribe to the judgment of those writers who maintain that of all the differences between man and the lower animals, the moral sense or conscience is by far the most important."[17] Plainly he fears that, without some account that links human moral deliberation to precursor capacities in nonhuman animals, the way will be open for others—even others like Wallace, who support the general evolutionary view—to conclude that some special creative act played a role in the origin of our own species. Contemporary thinkers are likely to be far less troubled by this thought. Convinced that *Homo sapiens* descends from an ancestor that has also given rise to contemporary chimpanzees and bonobos, they see no need to campaign for gradualism across all important psychological traits. The moral sense might turn out to be a relatively sudden acquisition, the byproduct of some other change in the psychological constitution of our ancestors. Many philosophers are skeptical of the idea that an evolutionary account of morality can be given, or even, if it can, that it will offer any illumination of ethical life.

Darwin thought differently. Although the threat of invoking special creation for the special case of human origins evidently moved him to take up the topic, by the end of the second paragraph of chapter 4 of *Descent* he was ready to announce a higher ambition: "The investigation possesses, also, some independent interest, as an attempt to see how far the study of the lower animals throws light on one of the highest psychical faculties of man."[18]

The strategy for ruling out appeals to special creation consists in reducing the moral case to the ones already discussed. Darwin emphasizes the "sociability" of many nonhuman animals. Given the "social instincts," the capacities for sympathy with others of the same species, all that is needed for morality is the further development of the "intellectual powers"—and, as he later adds, the evolution of language. The proposition to be defended is stated at the beginning of his discussion: "Any animal whatever, endowed with well-marked social instincts, the parental and filial affections being here included, would inevitably acquire a moral sense or conscience, as soon as its intellectual powers had become as well, or nearly as well developed as in man."[19] If his previous chapters have settled doubts about the continuity of human and nonhuman intellectual capacities, then, given this proposition, the linkage extends to the moral domain, connecting human beings with other social animals.

Darwin's defense of his crucial proposition proceeds by pursuing his more ambitious goal, using "natural history" to illuminate ethical life or, more exactly, to offer a revisionary account of it. Fundamental to morality, he claims, is the ability to sympathize with those around us, initially those who belong to a small social group. As animals are better able to remember and to compare their previous experiences, they naturally come to reflect on the occasions on which their individual impulses have overridden their social instincts, and because of the enduring pressure of the latter, they come to feel "dissatisfaction" or "misery." Such feelings are reinforced once language has been acquired, and it is possible for members of the group to discuss their conduct with one another. So animals come to internalize "the wishes and judgment of the community."[20]

"Natural history" of this sort provides a picture of ethical life, as we know it, as having been gradually assembled from the development of psychological capacities. The beginnings were almost certainly crude, as a basic ability to recognize actions that brought undesirable consequences, allied to a primitive capacity for suppressing the recurrent impulses that gave rise to them, yielded a diminution of antisocial behavior. To go beyond this to a state in which more refined emotions come into play—in which conduct is motivated not simply by fear of reprisals but by a sense of solidarity with fellows or a respect for the patterns of behavior on which the group has explicitly agreed—requires further steps. So too does the extension of morality to actions whose effects on group welfare are indirect, as with imperatives to cultivate talents. Even more evidently, contemporary moral thinking has broken the narrow boundaries of the local band—in a famous image, the circle has expanded.[21] Darwin's account of this last step is hardly satisfactory. He writes:

As man advances in civilization, and small tribes are united into larger communities, the simplest reason would tell each individual that he ought to extend his social instincts and sympathies to all the members of the same nation, though personally unknown to him. This point once being reached, there is only an artificial barrier to prevent his sympathies extending to the men of all nations and races.[22]

This seems blithely indifferent to the long struggle to abolish chattel slavery (oddly so, given Darwin's fierce opposition to the practice), and overoptimistic about human xenophobia. Its principal deficiency, however, lies in the fact that the events taken as the cause of enlarged sympathies—the uniting of communities—seem already to presuppose the extended moral practice that expanded sociability is supposed to produce.

Darwin's attempts to explain the refinement of moral motivation and the emergence of precepts for self-regarding actions do better. In both instances he points to the effects of "the praise and the blame of our fellow-men."[23] So he suggests that the original "low motives," such as fear and self-interest, for conforming to agreed-on rules and customs are joined by a sense of solidarity with other members of our social group, largely fueled by the need for approval from those around us.[24] Similarly appreciation of self-regarding virtues derives from increased awareness of these as preconditions for the success of the various kinds of cooperative ventures that ethical life has already made available, and a resultant community decision to react to their presence or absence with praise or blame.[25]

In summary, Darwin's "natural history" of morality starts from the picture of humans as social animals, whose responsiveness to one another enables us to live together, even though the limitations of that responsiveness cause recurrent conflicts and constrain our fruitful cooperation. Given a primitive ability to override some desires and impulses, coupled with an ability to recognize the undesirable consequences of actions moved by those desires and impulses, our ancestors were able to initiate a practice of systematically restraining forms of antisocial conduct and fostering forms of cooperative behavior. Language enabled them to work out the patterns of their joint life, and thus launched the human lineage on a series of "experiments of living," out of which the ethical codes of the present have emerged. In the course of the gradual evolution of ethical life, motivations have been refined, new types of emotions and aspirations have emerged, and the boundaries of moral protection have been radically expanded. The process should be seen not as the discovery of some independent moral truth but as the collective construction of ethical life, in response to problems posed for us by enduring characteristics of our species (in particular our need for social life and our limited capacity for the responsiveness social life demands). We invented the ethical project; we cannot envisage human life without it; and it is permanently unfinished.[26]

Darwin, like Peter Singer after him, suggests a way in which that project might be further continued. Summarizing his account of how an "anthropomorphous ape" might move in the direction of morality, he notes that the extension of sympathy would probably be restricted, falling short of "that disinterested love for all living creatures, the most noble attribute of man."[27] Late in the *Descent* he returns to the same theme, seeing moral progress as residing in the fact that human sympathies have "been rendered more tender and widely diffused," and seeing the summit of our "exalted powers" in that "benevolence which extends not only to other men but to the humblest living creature."[28] As I will now suggest, continuing the ethical project in the manner envisaged here would raise a new problem for moral and social theory: how to govern Darwin's world?

DARWIN AND PEACEABLE KINGDOM THINKING

Darwin transforms older issues about dominion or stewardship. Given his evolutionary account of morality—and the fact that we cannot directly negotiate with nonhuman animals—any future extension of the ethical project to include them must represent nonhuman perspectives by proxy. A second mode in which the questions are changed stems from the conception of the organic world offered in the *Origin*. Central to that conception is the idea of the struggle for existence. Life is organized so that conflict is inevitable, and even if selection does not always generate a nature red in tooth and claw, it frequently does so. Those who envisage a perfect extension of sympathy, in which it flows out evenly across the animal kingdom, are doomed to disappointment. To sympathize with the predator is to withhold sympathy from the prey, and conversely. Darwin thus disrupts a style of thought that surely permeated earlier religious approaches to the stewardship of creation at their most enlightened and benign and that continues to linger in the writings of environmentalists and those most committed to animal welfare or to animal rights. I shall call it "Peaceable Kingdom Thinking."

Peaceable Kingdom Thinkers tacitly assume a benign nature, disturbed only by morally problematic human interventions. They see the world through the lens of the Anglican hymn "Where every prospect pleases, / And only Man is vile." In consequence their vision of governance embodies a simple principle: Human beings should act only in ways that do not cause any harm or suffering to sentient animals.[29] So they distinguish episodes in which human actions produce animal suffering from those in which very similar suffering is inflicted by nonhuman animals. It is surely indisputable that members of our species can be very creative in their cruelty, but we do not have a monopoly on actions that prolong pain. Many cat owners have seen their pet toy with a captive mouse. During my own observations of bonobos—a famously "peaceful" species—I witnessed a squirrel, caught almost by accident, used as a plaything for a period of half an hour, beaten against rocks, tossed from one bonobo to another, pulled and twisted while it still twitched, until it was eventually thrown aside. (I am not sure whether it was dead at that point.) From a Darwinian perspective, we should not be surprised that the struggle for existence often entailed massive suffering long before our species came to dominate the selective environment. We might also ponder Darwin's comment that we need no longer

"marvel... at ichneumonidae feeding within the living bodies of caterpillars."[30]

It should come as no surprise, then, that if we take the further expansion of the moral community seriously, the problem of governance
is difficult and that optimal solutions are rarely available. I will briefly
consider a few examples before offering an alternative to Peaceable
Kingdom Thinking.

(1) Probably no supporter of human restraint in dealing with the
    nonhuman world would object to the claim that we are sometimes
    justified in trying to eliminate disease vectors. Bacteria are
    beyond the range of sympathy. Sometimes, moreover, the only
    effective means for affording protection is to focus on a particular
    stage of the bacterial life cycle, during which it has infected a
    sentient animal host.

(2) Many champions of animal welfare or animal rights quite
    reasonably object to practices of environmental degradation
    that increase the difficulties for members of endangered species,
    and they favor attempts to prevent the hunting of the pertinent
    animals. Frequently such practices arise from the pressures on
    the human population in the pertinent environment: clearing a
    patch of forest or shooting an elephant is the only way for the
    inhabitants to feed the children or to afford the medicines they
    need. From a Darwinian perspective, the human agents are
    using adapted forms of behavior to compete in the struggle for
    existence—just as the lion does when it pursues a gazelle.

(3) One of the great achievements of the "animal liberation"
    literature of the past forty years (from Peter Singer's seminal
    book onward) has been its raising of consciousness about the
    usage of nonhuman animals in the mass production of food.[31]
    It is beyond question that factory farming creates conditions
    under which hundreds of millions of sentient animals (annually)
    live hideously distorted lives, full of pain and suffering. Yet

even in wealthy countries, large segments of the population have no access to alternatives.

Recognition of the continuity between human beings and other animals prompts the aspiration (shared, as we have seen, by Darwin) to extend the moral community. Once that potential expansion is framed by his conception of the organic world as an arena in which living things struggle—and typically compete—for existence, we should recognize that the problem of governance will be complex and that simple slogans are unlikely to be adequate.

The alternative I propose to Peaceable Kingdom Thinking is pragmatic. Because the struggle for existence pervades life, it is utopian, even foolish, to think in terms of eliminating suffering or achieving some morally perfect state. The aim should be simply to improve the existing situation, to clear up as many of the most glaring problems as we can. Even if human beings are the only potential legislators (the only animals who have evolved a moral sense), our ability to govern the entire animal kingdom is obviously extremely limited. This is as much a matter of incomplete knowledge as restricted power. As Darwin pointed out, the causal connections among selective pressures are often hard to trace, and human interventions frequently have remote consequences for populations that do not figure in our deliberations.[32] Responsible governance might well begin by recognizing that past human actions have already brought into being new subspecies[33] with which our lives are causally interwoven.[34] Instead of thinking broadly about the moral reform of the animal kingdom, we might engage in piecemeal attempts to address the problems of the groups we have created: the domesticated animals.[35]

ANIMALS AND THE MORAL COMMUNITY

Darwin's account of the evolution of morality suggests a general approach to problems of governance. Recall two of its important features. First, the moral community is bound together through the use of language to express the patterns of conduct that deserve praise or blame; second, the expansion of the moral community does not involve discovery of some prior ethical fact but is achieved through the construction of a new framework, addressing the problem that prompted the extension. As I have elaborated the Darwinian view, the initial formation of a moral community—the start of ethical life—begins out of reaction to the fundamental difficulty of our limited responsiveness to others. The best hypothesis is that the problem was tackled by involving all adult members of a small band in discussion, with the aim of finding approved patterns of behavior with which all could live. This, as anthropologists have pointed out, is the practice of those surviving groups whose environments and ways of life are closest to those of ancestral human bands (contemporary hunter-gatherers).[36] Moreover, given the character of the problem, it is a straightforward solution (even the obvious one): to try to widen the limits of responsiveness, you aim to include all points of view.[37]

In viewing language acquisition as a crucial step in the evolution of ethical life, Darwin points toward an obvious method of ethical decision. To address a problem, you try to embrace all points of view, to refine those points of view in the light of the best available factual information, and you attempt to find a solution with which all parties can live.[38] In the envisaged expansion of the moral community to include the standpoints of nonhuman animals, it is not possible for many of the participants to plead their own case. Yet, that holds with respect to some human subgroups (the unborn, the very young, the severely damaged, many of the elderly). It is, of course, important that those who cannot represent themselves should be well represented, that the proxies should understand and identify with their perspective. Equally, it is crucial that discussion proceed in the "cool hour," so that the urgency felt at the moment of conflict gives way to a serious attempt at mutual engagement, a concern for each point of view and for the needs and aspirations of all parties.[39]

We have already taken steps to expand the moral community by including nonhuman animals, and already begun the approach to governance just envisaged. With respect to the use of animals in experiments, oversight committees have been established, and some of their findings are already incorporated into codes of proper behavior. The Darwinian approach I am elaborating (and recommending) sees these developments as positive steps but recognizes ways in which committee discussion might be refined. I shall briefly consider two main lines of modification.

Contemporary moral discussions often proceed on the basis of a dangerous myth. It is widely assumed that there are ethical experts with the authority to pronounce a definitive verdict on the case at hand. Darwin's approach to ethical life does not license that kind of expertise. Authority does not lie in the individual but in the group, insofar as it approximates the conditions of inclusiveness of perspectives, freedom from factual error, and mutual engagement. There is no prior moral order accessible to particularly privileged people who can enlighten others about its character; there is only a particular form of conversation.[40] The myth of individual ethical authority arises from the distortion of the ethical project through embedding morality within religion and then crediting particular people with special access to the supernatural; in a secular world the supernatural beings give way to a background moral order and the philosopher or professional ethicist succeeds the shaman or the priest.[41]

To suppose that no single person has the last word is not to deny a different form of expertise. Particular individuals, those who have read widely or reflected deeply, may be particularly good at facilitating discussion, at framing questions and promoting mutual engagement. It is a very good thing to have John Rawls in the room, even if he is not assigned the role of issuing a definitive judgment. By the same token, it is a very bad thing if apparently authoritative participants insist that points of view essentially dependent on factual mistakes are allowed. Conversation will not go well if some of the parties are adamant about the factual truth of Genesis and conclude that human beings have un-limited rights to use the "lower animals" as they see fit.

The second envisaged refinement takes up the complaint, frequently made by animal sympathizers, that their voices are underrepresented (even unrepresented) in discussions of experiments on animals. Concerns of this kind are easy to understand. Research groups and hospitals typically staff oversight committees with medical profession-als, leaving only a small number of places for others. Yet it is important to distinguish advocates for the particular animals whose lives will be affected from advocates of animal rights. In many instances—those in which the proposed experiment is directed toward a specific disease, for example—the principal affected parties are the animals who may suffer from the experimental treatment and the animals (often but not always human) who need relief from the disease. Arguably both of these parties should be well represented in the discussion by people who know and can make vivid both the consequences for the experi-mental animals and the consequences for those afflicted with the dis-ease. Doctors who might carry out the procedures have an important role to play in explaining what would be done, and a secondary interest that arises from their pursuit of a line of research. The issue of how to strike a good conversational balance is probably one to be settled through empirical trials. I am inclined to start by proposing significant representation both for disease sufferers and for the animals (with ex-perts on their physiology and life cycles, as well as experts on pain), together with a smaller number of medical researchers (both those interested in the line of experimentation under consideration and those able to make a detached appraisal of its promise), complemented by a large cluster of open-minded outsiders, willing to immerse them-selves in the scientific details and ready to sympathize with all the parties affected.[42]

These are general ways of elaborating Darwin's approach to morality to tackle the problems of governing a Darwinian world. I shall con-clude by considering the proper use of experimental animals in a little more detail, in the hope that a Darwinian perspective might liberate us from familiar impasses.

IMPLICATIONS FOR ANIMAL EXPERIMENTATION

In the summer of 1921 two young Canadian researchers, Frederick Banting and Charles Best, isolated a substance, insulin, that enabled a dog whose pancreas had been removed to survive for ten weeks.[43] During the course of their experiments, at least ten dogs died as a result of the diabetes that had been artificially induced in them. Banting's subsequent ability to obtain insulin in large quantities from other domestic animals (initially cattle) allowed for the mass production of the treatment, and by 1923 it was available in many countries. From that point on, millions of people have been able to live fulfilling lives despite the fact that in childhood or adolescence or young adulthood they contracted a disease that had been, for millennia, a death sentence.

Many discussions of the use of nonhuman animals in scientific experiments begin with this particular example because the benefits of the research are so striking (millions saved, not all of them human beings), while the costs are relatively low (a small number of unfortunate animals).[44] While it is a parade case, the research of Banting and Best is hardly typical. Relatively few animal experiments have so direct a target (a specific program for treating a common disease), and few promise such enormous and immediate positive consequences. In many instances it is reasonable to ask in advance about the significance of the planned research, and responsible answers often have to appeal to the general fruitfulness of enhanced understanding of basic features of animal metabolism or animal development. "Basic research" can be defended on its track record, but the defenses would be more convincing if there were a general practice of systematic and sober appraisal of the benefits achieved by particular types of experimental investigation on particular types of problems.[45] It is neither unreasonable nor callous to conduct experiments that have small chances of contributing indirectly to a body of knowledge that will ultimately deliver benefits (for human beings and nonhuman animals), especially if, as is almost invariably the case, in the initial stages where the probabilities are tiny, the experimental organisms involved do not raise concerns about animal suffering.

The Darwinian approach to the governance problem, outlined in the previous section, envisages a group of mutually engaged discussants assessing both the promise of a particular research program and the animal suffering it will entail. Some future cases will resemble that of Banting and Best, in having a clear and direct target of relieving suffering. The consequences of others will be far more nebulous, and, as I have emphasized, here it is important to achieve a firm analysis of the results of prior lines of investigation, and also to use only certain kinds of organisms (those to whom we cannot attribute a "point of view") until the likely fruitfulness of the inquiry has been demonstrated. In yet other instances, perhaps the majority in today's world, a world increasingly dominated by commercialized research, the supposed benefits themselves should be carefully scrutinized. As animal sympathizers rightly remind us, many laboratory animals suffer in attempts to produce things that nobody needs but that can add to the profits of those who fund the experiments.[46] If the ethical discussions were well set up, those experiments would vanish.

The approach I have sketched so far is aligned with the so-called Three Rs framework, which attempts to address concerns about the experimental use of animals by advocating replacement, reduction, and refinement. Replacement consists in using dead animals or animals without highly developed nervous systems, when that is possible; reduction attempts to minimize the number of animals on which experimental procedures are performed; and refinement introduces methods (such as administering analgesics) for diminishing suffering. Although few people would deny that this framework is an improvement on the unrestricted use of laboratory animals, most animal sympathizers believe that it fails to go far enough.[47] I agree that the framework itself needs refinement, but, as I shall hope to show, this refinement should be guided by a Darwinian perspective.

Start with a style of experimentation that receives little attention in discussions of the legitimacy of using animals. It is no exaggeration to say that the majority of basic biological knowledge has been obtained by studying organisms of five kinds, four of them being the bacterium *E. coli*, the sea slug *Aplysia*, the nematode worm *C. elegans*, and the fruit fly *Drosophila melanogaster*. (The fifth will make its entrance later.) All these organisms have been modified and invaded in extraordinary ways. Researchers create a wide variety of mutant forms, halt the life cycle when they please, inject fluorescent proteins so they can track development—and out of their investigations comes an understanding of basic genetic mechanisms, fundamental insights into the behavior of neurons, a "fate map" that reveals where each of the 959 somatic cells of the nematode comes from, and the identification of the genetic mechanisms responsible for the first stages of development in the fruit fly. This last accomplishment, which earned a Nobel prize, was achieved by Christiane Nüsslein-Volhard, who bred mutant flies whose development was halted at successive early stages. Through careful analyses of these flies, Nüsslein-Volhard was able to trace the molecular interactions that generate the head-tail axis of the larval fly and that fix its normal segmentation pattern. If, a century from now, developmental biology facilitates programs of treatment for major developmental disorders in humans and other sentient animals, significant credit must go to Nüsslein-Volhard as the founder of the enterprise.

Yet what she did was profoundly invasive. She deliberately created mutant flies that would be grotesquely deformed and that would lead exceptionally short lives. In the numerous discussions on the experimental uses of animals that I have read, her experiments, and others like them, do not rate a mention. Why is that? Surely because the flies in question are not viewed as being harmed. Some of their luckier fellows within the lab may live a few days, even copulate a bit. Those who fly around in the wild will be more or less fortunate. Given the mechanisms on which Darwinian evolution depends, there will be genetic variation, occasionally producing flies just like those Nüsslein-Volhard studied, and there will be rigorous selection, so that life for many flies will be measured in hours, or even minutes. It is hard to focus on "fly pain" or to conceive a normal life cycle as something important to preserve or to assign flies a place in the Peaceable Kingdom.[48]

In subsequent work Nüsslein-Volhard and her colleagues extended the investigation of early development to a vertebrate, the zebrafish. There has been some discussion of the capacities of zebrafish for pain and for anxiety, and consequent concerns about the work that follows Nüsslein-Volhard's experimental paradigm. But I want to focus on an example in which laboratory practice is even more invasive, and in which there are no serious doubts about whether the species from which innumerable variant strains are derived can suffer. My fifth species, the laboratory mouse, is the model organism par excellence.[49]

The activist group People for the Ethical Treatment of Animals (PETA) surely goes beyond what has been scientifically confirmed (in just the types of experiments it opposes) when it claims that mice "feel pain and suffer as much as dogs, cats, and rabbits do."[50] Yet that there is a rough correspondence of the sensitivities of all these kinds of mammals is uncontroversial. Despite the fact that, in other contexts, animal rights activists insist on the *dissimilarities* between mice and *Homo sapiens*, denying that experiments on mice can teach us anything about human physiology or development or neurology, there are many scientific purposes for which the differences do not matter: a mammal is a mammal is a mammal (as Gertrude Stein unfortunately did not say). The evidential value of many experiments on mice is beyond question and, of course, well supported by the facts of our evolutionary kinship.

The extent to which individual mice suffer varies enormously from experiment to experiment. As with Nüsslein-Volhard's creation of mutants, some of the changes inflicted on laboratory mice are extremely invasive, effectively introducing disease conditions deliberately intended to mimic those that afflict human beings, or gross disruptions of development and behavior. What needs emphasis, however, is the artificiality of not just some but all of these mice. Many of them bred in a professional service facility (the Jackson Laboratory, or "Jax Lab"), they are further modified in numerous laboratories all over the world (often a lengthy and difficult process) so that they will acquire the genomic background needed by the experimentalist.[51] All laboratory mice are sufficiently removed from their wild forebears as to constitute a separate subspecies—*Mus musculus laboratorius*, as it is sometimes (not altogether jokingly) designated.[52] The vast number of individual strains within the subspecies are each derived from at least twenty brother-sister matings (designed to standardize the pertinent aspects of the genotype). Many strains show chromosomal aberrations and modifications of normal development.

When these features are clearly in view, it is not hard to appreciate concerns not only about the lives of mice within the laboratory but also about the processes by which they came to be there. The Jackson Laboratory, like the investigators who cleverly tinker with its basic strains, seems to be creating animals who are set up for suffering. Yet that need not be so. It is in principle possible for animals bred to replicate a human disease to receive a carefully orchestrated program of pain management; they may suffer no more than the unfortunate children with major genetic disorders who are palliated throughout their short lives.[53] If we imagine an oversight committee considering a proposed experiment on laboratory mice, we should expect them to inquire into the pain likely to be inflicted. Assume they learn that pain will be managed, that the animals will suffer no more than any typical wild mouse in any of its standard environments—and possibly, because it will always be well fed, rather less. Does that settle the matter?

Advocates for animals often think that it does not. Their worries begin from conceiving the mice as being "subjects of a life" that opens them to harm and deprivation when their normal life cycles are distorted.[54] It is tempting to think that the lab mouse does not have much of a life—but this is to fall victim to a pre-Darwinian attitude. The laboratory mouse is a distinct subspecies. To place it in the environment of its wild-type ancestors would be an act of gratuitous cruelty. Lamenting its inability to frolic in nature is as misguided as regretting the fact that contemporary wild horses cannot run in the environment of *Eohippus*. The crucial matter for sympathetic deliberators is to ask whether the scientists who have evolved these specially designed animals can provide them with an environment in which their drives (including those drives they continue to share with their ancestors) can be satisfied.

Codes for treating laboratory animals sometimes take steps to address that critical question. They stipulate that cage sizes must be regulated, that social needs must be met, that animals should be isolated only for welfare, for veterinary reasons, or for the purposes of the experiment. Interestingly the issue of whether to provide a richer than normal structure in the local environment is often debated not from the perspective of the research budget but on the basis of efforts to assess the animals' welfare: mice in cages equipped with devices for play and exploration sometimes show higher levels of stress hormones, raising questions about whether this is welcome stimulation or a cause of anxiety.[55]

Peaceable Kingdom Thinking supposes that there must always be a loss when animals are removed from a supposedly benign natural environment or deprived of the characteristics needed for living in that environment. Laboratory mice plainly do not have access to all the possibilities of their wild ancestors—including, we may note, the thrills of evading the hungry owl.[56] Taking Darwin seriously entails recognizing that different animal species (and subspecies) adapt to different environments. Animals are not necessarily deprived if they do not interact with their surroundings in the ways characteristic of their evolutionary relatives. Assessments of their welfare ought to rest on an understanding of the dispositions to behavior they have—many of them, but by no means all, similar to those of their ancestors—and on whether those dispositions are satisfyingly activated in the environments provided for them.

Many people, including people with highly developed sensitivity to animals, recognize that some of the animals with which human beings interact most frequently have lost capacities possessed by their feral ancestors. The most dedicated pet owners work hard to provide environments in which the impulses the animals share with their wild relatives can be safely satisfied. Existing manuals for the management of laboratory animals often reveal a dominant concern for the health and safety of the personnel who will interact with them—with details on how to handle the animals so as to avoid being bitten, for example[57]—but, as discussions of the need for space, social interaction, and the potential benefits of an enriched environment make clear, there is already a nascent sympathy to the animals' needs. Deliberations about specific experiments might insist on developing that sympathy further, emulating the attitude of the responsible pet owner.

Some advocates for animals would deny that any environment at all can replace life in the wild. A consequence of this position is that the 10,000-plus year history of animal domestication was a moral blunder, requiring us to undo it as speedily and humanely as possible. This view is perhaps the ultimate in Peaceable Kingdom Thinking. It fails to appreciate the Darwinian insight that the work of breeders is akin to the selective processes that pervade the living world. There is no more reason to take as privileged the species that were the immediate feral ancestors of our domestic strains or to suppose that their environments are the only ones in which animal welfare can be realized. Any dog owner who lives in proximity to half-starved coyotes should appreciate the point.[58]

It may seem, however, that all this is beside the point. However we provide for a well-fed existence among other mice in a comfortably appointed cage, the life of the laboratory mouse will usually be truncated, and often it will be pervaded by the effects of a deliberately introduced disease. Even supposing that there is little pain, can we suppose lives of this sort to be worth living? Everything depends on the details (the particulars that the oversight committee should consider). The average life span of a free-living mouse is about one year; mice that live commensally with human beings have a higher expected life span (about eighteen months); and laboratory mice can enjoy greater longevity. It is not immediately obvious that mice allowed a significant number of months before the experimental procedures begin have been deprived or harmed.[59]

I will close by returning to Banting and Best and to the dogs that died at their hands. Unlike laboratory mice, those dogs were not carefully manufactured to meet the experimental needs. They were descendants of wild canids, belonging to varieties selected by generations of breeding. If they were harmed by the experiments, that harm consisted in depriving them of the kind of environment a considerate owner might have provided and in subjecting them to procedures that shortened their lives. The rhetorical value of this particular case is not exhausted by the features with which I began—the relatively small number of animals and the extraordinary relief of subsequent suffering. Beside those are the well-known pictures, in which the dogs appear with the two young experimenters very much as if they were with their kindly owners. Neither the pictures nor what is known about the conduct of the experiments suggests anything other than sympathy. It is easy to imagine that these dogs behaved like the one in Darwin's vivid example, licking the hands performing the operations that would bring about their deaths.

Almost certainly those deaths were premature. But suppose that were not so, that the dogs had been carefully chosen, selected because they had lived long and had been well treated—and recently diagnosed with a disease certain to bring death in a few weeks or months, a disease whose presence would in no way compromise the experimental results. The details do matter in our attempts to govern Darwin's world.[60]

CHAPTER ELEVEN

Morgan's Canon

ANIMAL PSYCHOLOGY IN THE TWENTIETH CENTURY AND BEYOND

Helen Steward

An enormously important role has been played in twentieth-century animal science by the principle known as "Morgan's Canon," first formulated in the nineteenth century by Conwy Lloyd Morgan (1852–1936), a British ethologist widely regarded as one of the most influential founders of comparative psychology. The principle was expressed by Morgan over the course of his lifetime in a number of different ways, but the one that seems to be most often quoted in the literature is from the first edition of his *Introduction to Comparative Psychology*: "In no case may we interpret an action as the outcome of the exercise of a higher psychical faculty, if it can be interpreted as the outcome of the exercise of one which stands lower in the psychological scale."[1] The influence the principle has had on the conduct and methods of comparative psychology over the succeeding 120 years cannot be overestimated; it has been described by one writer as "possibly the most important single sentence in the history of the study of animal behavior."[2] It was

certainly implicated in the widespread adoption of radical psychological behaviorism during the middle decades of the twentieth century,
but its impact has outlasted the demise of that doctrine. The Canon is
still regularly explicitly invoked by scientists working on animal behavior and is perhaps even more often silently applied as part of an implicit
orthodoxy concerning the appropriate methodology for a sober psychological science.[3]

However, the Canon has been severely criticized in recent years by
some powerful detractors. Daniel Dennett,[4] Elliott Sober,[5] and Jerry
Fodor[6] have all argued, in different ways, that Morgan's Canon is either
redundant, defensible only on a quite seriously modified interpretation of its meaning, or simply silly. A number of other philosophers
have also contributed excellent critiques.[7] Historians of science, moreover, have shown convincingly that the Canon has been utilized by
scientists of animal behavior in ways that were never intended and,
moreover, would have been deplored by Morgan himself.[8] The case
against the Canon has been thoroughly made with considerable power,
in more than one way, by a range of philosophers and historians. Why,
then, write yet another critique of Morgan's Canon?

One reason for thinking that there is room for another nail or two
in the coffin of the Canon is that, as already noted, the principle appears as yet to be thoroughly undead in the disciplines to which it is of
direct relevance. It still stalks the corridors of psychology departments,
making its unholy presence firmly felt,[9] and though this is rarely noted,
its influence also continues to be discernible well beyond the academy.
The anthropomorphic tendencies of the general public, delighting to
tell anecdotes supposedly revelatory of the reasoning powers, emotional sophistication, and general intelligence of their pets, have long
been deplored by many Canonized practitioners of animal science. But
in fact many people reveal, even as they offer up these anecdotes, an
astonishingly high level of awareness of the possible perils of overimag-
inative interpretation, often laughingly following their tales with em-
barrassed acknowledgments of the foolish anthropomorphisms they

take to be thereby exhibited. One reason for this high level of awareness is that the cautious and purportedly objective descriptions of animal behavior which have been supposed part of a respectable scientific animal psychology have thoroughly permeated the broadcasts and publications by means of which the public gains much of its scientific understanding of the animal world. To take one instance, the banter between Chris Packham and Michaela Strachan on recent editions of *Springwatch* and *Autumnwatch*, BBC nature programs that may be familiar to British readers, regularly involves the attribution of high-level psychological states to the creatures observed by the giddy Michaela, lover of animals, who is gently put right on the matter by the sober and biologically better-educated Chris, urging caution and the strenuous avoidance of anthropomorphism.[10] The message that often emanates from these and many other wildlife programs, and from the language in which their descriptions of animal behavior are cautiously couched, is that anyone who knows anything about the science of animals knows also that their activity ought not to be interpreted by means of the tools that often seem to come naturally to human observers: the tools made available by intentional descriptions, and the assumption of such things as agency and perhaps even consciousness, in the creatures being observed. Real scientists, we are encouraged to think, know better. But do they know better? The extent to which Morgan's Canon may be responsible for a now thankfully teetering orthodoxy needs to be appreciated before this question can hope to receive a serious answer.

A second reason for thinking that Morgan's Canon deserves another airing is that the debate about the principle is far less widely known outside psychology than it ought to be. Among philosophers of mind and action, for instance, the Canon is rarely mentioned. I had been working, in the philosophy of mind for many years when I first heard of it, my attention directed to its influence and interest not by a fellow philosopher but by a colleague working in the history of science, Greg Radick, who had himself written about the Canon.[11] I suspect a poll of philosophers of mind would reveal similar

levels of general ignorance. And yet the principle is enormously significant. The question of whether it is to be endorsed or rejected is utterly
central to the pursuit of questions about animal mind, to questions
about other minds in general, to questions about humanity's place in
nature. Philosophers of mind need to know about it, and they need to
know about the influence it may have had on the psychological work
from which they increasingly frequently take their inspiration. Not to
know is to risk mistaking the products of various contingent historical
factors for the nonnegotiable outcome of the inevitable onward march
of an increasingly objective science.

A third and final reason for thinking that more needs to be said
about Morgan's Canon is that the existing literature is rather confus-
ing. Not everyone who criticizes the Canon is criticizing the same version of it; moreover interpretations of its crucial terms differ, so that
not everyone who appeals explicitly to the Canon really has quite the
same principle in mind. Some points made in opposition to the Canon
ought never to have been made, for they are very easily met and ought
to be discarded in favor of the more powerful arguments that are available. And in addition one needs, of course, to give proponents of the
Canon a fair hearing and to respond to their anxiety that to lose the
Canon might be to open the door to an absurd degree of anthropomorphic license. Simon Fitzpatrick has argued that many endorse the
Canon only because they fail to see that the work they believe it is
needed to do can be done instead by an alternative scientific principle,
a principle Fitzpatrick calls "evidentialism." Scientific evidentialism, in
its most general form, simply states that in no case should one endorse
any scientific theory or explanation if the available empirical evidence
gives us no reason to prefer it to an alternative theory or explanation.
Formulating a version specifically directed to the interpretation of
animal behavior, Fitzpatrick offers the following:

> *Evidentialism*: in no case should we endorse an explanation of
> animal behaviour in terms of cognitive process X on the basis of the

available evidence if that evidence gives us no reason to prefer it to
an alternative explanation in terms of a different cognitive process
Y—whether this be lower *or* higher on the "psychical scale."[12]

Evidentialism supports the view that in circumstances in which we
genuinely have no proper empirical reason of any sort to prefer one of
two theories to another, the correct response is *agnosticism*, together,
perhaps, with a redoubling of efforts to ascertain (by means of experimentation or further observation) which of the two theories really
does offer the better explanation.[13] But *endorsement* of either theory
until these efforts have been made successfully would go too far. And
endorsement is what Morgan's Canon purports to justify. Evidentialism,
then, opposes Morgan's Canon. And I shall concur with Fitzpatrick in
arguing that it is evidentialism, and not the Canon, that ought to be
the touchstone of good science.

In some ways, I confess, it just seems obvious to me that if we are
looking for a quite general principle of theory choice in the realm of
comparative psychology, evidentialism embodies a much safer scientific attitude than does Morgan's Canon. (In case this is not plain,
I shall offer below some examples that make clear that Morgan's Canon
both can encourage and has in fact resulted in the endorsement of
unsafe verdicts on animal behavior.) The interesting question is really
how, and why, Morgan's Canon has managed to last so long. In an attempt to answer this question, I shall look at some of the arguments
that might conceivably have convinced some of its proponents of its
legitimacy, and will seek to undermine them. But the correct explanation of its tenacity may ultimately be one that cites causes rather than
reasons. Morgan's Canon has been of the utmost importance to the
attempts of psychology to escape such evils as anecdotalism and intro-
spectionism and to psychology's struggle to establish itself as a proper
scientific endeavor alongside the "hard" sciences. To discard it may feel
to the practitioners of that science like a dangerous step in an unwanted
direction. I shall add to the attempts that others have made to allay this

concern. Like a mercenary once recruited for a good cause but now exhausted and capable of being induced to fight for the other side, Morgan's Canon is now itself the danger to good science.

THE CANON ACCORDING TO MORGAN

As already noted, Morgan's Canon states, "In no case may we interpret an action as the outcome of the exercise of a higher psychical faculty, if it can be interpreted as the outcome of the exercise of one which stands lower in the psychological scale."[14] The first duty of any philosopher tasked with arriving at a good understanding of Morgan's Canon is evidently the interpretation of the crucial terms "higher" and "lower." But before embarking on an attempt to decide how best to understand the nature of the hierarchy implied by these terms, it is worth pausing to take note of a number of additions and clarifications that were made by Morgan himself.

One addendum Morgan made almost immediately after stating his Canon expresses a certain discomfort at his own use of the word "faculty." Suspicion of "faculty psychology" was in the air in the late nineteenth century; in his *Grundzüge der physiologischen Psychologie*,[15] first published in 1874, Wundt had already criticized the misleading "mythological" conception of a psychological faculty as something that itself acts. Morgan suggests as an alternative for those who are worried by the use of the term "faculty" a restatement of his Canon in terms of an ontology of processes: "In no case is an animal activity to be interpreted in terms of higher psychological processes, if it can be fairly interpreted in terms of processes which stand lower in the scale of psychological evolution and development."[16] This restatement offers not only an alternative ontological framework for the understanding of the Canon, one that modern practitioners of psychology and philosophy might find more appealing than the faculty-based formulation, but also a clarification of the relevant notion of a "psychological scale." We are told here that the "scale" according to which the processes can be ranged in a hierarchy is a "scale of psychological evolution and development." I shall turn presently to some possible concerns about this suggestion.

Another important elucidation is that when Morgan speaks in the original formulation of his principle of "an action" ("in no case may we interpret an action…"), he is speaking not of what contemporary philosophers would call act *tokens* but rather of act *types*, so that the question is not whether, on a given occasion, we should attribute a piece of animal behavior to this or that faculty, this or that process, a decision that, as Morgan notes, would be "a purely individual matter of comparatively little moment,"[17] given the independently evidenced assumption that the creature in question possesses both faculties (or utilizes both processes). The question is whether a type of activity *in general*— a pattern of activity one sees repeated on a number of occasions across different individual members of the same species, or even across members of many species, in different times and places, such as web spinning in spiders, the broken-wing behavior in certain waders, plovers, and doves,[18] grooming in primates, and so on, and capable of being interpreted as the "outcome" either of a "higher" or a "lower" process—should, in the absence of any further, independent evidence, be attributed to the "higher" or to the "lower" one. Morgan is absolutely clear that "it should be added, lest the range of the principle be misunderstood, that the Canon by no means excludes the interpretation of a particular activity in terms of the higher processes, if we already have independent evidence of the occurrence of these higher processes in the animal under observation."[19] The principle applies only when one does *not* have such independent evidence. One may not, therefore, on Morgan's view, use the Canon to insist upon "lower" interpretations of behaviors in certain animals if one already has evidence of relevant capacities in those animals that might permit "higher" interpretations to be more plausible.

What, then, should we make of Morgan's talk of "higher" and "lower" faculties and processes? The first and most important point is that Morgan's own distinction is a distinction among faculties or processes *all of which are "psychical."* This is easy to miss, particularly in view of the widespread appropriation of the metaphor of hierarchically ranged levels in contemporary thought to understand the relation between different sciences and their theories, explanations, and vocabularies. Confusion on this score might well incline us to leap immediately to the conclusion that Morgan's Canon tells us to prefer the explanations of the sciences ranked lower in this hierarchy (for example, those of neurophysiology or biochemistry) to those ranked higher (such as those of psychology), where they are available. But this was no part of Morgan's own view. Morgan's conception of psychology was organized in terms of a hierarchy of powers or faculties that might be invoked in the explanation of behavior, at the bottom of which was to be found "mere instinct" and at the top, reason. The distinction between the two had already been discussed in the introduction to Romanes's work, *Animal Intelligence*, and this discussion represents the starting point for Morgan's methodological deliberations in his own *Introduction to Comparative Psychology*. Morgan's distinctive advance on Romanes was to argue that between these two domains of psychic life, we must recognize "a vast field of animal and human activity which... [should be] distinguish[ed] from both by the application of the term 'intelligence.'"[20] For Morgan, it is clear that we are going to need (at least) a threefold distinction between instinct, intelligence, and reason for the interpretation of animal behavior. One thing the Canon clearly entails for Morgan, then, is at least this: that what we can perfectly well interpret as the product of instinct, we should not seek to explain by means of the attribution of intelligence, and what we can understand as an exercise of mere intelligence, we should not consider to be a demonstration of reason.[21]

It need hardly be said that the Canon's directive has not always been interpreted in this strictly intrapsychic way by many modern and not-so-modern psychologists. Very often the Canon has been thought to sanction a preference for explanations that do not involve the attribution of consciousness over those that do; for explanations that are mechanistic rather than intentional; for explanations of behaviors in terms of such things as fixed action patterns, stimulus-response mechanisms, tropes, and reflexes rather than anything that might be better understood by reference to such things as judgement, decision, or even emotion—without any essential reference, indeed, to *anything* that might make the psychological grade. Of course it is a vexed matter to say what it is for any kind of faculty or process to make the psychological grade, but most philosophical attempts at defining the psychic have made some kind of reference or other either to consciousness or to intentionality, or both. Morgan's Canon has been assumed to justify the general privileging of the nonpsychic over the psychic. But that is certainly not how Morgan intended it. Indeed Morgan himself would be turning in his grave if he knew how the Canon had been deployed within the science of comparative psychology, of which he has a good claim to be regarded as one of the founding fathers. Following his discussion of animal memory, he makes the following request:

> I will only ask the reader...to be good enough to credit me with an unbiassed desire to interpret the phenomena of animal psychology without exaggeration, either in the direction of excess *or defect* of mental power and differentiation. As an evolutionist who believes that the whole range of the mental faculties have been developed by natural processes, *the tendency of my bias would assuredly not be in the direction of setting a gulf between the faculties of animals and the faculties of man.*[22]

Morgan himself is in the business of defending the principle that mind is likely to be found throughout the animal kingdom, though reaching different degrees of sophistication in different animals. A "gulf," it is worth bearing in mind, is what he never would have countenanced. And yet a gulf is what the practical application of his Canon has often suggested.

Extending the Canon?

It might be said that what Morgan himself intended is really of only secondary and purely historical interest. Even if his was, as I have suggested, intended to be an intrapsychic scale, it might be alleged that there is no good reason to be so restrained in the application of the Canon. Allen-Hermanson, for example, "can see nothing incoherent about extending the Canon to include showing a preference for *nonmental* faculties over ones that are psychological."[23] But it seems to me, on the contrary, that once one makes this step, certain difficulties at once present themselves. The reason is that if we interpret the Canon as endorsing a preference for nonpsychic over psychological explanations, it will almost certainly end up by licensing far too much. A first attempt at expressing the worry here might go as follows: It is *always* possible to offer nonpsychological explanations of patterns of behavior, alongside the psychological ones we might also think correct. This is true even in the human case. For example, I (and millions of other human beings) leave our homes each morning for a job where we intend to earn the money to support ourselves and our families. To mention the aim of earning money is to offer a psychological explanation in terms of intention and purpose—making the activity into one that can be readily understood as a prime case of the operation of practical reason. But there will also be a range of lower-level explanations available of this widespread variety of human behavior. There will, for example, be a physiological account to be given of the causal origin of the walking movements we make in leaving (and in opening doors, stepping outside, closing our doors behind us, setting off down the road, and so on) in terms of activity in the motor cortex, responses to incoming perceptual data, perhaps the setting in train of certain habitual mechanisms (we know without looking where our own door handle is, what sort of force will be needed to turn it, and so on). We do not normally suppose that the existence of the second sort of explanation excludes the relevance and importance of the first. Yet Morgan's

Canon, extended in the way envisaged by Allen-Hermanson, might seem to advise us to dispense with the intentional explanation entirely, in favor of the purely physiological one.

It might be said in response—and it would be rightly said, in my view—that this argument is too quick. For it assumes that the physiological explanation in such a case would be an explanation *of the very same thing* as the intentional one—and that this is not in fact the case. The psychological explanation explains why a certain pattern of intentional activity has occurred, whereas the physiological explanations merely explain *why such and such bodily motions took place*. We have here two explananda and not one, and that is why two distinct explanations are admissible. But so far as animals are concerned, the very thing that is likely to be in question, when an application of Morgan's Canon is envisaged, is whether or not one can distinguish in this way between similarly differentiated explananda—whether or not, for example, there really is, in a given case, something it might make sense to think of as an intentional action present, in addition to a mere set of movements. Is the Australian jewel beetle trying to mate with the beer bottle it mistakenly believes to be a female? Or should we simply say that certain features of the bottle have triggered (in an entirely mechanistic way) the "release" of certain behaviors? We face in such cases as this a question about how the general phenomenon, an instance of which we are currently observing, is to be *described* before we can begin to even approach the question of how it is to be explained. It is simply not the case, as the formulation of Morgan's Canon rather takes for granted (in speaking of "an action" that is "the outcome" of a given process), that we can offer an entirely neutral description of some single pattern of activity that then might admit either of a psychological or of a nonpsychological explanation. As Dennett has often argued, what we face in these cases is rather the more general, holistic question of whether there is a psychological *pattern* to be found across what is perhaps quite a wide range of behavior in different kinds of context, a psychological pattern that would be explanatorily and predictively helpful to us in our quest to interpret the world—and the answer to this question will dictate the description of the activity or behavior we want explained in the first place, as well as the form of the explanation itself.[24] As Dennett sees it, the crucial question is this: Does the intentional stance pay significant dividends in the attempt to understand the overall workings of a certain organism, or not? And it is not really clear how Morgan's Canon is to be applied, once this difficulty is recognized. If we interpret it as telling us always to favor a nonintentional, more mechanistic stance wherever we can do so—to look upon a creature as a mere mechanism wherever that is possible—we seem to be in danger of outlawing psychology altogether. For the trouble is that in a certain sense, it is always *possible* to take a mechanistic stance to a pattern of activity. We can always decide (even in the case of human action) that our explanandum is merely a set of bodily motions and resolve to seek merely to explain *those* in terms of their proximate neurological causes. But presumably we (mostly) think we would miss an utterly enormous amount, were we to restrict ourselves in this way, in the human case. Why, then, think that the decision to do so is not similarly likely to lead us astray in the case of other animals?

It might be said that this conclusion would follow only if we overlook Morgan's own clarification that we are allowed to offer a "higher" process in explanation of a phenomenon *in a case where we have independent evidence of some sort that it exists*. That is what we have in abundance, it might be said, to justify the application of psychological interpretations in our own case, and perhaps we might be happy to concede its existence (in the form of hugely increased general explanatory and predictive power) also in the case of certain other higher animals, such as primates and dogs. It might be doubted, I imagine (and I would myself doubt), that we have such independent evidence in the case of the jewel beetle. Morgan's Canon is to function, it might be insisted, merely as a "tie-breaker," to be brought in only when, having taken all available evidence into account, there *still* seems to be no clear reason to prefer the adoption of the intentional stance to a nonintentional or even entirely nonpsychological form of explanation. It is merely a directive that takes effect, other things being equal. But there would be two serious worries about trying to defend Morgan's Canon on this more limited basis. One is that we might reasonably have the suspicion that the number of cases in which all else really *is* equal is likely to be vanishingly small—indeed that it might end up being a null class. A situation in which even when all the evidence that could possibly be relevant to the interpretation of a piece of behavior is taken into account, there might be *nothing* that tips the balance in favor of the view that one or other of the competing hypotheses is the more probable, is hard to imagine. The other is, of course, the question already raised of what would *justify* the use of the Canon in such a case, to break the tie—of why agnosticism would not be the proper response instead. I shall turn shortly to consider some possible answers to this important question. But first, having cast doubt on the idea that it is safe to extend the Canon beyond Morgan's own intrapsychic application, let us return to the question I raised earlier, namely, the question of how we might interpret the difficult terms "higher" and "lower."

"Higher," "Lower," and the Psychic Hierarchy

As I have already explained, Morgan was operating with a basically tripartite understanding of the psychic "faculties" that might underlie animal behavior—instinct, intelligence, and reason—though he seems to have been perfectly aware that this division was strictly *pro tem* and likely ultimately to be superseded by a more complex set of divisions, particularly within the vast category that he calls "intelligence." Undoubtedly Morgan's own suggestion that these powers can be arranged hierarchically was underwritten, and perhaps made to seem more obvious than it really is, by assumptions that are false, in particular the assumption that evolution "always marches from simple to complex," as Sober puts it, and the vestiges of the linear conception of a scale of nature that Darwinism refutes, according to which every species can be ranked as "higher," "lower," or "equal to" each of the others. In particular we must suspect Morgan of having taken for granted the thought that "higher" implies "more characteristic of, or closer to, distinctively *human* behavior," and hence the assumption that man is the measure of all things cognitive. From a less anthropocentric viewpoint, one might indeed be tempted to claim, as Sober suggests at one point, that "it makes no sense to ask whether the ant's use of pheromones is higher or lower than the plover's use of deception. Both have their place in life's diversity."[25]

But even if we must beware of anthropocentrism in the very establishment of the scale in terms of which we are to understand Morgan's Canon, it is surely not true that we can make *nothing* sensible of the idea that some interpretations of creatures' behavior are more sophisticated than others. It is not, of course, that the operations of instinct are any less *impressive* than the workings of reasoned thought; indeed in some ways the reverse is true. It is *astounding* that a spider can spin a web and a bird build a nest without practice, without forethought, without teaching. Nor is the concept of *complexity*, I suggest, the most useful way to think about the question of which powers are "higher." There are just too many different ways in which to measure complexity for this to be a very useful suggestion. The processes behind the operation of many instincts, for instance, must be staggeringly complex, and in some ways might even seem to exceed in complexity the sorts of simple logical operations that are involved in some of the most basic varieties of reasoning.[26] What makes us regard certain interpretations of behavior as "higher," I suggest, is what they seem to imply about the overall capacities of the behaving *agent*. Where a behavior is attributed to instinct, comparatively little is left for the operation of judgment, decision, or thought to settle at the time of action, and few resources are presupposed that require such things as the consideration and weighing of *alternative* means to given ends. A spider may have to find a reasonable place to build her web, but web spinning itself is an ability she will not need to have learned or have practiced and that we can think of, more or less, as involving simply the execution of an entirely domain-specific program with which the spider comes equipped. Some degree of flexibility and adaptability is doubtless required, but the calls on the spider agent, deliberating in the moment, to come up with spur-of-the-moment solutions to unforeseen difficulties are plausibly not many. And should the spider for some reason be unable to construct an effective and successful web, she is unlikely to come up with many ideas about what she might do instead to get a meal. She will not, for example, be inventing wholly new kinds of fly trap or discussing interesting alternative possibilities with her conspecifics. If an instinctive behavior cannot be made to do the job for which it is intended (and no "backup" mechanisms have been selected for), then that is more or less that.

Moving up into the realms characterized by what Morgan called "intelligence," there is likely to be more flexibility and adaptability on show. New Caledonian crows can seemingly put together various parts of mechanisms they have learned to manipulate in order to reach food in such a way as to hatch a successful plan when confronted with a new and more complex mechanism than any they have hitherto seen. This cannot be explicated by means of instinct alone; the situation they face is new and requires immediate, on-the-spot assessment by something it is very natural to suppose must be a kind of thinker. But we need not suppose the existence of thought that is in all respects like our own in order to make sense of the postulated abilities. We need not attribute, for example, such things as episodic memory, arithmetical abilities, a sense of self, or conceptual thought, at least not where we have no other behaviors to go on. What we attribute is a level and type of intelligence of the sort necessary to explain the kind of problem solving revealed by the crows: no more.

Reason—a category as unsatisfactorily vague in its own way as intelligence—is at the top of Morgan's hierarchy for several reasons, I think. One is obviously its traditional place as the differentia of the human species and its traditional associations with the presence of linguistic abilities, via the concept of *logos*. Another, less anthropocentric justification one might offer for thinking that it truly belongs there is that "reason" is often used to refer to a set of abilities to manipulate information that are potentially entirely domain-general; inferential abilities, for example, can be applied, in principle, to problems that share the same logical shape, no matter what the topic of the reasoning involved. It is true that evidence suggests we cannot always exercise our reasoning abilities on some kinds of problem as well as we can on others; there may be more domain specificity in human thinking that has hitherto been recognized.[27] But still, the applicability of general logical principles, mathematical reasoning, etc. to diverse puzzles about the construction of buildings, the calculation of prices, the drawing of maps, the prediction of the motions of planets, etc. is striking, and there seems to be little evidence of such very diverse applications of inferential thinking in creatures other than ourselves. We are probably less inclined than Morgan would have been to suppose that evidence of the application of reason is necessarily evidence of an agent consciously thinking, for unlike Morgan, we have seen what mere machines are able to do in the realm of calculation, inference, and problem solving and how domain-general are the abilities they display; perhaps we are also less likely to think that reason and language necessarily go hand in hand. But the presence of the two together certainly appears exponentially to expand the range of a creature's abilities. We may additionally associate with reason such things as the ability to think about things in their absence; to engage in counterfactual thinking; to think utterly freely about future and past; to form new concepts and categories, building on those that already exist—all things that seem to have been crucially important in human development and to have put within the reach of their possessors a range of capacities to act on the world of which no other animal has so far been capable. Morgan's categories are doubtless too broad, too vague, and too all-encompassing. But it cannot be said that we have no idea at all what to make of the suggestion that some processes offer "higher" interpretations of creatures than others. We can at least make rough-and-ready sense of what is at issue—enough sense, anyway, to make Morgan's Canon definite enough in its specific directives to be practically usable.

Suppose, then, that we adopt, roughly, the suggestion offered earlier as to how we are to understand the terms "higher" and "lower." "Lower" processes carry with them fewer commitments to further abilities; they are less flexible in the face of unexpected failure or alteration in circumstance; they are more domain-specific. Is there any reason to suppose that if we have no empirical evidence to prefer an interpretation of animal behavior in terms of "higher" processes to one in terms of possible "lower" processes, we should endorse the lower? I want now to consider whether there is anything to be said for Morgan's Canon, thus understood.

THE JUSTIFICATION OF MORGAN'S CANON

There seem to be roughly three kinds of argument available for the possible justification of Morgan's Canon. One variety of argument—perhaps the most common—suggests that it is simply a version of some very widely endorsed scientific principle of theory choice: either a principle of *parsimony* or perhaps a principle of *simplicity*. A second suggests that it is a principle that has a specifically biological grounding of some sort. A third idea is that it is required in order to correct for an inherent bias toward anthropomorphism. All these possible justifications have been thoroughly worked over and in my view successfully demolished in the literature. I do no more here than simply summarize and modestly supplement points that have already been very clearly made by others.[28]

The idea that Morgan's Canon can be justified on grounds of parsimony or simplicity raises the prior question of how such generic principles of theory choice are themselves to be justified, but let that pass. Some of those who have invoked the idea that the Canon is simply one application of such a principle have been willing to bite the bullet and accept that such principles cannot be justified but must simply be assumed.[29]

But it is *not* a parsimony principle, and though it seems to me arguable that it *is* a variety of simplicity principle, there are many kinds of simplicity, and very much more argument than has been offered would be needed to support the view that the kind of simplicity it approves must be preferred over the other varieties. Parsimony first: there is more than one kind of parsimony one might have in mind in putting forward a parsimony principle, for example, straight ontological parsimony, of the sort advocated by Ockham's razor; parsimony of theoretical assumption; cladistic parsimony (i.e., parsimony of separate evolutionary origins for a given trait). But parsimony is always about getting by with *fewer* of something; it is not about getting by with "lower" rather than "higher" faculties and processes.[30] Simplicity, admittedly, is a different virtue from parsimony; perhaps a preference for interpretations in terms of "lower" processes does indeed amount to a preference for one kind of simplicity. But as Fitzpatrick and Fodor both convincingly argue, there are many varieties of simplicity, and we will still need to know how to trade off the different kinds against each other. To take a nice example from Fodor,[31] on one conception of simplicity the simplest way to play tic-tac-toe is to memorize all the possible games and play by rote. But that is not the way anybody in fact plays, nor would it be sensible to program a machine to play that way since there are rule-based solutions that work just as effectively but use less computational power. If "rote learning" is "lower" than the application of rules, as might seem intuitive, Morgan's Canon looks as though it would suggest the wrong result in a case like this. To take a case from Fitzpatrick, it is plausible that it is "simpler" in one sense to suppose that we should use similar psychological explanations for similar behavior, where the behavior is found in more than one species.[32] But suppose we had abundant evidence that in one of these species, the behavior was produced by way of a "higher" process? Morgan's Canon would seem to insist that we nevertheless prefer the "lower" process as an account of what is going on in the other species, but it is not in the least obvious that we ought to do so.

Morgan's own attempt to justify the Canon does not go by way of simplicity; indeed Morgan assumes that simplicity would dictate utilizing the most anthropomorphic explanation available. His own justification appears to invoke the idea that the psychic powers arrayed in his hierarchy evolve from one another, and hence looks to be intended as a specifically biological justification: "It is clear that any animal may be at a stage where certain higher faculties have not yet been evolved from their lower precursors; and hence we are logically bound not to assume the existence of these higher faculties until good reasons shall have been shown for such existence."[33] But as Sober argues, this is not enough to justify the Canon. There is no reason to suppose, even if it were true that the higher faculties were evolved from the lower, that the lower ones are more likely to explain any given piece of animal behavior than the higher. The evolution of the higher capacities might well involve the atrophy of the lower: faced with a given pattern of activity, then, there is no prior probability that it is a lower rather than a higher capacity that explains it.

Someone might think that the best justification for Morgan's Canon is that it guards against an opposing bias that is present in all of us: a bias toward anthropomorphic explanations and interpretations. I think it may well be true that human beings do have such a bias. We are good at searching for mindedness in the world, and it is undeniable that we have historically found it in many places where it turned out not to exist, inventing gods and demons, spirits and fairies, ghosts and goblins to explain phenomena that did not need to be thus explained. But in general it is not true that the best way to compensate for one bias is to introduce another. Evidentialism alone will do the trick and is far safer. All that is needed, when a suspiciously anthropomorphic explanation appears to be on the cards, is the caution that other possible explanations of the behavior in question may need to be investigated and empirical reasons found for preferring one of the rival explanations over the other.

Might it be objected, though, that evidentialism faces difficulties of its own? One might worry, perhaps, that "higher-level" explanations of any given pattern of observed animal behavior are always available in principle, and that without Morgan's Canon there is simply no way to discard these explanations, despite what might be alleged to be their intuitive extravagance. Consider, for example, a behavior of which we might suppose ourselves to have at least the basis of an entirely satisfactory, relatively "low-level" explanation—say, the tendency of worker ants from the same colony to respond effectively and instantly to danger to the nest, and in particular to its queen and larvae. In cases of serious danger, the whole nest is sometimes moved in response to an attack that cannot be successfully repelled by soldier ants, with worker ants carrying the vulnerable larvae to a safer place. The role of instinctive, pheromone-guided behavior in eliciting appropriate responses from individual worker ants has been intensively studied, and much scientific literature now exists on how these processes work to ensure the protection of the colony.[34] But of course it would be possible to envisage other, "higher-level" explanations of the same behavior. Perhaps, for example, someone might suggest that the response is mediated by emotion, by love for the colony, say, on the part of the ants, who then respond protectively in the light of their love. Without Morgan's Canon, it might be wondered whether there is any way decisively to rule out a suggestion that might strike some as intuitively absurd.

One possible riposte here would be to try to argue that evidentialism could lead only to the suggestion that we ought to suspend judgment about this case if an inappropriately restrictive interpretation of what could constitute a "reason to prefer" one theory over another is adopted. In this particular case, perhaps, one might expect that the "love" hypothesis could be rendered deeply improbable by further experimentation. But even if no such experiment could be devised, the point could be remade that reasons to prefer one theory over another may relate not only to observations that are strictly of the specific behavior to be explained but also to far more general considerations— such as, for example, the necessary conditions for the attribution of emotions such as love to a species of creature. These might involve a much more holistic view on the overall active repertoire of a given species of animal, and indeed might perfectly well include philosophical as well as scientific considerations. It seems plausible, for instance, that to attribute the capacity for love to a creature one would require evidence not only of a well-organized behavioral response to an attack on the purportedly loved entity but also of distress in response to the death or destruction of that entity; of specifically emotional forms of attachment, such as comforting and touching, for example; and an altogether more flexible repertoire of response to different kinds of threat to the survival and well-being of the larvae than ants are capable of displaying. Another possibility would be to invoke neurological evidence of a general kind relating to the supposed neural basis of the capacity for emotional response. At any rate, it seems very unlikely that there are cases in which *no* such general considerations would be available to provide reasons to allow one hypothesis to prevail over another. But in cases in which there truly were no such considerations, arguing for a reason to prefer the lower-level explanation over the higher, I would be inclined to stand by the verdict of evidentialism. If no reason, either scientific or philosophical, can be given for supposing that insects such as ants do not feel emotions, then we should remain agnostic until such time as reasons can be brought forward for preferring one explanation over the other. The danger otherwise is that in attempting to adopt a bias thought to be opposed to our natural anthropomorphic tendencies, we shall underestimate some of our fellow creatures.

Moreover when a bias is embraced by the scientific establishment in some discipline, things are likely to go particularly badly wrong. The very experiments that might serve (in a world where evidentialism held sway) to undermine the bias are likely to be discouraged, and if undertaken at all, their results may be treated with undue skepticism. In 2008 Franklin D. McMillan was still able to write that "it is still politically wise to present oneself as soundly behaviorist, if not radically so."[35] The particular bias in question in this case may interact in dangerous ways with other societal forces. There may be a gender component to anti-anthropomorphic sentiment in science; one can readily enough imagine it being supposed that it is foolish and oversentimental women who attribute mindedness to animals, and only men who are able to maintain a truly objective attitude. And human self-interest may also play a role. If animals are complex automata, we do not have to worry so much about agricultural methods, animal experimentation, the destruction of habitat, and so on. We have to be on our guard against the possibility that what masquerades as a sober methodological imperative in fact simply enshrines the prejudices that are most useful to us.

Is it mere speculation to suggest that Morgan's Canon may have been unneeded in psychology (given the availability of the evidentialist alternative) and could also prove actually to have been damaging? To conclude my discussion, I shall offer two examples of cases that shed light on this question in different ways. The first is a case discussed by Simon Fitzpatrick in his excellent critique of the Canon, a case in which the methodological imperatives of the Canon were ignored, to famously productive effect. The second is an instance in which they seem to have been followed, but where conclusions stronger than those really admissible appear to have been drawn in consequence, arguably as a result of Canonesque thinking.

Pernicious Effects

If one believed in Morgan's Canon, how might this affect one's research strategy? Plausibly it might affect one's sense of what one's working hypothesis ought to be in any given case. As Fitzpatrick notes, it might make plausible what he calls the "scaling up strategy"—that "in any given area of research into animal behavior, the working hypothesis should always be the least cognitively sophisticated explanation consistent with the available data."[36] But Fitzpatrick claims that there are many examples from the recent history of animal psychology where this was *not* the working hypothesis—and where exciting results were discovered in consequence. The case he discusses in detail is that of the discovery by Karl von Frisch of the famous honeybee dance and its role in the communication of bees about the location of food sources.[37] Von Frisch discovered that the bees' figure-eight-shaped "waggle dance" encodes three pieces of information: (1) the direction of the food source (encoded in the angle of the waggle movements through the center of the figure eight relative to the vertical, which represents the angle of the direction in which the food is located, relative to the angle of the sun); (2) the distance from the hive of the source, encoded in the duration of the waggle runs through the center of the figure eight; and (3) the quality of the food source, encoded in the vigor of the dance.

Who would have dreamed that bees possessed such a sophisticated communicative device? In the years immediately following the publication of von Frisch's findings, many were extremely skeptical of his claims, and critics defended an alternative "lower" hypothesis in terms of olfaction. If von Frisch had adopted similar views as his working hypothesis, it seems exceedingly unlikely that the significance of the honeybee dance would ever have been discovered. The exciting explanation he eventually offered of the ability of honeybees to use the waggle dance as a means of finding food was discovered only as a consequence of his conviction that the dance was a communicative strategy and his willingness to pursue this hypothesis with dedication. The lesson to be learned here, as Fitzpatrick suggests, is that researchers should be free to investigate whatever hypotheses suggest themselves, all things considered, untrammeled by a priori methodological assumptions. I turn now to a second case in which the perils of the Canon can be discerned in a somewhat different way.

In a paper entitled "Distress Vocalizations in Infant Rats: What's All the Fuss About?," Mark Blumberg and his coauthors report on their investigations into ultrasonic vocalizations emitted by infant rodents on being separated from the nest. Such vocalizations had previously been interpreted by some investigators as cries of distress; Blumberg et al. wanted to investigate the alternative hypothesis, that the vocalizations were merely "acoustic by-products of a physiological manoeuver, the abdominal compression reaction (ACR) that increases venous return to the heart when return is compromised."[38] This had been suggested to them by the existence of two other contexts known to reliably elicit ultrasound production: extreme exposure to cold and administration of clonidine. Each of these two contexts produces a decreased cardiac rate, against which the ACR maneuver provides some protection. Their experiments revealed that administration of clonidine did indeed increase venal return to the heart (as well as ultrasound emission). These results, they suggest, "provide strong, direct support for the ACR hypothesis, and, by doing so, underscore the potential pitfalls of anthropomorphic interpretations of the vocalizations of infant rats."[39]

If the ACR hypothesis is the hypothesis that the vocalizations produced by infant rats when removed from the nest are mere byproducts of a physiological maneuver, we must ask what it means to say that the experimental results "provide strong direct support for the ACR hypothesis." It is legitimate to say that *relative to the state of the evidence prior to these experiments having been done*, there is now more reason than there was previously to think the hypothesis is a possible explanation of the vocalizations—because we now know of another context in which ultrasound production and increased venous return go together. But that is *all* we can say. We cannot make any further judgments. The ACR hypothesis is somewhat more likely *than it was before* to be true, but we cannot say (on the basis of these experiments alone) that it is now more likely to be true than the explanation in terms of emotional distress. So the results do not provide strong or direct experimental support for the ACR hypothesis *as against the distress hypothesis*. We are still entirely in the dark about which hypothesis offers the better explanation of the phenomenon observed.

In light of this, what entitles Blumberg and his colleagues to make the claims they do about the perils of anthropomorphic interpretation? We have no reason whatever, as yet, to suppose that the explanation in terms of emotional distress is mistaken. We *do* have reason to think that we should, for the moment, be agnostic until further inquiry has given us reason to think one or other explanation is definitely better. Perhaps Blumberg et al. merely mean to make the point that other explanations for the infant rat vocalizations may be possible and should have been considered before the distress vocalization hypothesis had been endorsed. That is true enough, and mere evidentialism would support it. But it seems to me that Blumberg and his colleagues mean to go further than this. In a follow-up paper they suggest that their theory, which claims that "a common physiological event triggers ultrasound production regardless of the context or manipulation used," is more parsimonious than that offered by the distress hypothesis— a claim that in this context is perilously close to an invocation of the Canon, a plea to favor the "lower" process, which seems to offer a good explanation in the clonidine case, over the "higher," which attributes an emotional state to the infant rats. But considerations of parsimony cut both ways. For we know that emotional distress is the reason some infant animals vocalize, so there is a variety of explanatory parsimony one can draw on to support the "higher" explanation too. Blumberg and his coauthors are right that "it certainly does not follow that all infant vocalizations are emitted for a communicatory purpose."[40] But once again the correct response is agnosticism and further investigation. One can draw, I suggest, no conclusions at all about the relative likeliness that ACR explains the ultrasonic vocalizations, as opposed to the hypothesis of emotional distress, from the research they cite.

CONCLUSION

It is almost impossible for an armchair philosopher criticizing the practices and assumptions of working empirical scientists to avoid courting opprobrium. So perhaps it is necessary to say, in conclusion, that I hold no brief for anecdotalism, nor for inappropriately anthropomorphic interpretations of animal life, and I have the utmost respect for empirical methods. But one should not confuse the application of the Canon with the careful interpretation of empirical results. The role it has played amounts, in my view, to a rejection of the cautious agnosticism that ought to be the proper response to an as yet empirically unsettled question as to what mental capacities truly account for a particular instance of animal behavior.

CHAPTER TWELVE

The Contemporary Debate in Animal Ethics

Robert Garner

It is useful to consider the development of contemporary animal ethics within the prism of three historical periods. Up until the 1970s, with a small number of exceptions, the moral worth of animals was widely regarded, in theory and practice, as inferior to that of humans. This inferior moral status was challenged in the 1970s and later by philosophers invoking rights-based, utilitarian, and contractarian frameworks in order to establish a moral status for animals that is much closer to that which is commonly attached to humans. This was accompanied by a reinvigorated and radicalized animal protection movement emphasizing grass-roots campaigning and an animal rights ideology. Since the 1990s the debate in animal ethics has fragmented, with attempts to provide a more nuanced animal rights position together with the development of relational approaches based on the care ethic, drawn from the feminist tradition, and citizenship, from political philosophy.

The Dominance of the Animal Welfare Orthodoxy

Prior to the nineteenth century animals were commonly regarded, in theory and practice, as having no moral standing.[1] This was typified, philosophically, by Descartes's assertion that animals lack sentience and Kant's claim that animals are not moral agents in the sense that they are not capable of recognizing right from wrong or capable of participating in moral agreements.[2] For those who hold that animals have no moral standing, the only duties we have toward them are indirect ones. That is, harming animals becomes morally significant only if it harms the interests of other humans, such as in the common argument that those who are cruel to animals are likely to be inclined to treat humans in the same way. This alleged link, it has been suggested, was the rationale for much of the early nineteenth-century animal protection law.[3]

There are still some contemporary moral philosophers—most notably Peter Carruthers[4]—who argue, usually from a contractarian perspective, that animals have no moral standing. For the vast majority of contemporary moral philosophers (or at least those who have written about the matter), however, animals are sentient, possess some direct moral worth, and are therefore owed something from us. Of crucial importance in transforming the intellectual climate was the advent of utilitarianism in the nineteenth century. Jeremy Bentham set the scene for this transformation in the moral status of animals when he wrote, in an oft-quoted passage, that "the question" of moral status is not "Can they reason? Nor, Can they talk? But, Can they suffer?"[5] The utilitarian position that sentience provides the benchmark for moral standing has had a considerable influence on debates about the moral worth of animals leading to the acceptability, in theory and practice, of the animal welfare ethic. As we shall see, the contemporary utilitarian Peter Singer invokes the sentience criterion to go beyond the animal welfare ethic. Animals' lack of moral agency (and, in general terms, their lack of the collection of capacities usually described in shorthand as autonomy) is still, for some, philosophically important, but it is now more often than not invoked to deprive animals of an increase in moral status rather than the existence of any moral standing at all. There is a consensus, in other words, that the sentience of animals means that we have some moral obligations to them.

The central feature of the animal welfare ethic is an insistence that humans are morally superior to animals but that, since animals have some moral worth, we are not entitled to inflict suffering on them if the human benefit thereby resulting is not necessary. The principle of *unnecessary suffering*, therefore, can be invoked if the level of suffering inflicted on an animal outweighs the benefits likely to be gained by humans. The political philosopher Robert Nozick provides a concise but admirably effective definition of animal welfare when he writes that it constitutes "utilitarianism for animals, Kantianism for people."[6] Sacrificing the interests of animals for the aggregative welfare, then, is permissible providing that the benefit is significant enough, but treating humans in the same way is prohibited whatever the benefits that might accrue from so doing.

The animal welfare ethic became the dominant position in the animal ethics literature and still remains the dominant force behind state approaches to the treatment of animals. There are two observations I would make about the animal welfare ethic, both of which help to clarify and deepen understanding of the position. The first is to emphasize that animal welfare as an ethic differs from animal welfare as a science. The study of animal welfare in a scientific context dates back to the 1960s and is now a recognized and respected part of veterinary science.[7] This discipline studies what is necessary for the physical and psychological well-being of animals. It is, in general, true that the development of animal welfare science was largely a product of ethical concerns about the well-being of domesticated animals.[8] Likewise a scientific evaluation of an animal's welfare is a crucial component in assessing the ethical validity of a particular practice. The fact, for instance, that animal welfare scientists tell us that a certain husbandry system causes animals to suffer is clearly morally significant. Such an empirical observation, however, does not, by itself, determine whether or not this husbandry system is permissible from an ethical perspective since it does not tell us whether or not it is deemed to be necessary.

A second thing to note about the animal welfare ethic is how vague and therefore flexible the concept of *unnecessary* suffering is. What is characterized as unnecessary will vary over time and place. While this flexibility may be useful in a political context, from an ethical point of view it is less than ideal. A number of scholars have sought to fill in the gaps here by offering more rigorous accounts of what exactly this means for animals in terms of how far their interests are discounted. A typical analysis is the one offered by Rachels, who distinguishes between a "radical speciesism" and a "mild speciesism."[9] The former is where "the relatively trivial interests of humans take priority over the vital interests of nonhumans." The latter is where "we may choose for the nonhuman" when "the choice is between a relatively trivial human interest and a more substantial interest of a nonhuman." Becker's category of "absolute speciesism" goes further than Rachels's "radical speciesism" by refusing "to rank any animal interest (no matter how serious) above any human interest (no matter how trivial)."[10] Such a position, though, comes close to denying any moral concern for animals and therefore might be regarded as inconsistent with an animal welfare ethic.

Rachels's two categories are best seen as representing the extremes of the animal welfare ethical continuum, a position he describes as "qualified speciesism."[11] Which point on the continuum is chosen in practice, and enshrined in law, will depend upon geographical and historical factors. Brody, probably correctly, suggests that the United States operates a regime for animal experimentation that is closer to radical speciesism, as Rachels defines it, while the European approach is closer to a mild speciesism position.[12]

THE SINGER-REGAN DEBATE

The animal welfare ethic began to be challenged in the 1970s onward. Indeed this era marked an astonishing growth of academic interest in animal ethics. In his extensive bibliography, Charles Magel allocates ten pages for philosophical material on animals up to 1970 and no fewer than thirteen pages for material published in the subsequent two decades.[13] Since the late 1980s this literature has mushroomed even further. Our treatment of animals is now taken seriously as a main-stream branch of applied ethics, to be examined along with other moral questions such as abortion and euthanasia in degree-level phi-losophy courses and is increasingly a topic for discussion in schools.

Much of the post-1970 academic literature sought to challenge the moral orthodoxy. The academic debate was, initially at least, dominated by two philosophers, the Australian Peter Singer and the American Tom Regan. What is significant about these challenges to the moral orthodoxy is that they utilize previously existing and con-ventional traditions of thought. The first to do so (at least in book form) was Singer.[14] Somewhat ironically, a fact not lost on Regan and others, Singer is not an advocate of rights but is an exponent of utilitar-ianism, the heir of Bentham. Singer suggests that we ought to treat like interests alike (the equal consideration of interests), and since at least some animals are sentient it is morally illegitimate to prioritize the human interest in not suffering on all occasions. In some situations, indeed, there may be a case for saying that animals can suffer more than humans and therefore their interests should prevail. This, Singer argues, is the conclusion Bentham ought to have reached.

Singer's utilitarian position was challenged by critics of the attempt to justify an enhanced moral status for animals. Perhaps the most sus-tained critique, though, came from those philosophers who argued that Singer's position did not provide a firm enough foundation for the enhanced moral status he sought to establish. Central to this strand of thought is Regan's animal rights position.[15] Regan seeks to show that at least some animals are what he calls "subjects-of-a-life," possessing enough mental complexity to be morally considerable. Because at least some animals have the relevant capabilities, Regan argues that they have a welfare that may be harmed not only through pain and deprivation but also by death, since it forecloses all possibilities of finding satisfaction in life. The key point is that rights are not granted to animals by virtue of their sentience (although this was in fact Regan's early position) but because they are "subjects-of-a-life"—that is, beings with considerable cognitive capabilities.

I describe Regan's position as a species-egalitarian version of animal rights, on the grounds that, to all intents and purposes, it advocates moral equality between humans and animals, in that they each share an equal right to life and liberty. A corollary of this is that—for most animal rights philosophers, animal rights activists, and, indeed, their opponents too—animal rights and abolitionism are synonymous. The abolitionist position draws its inspiration from the work of Regan, and its best known contemporary advocate is probably Gary Francione, who has written extensively on the subject.[16] Abolitionism seeks, on the grounds that animals have a right to life and liberty, a prohibition on the use of animals by humans *irrespective of the ways in which they are treated*. Thus, for Regan, the animal rights movement "is abolitionist in its aspirations. It seeks not to reform how animals are exploited…but to abolish their exploitation. To end it. Completely."[17]

Not surprisingly, perhaps, debates between the Singer and Regan camps tended to overshadow critical responses from exponents of the moral orthodoxy. It is particularly important here to tackle the major contours of the debate surrounding Singer's work. There are at least three aspects to this. The first is the claim, often made by animal rights abolitionists, that Singer's position is equivalent to the animal welfare position. To fully assess this claim, we have to go back to Bentham. The logic of Bentham's position is to equate the like suffering of humans and animals. Indeed the emphasis he placed on the moral importance of sentience led his critics to claim that he was promoting the base pleasures and therefore encouraging individuals to live debased lives of sensual indulgence. For our purposes, though, what is crucial is that the emphasis on sentience in the classical utilitarianism of Bentham played an important role in putting animals on the moral agenda.

Bentham, for whatever reason, failed to draw the radical implications that seemed to follow from his ethical theory. Indeed he seemed to settle on a version of animal welfare, supporting, for instance, the use of animals in medical research.[18]

Singer does draw such radical conclusions from utilitarianism. It is true that, all things being equal, Singer does seem to regard animal life as less important morally than human life because humans, as autonomous beings, can have richer lives than animals. In a sense, though, this is not a theoretically significant observation for utilitarians because for them the morally important criterion is sentience, or the ability to suffer, and therefore the question of life and death for either animals or humans is not of primary concern philosophically. Singer's position is often, incorrectly, equated with the animal welfare ethic because he does not use the concept of rights for animals. However, the key point is that Singer does not attach rights to either humans or animals. A morally correct action, on his view, is one that maximizes pleasures or preferences, whether of humans or of animals. For Singer, to prioritize human interests in the way that the animal welfare ethic does is speciesist because it is basing moral superiority on species membership rather than a morally relevant characteristic. Thus, while the animal welfare ethic would not countenance the sacrificing of nontrivial human interests, whatever the benefits of this were to animals, the logic of Singer's utilitarianism would allow this.

The second debate surrounding Singer's work relates to the value of animal lives. There is a widely held perception that Singer thinks there is nothing wrong morally with killing animals, provided that replacements are forthcoming to maintain the same amount of pleasure in the world, and that what is morally wrong about our treatment of animals is the infliction of suffering on them. This position is based on the assumption that, by itself, killing an animal does no harm to the animal. This, in turn, is based on the claim that animals are not self-conscious, and therefore have no sense of themselves existing over time. As a result it is permissible morally to kill animals painlessly provided that they are replaced by beings who live equally pleasant lives. Hare adopts this interpretation: "For utilitarians like Singer and myself, doing wrong to animals must involve harming them. If there is no harm there is no wrong."[19] As a result killing them is not a moral problem. All that matters is that those animals that are killed are replaced by others who live equally pleasant lives.

However, this is not quite Singer's position. It is true that he accepts that in the case of animals who are not self-conscious, and therefore have no sense of themselves existing over time, it is permissible morally to kill them provided they are replaced by beings who live equally pleasant lives. In this sense eating animals that have had pleasant lives and that are killed painlessly presents no moral problem.[20] However, Singer also argues that for animals that are self-conscious there *is* a direct loss to them caused by death (in the form of the denying of the preference that such individuals have for continued life). Therefore these preferences should be taken into account.[21] In other words, the individual lives of self-conscious animals do count morally.

The third area of debate surrounding Singer's position is the aggregative character of utilitarianism. Singer is an act utilitarian.[22] As such, when judging the ethical permissibility of a particular use of animals he is required to weigh the total number of preferences, including preferences to go on living, that would be satisfied if that use is prohibited. The problem for Singer, as noted by his animal rights critics, is that if we factor in all of the consequences likely to follow a particular improvement to the way that animals are treated, the improvement may not prove to be justified on utilitarian grounds. It may be doubted whether Singer is right that, on a utilitarian calculation, we should not farm animals for food or use them as experimental subjects. Assuming that we can realistically hope to weigh all of the preferences involved, there would seem to be numerous human preferences that would be served by continuing these practices. In the case of animal agriculture, for instance, it is clearly not the case that all we have to do is simply weigh the most fundamental interests of animals against the most trivial interests of humans. Rather, to what might be regarded as a trivial interest—the fact that many humans like the taste of meat—must be added less trivial human interests, such as the undoubtedly significant economic costs of the elimination of all forms of animal agriculture.[23]

The key point is that, at the very least, "it is not *obviously* true" that the end of animal agriculture would result in a surplus of preferences met.[24] A utilitarian calculation does not even necessarily justify the end of factory farming, although there is clearly a stronger case for this conclusion since animals do not live pleasant lives in factory farms, and moreover there are plenty of human-interest grounds—environmental protection, better human health—for eliminating it. One would have thought, too, that a utilitarian case for ending all animal experimentation would, if anything, be even harder to sustain given the claim that this use of animals can have very beneficial health consequences for both humans and animals, in addition to the economic costs of abolishing it.

A Contractarian Diversion

The work of Singer and Regan (and the rights and utilitarian traditions, which have a long history in Western thought) have tended to dominate the animal ethics debate. One less well known strand is drawn from the social contract tradition in Western political thought. This has centered on the work of John Rawls, a central figure in contemporary political philosophy.[25] Rawls reinvigorated the social contract tradition, associated most notably with Locke and Hobbes. In Rawls's imaginary negotiating position (which he describes as the original position) parties to the contract meet to determine principles of justice behind what he calls a "veil of ignorance," where the participants know nothing about their particular abilities, tastes, and position within the social structure. Rawls explicitly excludes animals as beneficiaries of a theory of justice because, lacking moral agency, they are unable to participate in a contractarial agreement—although it should be pointed out that he does not exclude animals as beneficiaries of a wider theory of morality, as do other contractarians, such as Carruthers.[26]

Some philosophers, most notably Mark Rowlands, have sought to adapt Rawls's social contract in a way that allows for the inclusion of animals, therefore providing a third strand of the challenge to the moral orthodoxy.[27] In traditional accounts of the social contract, animals are excluded because, lacking moral agency, they cannot be part of the (hypothetical) negotiations whereby participants meet to discuss what principles would serve their self-interest. For Rowlands, this type of contract is Hobbesian. But there is another version of the contract, a Kantian version, and Rowlands argues not only that this version enables us to include animals but also that this is the version that Rawls, in the main, adopts. In a Kantian version of the contract, the principles of justice adopted are not merely constituted by the participants. Rather the principles arrived at through the contract have to be continually checked against preexisting moral principles that exist independently of the contract and the contractors. Rowlands argues that the key "moral law" that Rawls advocates is "equal consideration," or what Rowlands calls the "intuitive equality argument" (IEA). This is the argument that individuals should not benefit from the possession of characteristics, such as ability or rationality, for which they are not responsible. The principles of justice emanating from the contract, then, must, for Rowlands, be consistent with the IEA.

If we adopt this principle, Rowlands suggests, there is nothing to stop us from including nonmoral agents, such as animals and marginal humans, as beneficiaries of principles of justice. For Rowlands, the IEA insists that we include animals (and marginal humans) because rationality itself is not a characteristic that we have earned. Rather we just have it as a matter of luck. Thus, just as specific human abilities—and more general characteristics such as age, gender, race, and class—are hidden behind the veil of ignorance, rationality is an equally undeserved natural advantage that also ought to be hidden. Including species as an unknown characteristic behind the veil of ignorance means, then, that the participants in the original position do not now know if they are going to turn out to be moral agents or non-rational entities such as animals or marginal humans.[28] Once it is allowed that knowledge of one's species should be one of those things excluded by the veil of ignorance, it would be just as irrational to opt for a system that permitted harmful or injurious treatment of nonhumans as it would be to opt for a system that permitted the same sort of treatment for humans.

Three major criticisms can be made of Rowlands's attempt to amend Rawls. The first questions whether it is possible for participants behind the veil of ignorance to be ignorant of their status as human beings.[29] Rawls imputes to the contractors a number of intellectual capacities, and it is doubtful whether they could be ignorant of their species. Of course Rowlands and others would respond by saying that this does not preclude the possibility of the human contractors simply imagining that they may still turn out to be nonhumans once the veil is lifted. The second criticism is to question whether, even if the participants know they might turn out to be animals once the veil of ignorance is lifted, they would adopt a risk-averse strategy and opt for an end to the exploitation of animals. They might, in other words, risk being animals once the veil is lifted. They might rationalize, for instance, that, as animals, they would not be autonomous agents and therefore would have less to lose by death.

The third criticism of Rowlands's revision of Rawls relates to his Kantian interpretation of the contract.[30] We can readily accept that this is closer to Rawls's own position than the Hobbesian version. However, the problem with accepting that there are moral principles we value independently of what is decided by the participants in the contractual situation is that it reduces the importance of the contract device. It amounts to saying that the contract must be so organized as to reflect these important preexisting moral principles, or at least to consider them seriously. Thus, even though the consequences of adopting a Hobbesian version of the contract is the exclusion of animals because they lack the moral agency required to participate, Rawls's exclusion of animals is arguably made prior to his use of the contractual device. That is, by concluding that only moral agents should be beneficiaries of justice Rawls has already made the decision that animals ought to be excluded from his theory of justice. Principles emanating from Rawls's contract are therefore not the result of an objective account of what participants in the original position would choose but reflect preexisting normative judgments, one of which is that justice applies only to persons. Why, then, it might be asked, does Rowlands bother to reinterpret the Rawlsian contract when most of the work is being done by principles that can be justified independently of it?

The Backlash against Singer and Regan

The arrival of Singer's and Regan's work—along with a considerable body of literature from other moral philosophers in one or other of the camps[31]—produced a backlash. A number of philosophers sought to reassert the moral superiority of humans. Traditional defenses—based, for example, on claims about the human possession of an immortal soul—seem unlikely to succeed in a more secular age. Another obvious defense is to adopt a position that regards human species membership alone as sufficient to justify differential treatment. Without an argument to explain *why* it is that humans should be regarded in a superior light, this position does not seem to pass a qualifying test either. For one thing, the same kind of justification invoked to privilege human moral status in this defense could be used to grant a privileged moral status to, say, a particular gender or race.[32]

In order to defend the moral superiority of humans, advocates of the animal welfare ethic tend to argue that humans have morally significant characteristics not possessed by nonhuman animals. As Steinbock states, "We do not subject animals to different moral treatment simply because they have fur and feathers, but because they are in fact different from human beings in ways that could be morally relevant."[33]

Humans, it is typically said, are rational, self-conscious, autonomous persons, able to communicate in a sophisticated way and to act as moral agents. This is often converted into a shorthand claim that humans are persons, while animals are not (the personhood position). From this empirical evidence, it is argued, can be derived a justification for regarding humans as morally superior to nonhumans and therefore providing a defense of the moral orthodoxy.[34]

Regan, as we have seen, does claim that at least some animals are not merely sentient but are what he calls "subjects-of-a-life," characterized by beliefs and desires and capable of acting intentionally to satisfy their preferences. All subjects-of-a-life for Regan (including both humans and animals) have inherent value. Regan is surely correct to claim that at least some animals do possess more than mere sentience. It is still difficult to establish, though, that the cognitive characteristics possessed by animals are anything remotely approaching those possessed by most humans. This point is well drawn out by Raymond Frey.[35] He distinguishes between control and preference autonomy. Normal humans can exercise "control autonomy," which is equivalent to a Kantian notion of autonomy. This involves individuals themselves choosing what they want to achieve and organizing their lives in pursuit of this goal. We will not be autonomous to the extent that we allow ourselves to be coerced by others and to the extent that we allow our life plan to become subservient to our "first-order" desires—eating, drinking, drugs, and so on.

Animals, Frey continues, can exercise only "preference autonomy," which requires merely that beings be able to have desires, or preferences, and have the ability to initiate actions with a view to satisfying them. Absent from this notion of autonomy are the key features of control autonomy. The latter involves a much higher quality of life and the capacity to assess desires rationally and to shed or moderate some, particularly first-order, desires if they are not consistent with an individual's conception of the good life. At most, then, animals are capable of dealing only with a very basic set of first-order desires, which denies them "means to that rich full life of self-fulfillment and achievement" that is "quite apart from any satisfaction and fulfilment that comes through the satisfaction of our appetites."[36]

The distinction Frey makes is of particular importance when we come to the issue of the respective interest humans and animals have in life itself. Here it is clear that many, if not most, animal ethicists who agree that animals ought to be granted a higher moral status than the moral orthodoxy allows, do accept that, although at least some animals have an interest in continued life, those normal adult humans who possess the characteristics of personhood—rationality, autonomy, a sophisticated communication system, moral agency, and so on—have a greater interest in continued life. The argument that the duty not to kill animals is as strong as the duty not to kill humans is, in DeGrazia's words, "very hard to believe."[37] Likewise for McMahan it is "uncontroversial" to regard the killing of an animal as less seriously wrong than the killing of a human.[38]

Nevertheless animal ethicists who dispute the moral force of the personhood view have responded in a number of ways to the claim that humans, because of their status as persons, should be regarded as morally superior to animals. A dominant response to the personhood view is to deny either the differences between humans and animals or the moral significance of those differences. One version of the former approach points to the cognitive capacity of "higher" nonhuman animals, such as the Great Apes, which it is argued ought to put them on a par morally with most humans.[39] It is clear that some species of nonhuman animals have at least some of the characteristics of personhood. It makes sense, therefore, to give these species the benefit of the doubt and treat them as if they have the same interests as most humans.

However, important though it may be to acknowledge that more needs to be done to protect the interests of the "higher" nonhuman animals, all this recognition does is to create a new moral boundary, above which are most humans and those nonhuman species that possess at least some of the characteristics of personhood, and below which are the vast majority of other nonhuman animals. It does not, in other words, provide a justification for the kind of broad application of rights to animals that is usually regarded as the aim of animal rights advocacy.

A more fundamental response is to deny that the possession of personhood has the moral weight that defenders of the moral orthodoxy claim for it. There are at least two versions of this critique. One is to argue that, since humans possess the characteristics of personhood to varying degrees, the personhood position commits us to a sliding moral scale, with the most cognitively endowed having considerable moral status and the least endowed having the lowest moral status, with gradations of moral status in between. A possible answer to this objection is to identify a threshold beyond which all have the equal moral status of personhood.[40] It is justifiable, it seems to me, to say that those above this threshold, exhibiting the characteristics of personhood, have a similar interest in life, liberty, and the avoidance of suffering, even though there may be variations in the psychological capacity of individuals above this threshold. Drawing the line, though, is difficult.

The stronger version of the denial that the possession of personhood has the moral weight that defenders of the moral orthodoxy claim for it is the so-called argument from marginal cases (AMC). Those humans deemed to be "marginal" are infants, anencephalic babies—a condition where a baby's brain is seriously underdeveloped—the permanently comatose, the severely retarded, those who have suffered severe mental impairment through strokes, those with advanced dementia, and so on. The AMC is ubiquitous in the animal ethics literature, providing the major critique of the personhood position.[41] There are, in fact, two versions of the AMC. In what Pluhar[42] describes as the "bioconditional" version, it is argued that *if* marginal humans are regarded as having the same moral status as other, nonmarginal humans, then consistency demands that animals of cognitive ability similar to the former ought to be accorded the same moral worth as the latter. The second version of the AMC, what Pluhar calls the "categorical" version, holds that *because* marginal humans (or human nonpersons) are deemed to have maximum moral significance, consistency demands that animals with a cognitive capacity equivalent to theirs are accorded the same moral status as they. The difference between the two versions is that the former, bioconditional version could be used to justify excluding both animals and marginal humans from maximum moral significance.

Defenders of the personhood position have sought to deny the force of the AMC in a number of ways. The most common device is the "appeal to thwarted potential."[43] Here it is argued that it is justifiable morally to treat those with the potential to become persons as if they were persons, since to fail to do so is to thwart this potential. There is, however, a question mark against the moral importance of potential, one implication being that it makes abortion, and even the use of contraception, a serious wrong.[44] In addition it has limited application, applying only to infants and not to other marginal humans.

Other critiques of the AMC have a more general application. Two (in my view weak) responses are, first, the slippery slope justification,[45] whereby nonmarginal humans may be mistaken for marginal humans, and, second, the claim that marginal humans are the same "kind" as "normal" humans and are therefore different from animals.[46] Against the first, there is little evidence that societies have had difficulty in distinguishing between marginal and nonmarginal humans. In any case, what matters philosophically is not whether these groups are mistaken for one another but whether there is actually a difference between them. In the case of the second, it is difficult to see how a biological criterion, such as species, can have any moral significance.[47]

There are a number of more promising critiques of the AMC. The first is the "difference in kind" argument, which suggests that most, if not all, marginal humans still have cognitive characteristics closer in kind to "normal" humans than they do to most species of nonhumans.[48] This objection to the AMC depends, of course, on an empirical examination of the respective psychological characteristics of marginal humans and animals. Much will therefore depend on the level of cognitive impairment encountered by the marginal human and the species of animal it is being compared with. What can be said is that it is undoubtedly true that, in some cases at least, the psychological capacities of some animals compare favorably with those of some marginal humans. For example, anencephalic infants are born without the capacity for consciousness, and those with advanced Alzheimer's disease have little capacity for thought and perception, to the point that they have arguably ceased to exist as a person.[49]

A second, more promising response to the AMC is a relational argument, whereby the relevant difference between animals and marginal humans relates to extrinsic relational factors and not to intrinsic psychological characteristics. One version of this argument is provided by McMahan.[50] It can be argued, he suggests, that it is the special relations we have with marginal humans—primarily as relatives—from which we can derive moral reasons to treat them more favorably than animals with similar psychological characteristics. The problem with this argument is that marginal humans are dependent for the existence of the full panoply of rights on relations they have with other, nonmarginal humans. In other words, those marginal humans who do not have such relationships—such as orphans or those with callous and unfeeling carers—do not, according to the relational position, possess the same moral status as nonmarginal humans.[51] The arbitrary nature of this allocation of moral value would seem problematic.

FRAGMENTATION, PART 1: A NUANCED
ANIMAL RIGHTS POSITION

In more recent years the animal ethics debate has moved beyond the Singer/Regan axis. In the first place, there have been challenges to the commonly held position that defending animal rights is synonymous with the abolition of all uses of animals. Central to this challenge to the animal rights orthodoxy is the adoption of an alternative theory of rights. As we have seen, the abolitionist assumption derives from Regan's claim that to use animals, irrespective of how they are treated while being used, is to infringe on their right to respect, which, in turn, derives from what Regan sees as their inherent value. Such an account depends upon the employment of a particular, Kantian approach to rights, which holds that the function of rights is to establish arenas within which individuals can exercise choices.[52]

There is, however, an alternative theory of rights, based on interests. The interest theory of rights holds that the function of rights is to uphold individual well-being.[53] The possession of an interest therefore leads to a duty on others to ensure that the right, the existence of which follows directly from the existence of an interest, is upheld. Advocates of an interest-based theory of rights are not suggesting that all interests can be translated into rights, only that rights derive from interests. It may be that we decide that some, relatively trivial interests are not strong enough to be translated into rights, whereas others clearly are, or that some interests ought not to be promoted because they harm others.[54] Obviously, this insight has important ramifications for an interest-based theory of animal rights.

Adopting an interest-based theory allows for a much more nuanced, and arguably more convincing, theory of animal rights. This alternative theory of rights has been present for a long time in the animal ethics literature, in the work of philosophers such as Rachels and Feinberg, but it has been overshadowed by the Regan position.[55] The first comprehensive interest-based theory of animal rights was that of Alasdair Cochrane.[56] He begins by arguing, in line with defenders of the moral orthodoxy, that animals do not possess an interest in liberty because, unlike humans, they are not autonomous agents. As a result they do not have an automatic right to liberty. But for Cochrane a lack of autonomy does not imply a lack of rights. For example, on his view animals do have an interest in avoiding suffering (and therefore a right not to have suffering inflicted on them), and so in cases where the use of animals does infringe on this right it ought to be prohibited. The effect of this analysis, then, is to "decouple animal rights from animal liberation."[57]

Being able to identify particular interests that animals (and humans) possess allows us to develop a much less rigid theory of animal rights than the version associated with Regan. Rachels made a similar observation as far back as 1990. His approach, which he describes as "moral individualism," emphasizes that how an individual should be treated ought to depend on his or her own particular characteristics. Once attention is directed away from species membership and toward particular characteristics of individuals, the door is left open to emphasize those characteristics possessed by nonhuman animals and humans alike, and at the same time to be aware that not all humans have the same characteristics.[58]

In my view, this revised version of animal rights enables us to critique the moral orthodoxy as well as the species-egalitarian strand of animal rights.[59] The major problem with the moral orthodoxy is the assumption that the identification of characteristics unique to humans—in this case rationality, autonomy, language, and so forth—is sufficient for the claim that all human interests are morally superior to all animal interests. An interest-based theory of animal rights would, as we have seen, allow us to say that, while animals may not possess an interest in liberty and continued life—or at least have less of an interest than humans do—animals may nonetheless possess a considerable interest in other things, not least an interest in avoiding suffering. If this interest translates into a right, it clearly places limits on what might be done to animals in pursuance of human benefit and certainly does not justify the blanket exploitation of animals allowed by the moral orthodoxy. In particular, if humans and animals are capable of suffering in an equivalent manner, then why is this capacity of animals downgraded on the grounds that humans also possess the characteristics of personhood? The fact that humans are persons and animals are not cannot justify the whole range of differences in our treatment of humans and animals that the moral orthodoxy wants it to. To put it simply, torturing an animal is wrong because it hurts. Here the fact that the animal does not have the characteristics of personhood would seem to be irrelevant. As Rachels points out, "Autonomy and self-consciousness are not ethical superqualities that entitle the bearer to every possible kind of favorable treatment."[60]

This more nuanced animal rights position allows us to avoid the blanket inegalitarianism contained in the moral orthodoxy. Equally it enables us to avoid the blanket egalitarianism that is a central feature of the Regan-inspired strand of animal rights. Like the personhood view, Regan's approach is concerned with identifying a single characteristic (inherent value) that can explain the possession of rights for animals. The moral orthodoxy is flawed because it does not take into account the fact that, like humans, animals have important interests—such as avoiding suffering. These interests do not presuppose possession of the characteristics of personhood—rationality, autonomy, language, and so forth. The species-egalitarian version of animal rights is similarly guilty, but rather than failing to take into account the importance of nonpersonhood interests, it fails to take into account the moral significance of those interests associated with persons. In other words, the species-egalitarian strand of animal rights is flawed because it is difficult to argue against the claim that the differences between "normal" adult humans and adult animals are both substantial and morally significant. An individual's level of complexity affects what can be a harm for it, and thus the nature of its interests.

In particular the fact that most animals lack the characteristics of personhood challenges the claim that they have equivalent levels of interest in life and liberty to "normal" humans. Moral egalitarianism between humans and animals founders on the fact that humans and animals do not have equally important interests in life and liberty. From this we might want to conclude that the interest animals have in life and liberty are not strong enough to be translated into a right. The more nuanced animal rights position enables us to differentiate between the interests of humans and nonhuman animals in a way that the species-egalitarian strand of animal rights is unable to do. This alternative animal rights position does not necessarily entail moral equality between humans and animals. Instead the like interests of humans and animals are to be treated equally, and their unlike interests are to be treated unequally. Differentiating between the interests of humans and those of animals allows us to paint a much more complex, and realistic, picture of our moral obligations to animals.

FRAGMENTATION, PART 2: THE RELATIONAL TURN IN ANIMAL ETHICS

The animal ethics debate has fragmented in other ways too. New approaches—utilizing the virtue ethics tradition, on the one hand, and the notion of capabilities, on the other—have been applied to animals.[61] Animal ethics has also taken a relational turn. Traditionally animal ethics has used what Palmer calls a "capacity-oriented" approach.[62] According to this approach, moral status or worth is granted on the basis of the possession of some capacity or other, whether it be mere sentience or greater cognitive capacities. A major alternative approach is the adoption of a relational ethic, whereby, in its pure sense at least, the moral status of an individual is based not upon her capacities or interests but upon the relationship she has with others.

The relational approach has its roots in the feminist care ethic tradition. The emphasis on care derives from the work of Carol Gilligan, who posits a dualism between a masculine focus on rights, justice, and autonomy and a feminine tendency to focus on caring, responsibility, and interaction with others.[63] Care ethicists have argued that we should value emotion and sentiment over reason and that our moral obligations should derive from the relationships we develop and not as a result of impartial rules. Applied to animals, then, our duties to them are based not on the grounds of impartial and abstract principles but on our duty to care about those animals with whom we forge relationships.[64]

The overriding problem with relational ethics in general, and the care ethic in particular, is that if we adopt a theory that grounds moral duties in the relationships we forge, it is difficult to see how moral duties can be applied to those with whom we do not forge a relationship. In the case of animals, for instance, some animals are likely to fare better—companion animals rather than farm and laboratory animals, for instance—and it could be argued that the protection of animals is in fact less likely to be ensured by an ethic that focuses on partial relationships, since our relationships with members of our own species are likely to be stronger than the ones we develop with nonhumans.[65] It would seem intuitively mistaken, because morally arbitrary, to deny moral entitlements to animals (and indeed humans) with whom we do not have a relationship, irrespective of their cognitive capacities.

One area wherein the relational ethic is more convincing than the traditional capacity-based approach, though, is in its apparent potential to account for the different ways we regard domesticated and wild animals. That is, it is more able to account for the "laissez-faire" intuition whereby it is permissible morally to leave wild animals to their fate, while it is unacceptable to neglect domesticated animals in the same way, irrespective of the cognitive capacities of the animals concerned.[66] A relational ethic can justify leaving wild animals alone and therefore avoid debates about whether we ought to intervene to prevent the suffering of wild animals not least when this suffering is caused by other animals, as in predation. By contrast, domesticated animals, because of the relationship we have with them, can expect us to intervene in a positive fashion to prevent and alleviate suffering, at least when it is not against our interests to do so.

There are two critical observations we can make here. In the first place, it might be argued that, in certain circumstances at least, there is a moral case for intervening to protect the interests of wild animals, and this is precisely what happens in practice. Humans do, for instance, sometimes intervene to prevent predation (as in the case of trying to prevent domestic cats from killing birds), and do seek to prevent other humans from preying on wild animals, as in the case of whaling.[67] A strict dichotomy between the moral rules we apply to domesticated and wild animals, then, would not seem to be correct. In any case, second, a "pure" relational ethic would deny any moral worth at all to animals with which we have no relationship. Applied strictly, then, the relational ethic represents a free-for-all in the case of wild animals, and not just a prescription of noninterference.

An answer to the second criticism, if not the first, might be available in an account that combines relational and capacity-oriented strands. Such an account is offered by Donaldson and Kymlicka.[68] In an innovative analysis they argue that it is useful to map our obligations to animals through citizenship theory. In other words, the moral worth of animals is cashed out, at least in part, through their membership in political communities and the relationships they have with us.

Donaldson and Kymlicka envisage three categories of animals, informed by a relational ethic based on citizenship theory. Domesticated animals, those who are part of our societies, are equivalent to co-citizens and have certain particular rights because of their relational status with humans. Those animals who live among us, but who are not domesticated, so-called liminal animals, are equivalent to co-residents who do not have the rights of full citizenship. Finally, genuinely wild animals are equivalent to separate sovereign communities that ought to be regulated by norms of international justice. In short, only those domesticated animals who are citizens have certain particular positive rights because of their relational status with humans. By contrast, genuinely wild animals are equivalent to separate sovereign communities, and the assumption here is that they should be left alone by other, human communities.

Donaldson and Kymlicka's relational approach provides a rich analysis of human-animal relations which has led to considerable scrutiny by the animal ethics community.[69] There is considerable doubt, for instance, whether animals can be regarded as citizens in any meaningful sense. For the purposes of the present discussion, however, two points are worth noting. The first is that Donaldson and Kymlicka underestimate the degree to which humans do intervene to protect wild animals, and therefore overestimate the utility of the laissez-faire intuition. Second, it is important to note that the relational approach plays a relatively small role in their analysis, and as a result the case for regarding their approach as genuinely different can be challenged. This is because their starting point is the acceptance, as a baseline, of a traditional species-egalitarian abolitionist animal rights agenda based on a capacity-oriented ethic.[70] That is, they accept that animals have a right to life and liberty that "prohibits harming them, killing them, confining them, owning them, and enslaving them."[71] This has the effect of ruling out the domestication of animals for exploitative human purposes. Animal agriculture and animal experimentation are therefore morally illegitimate, on the grounds that to use animals in such a way is to infringe their rights. This severely restricts the type of domesticated animals that would have citizenship status. Indeed presumably only companion animals would be included.

Donaldson and Kymlicka's work has drawn attention to the relationship between animal ethics and politics. As I have shown, their work gives animal ethics a political twist by situating relations between humans and animals within the context of group-differentiated rights (that is, rights held by a group *qua* group rather than by its members individually) utilized in the political philosophy literature on citizenship.[72] They certainly do offer a political theory of animal rights (the subtitle of their book), but it might be more accurately described as *one* political theory of animal rights. For one thing, the unstated assumption that traditional animal rights ethics is not political is mistaken. The traditional approach is equally political in the sense that it places a moral obligation on the state, or the international community, to recognize and act upon the rights of animals. In this sense, animal ethics is inextricably linked with justice, a central political concept. In contrast to Donaldson and Kymlicka's account, however, the traditional approach to animal rights represents an alternative (and mainstream) political tradition centering on a universalistic and cosmopolitan theory of rights.[73]

CONCLUSION

The summary of contemporary animal ethics in this chapter has revealed a remarkable expansion of interest in the field since the 1970s. After the early dominance of the Singer/Regan challenge to the moral orthodoxy, the debate has increasingly fragmented. Indeed constraints of space have prevented me from considering all of the various directions this debate has traveled in and from even mentioning, until now, the critical theory strand of animal ethics and the debate between advocates of individualistic animal ethics and the holistic focus of environmental ethicists.[74] The fact that the contemporary development of animal ethics as an academic subject has been accompanied by, and has been partly responsible for, the development of an increasingly large and influential social movement has given animal ethics extra momentum and credibility.

Notes

1. In natural English the word "animals" can be used in both an inclusive sense (e.g., "human and nonhuman animals") or an exclusive sense (e.g., "humans as opposed to animals"). In this book both uses appear, with context, for the most part, indicating which of the two senses is meant. The meaning will be explicitly stated when context alone does not make this clear.
2. Aristotle, *Parts of Animals*, 644b. (See Barnes, *The Complete Works of Aristotle*.) The reader should note that the primary literature bibliography in this volume lists works under the names of editors/translators where possible. Chapter notes thus direct the reader to the relevant editions of primary texts so that they may be located in the bibliography. When names of editors/translators are unavailable or unhelpful, works have been listed under original author name.
3. De Waal, *Are We Smart Enough*, 26, 122.
4. By contrast Darwin himself remarked in a letter, "Linnaeus and Cuvier have been my two gods...but they were mere schoolboys to old Aristotle." See Gotthelf, "Darwin on Aristotle." Our thanks to Daniel Lindquist for the reference.
5. The more basic tendency to define the human in opposition to the animal is as old as the oldest human literature that still exists. For this theme in cuneiform

literature, see Foster, "The Person in Mesopotamian Thought," 118–19. One could argue that Akkadian and Babylonian literature also already points to the blurriness of the contrast, as with the initially animalistic portrayal of Gilgamesh's ally Enkidu before he is socialized by encountering a human woman.

6. For recent collections devoted to these three topics see Lurz, *The Philosophy of Animal Minds*; Beauchamp and Frey, *The Oxford Handbook of Animal Ethics*; Blatti and Snowdon, *Animalism*.

7. For this example see Adamson, "Abū Bakr al-Rāzī on Animals," 261.

8. See recently on this debate Riskin, *The Restless Clock*.

9. Astonishing, but not impossible: when reading male ancient and medieval philosophers on the capacities of children and women, one sometimes wonders whether they have ever met a human who is not an adult male.

10. Translation taken from Ryan, *Dante*, §3.7.

11. Consider for instance the remark made by Philip Thicknesse in a letter composed in 1789, concerning a baboon: "He understood everything said to him by his keeper, and had more sense than half the brutes erect we meet in the street" (quoted in the *London Review of Books*, December 15, 2016).

12. We would like here to register our gratitude to LMU Munich, Washington University in St. Louis, and the British Society for the History of Philosophy, who provided funding for an exploratory workshop that led to this volume, and to King's College London for hosting the workshop. We are also grateful to Hanif Amin and Michael Lessman for their work in preparing the volume for press.

CHAPTER ONE

1. I am grateful to Peter Adamson and G. Fay Edwards for useful feedback on my paper as well as to my team of research assistants for helping compile material (Matthew Watton, Cecilia Li, Adam Woodcox, and Paola Chapa Montes). All translations of Aristotle are my own, unless otherwise stated.

2. It is important to note that Aristotle thinks of humans as animals, though he has a tendency to speak of them as though they constitute a distinct kind of organism (e.g., *On Generation of Animals*, II 1, 732a1–2).

3. For a useful discussion see Gregoric, *Aristotle on the Common Sense*, s.v. perceptibles, accidental; Johansen, *The Powers of the Aristotelian Soul*, 180–85.

4. Cashdollar, "Aristotle's Account of Incidental Perception," 167, 170.

5. By saying that the lion might see a gazelle I do not mean to suggest that Aristotle thinks they perceive the universal. For he is explicit in *Posterior Analytics* II 19 that this requires *nous*, which belongs to the rational part of the soul. For more on the content of sense perception in nonhuman animals see Sorabji, *Animal Minds*, ch. 3.

6. Shields, "Aristotle's Psychology." Aristotle uses visual, especially pictorial, language in his talk of *phantasia* but seems to suppose that it deals with mental representations from all sense modalities.

7. Hence Aristotle thinks it is involved in such cases as its appearing to be the case that a figure in the distance is Socrates.

8. *On Dreams* III. Aristotle says that because mental images persist in the agent and resemble sense perceptions, animals frequently act in accordance with them: some (i.e., nonhuman animals) because they lack intellect (*nous*), others (i.e., humans) because the intellect is temporarily obscured by emotion, disease, or sleep (*On the Soul*, 429a4–8).

9. Aristotle is clear, in *On Memory*, that any animal that has memory also has a concept of time, since remembering something implies the ability to recognize that the event occurred in the past (449b28–30, 450a). What nonhuman animals do not have, however, is the ability to engage in the process of recollection (*anamnēsis*) (453a6–14). Suppose a lion makes a kill and then wanders away from the kill site. She may have a memory image of the scene of the kill, and so she would recognize it were she to follow the scent back. But she cannot mentally retrace her steps in order to determine how to get back there. This kind of mental operation, Aristotle thinks, is inferential and "can only belong by nature to those that have the capacity for deliberation (*to bouleutikon*); for deliberation is also a kind of inference."

10. This refers to knowing only in the weaker sense that involves some kind of cognitive grasp and not the stronger sense of knowledge that only animals with reason have. The word Aristotle uses here, *gnōsis*, is the same word he uses at *On Generation of Animals* 731a32, where he says that all animals have a share in knowledge insofar as they have sense perception: "For sense-perception is a sort of knowledge (*gnōsis tis*)." Cf. *On Memory*, 450a9–14, where *gnōsis* is used in connection with our grasp of magnitude and time, the latter of which is ascribed to some nonhuman animals. Gregoric (*Aristotle on the Common Sense*, 121n17) offers more references.

11. Alexander's commentary on the *Metaphysics* at Alexander of Aphrodisias, in Hayduck *Aristotelis Metaphysician Commentaria*, 5, 1–2, appears to treat this as a function of reason insofar as it requires "comprehension" (*perilēpsin*).

12. In the passage from *Metaphysics* I 1 (980b26ff.) Aristotle seems to equate experience with the set of memories taken individually before they have been connected into a single universal judgment. The latter, he says, is at the province of craft and (presumably) science. This is compatible with my reading if we take 980b29–981a12 to be talking about the richer sort of experience whose content includes universals.

13. *Nicomachean Ethics*, VII 3, 1147b3–5 says that nonhuman animals "do not have universal apprehension but only *phantasia* and memory of the particulars" (*ouk*

echei katholou hupolēpsin alla tōn kath' hekasta phantasian kai mnēmēn). Cf. *Metaphysics* I 1, 980b25–26.

14. Cf. Meyer, *Aristotle on Moral Responsibility*, 24–29.

15. This passage is translated after that contained in Barnes, *The Complete Works of Aristotle*.

16. Cf. Sorabji, *Animal Minds*, 36–38.

17. Meyer, *Aristotle on Moral Responsibility*, 30.

18. *Parts of Animals,* 650b19–20: "Now some of these animals have a more refined intelligence, not because of the coldness of their blood, but because it is thin and pure." *History of Animals,* 612b19–26: "Acute intelligence (*tēn tēs dianoias akribeian*) will be observed in small animals more than in larger ones, as is exemplified in the case of birds by the nest-builders among the swallows. For in the same way as humans do the sparrow mixes mud and chaff together; if it runs short of mud, it souses its body in water and rolls about in the dust with wet feathers. Moreover, just as humans do, it makes a bed of straw, putting hard materials below for a foundation and adapting all to suit its own size." *History of Animals,* 623a8: "There is a third species of spider [whose web construction] is most clever and skillful (*sophōtaton kai glaphurōtaton*)." *History of Animals,* 614b19–21: "Many indications of intelligence (*phronima*) are thought to occur in the case of cranes. They will fly to a great distance and high up in the air in order to command an extensive view. If they see clouds and signs of bad weather, they will fly down again and remain still." *History of Animals,* 618a25–27: "The cuckoo is thought to exhibit wisdom (*phronimon*) in the disposal of its progeny; for, owing to her awareness of her own cowardice, and because she is unable to help her young, she makes it a suppositious child in a foreign nest for the sake of its own preservation."

19. This is the standard interpretation of the passage (e.g., Sorabji, *Animal Minds*, 119), but not the only way to read these remarks (see below).

20. With the following see Leunissen, "Aristotle on Natural Character"; Lennox, "Aristotle on the Biological Roots of Virtue." Aristotle discusses the moral virtues in *Nicomachean Ethics*, II 5–IV 8. He discusses the intellectual virtues in *Nicomachean Ethics* VI.

21. This passage is translated after that contained in Barnes, *Complete Works*.

22. This passage is translated after that contained in Barnes, *Complete Works*.

23. Again, see Lennox.

24. Aristotle goes on to say that one comes to possess the character virtues only when she comes to possess practical wisdom; they all come to be present together (1145a1–2).

25. *On the Soul* distinguishes between perceptual *phantasia* and calculative or deliberative *phantasia* (433b27–31, 434a5–12). The former is what triggers appetite in

nonhuman animals, while the latter occurs in humans and triggers decision (which is a desire formed on the basis of deliberation).

26. Cf. *On the Soul*, III 9, 432a15–17.

27. *Nicomachean Ethics* VI 2 argues that thought and desire are two aspects of the same unified state, decision, which is the efficient cause of action. See Charles, "Aristotle on Practical and Theoretical Knowledge."

28. This impression would be mistaken, however. First Aristotle does not say that animals are automatons. He thinks there are important points of analogy between animals and self-moving automatons, which makes them a good model for understanding the mechanics of animal motion. But there are also important disanalogies, specifically, animal motion is caused by mental states (desires, sensations, mental representations, thoughts) that can only occur in living things equipped with souls. Second, Aristotle is explicit that the analogy extends to the movements of human animals as well. And he hardly thinks of human beings as mere machines.

29. In *On Generation of Animals* V Aristotle defines an *archē* in the causal sense as that which is the cause of other things but of which nothing prior is the cause (788a14–16). Assuming Aristotle is using *archē* in the same sense here, by saying the *archē* of the action must be internal to the agent he means that the agent is the beginning or originating source of her motion. By contrast, her action is compelled (and therefore involuntary) whenever the originating source is external to her (*Nicomachean Ethics*, III 1). For example, if you rear-end me at a stop sign, which forces my car into the intersection, resulting in my hitting a child, while I might bear some causal responsibility for hitting the child, Aristotle would deny that my action was voluntary since its *archē* (the beginning of my motion) was external to me.

30. In *Eudemian Ethics* II 8 Aristotle connects the concept of an internal origin to the idea that it is "up to" the agent to do X or not do X, and this is sometimes thought to be inconsistent with his claim in *Nicomachean Ethics* and *Movement of Animals* that nonhuman animals can behave voluntarily. I think Aristotle is best understood to believe that the tiger that kills the chimp could have done otherwise, making the killing "up to" her and voluntary, even though she lacks the ability to make genuine decisions. For a defense of this reading see Sorabji, *Animal Minds*, 108–12.

31. Meyer, *Aristotle on Moral Responsibility*, 23.

32. Sorabji, *Animal Minds*, 108–12.

33. For an argument against this model of deliberation, see Nielsen, "Deliberation as Inquiry."

34. Meyer, *Aristotle on Moral Responsibility*, 3.

35. Meyer, *Aristotle on Moral Responsibility*, 4.
36. With the following see Sorabji, *Animal Minds*, 175–78. Sorabji argues, convincingly, that Theophrastus's account goes beyond sacrifice and includes moral restrictions on eating animals.
37. This translation is from Taylor, *Porphyry On Abstinence from Animal Food*. For the idea that animals are the possession of the gods, which they gave to us for our use, cf. Sorabji, *Animal Minds*, 199. Compare Socrates's argument against suicide in Plato, *Phaedo*, 62bc (see Cooper, *Plato: Complete Works*).
38. In fact it was a common ancient Greek sacrificial practice to sprinkle an animal's head with water in order to make it nod its assent to being sacrificed. For more on this practice see Waldau and Patton, *A Communion of Subjects*, 396. There are also far-fetched stories of animals voluntarily taking themselves to the altar ready for sacrifice in Porphyry, *On Abstinence*, 1.25.6–9 (see Clark trans.).
39. Theophrastus adds that we are not violating any moral principles when we collect honey from bees. For the beekeeper invests his own labor in the process, so that "it is fitting that we should derive a common benefit from it." Since the honey is useless to them, and beneficial to us, we are extracting our reward without depriving them of anything they need. However, he says that when we collect the honey we must be sure that the bees suffer no harm in the process.
40. Compare Aristotle's remarks in *History of Animals* VIII (discussed earlier).
41. Sorabji, *Animal Minds*, 119, 177–78.

CHAPTER TWO

1. I would like to thank Peter Adamson and the other contributors to this volume for providing useful feedback on an early draft of this paper, as well as Stephen T. Newmyer, who very helpfully went to great lengths to ensure that I had access to his work on Plutarch on animals.
2. Plutarch's three main works of relevance to this chapter (*The Cleverness of Animals*, *On Flesh-Eating*, and *Beasts Are Rational*) can all be found in Helmbold, *Plutarch: Moralia*, vol. 12, from which all translations are taken.
3. Clement, *Stromata*, 7.32.9 (found in Stählin and Früchtel, *Clement of Alexandria: Stromata*).
4. Porphyry, *Life of Plotinus*, §2. The *Life of Plotinus* is Porphyry's introduction to the works of Plotinus, which he edited and arranged into their current format. It can be found in Armstrong, *Plotinus. Ennead I* (1969).
5. For an edition of this work see Most.
6. Plato's works can be found in Cooper, *Plato: Complete Works*, from which all translations are taken.

7. Porphyry, *On Abstinence*, 2.7.2, 2.9.1, 2.10.3, 2.12.1; Plutarch, *On Flesh-Eating*, 993cd.

8. Diogenes Laertius, *Lives*, 8.33 (see Hicks trans.); Plutarch, *On Flesh-Eating*, 993a, 997e, 998a, and *Cleverness*, 964de; Porphyry, *Life of Pythagoras*, § 7, § 36, and *On Abstinence*, 1.3.3, 3.1.4, 3.6.7; Porphyry's *Life of Pythagoras* can be found in Guthrie, *Pythagoras Sourcebook and Library*.

9. Plutarch, *On Flesh-Eating*, 996a, *How to Profit by One's Enemies* (in Helmbold, *Plutarch: Moralia*, vol. II), 91c, and *Cleverness*, 959f–60a = Porphyry, *On Abstinence*, 3.20.7, Porphyry, *On Abstinence*, 1.23.1–1.24, 3.26.6–8; Clement, *Stromata*, 2.18; Iamblichus, *Life of Pythagoras*, ch. 30, 168, 186 (see Taylor trans.).

10. Plutarch, *On Flesh-Eating*, 998c; Seneca, *Epistles*, 108.19 (see Gummere trans.); Porphyry, *Life of Pythagoras*, § 19; Diogenes Laertius, *Lives*, 8.4. Cf. Porphyry, *On Abstinence*, 1.6.3, 1.19.1–3, 4.16.2.

11. E.g., Plato, *Timaeus*, 42bd, 91d–2c, *Phaedo*, 81d–2b, *Republic*, 620ad. Although see also the denial that humans can reincarnate as animals at *Phaedrus*, 249b.

12. Although compare the opponents' argument that reincarnation makes killing animals a good thing, since it will return their souls more quickly to human form. See Porphyry, *On Abstinence*, 1.19.1–3, 1.20.1.

13. Plutarch, *On Flesh-Eating*, 997e, 998d.

14. Aeneas, *Theophrastus*, 12, 11–20 (893ab), for which see Gertz, Dillon and Russell, *Theophrastus: Aeneas of Gaza*.

15. Proclus, *Commentary on Plato's "Republic,"* II, 309, 28–310, 6, and *Commentary on Plato's "Timaeus,"* II, 334–37 and III, 294, 21 (see Baltzly and Tennant trans.).

16. Plotinus has several passages on reincarnation (*Ennead*, I.1.11, III.3.4, III.4.2, V.2.2, VI.7.6). For a discussion of his position see Rich, "Reincarnation in Plotinus."

17. Porphyry's views on transmigration are notoriously difficult to determine. For more, see Helmig, "Plutarch of Chaeronea," esp. n9.

18. All translations of this work are from Clark, *Porphyry: On Abstinence from Killing Animals*, unless otherwise stated.

19. For more on the Stoic position, see Porphyry, *On Abstinence*, 1.4.1–2, 3.1.4; Cicero, *On the Laws*, 1.23 (see Keyes trans.); Seneca, *Epistles*, 76.9–10 = LS 63D; Diogenes Laertius, *Lives*, 7.129; Cicero, *On the Nature of the Gods*, 2.78 (see Rackham trans.); Epictetus, *Discourses*, II.8 (see Oldfather trans.); Cleanthes passage translated in Long and Sedley, *The Hellenistic Philosophers* (hereafter LS), 54I.

20. Compare, for example, 972b with 977d.

21. Compare, for example, the contradictory assertions at 969ab.

22. Compare, for example, *Cleverness*, 972df, with *Beasts Are Rational*, 991a, 988f.

23. These individuals are the Stoics.

24. Newmyer, "Animals in Plutarch," 224; Helmbold's introduction to the Loeb edition of *Cleverness*, 312; Sorabji. *Animal Minds*, 179.

25. Schuster, *Untersuchungen*.

26. Sorabji, *Animal Minds*, 182; Osborne, *Dumb Beasts*, 228; Clark in her introduction to *Porphyry: On Abstinence from Killing Animals*, 3; Newmyer, *Animals in Greek and Roman Thought*, 108; Steiner, *Anthropocentrism*, 104–11; Passmore, "Treatment of Animals," 211; Walters and Portmess, *Ethical Vegetarianism*, 36; Barnes, *Porphyry: Introduction*, 111; Karamanolis, *Plato and Aristotle*, 268; Dombrowski, *Vegetarianism*, 116.

27. Plutarch, *Cleverness*, 969ab; Porphyry, *On Abstinence*, 3.6.3.

28. Plutarch, *Cleverness*, 974de.

29. Plutarch, *Cleverness* 960bd = Porphyry, *On Abstinence*, 3.21.1–6; Plutarch, *Cleverness* 961ab = Porphyry, *On Abstinence*, 3.21.8–9; Porphyry, *On Abstinence*, 3.8.1–6.

30. Plutarch, *Cleverness*, 961cf = Porphyry, *On Abstinence*, 3.22.3–5.

31. Plutarch, *Cleverness*, 961bc = Porphyry, *On Abstinence*, 3.22.1; Porphyry, *On Abstinence*, 3.1.4, 3.10.3.

32. Plutarch, *Cleverness*, 972f–3a; Porphyry, *On Abstinence*, 3.3–3.6.

33. Plutarch, *Cleverness*, 966df, 973ab, 983bc; Porphyry, *On Abstinence*, 3.15.1–2.

34. Plutarch, *Cleverness*, 967c, 977cd, 980ab; Porphyry, *On Abstinence*, 3.11.1.

35. Plutarch, *Cleverness*, 969c–70a, 984c; Porphyry, *On Abstinence*, 3.12.1–3.

36. Plutarch, *Cleverness*, 966b, and 962ab = Porphyry, *On Abstinence*, 3.22.7.

37. Plutarch, *Cleverness*, 967de, 977cd and 962be = Porphyry, *On Abstinence*, 3.22.7–23.5; Porphyry, *On Abstinence*, 3.10–13. Note that Plutarch elsewhere makes the opposite point—viz. that animals are more virtuous because they are irrational (e.g., *Beasts Are Rational*, 988de, which reflects Plato, *Laws*, 963e).

38. Plutarch, *Cleverness*, 963cf = Porphyry, *On Abstinence*, 3.24.2–5, *Beasts are Rational*, 992ce.

39. Plutarch, *Cleverness*, 961bc = Porphyry, *On Abstinence*, 3.22.1; Porphyry, *On Abstinence*, 3.9.6.

40. Porphyry, *On Abstinence*, 3.9.2–4. The reader might wish to compare Plutarch's *Beasts Are Rational* 991d–2e, which offers a short argument in favor of granting rationality to animals.

41. This work can be found in Helmbold, *Plutarch: Moralia*, vol. 13, part 2.

42. Plutarch, *Cleverness*, 961cd = Porphyry, *On Abstinence*, 3.22.2–3; Plutarch, *Cleverness*, 960de = Porphyry, *On Abstinence*, 3.21.4.

43. See, for example, Longinus, frag. 42, lines 154–57; (see Patillon and Brisson, *Longinus: Fragments*); Alexander of Aphrodisias, *Quaestiones*, 1.3 (see Sharples trans.) and *On Aristotle Topics*, 355.18–24 (see van Ophuijsen trans.); Galen,

Exhortation to Study the Arts, 9, vol. 1, pp. 21.4–6K (see Walsh trans.); Sextus, *Against Professors*, 11.8–11 (see Bury trans.) = LS 30I; Cicero, *Academics*, 2.21 (see Rackham trans.) = LS 39C; Diogenes Laertius, *Lives*, 7.60–2 = LS 32C. Porphyry apparently subscribes to the traditional division; see, for example, Porphyry, *On Aristotle's Categories*, 63, 23–25 (see Strange trans.), and *Introduction*, 11, 15–16 (see Barnes ed.). For more on his position see Edwards, "Irrational Animals."

44. Although cf. Plato, *Timaeus*, 91d–2c, *Laws*, 961d, and *Statesman*, 263d.

45. There is disagreement over whether a belief in human-animal reincarnation requires the rationality of animals. Compare Sorabji, *Animal Minds*, 10, with Karamanolis, *Plato and Aristotle*, 268–69.

46. Plutarch, *Cleverness*, 969ab; Porphyry, *On Abstinence*, 3.6.3; Sextus Empiricus, *Outlines of Scepticism*, 1.69 (see Annas and Barnes trans.); Aelian, *On the Nature of Animals*, vi.59 (see McNamee trans.); Philo, *On Animals*, 45. Philo's text, which was preserved only in Armenian, is translated into English in Terian, *Philonis Alexandrini De Animalibus*.

47. Following Plato, *Theaetetus*, 186d. Cf. Aristotle, *On the Soul*, 432a22–b7.

48. For more on rationality as the grasp of conceptual relationships see Frede, "The Stoic Conception of Reason," esp. 54.

49. Helmbold trans. slightly modified.

50. Tuominen, *Apprehension and Argument*, 270.

51. E.g., Aristotle, *On the Soul*, 414b3–6, 427b7–8, 432b6–7, *Sense and Sensibilia*, 436b11–3, *Metaphysics*, 980a27. Aristotle is very clear, however, that only humans are rational, other animals irrational (e.g., *On the Soul*, 414b18–9, 427b13, 428a23–24, 429a5–8, 433a11–12, *Parts of Animals*, 641b7, *Politics*, 1332b4–5).

52. Aristotle used this same trick to distinguish the genuine skill, wisdom, understanding, virtue, and vice of humans from their merely analogous counterparts in animals (*History of Animals*, 588a29–30, *Nicomachean Ethics*, 1150a1–4, *Eudemian Ethics*, 1224a27).

53. For this Stoic position, see Cicero, *Academics*, 2.37.108 and 2.38; Aëtius, *Doxographi Graeci*, 396, 3–4 (see Diels trans.); Calcidius, *On Plato's Timaeus*, 220 (see Magee trans.); Plutarch, *On Moral Virtue* (in Helmbold, *Plutarch: Moralia*, vol. VI), 446f = LS 65G1; Galen, *On the Doctrines of Hippocrates and Plato*, 5.6.37 (see DeLacy trans.) = LS 65I4; Seneca, *On Anger*, 1.3.4, 2.3.5, which can be found in Basore, *Seneca: Moral Essays*, vol. 1.

54. Clark trans. slightly modified.

55. For more on my interpretation of Porphyry see Edwards, "The Purpose of Porphyry's Rational Animals."

56. This marks a departure from Pythagoras, who advised abstention from beans (Porphyry, *Life of Pythagoras*, § 43; Diogenes Laertius, *Lives*, 8.19).

57. This is clear from Socrates's comment that more cattle will be required "if the people are going to eat meat" when their diet is adapted to include luxuries (*Republic*, 373c).

58. Porphyry is concerned with restricting food quantity as well (e.g., *On Abstinence*, 1.43.2, 1.46.1, *Life of Plotinus*, § 8).

59. Porphyry says that only philosophers need to be vegetarian (e.g., *On Abstinence*, 1.27.1–1.28.4; 2.4.3). He appears to believe that meat consumption is necessary for bodily strength and that, while philosophers do not need bodily strength, individuals in physical jobs, such as soldiers and athletes, do (*On Abstinence*, 1.52.2, cf. 1.34.4).

60. Osborne, *Dumb Beasts*, 226–31.

61. Porphyry's opponents suppose the exact opposite—viz. that meat-eating preserves health (*On Abstinence*, 1.15.2, 1.17.1–3, 1.25.1).

62. This threefold division is originally made by Epicurus in his *Letter to Menoeceus* (recorded by Diogenes Laertius, *Lives*, 10.127).

63. Cf. Porphyry, *On Abstinence*, 3.10.4–5; Philo, *On Animals*, 48.

64. Although, oddly, this is immediately contradicted by Gryllus's assertion at 990e that cockerels that mount one another get burned alive.

65. Note that this is contradicted by *Cleverness* 972df, where animals are said to fall in love with human beings (an attempt to prove that animals possess emotion).

66. Cf. Porphyry, *On Abstinence*, 3.10.4–5; Plutarch, *Cleverness*, 962e.

67. Cf. *Cleverness*, 959e, where weasels and cats are said to eat meat only out of "hunger," and Porphyry, *On Abstinence*, 3.1.3, where what is right for wolves and vultures is contrasted with what is right for humans.

68. See above n57.

69. E.g., Seneca, *Epistles*, 15.2.

70. I thank Rachana Kamtekar for this thought. This position is recorded and challenged in Porphyry, *On Abstinence*, 3.20.1–6.

71. E.g., Musonius Rufus, *On Food*, frags. 18a and 18b, translated by Lutz, "Musonius Rufus: The Roman Socrates"; Seneca, *Epistles*, 108, 13–22.

CHAPTER TWO: REFLECTION

1. For an overview of our sources for Aesop's fables in Greek and Latin, see Holzberg, *The Ancient Fable*; cf. Lefkowitz, "Aesop and Animal Fables."

2. Zafiropoulos, *Ethics in Aesop's Fables*, 26–36, provides an excellent survey of scholarship on the Greek fable's ethical content and function.

3. On the relationship between fable and satire, see Cozzoli, "Poesia satirica latina"; del Vecchio and Fiore, "Fabula in satura"; Cavarzere, "Ego Polivi Versibus Senariis"; cf. Holzberg, *The Ancient Fable*, 31–35.

4. Ancient writers use several different terms for the pithy messages attached to fables (e.g., *epimuthion, promuthion, epilogos, paramuthion, perimuthion*), though none of them carries the ethical connotations of "moral" in English. See Perry, "The Origin of the Epimythium"; Nøjgaard, *La fable antique,* 1:122–28.

5. On animal fables as a useful way to lighten the mood and provoke laughter, see, e.g., Aristophanes, *Wasps,* 566, 1256–61 (see Henderson trans.); Cicero, *De Inventione,* 1.17.25 (see Hubbell trans.); Quintilian, *Inst.* 1.9.1–3; 6.3.44 (in Russell, *Quintillian: The Orator's Education*); Plutarch, *Moralia,* 14e and 162bc (see Helmbold trans.).

6. Numbers refer to fables collected in Perry, *Aesopica.*

7. All translations are from Daly, *Aesop without Morals.*

8. Cf. Nøjgaard, *La fable antique,* 1:63. The treatment and distribution of speech (*logos*) is not straightforward here; the ass, for example, does not speak but is twice characterized as making animal sounds (*phthegxamenou, ogkōmenou*). Moreover the other animals that his lion costume is meant to frighten are characterized as "speechless" (*aloga*).

9. The animal fable did not, of course, originate in Greece, nor did the Greeks think it did; Greek authors associated it with various exotic figures (e.g., Conis the Cilician, Thouros the Sybarite, and Cybissus the Libyan) and with locales that had reputations as sources of venerable wisdom (e.g., Libya, Phrygia, Cilicia, Caria, Egypt); cf. Lefkowitz, "Aesop and Animal Fables."

10. A number of different terms could describe fable, including *logos, ainos,* and *muthos* in Greek, and *apologus, fabula,* and *fabella* in Latin; cf. van Dijk, *AINOI,* 79–111.

11. See the useful comments in Dover, *Greek Popular Morality,* 74–75.

12. The *Collectio Augustana,* usually placed in the first or second century CE, is our earliest surviving Greek fable collection; the *Augustana* fables can be found in Perry, *Aesopica,* numbered 1–231.

CHAPTER THREE

1. In Plato's *Politicus,* 262b–263a (see Cooper, *Plato: Complete Works*), we are warned against the false essentialism of presuming that wherever there is one word, there is one thing; "barbarian," for instance, collects together persons with nothing in common except their not being Greek.

2. This is not to say the notion was entirely alien. Chakrabarti, "Rationality in Indian Philosophy," observes that the *Durga Saptasati's* declaration that animals are capable of knowledge must have been speaking to a presumption that they were *not.*

3. For an edition of this work see Most.

4. Sorabji, *Animal Minds*, 14–21.

5. For a translation of this work see Olivelle. Not all the sources cited in this chapter are easily accessible in English translation. Where such translations are available, references have been given.

6. Dating anything in classical Indian literature is a minefield. So I would not go to the wall for a third-century BCE dating of the *Pañcatantra*. The *Hitopadeśa* quote is from the introduction, at verse 25: "With beasts we share a similar nature / in fear and hunger, sex and rest. / Virtue is man's special feature: / without it, he's a beast at best" (for an edition of this work see Haksar, from which this translation is taken).

7. For a translation of this work see Cowell.

8. This intuition is not universally shared—Mark Rowlands's recent monograph, *Can Animals Be Moral?*, contests it—and I do not claim here that this intuition is correct.

9. "From the moral perspective, animals are constitutionally disposed to acts of violence and sexual misconduct. They are inclined to disregard the taboos that bind human society together and this propensity, on occasion, may result in the crimes of cannibalism or incest. Goats, sheep, chickens, pigs, dogs and jackals are particularly blameworthy in the latter respect" (Harris, "Buddhism and Ecology," 121). See, e.g., *Dīgha Nikāya* iii.72: "Among those of a ten-year lifespan no account will be taken of mother or aunt, of mother's sister-in-law, of teacher's wife or of one's father's wives and so on—all will be promiscuous in the world like goats and sheep, fowl and pigs, dogs and jackals." (For a translation of this work, see Walsh, *The Long Discourses of the Buddha*.)

10. Due to the wide scope and flexibility of the word *dharma*, it may also be possible to say instead that in Hindu thought each sort of animal has its own *dharma*—what is given it to do, given its nature and overall place in the scheme of things. I thank Elisa Freschi for the suggestion. At issue here, however, is the restricted sense of *dharma* at work in the *Hitopadeśa* text quoted.

11. See *Majjhima Nikāya* (hereafter *MN*) 12, "The Greater Discourse on the Lion's Roar" (*Mahāsīhanāda Sutta*), §35 (PTS: i.73). *MN* 97, "To Dhānañjāni" (*Dhānañjāni Sutta*), §30, offers another example within a Buddhist text, more finely differentiated in the divine worlds; the context is a conversation with a non-Buddhist, so the recognized distinctions as well as their rank more likely reflect the non-Buddhist common view, some or all of which a Buddhist might reject. (For a translation of *Majjhima Nikāya*, see Ñāṇamoli and Bodhi, *The Middle-Length Discourses of the Buddha*.)

12. Olivelle writes, "There is, then, no unbridgeable gulf between gods, humans and animals within the Indian imagination" ("Talking Animals," 17).

13. Xenophanes, fr. 7 (Diogenes Laertius VIII, 36) in Kirk et al., *The Presocratic Philosophers*, 219.

14. This implication of rebirth was not overlooked: consider the *ṛṣi* of *Mahābhārata* XIII.117, persuading a worm to get itself run over by a chariot so it can be reborn as a Brahmin. Rāmānuja defends Vedic animal sacrifices on the same grounds: one is doing the animal a favor, releasing it from a lower and sending it to a higher rebirth (*Brahma-Sūtra* III.1.25); cf. Śaṅkara's *Brahmasūtrabhāṣya* III.1.25 for his defense of animal sacrifice. (For the *Brahma-Sūtra* and *Brahmasūtrabhāṣya* see Bapat, *A critical edition of the Brahmasūtras*.)

15. Chapple, *Nonviolence to Animals*; Dundas, *The Jains*, 160–61.

16. In the *Mahābhārata* XIII.116, "*ahiṃsā* is the highest *dharma*… the best austerity (*tapas*)…the greatest gift. *Ahiṃsā* is the highest self control…the highest sacrifice…the highest power…the highest friend…the highest truth…the highest teaching," reiterated at XIII.125, "*ahiṃsā* is the *dharma*. It is the highest purification. It is also the highest truth from which all *dharma* proceeds."

17. Olivelle, "Food for Thought."

18. The Jaina *Ācārāṅga Sūtra* I.4.1 (quoted in Dundas, *The Jains*, 41–42).

19. Perrett, "Moral Vegetarianism," writes, "Sentience, rather than species membership, is widely acknowledged in India as a basis for direct moral concern" (96); for the reasons given, however, I would hesitate to characterize this as moral *extensionism*.

20. The Jains thought sentience went all the way down: "The soul is never bereft of sentience, however feeble and indistinct this may be in underdeveloped organisms." This is from Umāsvāti's second-century BCE *Tattvārtha Sūtra*, quoted in Vallely, "Being Sentiently with Others," 43. "According to Jainism, rocks, mountains, drops of water, lakes, and trees all have life force or *jīva*," Chapple writes (*Nonviolence to Animals*, 11)—and this was considered grounds for extraordinary restrictions on what one could do or eat. Buddhists, not inclined to such austerity, were faced with what L. Schmithausen discusses as "the problem of the sentience of plants in earliest Buddhism." The problem of what to eat was resolved by declaring plants insentient, and therefore not alive. E. B. Findly examines this debate in *Plant Lives*, for discussion of which see E. Freschi's review in *Philosophy East and West*. Freschi gathers and discusses a wide range of Indian philosophical texts concerned with plant sentience in "Systematising an Absent Category."

21. Doniger, "A Symbol in Search of an Object."

22. For a translation see Olivelle, *The Law Code of Manu*.

23. Translation from Olivelle. See also *Mahābhārata* XIII.115–16. The *Laws of Manu* are traditionally given unfathomably ancient provenance; its current form might have been fixed anywhere from 300 BCE to AD 300 L. Nelson

describes the substitution and retention with justification in "Cows, Elephants, Dogs," 184.

24. Olivelle, *The Law Code of Manu*; discussed also by Chapple, *Nonviolence to Animals*, 16. C. G. Framarin, *Hinduism and Environmental Ethics*, argues that overall the *Laws of Manu* grant nonhuman animals direct moral standing; animal sacrifice was an exception and stood in need of special justification. This does not necessarily preclude animal sacrifice but surely complicates our understanding of it.

25. Kumārila explicitly makes this comparison in his justification for ritual sacrifice at *Ślokavarttika* II.248–58.

26. See, for instance, *MN* 57.

27. At the level of the ideal, however, the evidence is mixed: For instance, a story preserved in the *Dhammapada Commentary* depicts the Buddha refusing an offering of honey until the insect eggs hidden within it are removed. See the translation in Burlingame, *Buddhist Legends*, 180.

28. Early Buddhist attitudes toward eating meat are discussed with great scholarly mastery and subtlety by Schmithausen and Maithrimurthi, "Attitudes towards Animals," and Seyfort-Ruegg, "*Ahiṃsā* and Vegetarianism."

29. "You are irreligious, unworthy men, devoted to foolish pleasures, who say that partaking heartily of this meat you are not soiled by sin" (*Sūtrakṛtāṅga* II.6.38, in Jacobi, *Jaina Sutras*).

30. There is perhaps a different cosmological view animating the Jaina position and explaining its difference from non-Jaina Indian views, but it was not a revision of rebirth. This will be discussed below.

31. Framarin arrives at the same conclusion via a different route (*Hinduism and Environmental Ethics*, ch. 3). Schmidt-Raghavan, "Animal Liberation and *Ahiṃsā*," and Jaini, "Animals and Agents," may be taken as representative of the not-uncommon opposite presumption.

32. Olivelle, "Talking Animals," 18.

33. In "Food for Thought," Olivelle offers a detailed survey of the various taxonomies of animals, together with their associated implications.

34. Nelson, "Cows, Elephants, Dogs," 185, has examples from the *Laws of Manu* showing "rebirth as an animal is a frightening punishment" (*Laws of Manu* 12.59, 69); see also the *Chāndogya Upaniṣad* (5.10.7–8). In the *Middle-Length Discourses of the Buddha*, "there are two destinations for one with wrong view, I say: hell or the animal realm" (*MN* 57: *The Dog-Duty Ascetic* [*Kukkuravatika Sutta*] i.389); this offers a particularly relevant case, since the wrong view that will land these ascetics in an unpleasant rebirth is their pointless mimicry of animals as a form of practicing austerities. Regarding the Jaina view see Chapple, "Inherent Value," 242.

35. On the Buddhist side, according to *The Greater Discourse on the Lion's Roar* (*Mahāsīhanāda Sutta*), one in the animal realm "is experiencing extremely painful, racking, piercing feelings," and its fate is compared to falling into a cesspit of filth (*MN* 12, § 38). According to the *Mahābhārata* XII.180, nonhuman animals experience much more physical discomfort than humans, some of it caused by humans whose hands and articulacy enable them to subjugate other animals. In his section titled "How Humans Are Special" from his "Rationality in Indian Philosophy," Chakrabarti identifies three things that make animal lives inferior to human ones in the Hindu tradition: self is less manifest in animals; animals cannot anticipate future results from current actions; and animals cannot do metaphysics. N. Dalal and C. Taylor note that "rebirth minimizes human and nonhuman animal dichotomies and hierarchies.... However; rebirth and *karma* ironically provide hierarchy, for nonhuman animal births are generally considered lower ones resulting from negative *karma*. Nonhuman animals are perceived to live in great suffering, and are unlikely or unable to gain liberation due to a lack of wisdom, are unaware of morality, do not have an aptitude for ritual, and may not be able to produce positive *karma*. The Indian traditions tend not to explore this ambivalent tension" (*Asian Perspectives on Animal Ethics*, 5).

36. While humans know of heaven and hell, animals know only hunger and thirst, says the *Aitareya Aranyaka* II.3.2, and so cannot plan for tomorrow nor strive for immortality. Śabara explains that animals desire only what is immediately present before them and so cannot perform the rituals properly, for the sake of *dharma*, or make connections between action and result (*Mīmāṁsā-Bhāṣya* VI.1.5).

37. According to the *Yogavasistha Ramayana* II: 14, humans are capable of spiritual inquiry into the nature of self and the causes of *saṃsāra* necessary to end all sorrow. See Venkatesananda, *Vasistha's Yoga*, 42.

38. Nelson, "Cows, Elephants, Dogs," 184–85.

39. The *Mahābhārata* introduces the bird Jaritari, trapped in the gleeful burning of the Khandava Forest, who must decide whether to die with her young, whom she cannot carry to safety, or to abandon them for the sake of preserving the future of the species; she even gives her siblings teachings on the virtue of equanimity (*Mahābhārata* I, Khandava-daha Parva). A forest fire also elicits exceptionally virtuous animal behavior in a famous Jaina tale: as the animals crowd together in a place of safety, an elephant lifts his leg to scratch an itch, and a rabbit darts into the remaining space. In order not to crush the rabbit, the elephant stands with his leg lifted for three days, until the raging fire passes. When the animals disperse, the elephant can finally lower his foot, but dies of exhaustion. This is recounted in Jaini, "Ahimsa and 'Just War,'" 49. Nelson, "Cows,

Elephants, Dogs," 187–88, offers three examples of animals attaining liberation in the Hindu tradition. Two of these are from lives of saints, one living in the sixteenth century, the other in the twentieth; the third story is from classical literature (the *Bhāgavata Purāṇa* 8.2–4). Note that none is from the *Hitopadeśa* or *Pañcatantra*, where one might object (wrongly, in my view) that the anthropomorphizing is so strong that we cannot take what happens there to indicate anything about what was thought about actual nonhuman animals.

40. McDermott, "Animals and Humans," 270.

41. See for instance the sorry, but ultimately promising, tale of the elephant Pārileyyaka who attends the Buddha faithfully during the latter's forest retreat. When the Buddha quits the forest, he sends the elephant back to the forest with the parting words, "Pārileyyaka, I am going now, never to return. You cannot hope in this existence to enter into states of trance, or to attain spiritual insight, or the path or the fruits. Halt!" (Burlingame, *Buddhist Legends*, 182). But when Pārileyyaka then dies of a broken heart full of faith in the Buddha, he is reborn in a divine realm. As an elephant, Pārileyyaka cannot attain final insight; but he can exemplify a central virtue enjoined upon all the Buddha's followers, namely *faith*. (This virtue is especially emphasized in the collection of Buddhist tales known as the *Divyāvadāna*, translated in Rotman, *Divine Stories*.)

42. McDermott, "Animals and Humans," 269–70. The *Vinaya Piṭaka* is the collection of texts on monastic discipline (for a translation, see Horner, *The Book of Discipline*). They do not give universal prescriptions nor even universal principles, for their primary aim is to describe how Buddhist monastics should live together such that they might all best support each other in reaching *nirvāṇa*. As Seyfort-Ruegg points out, this makes the purpose of the *vinaya* texts "neither philosophical nor even ethical" ("Ahiṃsā and Vegetarianism," 239). They remain nevertheless an excellent source of detailed cases and prescriptions, often with reasons.

43. There will of course be much more of this sort of thing when we turn to fable literature, and specifically in this context to the *Jātaka* tales.

44. McDermott, "Animals and Humans," 270–71.

45. The *Jaina Sutras*, *Sūtrakṛtāṅga* II.6.26–28, imagine a person mistaking a baby for a gourd, splitting and eating it, but blameless in Buddhist eyes, while the person who makes the opposite mistake and ends up eating a gourd ends up in hell. The criticism is more trenchant than absurd in light of Buddhist texts from the *Vinaya Piṭaka* such as *Pācittiya* 61.1.1–3, which declares, "If [one] thinks that it is not a living thing when it is a living thing, there is no offence. If he thinks that it is a living thing when it is not a living thing, there is an offence of wrong-doing"—and this not just in reference to a crow killer but also regarding

the man who accidentally sits down on a baby, suffocating it in front of its mother. See Horner, *The Book of the Discipline*, 890–91.

46. And perhaps also ethical advantages: P. Harvey, *An Introduction to Buddhist Ethics*, 160, observes that in the Theravada tradition meat-eating is permissible as (1) not depriving laypeople of the merit of giving alms-food, (2) preventing monastics from getting picky about the food they receive from laypersons, and (3) preventing negative attachment to meat (that is, aversion, or attachment to the negative evaluation of meat). "If they were given fleshfood, and it was 'pure'...to refuse it would deprive the donor of the karmic fruitfulness engendered by giving alms-food. Moreover, it would encourage the monks to pick and choose what food they would eat. Food should be looked on only as a source of sustenance, without preferences"; and "vegetarians can in time become disgusted with meat, which can be seen as a form of negative attachment." By contrast J. Stewart, "The Question of Vegetarianism," argues that the Buddha's nonvegetarian stance was purely strategic, and indeed, as Sherice Ngaserin reminds me, vegetarianism was in fact one of the five austerities Devadatta sought to require in order to sow dissent within the *saṅgha*. The Buddha maintained that it should remain optional.

47. And it is certainly related to the apparent lack of moral *theory* among classical Indian philosophical texts, on which see Matilal, *Ethics and Epics*, 19 and Dreyfus, "Meditation as an Ethical Activity."

48. *Karuṇā* is more usually translated as "compassion"—and then immediately qualified as not being just a feeling (com*passion*) but a disposition to engage helpfully. Given the common root of *karma* and *karuṇā* (*kṛ*), I select "care" as a closer equivalent, containing both emotional and active elements.

49. "Proper human/animal relationships are to be governed by the same universal, positive virtues or divine attitudes—the *brahma vihāras*—that govern human inter-relationships, namely: loving kindness (*metta*), compassion (*karuṇā*), sympathetic joy (*muditā*), and equanimity (*upekkhā*)," writes McDermott ("Animals and Humans," 277). "The texts make it explicit that these are intended to apply to all living beings."

50. For an edition, see Red Pine, *Laṅkāvatāra Sūtra*.

51. Put in this acute form, the argument may appear utterly implausible; if it does so, however, it is worth reflecting on the presumptions that make it appear so—for instance, that there is a chasm to be leaped here, and not a slope at all.

52. Compare *Mahābhārata* XIII.114, which describes how meat (the tastiest food there is; XIII.116) "gradually attracts the mind and enslaves it" until "stupefied by its taste"; one becomes incapable of appreciating higher pleasures.

53. Compare again *Mahābhārata* XIII.114, where the meat of animals is like the flesh of one's own son.

54. We might think of Diamond's "Eating Meat and Eating People" as one attempt to do just that—but also to make it clear that some such shift is what is at issue rather than an appeal to principles and rights.

55. Note that these are only the highest third of *three* orders of living being (Chapple, *Nonviolence to Animals*, 11).

56. Vallely, "Being Sentiently with Others," 38–39, disagrees. "There *is* an 'ontological' distinction between human and nonhuman animal in Jainism," she writes, but "hierarchical does not encode an exploitative relationship. The animal in Jainism, though ontologically distinct, is on the same essential trajectory as the human, and its claims to life are no less valid than those of any other sentient being." She goes on to say that Jainism's "attention to the nonhuman is not ideological (or, therefore, ethical), but relational, insofar as it inheres in the far more fundamental experience of being sentiently with others"; so whatever our differences in usages of "ontological" and "ethical," we seem to agree on the fundamental points.

57. Chapple, "Inherent Value," 242.

58. See for instance the very early *Ācārāṅga Sūtra*, which not only observes that all creatures dislike suffering, just like you (the hearer) do, but even further identifies the harm you do to others as harm done to yourself.

59. Chapple, "Inherent Value," 242. I discuss whether choice is or should be the gold standard of moral responsibility in Carpenter, "The Saṁmitīyas," and "Ethics without Justice."

60. There were, of course, Aesop's fables, which, if they did not actually come from India, are very likely at least to be evidence of rapid cross-cultural dissemination of tales across Mesopotamia and its trading partners. Aesop, however, neither had the stature nor the place of Homer and Hesiod in ancient Greek didactic culture; nor did Aesop's fables therefore have the centrality that the *Jātaka* and *Pañcatantra* tales had in ancient India. Moreover the great Indian epics, not just fable literature (unlike the Greek epics), feature talking animals. For recent work complicating and challenging this broad characterization, see Korhonen and Ruonakoski, *Human and Animal in Ancient Greece*.

61. Just how significant the absence of animal speech is may be measured by the important role speaking—in particular, reasoning with others about good and bad—had in ancient Greece. See Heath, *The Talking Greeks*. In India, by contrast, as Olivelle notes, animals *talk*: "It is easy to make the transition from human to animal.... If humans can become animals, then animals may assume human roles and even human speech" ("Talking Animals," 18).

62. Jamison, "The Function of Animals."

63. For instance in the *Śukapotaka-avadāna*, two faithful parrot chicks receive dharma teachings, take refuge, and are predicted to have good rebirths (Rotman, *Divine Stories*, Story 16).

64. Some of these Buddhist tales are beautifully retold in the fourteenth century by Ārya Śūra in the *Jātakamālā*, several involving virtuous animals (e.g. stories 6, 15–16, and 22, 24–27 in Khoroche, *Once the Buddha Was a Monkey*).

65. Since the dating of evolving texts in an oral tradition is notoriously difficult, and the situation probably fluid for many years, it is entirely possible that Buddhists drew on stories that were to become, perhaps only shortly thereafter, part of the *Pañcatantra*, and also that the Buddhist stories in turn were taken up by the non-Buddhist compilers of the *Pañcatantra*.

66. Vargas, "Snake-Kings, Boars' Heads," 218.

67. These descriptions are taken from Olivelle's introduction to the characters of the *Pañcatantra*.

68. Such "animal stories," Olivelle writes, "may be more effective tools of social control and instruction than learned discourses and śāstric writings" ("Talking Animals," 19). The stories, however, do not speak with one voice on these matters of, for instance, the scope of choice; they could perhaps rather be taken as a medium in which to discuss matters that were under debate rather than as tools for enforcing and policing unequivocal boundaries.

69. Olivelle, "Talking Animals," 20.

70. Deleanu, "Buddhist 'Ethology.'"

71. The proverb is discussed by Olivelle, "Talking Animals," 22 *et passim*.

72. *Jātaka Tales*, book 1, no. 128, Biḷāra-Jātaka, in Cowell, *The Jataka* (1895), 281–82.

73. I am particularly indebted to the scholarship of others who have come before me in each of the several specialized discourses within Indian thought. Many thanks are due to Matthew Dasti, Chris Framarin, Elisa Freschi, Patrick O'Donnell, Shyam Ranganathan for timely pointers and suggestions in this discussion. I also thank the contributors to this volume for their convivial discussion and helpful feedback on an earlier draft, as well as the editors for the same and for their patience. My thanks also go to Sherice Ngaserin for superb research assistance.

CHAPTER THREE: REFLECTION

1. For a full discussion of the historical development of the symbolic language of Chinese animal painting, see Sung, *Decoded Messages*, 207–44.

2. See "Autumn Flood (*Qiushui*)," in Watson, *The Complete Works of Zhuangzi*, 110.

3. Sung, *Decoded Messages*, 207–44.

4. See Zhang, *Zhongwen da Cidian*, 668.

5. These two tendencies can be seen respectively in *Fish and Water Grasses* (from the Southern Song dynasty, 1127–1279, held at the Nelson-Atkins Museum of Art), and Chou Dongqing's *The Pleasures of Fish* (Yuan dynasty, 1279–1368, dated 1291, held at the Metropolitan Museum of Art, New York). For detailed discussion of these paintings, see Sung, *Decoded Messages*, 221–27.

6. See *Shijing, maoshi, juan* 15, in Waley, *The Book of Songs*, 202; *Xuanhe huapu, juan* 9, in Anlan, *Huashi Congshu*, 91.

CHAPTER FOUR

1. *Yaḥyā Ibn 'Adī, Commentary on Metaphysics Alpha Elatton*, in Khalifat, *Yaḥyā Ibn 'Adī: The Philosophical Treatises*, 225–26. For more on this commentary see Adamson, "Yaḥyā Ibn 'Adī and Averroes on *Metaphysics* Alpha Elatton."

2. Averroes, *Commentarium in libros Physicorum Aristotelis*, proemium, fol.1b, h–i. My thanks to Juhana Toivanen for bringing the passage to my attention (this is his translation).

3. Much of this section summarizes arguments I have made in "Abū Bakr al-Rāzī on Animals," and "The Ethical Treatment of Animals."

4. See Bousquet, "Des Animaux"; Benkheira et al., *L'animal en islam*; Foltz, *Animals in Islamic Tradition*; Tlili, *Animals in the Qur'an*.

5. Quotations from the Qur'ān are from the Sahih International translation, sometimes slightly modified.

6. Interestingly, Porphyry, *On Abstinence*, 3.4.5, also credits birds with a special relation to the divine, presumably because the flights of birds were read as omens in antiquity. Plotinus also refers to this practice, for instance at *Enneads*, III.1.6.18–24.

7. For *ḥadīth* on showing mercy to animals see Bousquet, "Des Animaux," 40; Benkheira et al., *L'animal en islam*, 136; Foltz, *Animals in Islamic Tradition*, 19ff.

8. Sayeed, *Women and the Transmission of Religious Knowledge*, 28.

9. Van Ess, *Theologie und Gesellschaft*, 3:407.

10. Heemskerk, *Suffering*, 187–89.

11. Edited in Kraus, *Al-Rāzī*. For a full translation see McGinnis and Reisman, *Classical Arabic Philosophy*. All quotations from al-Rāzī are mine, cited by page number from Kraus's edition.

12. Hermarchus gives a similar rationale in favor of killing animals ap. Porphyry, *On Abstinence*, 1.19.2–3. For the proposal that killing animals does them a favor by liberating them from their current bodies, see also the chapters by Edwards and Carpenter in this volume.

13. Adamson, "Abū Bakr al-Rāzī on Animals," 264–67; see also Alexandrin, "Rāzī and His Mediaeval Opponents." It should, however, be noted that transmigration

was not unthinkable in the Islamic world. The Qur'ān itself says that God angrily turned certain sinners into apes and pigs (5:60), and figures other than al-Rāzī accepted, or were at least accused of accepting, animal-human transmigration. See on this Walker, "The Doctrine of Metempsychosis."

14. Goodman and McGregor, *Epistles of the Brethren of Purity*, cited by English and Arabic page number. On their views see also Lauzi, *Il destino degli animali*.

15. For editions see Gauthier, *Ibn Ṭufayl*, and Nader, *Ibn Ṭufayl*. An English translation can be found in Khalidi, *Medieval Islamic Philosophical Writings*. For a general introduction to the work see Kukkonen, *Ibn Tufayl*, cited by page number from the Gauthier edition.

16. See further Kukkonen, "Heart, Spirit, Form, Substance."

17. For instance by Naṣīr al-Dīn al-Ṭūsī: see his *The Nasirean Ethics*, in Wickens, 57.

18. See Henry's chapter for exceptions.

19. A good example is Miskawayh, whose works are marked by Platonic-Aristotelian harmonization. See Adamson, "Miskawayh's Psychology," 42.

20. Rocca, *Galen on the Brain*. The ruling faculty is not to be equated with reason: Galen and the Stoics both assume that animals have such a faculty despite being irrational. Rather it is the source from which such activities as bodily motion are controlled.

21. Galen, *That the States of the Soul Depend on the Body*, for which see Biesterfeldt, *Galens Traktat*.

22. See translation in Adamson and Pormann, *The Philosophical Works of al-Kindī*, §II.1–2.

23. Nemesius, *On the Nature of Man*. For a translation of this work see Sharples and van der Eijk.

24. See further Druart, "Al-Rāzī's Conception of the Soul"; Adamson, "Al-Rāzī on Animals."

25. Al-Rāzī, *Medical Introduction*, in de Benito, *Al-Rāzī: Libro de la introducción dal arte de la medicina o "Isagoge."* §§10–11.

26. For the question of what he means by "thought" (*fikr*) and whether it is found in animals, see Adamson, "Al-Rāzī on Animals."

27. This is more or less the position of Miskawayh too, except that he sees even less connection between intellect and the body. See Adamson, "Miskawayh's Psychology," 43–44. These ideas subsequently came into the Latin Christian tradition from the Arabic-speaking world. See for instance William of Conches, *Dragmaticon Philosophiae (A Dialogue on Natural Philosophy)*, in Ronca and Curr, §6.18.4. Here, drawing on Constantine the African, William (who died after 1154) seats imagination, reason, and memory in the brain.

28. See Wolfson, "The Internal Senses"; Black, "Imagination and Estimation"; McGinnis, *Avicenna*, 113–16. For the connection of the internal senses to the medical tradition see Pormann, "Avicenna on Medical Practice," 102–7.

29. Black, "Estimation (*Wahm*) in Avicenna." For the Latin reception of Avicenna's theory see also Hasse, *Avicenna's De Anima*.

30. Rahman, *The Philosophy of Mullā Ṣadrā*, 228.

31. For all this see Druart, "The Human Soul's Individuation"; Adamson, "Correcting Plotinus."

32. Kaukua, *Self-Awareness*, 164–67. On the Avicennan background see Marmura, "Avicenna's 'Flying Man'"; Black, "Avicenna on Self-Awareness." For the question of self-awareness in animals see also López-Farjeat, "Avicenna on Non-Conceptual Content." López-Farjeat has also pointed out evidence that Avicenna believed animals to be capable of meaningful sounds, if not full-blown language. See his "The 'Language' of Nonhuman Animals."

33. Arabic text in Zurayk *Miskawayh: Tahdīb al-Aḫlaq*. English translation in Zurayk, *Miskawayh: The Refinement of Character*.

34. This has led some to describe al-Rāzī's ethics as Epicurean in spirit, something I have argued against in "Platonic Pleasures" and "Al-Rāzī, *Spiritual Medicine*."

35. English translation in Mahdi, *Alfarabi: Philosophy of Plato and Aristotle*. For an edition in the original Arabic, see Mahdi, *al-Fārābī: Falsafat Arisṭūṭālīs*.

36. Cited by section number from Rosenthal, *Ibn Khaldun: The Muqaddima*.

37. Arabic edition and French translation in Genequand, *Ibn Bājja (Avempace): La conduit de l'isolé et deux autres épîtres*. English translation in Zidayah, "Ibn Bajja's Book Tadbir al-Mutawahhid." Cited by section number from Genequand in my own translations.

38. As noted by Druart, "Logic and Language," 78–79, Ibn Bājja suggests that some animals, particularly those that live in groups, can grasp universals in some sense.

39. Kraus, "*Kitāb al-aḫlāq li-Jālīnūs*," 25. Galen, *On Character Traits*, for an English translation see Singer, *Galen: Psychological Writings*.

40. The main exception is something I have not discussed at all in this chapter, namely contributions to zoology on the model of Aristotle's treatises on animals. The most prominent example, as so often, is Avicenna: see Kruk, "Ibn Sīnā on Animals."

41. My thanks to Anselm Oelze and G. Fay Edwards for helpful comments on a previous draft of this paper.

CHAPTER FOUR: REFLECTION

1. Lévi-Strauss, *Totemism*. 89. Why so few of the hundreds of species of animals sharing African environments with people are featured in visual and performance

arts is the central question of A. F. Roberts, *Animals in African Arts*. The present chapter is for Polly.

2. Fernandez, "Meditating on Animals." Also see Willis, *Signifying Animals*.

3. See Ceyssens, *De Luulu à Tervuren*. Further thoughts about this mask are offered in A. F. Roberts, "Why the Hero Lost His Teeth." How much is lost when one has no sense of particular masquerade events is evident in Anne-Marie Bouttiaux's writing about specific contemporary performances; see her "Guro Masked Performers."

4. Petridis, "Bwadi bwa Chikwanga," 58. On associations between fat-tailed sheep and atmospheric events among Luba and related peoples, see Weghsteen, "Haut-Congo." It may be noted that earlier Luba produced relatively few masks, and only the several known "lion" masks are explicitly zoomorphic; see M. N. Roberts and Roberts, *Memory*.

5. Buffalo are depicted in nineteenth-century masks fashioned by Tabwa people living just to the east of Luba lands, for example; see A. F. Roberts and Maurer, *The Rising of a New Moon*. To argue that one can discover the "right" answer to such questions is to miss the point of local epistemologies that encourage just such debate, and positivist perspectives may falsely defy a sense of symbols as purposefully multireferential. In other words, one can propose that for Luba, the horns of the mask may be both a ram's *and* a buffalo's. Indeed Luba delight in seeking just such "edification by puzzlement," to borrow an apt phrase from Fernandez; see his *Persuasions and Performances*.

6. Leakey, *The Wild Realm*, 48; Hallet, *Animal Kitabu*, 66. For Western naturalists' views of African buffalo, see Dorst and Dandelot, *A Field Guide*.

7. Bourgeois, "Mbawa-Pakasu," 21.

8. This hypothesis and these reflections are based upon Luba exegeses from the 1970s and 1980s; see M. N. Roberts and Roberts, *Memory*. Luba histories are presented in Reefe, *The Rainbow*, while versions of the Luba Epic are analyzed in de Heusch, *The Drunken King*.

9. Colle, *Les Baluba*, 275; see also Nooter, "Luba Art and Government."

10. Dichotomous representation is discussed in Needham, *Primordial Characters*, and Schoffeleers, "Twins." The hero is associated with other potent ambiguities, such as a blurring of gender; see M. N. Roberts, "The King Is a Woman," where the Luba helmet mask is briefly discussed.

11. On color symbolism among Luba and other Central African peoples, see A. F. Roberts, "Performing Cosmology." Reference to both past and present is necessary here, for while the adventures of Nkongolo and Mbidi are felt to have taken place at some very distant time, narratives and choreographies are performed in the present to facilitate reflection upon how the contrastive characteristics personified by the protagonists remain central to Luba philosophy and practices of everyday life.

12. Mudimbe, "Afterword," 246.

13. Durkheim, *The Elementary Forms*, 13; Fernandez, paraphrasing Durkheim, in "Principles of Opposition," 358.

14. Theuws, "Le Styx ambigu." 11.

CHAPTER FIVE

1. For Aristotle's works see Barnes, *The Complete Works of Aristotle*.

2. For a translation of this work see Silano.

3. For an overview that pays attention to the context of medieval discussions, see De Leemans and Klemm, "Animals and Anthropology." In the following piece, translations are my own unless otherwise stated.

4. Harvey, *The Inward Wits*, 4–61; Costa ben Luca, *De differentia spiritus et animae*, in Wilcox, *The Transmission and Influence*, 143–233.

5. This description originates in Aristotle (*On the Soul*, 1.1, 403a25–b19), and it was commonly accepted in the Middle Ages. See, e.g., Aquinas, *Summa Theologiae*, II-1.22.2. Aquinas explains the relationship between material and formal elements, e.g., in *Summa Theologiae* II-1.44.1 and 37.4. (For an edition of this work see Caramello.)

6. For a discussion, see Pasnau, *Thomas Aquinas on Human Nature*, 95–99.

7. Aquinas, *In duodecim libros Metaphysicorum Aristotelis exposition*, 7.11 [hereafter *In Met.*] (for an edition of this work, see Cathala and Spiazzi).

8. Porphyry, *Isagoge*, 9 (for which see Minio-Paluello, *Anicius Manlius Severinus Boethius Porphyrii Isagoge translatio*, I.6–7). Translation from Barnes, *Porphyry: Introduction*, 6.

9. Medieval philosophers followed different strategies to drive this point home, and in some cases they might have been uncomfortable with the expression "entity." For a discussion, see Bazán, "The Human Soul."

10. As can be seen, e.g., from logical exercises conducted in the arts faculties of medieval universities. "Omnis homo est animal" was one of the unquestioned premises. See, e.g., Peter of Spain, *Syncategoremata,* in de Rijk and Spruyt, 296–99; Henry of Ghent, *Syncategoremata*, in Braakhuis et al., 47–48.

11. I will not examine the problems, interpretations, and medieval discussions concerning the metaphysical picture that the *Introduction* draws. See Barnes "Commentary," in *Porphyry: Introduction*, 21–311.

12. *On the Soul*, 2.1, 412b18–22; *Meteorology*, 4.12, 390a10–13. See Aquinas, *Sent. DA*, 2.1, in Gauthier, *Thomas Aquinas: Sentencia libri De anima*, 71 (translated in Hibbs, *Aquinas on Human Nature*, 22, §226).

13. For Aristotle's idea of the continuous scale of nature, see, e.g., *History of Animals* 8.1, 588a16–b3; Albert the Great, *De animalibus*, 1:224 and 2:1341–42, 1348 (all references to this work use the numbering in Stadler, *Albertus Magnus: De animalibus libri XXVI*).

14. Ps.-Boethius of Dacia, Sup. An. Pr., Pro.: f.31ra, as quoted by Marno, "Anonymi Philosophia," 143 note f.

15. The anonymous author is alluding to the passage from Averroes quoted at the start of Peter Adamson's chapter in this volume.

16. For a discussion and references, see Bianchi, *Studi sull'Aristotelismo*, 41–61. Bianchi traces the discussions from the Middle Ages to the Renaissance and shows that the idea gained some degree of popularity among Renaissance philosophers. It is notable that some medieval authors drop the qualification "does not have aptitude to be able to be perfected by" speculative sciences, thereby making the claim even more radical. See, e.g., Aubry of Reims, *Philosophia*, in Gauthier, "Notes sur Siger de Brabant," 29–30.

17. Aquinas, *Sententia libri Politicorum*, 1.1/b 78b80–100.

18. Peter of Auvergne, *Quaestiones super libros Politicorum*, Paris BN Lat. 16089, fol. 276va.

19. Boethius, *Consolation of Philosophy*, book 4, part 3, in Slavitt, 118.

20. This idea is reflected, e.g., in Giles of Rome's *De regimine principum*, in Samaritanus, 1.4, 11: "A human being can be considered in three ways: first, as they are similar to animals; second, in themselves; third, as they participate in angels.... Therefore, everyone lives either like an animal, like a human being, or like an angel. Namely, one who lives a life of pleasures, lives like a beast; one who lives a political life, lives like a human being; and one who lives a contemplative life, lives like an angel. Philosophers distinguish therefore three lives or these three modes of living."

21. Köhler, *Homo animal nobilissimum* 1:419–43.

22. "Aliqua habent usum rationis sicut pygmei, alia non habent sicut simia" (Anonymous, "Utrum pygmei sint homines?," Paris BN lat. 15850, fol.16va–17rb).

23. Catherine König-Pralong has argued that Albert the Great distances human beings from other animals by emphasizing the rational and normative elements of human life at the expense of the biological elements. See König-Pralong, "Animal equivoque."

24. Montecatini, *In Politica Aristotelis Progymnasmata*, cap. 5, pars. 2, textus 23, 76.

25. For discussion, see Knuuttila and Kärkkäinen, *Theories of Perception*.

26. See, e.g., Walter Burley, *Expositio de somno et vigilia*, in Thörnqvist, "Walter Burley's *Expositio*," 423.

27. See, e.g., D. Gundissalinus, *Tractatus de anima*, in Muckle, "The Treatise *De Anima*," cap. 9, 70.

28. *Summa Theologiae* I.78.3.

29. Wolfson, "The Internal Senses" (1973), 1:252.

30. For a discussion and references, see Di Martino, *Ratio particularis*; Toivanen, *Perception*, 225–45.

31. Peter of John Olivi, *Quaestiones in secundum librum sententiarum* (hereafter Summa II), q. 62–66, 589–614 (all references to this work use the numbering in Jansen); Toivanen, *Perception*, 247–65.

32. Albert the Great (*De Animalibus*, 21.1.1, 1323) argues that even though animals may perceive more acutely than human beings, human senses are more perfect precisely because they convey more intellectual information. (See Kitchell and Resnick, *Albert the Great: On Animals*.)

33. *Summa Theologiae* I.78.4.

34. *De animalibus* 21.1.2, 1326–27. There are animals that cannot remember anything, Albert claims, and he mentions flies that return immediately after they have been driven off by slapping. His famous example of learning from experience is a weasel that knows how to use a leaf of a certain plant to fight off the poison of a serpent.

35. *De animalibus* 21.1.2, 1328–29.

36. *De animalibus* 21.1.2, 1327–28; 1.1.3, 18. Albert mentions practical reasoning and imitation of arts at 21.1.2, 1327 and 3, 1332.

37. *De animalibus* 21.1.2, 1328; See Resnick and Kitchell, "Albert the Great."

38. He claims that pygmies can reflect upon their experiences without abstracting universal concepts from them (*De animalibus* 21.1.3, 1328), which seems to suggest that pygmies are capable of entertaining some kind of proto-concepts.

39. Respectively, Albert the Great, *De homine*, in Borgnet, *Albertus Magnus: De homine*, q. 35, a. 1, 308; and John of la Rochelle, *Summa de anima*, in Bougerol, 2.101, 248.

40. Roger Bacon, *Perspectiva*, 2.3.9, 246–47. The translations of Bacon's work are from Lindberg, *Roger Bacon and the Origins of "Perspectiva" in the Middle Ages*, although I have occasionally amended them.

41. To the best of my knowledge, medieval philosophers do not develop this idea explicitly, and therefore this interpretation remains somewhat speculative.

42. Roger Bacon, *Perspectiva* 2.3.9, 250.

43. Perler, "Why Is the Sheep Afraid of the Wolf?" See, e.g., Albert the Great, *De anima*, in Borgnet, *Albertus Magnus: De Anima*, liber 3, tract. 1, c. 3, 319; Aquinas, *Quaestiones disputatae de veritate*, q. 24, a. 1, 680–81.

44. See the introduction to Heinämaa et al., *Consciousness*, 1–26. See also Toivanen, *Perception*, 173–75.

45. See, e.g., Summa II q. 58, 506 (a dog that dreams), q. 63, 601 (a dog that learns), q. 62, 588–89 (an animal that opens its eyes in order to see). Aquinas points out in *Summa Theologiae* II-1.26.1 that animals differ from inanimate nature because their desires follow apprehension, and that human beings differ from animals because their desires follow apprehension in such a way that there is a possibility of rational control. He does not think the crucial difference is awareness. See also *Summa Theologiae* II-1.6.2; Aquinas, *In Met.* 1.1.13.

46. Summa II q. 62, 587.

47. Summa II q. 62, 595 and q. 67, 615–16.

48. See Toivanen, "Perceptual Self-Awareness," 372–79.

49. See Hoffmann, "Intellectualism and Voluntarism."

50. Again the classification of various emotions varied from author to author. See Knuuttila, *Emotions*, 177–255.

51. Aquinas, for one, thinks that evaluative perception is the formal cause of an emotion. See King, "Aquinas on the Emotions," 214–15. For a detailed study, see Loughlin, "Similarities and Differences."

52. *Summa Theologiae*, I.81.3. For medieval discussions, see Perler, "Why Is the Sheep Afraid"; Black, "Imagination and Estimation."

53. *Summa Theologiae*, II-1.50.3 ad2; King, "Aquinas on Emotions," 215–16.

54. See, e.g., *Summa Theologiae*, II-1.6.2 ad 3.

55. All modern studies concerning these cases are based on E. P. Evans's pioneering work, which was published more than a hundred years ago, *The Criminal Prosecution and Capital Punishment of Animals*.

56. *Summa Theologiae*, II-2.64.1; Aquinas, *Summa contra Gentiles*, 3.112 (in Marc et al., *Thomas Aquinas: Liber de veritate catholicae Fidei contra errores infidelium seu Summa contra Gentiles*).

57. Mommsen et al., *Corpus iuris civilis*, 1.1.1.3–4.

58. *Summa Theologiae*, II-1.91.2.

59. Jean Gerson, *Oeuvres Completes*, in Glorieux 3:141–42; Brett, *Liberty, Right*, 83–85.

60. Aristotle, *Politics* 1.8, 1256b7–26.

61. Nicholas of Vaudémont (John Buridan, pseud.), *Quaestiones super octo libros Politicorum* (hereafter *QPol*), fol. 14ra.

62. Genesis 9:2–3.

63. See, e.g., Hassig, *Medieval Bestiaries*. A good example is Thomas of Cantimpré's *Bonum Universale De Apibus*.

64. See, e.g., Aquinas, *Sententia libri Ethicorum*, 7.5, 399–400. Aquinas mentions that these people may eat human flesh.

65. Nicholas of Vaudémont, among others, appeals to various senses of "being worst" that are based on a distinction between moral badness and "natural" badness. See *QPol.* 1.5, fol. 6vb–7ra.

66. This research has been funded by the Academy of Finland and Riksbankens Jubileumsfond. I am thankful to John Marenbon, Anselm Oelze, and the editors for their helpful comments.

CHAPTER FIVE: REFLECTION

1. There is biblical authority for this at Genesis 1:27–28.

2. As shown in Friedrich, *Menschentier und Tiermensch*.

3. Cormeau, *Walther von der Vogelweide*, tune 2, stanza II (in the new edition of T. Bein, 2013, given as stanza III with slight variations). See Colvin, *I Saw the World*.

4. Cormeau, *Walther von der Vogelweide*, C. 2.II, verses 12–16.

5. Colvin, *I Saw the World*, C. 2.II, verses 12–16.

6. Cormeau, *Walther von der Vogelweide*, C. 2.II, vers 19.

7. Instinctive behavior is also understood as a superior kind of intelligence. According to a poem written by the Marner (thirteenth century), ants undertake preparation for the winter "in an intelligent way (*kúndecliche*)": 1,1, vers 3, in Willms, *Lieder*.

8. Foerster, *Chrétien de Troyes*. For an English translation see Kibler, *Chrétien de Troyes*.

9. Benecke, *Hartmann von Aue: Iwein*. For an English translation see McConeghy, *Hartmann von Aue: Iwein*.

10. Benecke, *Hartmann von Aue: Iwein*, v. 4001–5.

11. McConeghy, *Hartmann von Aue: Iwein*, v. 4001–5.

12. Alexander, *Saints*, 24.

13. Sulpicius Severus, *Dialogi*, III.9.4, 207: *in nomine inquit Domini iubeo te redire.*

14. Alexander, *Saints*, 35.

15. Some legends explain the animal's behavior uncommon to animals by invoking God's will.

16. Salisbury, *The Beast Within*, 121, I take it that this also applies in cases where we are presented with human-animal hybrids or transformations. Such cases likewise assume, and thus confirm, the traditional boundary between human and animal. See further Friedrich, *Menschentier und Tiermensch*.

17. Roethe, *Die Gedichte Reinmars von Zweter*.

18. See further Gerhardt, "Reinmars von Zweter."

19. Pliny the Elder (Hist. Nat. X, §191) is an antique source for the idea of animals' superiority in sense perception, reflected in such medieval authors as Thomas of Cantrimpré (thirteenth century): *Homo in quinque sensibus superatur a multis: aquile et linces clarius cernunt, vultures sagcius odorantur, simia subtilius gustat, aranea citius tangit; liquidius audiunt talpe vel aper silvaticus. Unde versus: Nos aper auditu; linx visu, simia gustu/Vultur odoratu precedit, aranea tactu* (*Liber de natura rerum* 4, 1, 190–94, in Boese, 106). It is also reflected in Reinmar, in his *Sangspruch*,164. See also Pastoureau, "Le bestiaire."

CHAPTER FIVE: REFLECTION

* This essay is a radical abbreviation and reworking of J. Simpson, "Consuming Ethics: Caxton's *History of Reynard the Fox.*"

1. For larger, medieval Latin traditions, see Mann, "Beast Epic and Fable," 556–61. For the English texts, see J. Simpson, "Beast Epic and Fable," 111–12. The best critical book on medieval animal material is Mann, *From Aesop to Reynard.*

2. See Mann trans.

3. Flinn, *Le Roman de Reynart,* and J. R. Simpson, *Animal Body, Literary Corpus,* appendix one.

4. Caxton's text can be found in Blake, *William Caxton: The History of Reynard the Fox,* 263. Caxton's text was obviously popular, being reprinted in 1489, 1494, and 1525. For a translation see J. Simpson, *Reynard the Fox: A New Translation.* Chapter numbers cited here refer to this edition.

CHAPTER SIX

* All translations are my own if not stated otherwise. Initial research for this chapter was conducted while I was Ahmanson Fellow at Villa I Tatti—The Harvard University Center for Italian Renaissance Studies: I wish to express my gratitude to the Ahmanson Foundation for its support, and to my colleagues and friends at I Tatti—especially Angela Matilde Capodivacca, Guy Gelter, Giordano Mastrocola, and Eugenio Refini—for many fruitful conversations on the topic of my research. This chapter was completed while I was Fellow at the Warburg Institute, University of London, where I benefited from the use of its unique library, as well as from constant exchange with Guido Giglioni, whom I warmly thank.

1. Based on Anghiera, *Libretto,* chapter 5. See also Amerigo Vespucci's letter to Lorenzo di Pierfrancesco de' Medici (July 30, 1500), in Pozzi, *Il mondo nuovo,* 64: "From this people we know that those inhabiting the islands mentioned above were cannibals (*cambali*), and that they ate human flesh."

2. Also in the journal relating Columbus's first voyage, the cannibals are portrayed as frightening and aggressive indirectly through the report of other people encountered, yet the issue of communication and the possibility that there might have been misunderstandings are addressed. See Cristoforo Colombo, *Diario di bordo,* in Ferro, 104: "He says that all people he has encountered until the present day are very frightened of those of *Caniba* or *Canima*. . . . Since the captured Indians do not come back, they believe that they ate them. Every day we understand these Indians a bit better, and they us, even if we have often misunderstood."

3. See Anghiera, *Décades du Nouveau Monde,* in Gauvin, especially 23–25.

4. On the ways the descriptions of the Cannibals affected national identity see Wojciehowski, *Group Identity in the Renaissance World,* 76–128.

5. Scenes like this one have been visually represented by Theodor de Bry in the famous engraving contained in Staden, *Warhaftig Historia.*

6. The role of food in philosophical discussions of the human-animal distinction is understudied in comparison to historical and sociological reconstructions of the availability and culinary preparation of certain foods, and dietary prescriptions with regard to social status or religious belief. On the cultural history of food see Montanari, *The Culture of Food;* Montanari, *A Cultural History of Food;* specifically on the Renaissance: Albala, *Eating Right in the Renaissance.*

7. On Early Modern debates on the human-animal difference see especially Wild, *Die anthropologische Differenz.* Wild focuses on three main case studies: Montaigne, Descartes, and Hume. Many important studies have been published on Descartes's views on animals, emphasizing especially the (lack of) ethical consequences; see Cottingham, "'A Brute to the Brutes?'" Erica Fudge has focused on the status of animals in Early Modern England in *Perceiving Animals.*

8. On the ethical aspects of eating animals see Muratori and Dohm, *Ethical Perspectives.* I have considered the ethical approaches to diet, and the intertwining of discourses on cannibalism and vegetarianism in particular, in "Pitagora tra i cannibali."

9. On the name Zipangu (or Zipagu) see the explanation in Ruggieri's edition of Marco Polo's *Il Milione,* 378.

10. I translate from the version of the text printed in Milanesi's edition of Giovanni Ramusio, *Navigazioni e viaggi,* 3: 254. Cf. also Marco Polo, *Il Milione,* in Ruggieri, 247.

11. See for instance Milanesi, "Arsarot o Anian?," especially 42, about the fact that the new plant and animal species encountered had a key role to play in the definition of the Americas as a *new* world.

12. Antonello Gerbi has pointed out that Marco Polo, too, often compared the "new" animals he encountered with those known in Europe. On this see Gerbi, *Nature in the New World*, in Moyle, 5.

13. Vespucci, letter to Lorenzo di Pierfrancesco de' Medici (1502), in Pozzi, *Il mondo nuovo*, 77–78

14. Noteworthy is Augustine's skeptical position about the existence of inhabitants of the "opposite part of the globe (*contraria parts terrae*)" in *The City of God* (*De civitate Dei*), XVI, 9: *Quidam de antipodis fabulantur*. (For an edition of this work see Dods.)

15. Ramusio, *Navigazioni e viaggi*, in Milanesi, 3:7–8.

16. The Aristotelian legacy in Renaissance debates on animals is of course a vast topic. Specifically on the reception of Aristotelian zoology see Steel et al., *Aristotle's Animals in the Middle Ages and Renaissance*; Perfetti, *Aristotle's Zoology and Its Renaissance Commentators (1521-1601)*. An overview of university approaches to Aristotelian natural philosophy in the Renaissance can be found in Grendler, *The Universities of the Italian Renaissance*, ch. 8. Brian Cummings has explored the link between the Aristotelian problem of the human-animal distinction (as based on the conception of the passions) and the descriptions of the savages in the New World in "Animal Passions and Human Sciences."

17. As Markus Wild puts it, the focal point of the anthropological difference—that is to say, the definition of a border dividing humans from all other animals—lies in the philosophy of mind (see Wild, *Die anthropologische Differenz*, 3).

18. Cf. on this terminology Kahn, "Aristotle on Thinking."

19. Comparing several Aristotelian writings, and in particular those relating to biology (*History of Animals, Parts of Animals, On Generation of Animals*) with the psychological theory presented in *On the Soul*, complicates the picture of man's uniqueness simply based on rationality. See on this Laspia, "Aristotele e gli animali."

20. Longrigg, *Greek Rational Medicine*, 134: "Blood in Empedocles' system also serves as the seat and agent of thought (Frag. 105) and a human's sensitivity, intelligence and general ability is dependent upon the blending of the elements in its make-up."

21. This problem is addressed repeatedly in Muratori, *The Animal Soul*.

22. Vespucci, letter to Lorenzo di Pierfrancesco de' Medici from Lisbon (1502), in Pozzi, *Il mondo nuovo*, 79: "Now we come to the rational animals (*animali razionali*). We found that the whole territory was inhabited by fully naked people, men and women alike, who don't cover themselves and don't have any shame. Their bodies have a good shape and are well proportioned; they are white and

have long hair, and not much beard or at all. I struggled to understand their way of life and their habits, as I ate and slept with them for 27 days."

23. Vespucci, letter to Lorenzo di Pierfrancesco de' Medici from Lisbon (1502), in Pozzi, *Il mondo nuovo*, 79–80.

24. On the status of these indigenous people in relation to the question of their animality and the possibility of their conversion see Fudge, *Perceiving Animals*, 20–21. The topic is addressed repeatedly in Greenblatt, *New World Encounters*.

25. It should not be forgotten that, alongside the fascination for the cannibals, the myth of the "bon sauvage" also develops. See Lestringant, *Le Huguenot et le Sauvage*, especially ch. 8. See also Marcondes, "The Anthropological Argument," 41–42. A useful overview of positive and negative presentations of the indigenous populations encountered in the Americas can be found in Gliozzi, *La scoperta dei selvaggi*, 28–117.

26. Raber, *Animal Bodies*, 4. Raber is commenting here on the human-animal boundary in Giovan Battista Gelli's *Circe* (1549).

27. In Vespucci's *Mundus novus* the behavior of the cannibals is interestingly interpreted as being Epicurean (that is, based on sensation and pleasure) rather than Stoic (in Pozzi, *Il mondo nuovo*, 100–103).

28. Anghiera, *Décades du Nouveau Monde*, in Gauvin, 200.

29. *Mundus Novus* in Pozzi, *Il mondo nuovo*, 102.

30. Leonardo da Vinci, *Quaderni d'Anatomia II, in* Vangensten et al., fol. 14r (30a).

31. da Vinci, *Quaderni d'Anatomia II*, in Vangensten et al., fol. 14r (30a).

32. Michel de Montaigne, *Essais* I, in Tournon, 339. On the effects of Montaigne's skeptical approach to the question about the human-animal distinction, with particular focus on the conception of rationality, see Wild, *Die anthropologische Differenz*, 43ff.

33. See on this Mermier, "L'Essay *Des Cannibales* de Montaigne," esp. 29.

34. See Lestringant, "Le nom des 'Cannibales' de Christophe Colomb à Michel de Montaigne."

35. See for instance Schiefsky, *Hippocrates: On Ancient Medicine*, 29, 234, where Schiefsky notes that this theory is applied to the growth of plants as well as to human nutrition.

36. Girolamo Manfredi, *Liber de homine/Il Perché*, in Foresti et al., 75. The passage is commented upon by Camporesi in *I balsami di Venere*, 7.

37. A. J. Grieco has worked on the ways a hierarchical system among living beings was mirrored on the level of the choice of food as well, with certain aliments considered more suitable than others for each class of being. See Grieco, "Food and Social Classes in Late Medieval and Renaissance Italy."

38. Galen, *On the Power of Foods*, in Grant, 154–55. The passage continues as follows: "Athletes display the most striking proof of this fact, for if one day they eat an equal weight of some other food when training for their exercises, on the next day they grow weaker; if they continue this over several days, they not only grow weaker, but also clearly show signs of malnutrition." Cf. the same passages *Galen: On the Properties of Foodstuffs*, in Powell, 114–15.

39. On human-animal similarity in the history of vivisection see French, *Dissection and Vivisection*, 245–46. See also Galen, *On Anatomical Procedures*, in C. Singer, xxi.

40. On Galen Renaissance editions see Durling, "Galen in the Renaissance."

41. Marsilio Ficino, *Three Books on Life*, in Kaske and Clark, 181.

42. See Hogg, "Carthusian Abstinence."

43. Erasmus, *Colloquies I*, in Schoeck et al., *The Collected Works of Erasmus*, 39:330.

44. Galen, *The Thinning Diet*, in P. N. Singer *Galen: Selected Works*, 315. On this Galenic text see Wilkins, "The Contribution of Galen *De subtiliante diaeta.*"

45. With reference to the Hippocratic background of this theory see Langholf, *Medical Theories in Hippocrates*, 89–90: "As digesting the food was considered not only a 'cooking' process, but also a process of 'overcoming' the food, the harmful substance had to be 'overcome' by the body.... In the process of digestion either the body overcome the food, or the food overcome the body."

46. Cardano, *De rerum varietate*, in Spon, *Opera omnia*, 3:147b.

47. Cardano, *De subtilitate*, in Spon, *Opera Omnia*, 3:501b (English translation in Forrester, *The De Subtilitate of Girolamo Cardano*, 495: "As I said, bodies are altered by foods, and firstly the blood, and the habits, then the milk and the semen, and the fetus, and finally the flesh and the powers, specifically like magic. And so since the Germans are nourished mainly with the milk of beasts, especially cows, they are ill-tempered, fearless, and pastoral—bulls, that consume the same food, are like that.")

48. Cardano, *De subtilitate*, in Forrester, 495 (cf. Cardano, *De subtilitate*, in Spon, *Opera Omnia*, 3: 501b): "This is more apparent in animals than in human beings, and in plants than in animals, because they are not altered by other sources."

49. On the idea that "flesh nourishes flesh" see the example of the athletes' diet in Cardano, *Contradicentium medicorum*, in Spon, *Opera omnia*, 6:402.

50. Cardano, *De subtilitate*, in Forrester, 495 (cf. Cardano, *De subtilitate*, in Spon, *Opera Omnia*, 3: 501b).

51. Della Porta revised this work several times, from the first Latin edition (1586) to the latest vernacular translation (*Della fisonomia dell'huomo*, 1610). On the history of these editions see the introduction to Giovan Battista Della Porta, *De humana physiognomonia*, in Paolella, xii. See also A. Orlandi, *Le edizioni*

dell'opera di Della Porta Cf. also Della Porta, *De humana physiognomonia*, in Paolella, 65.

52. Della Porta, *Della fisionomia dell'uomo*, in Paolella, 76–77. Cf. Della Porta, *De humana physiognomonia*, in Paolella, 65.

53. Della Porta, *Della fisionomia dell'uomo*, in Paolella, 77. Cf. Della Porta, *De humana physiognomonia*, in Paolella, 65.

54. Cardano, *The Book of My Life*, in Stoner, 189.

55. Cardano, *De subtilitate*, in Spon, *Opera Omnia*, 3:525b (cf. Forrester's translation, *The* De Subtilitate, 565: "so this dog was trained to lead along those who are willing, and to mangle those who refuse, and to spar those who have fallen down. What these people credit to God's will and indulgence, I put down to feeding on human flesh, or to practice, or rather to demonic aid.")

56. Cardano, *De rerum varietate*, in Spon, *Opera omnia*, 3: 336b.

57. See Cardano, *De subtilitate*, in Spon, *Opera Omnia*, 3:507b (cf. Forrester, *The* De Subtilitate, 512).

58. See Cardano, *De subtilitate*, in Spon, *Opera Omnia*, 3:529b (cf. Forrester, *The* De Subtilitate, 577).

59. See Cardano, *De subtilitate*, in Spon, *Opera Omnia*, 3:526a (cf. Forrester, *The* De Subtilitate, 567).

60. Vanini, *De admirandis*, in Raimondi and Carparelli, *Tutte le opere*, 1336.

61. Francesco Zorzi, *L'elegante poema e Commento sopra il poema*, in Maillard, 116.

62. See Campanella, *Medicinalia*, 45.

63. Key passages for Campanella's view of human uniqueness are quoted and discussed in Ernst, "L'analogia e la differenza."

64. See Campanella, *Del senso delle cose e della magia*, in Ernst, 88: "Since in animals the processing of sensory input reaches little further than what they see and immediately feel [*poco discorrono più di quel che veggono e sentono presente*], and in humans this reaches many other similar things, and actions, and figures, and vices and virtues, and affairs at the same time, due to the fact that his internal [brain] cells are better [than in animals], the spirit [*spirito*] is purer, clearer, nobler, and this spirit is sharper in knowing thanks to the immortal mind which is united with it…so it happened that man is called rational and capable of discursive thinking [*è avvenuto che l'uomo si dica razionale e discorsivo*], and not the brutes, which are called only sensitive [*sensitivi*], not because they are not capable of discourse at all, but not much [*non perché non discorrano, ma poco*] just like plants are not called animals because they do not feel much."

65. Anton Francesco Doni, *I Mondi e gli Inferni*, in Pellizzari, 106.

66. See the discussion of this issue in Ernst, "L'analogia e la differenza."

67. See da Vinci, *Quaderni d'Anatomia II*, in Vangensten et al., fol. 14r (30a), where the description of the human act of eating animals is described in these terms: "by which [i.e., the gullet] you have tried to make yourself the sepulcher of all animals [*supulura dj tutti li anjmali*]."

CHAPTER SEVEN

1. References to Descartes's texts are from Adam and Tannery, *Oeuvres de Descartes* (hereafter *Oeuvres*). Unless otherwise indicated, translations are from Cottingham et al., *The Philosophical Writings of Descartes* (hereafter *Philosophical Writings*).

2. *On the Soul*, 412a17–27. For Aristotle's works, see Barnes, *The Complete Works of Aristotle*.

3. *Physics* 199a9–18.

4. According to Rosenfield, Descartes's first hints at the doctrine of animal automatism date from the period 1619–21. See his *Cogitationes privatae* (*Oeuvres* 10:219), where he alludes to the deterministic quality of animal actions (*Oeuvres* 10:231–32). The doctrine was, however, not fully developed until Descartes began work on *Le Monde* between 1630 and 1633. See Rosenfield, *From Beast-Machine to Man-Machine*, 5. On Descartes's experimenting with machines, see Descartes's biographer, Baillet: *La Vie*, 1:52. Francine was the same name Descartes gave to his daughter (b. 1635), but his automaton could have been named in honor of the Francini brothers, engineers of the automata in the gardens at Saint Germain-en-Laye.

5. Rosenfield, *From Beast-Machine to Man-Machine*, 8–9.

6. Gassendi, More, Cudworth, Highmore, Conway, Malebranche, and Cavendish all thought that mechanism was too impoverished to explain the order and regularity of organic nature. Gassendi and Malebranche appealed to God's intentions to fill the breach. Harvey, More, Cudworth, Conway, and Cavendish were instead attracted to various forms of vitalism—instruments of the divine craftsman that organized matter into regular forms or accounted for the animation of organs (e.g., the contractile power of the heart, in the case of Harvey). Leibnizian monads performed many of the functions of substantial forms and were imbued with various degrees of cognition (perception or apperception) as well as purposes. Summing up this common backlash to Cartesianism, Ralph Cudworth writes, "[Mechanists] make the world to be nothing else but a heap of dust, fortuitously agitated, or a dead cadaverous thing, that hath no signatures of mind and understanding, counsel and wisdom at all upon it" (*The True Intellectual System*, 147).

7. Descartes presents to Mersenne the view, similar to that advanced by the Stoics, that crystals occupy a middle status between the living and the nonliving (*Oeuvres* 2:525). For a more thorough account of the definitive characteristics of automata, see Sir Kenelm Digby's account in *Two Treatises*, 259, 265.

8. In Cotton, *Essays of Montaigne*, 4:439.

9. *Cogitationes privatae* (*Oeuvres* 10:219).

10. *De Sollertia Animalium,* 963B, in Goodwin, *Plutarch's Morals.*

11. Although the Stoics, Epicurus, and Hermarchus denied the possibility of contracts with animals (Diogenes Laertius, *Lives of Eminent Philosophers*, 10.150— see Hicks trans.), Lucretius allowed some contractual arrangements in which animals exchanged their services for security from hunger, thirst, and predators (Lucretius, *De Rerum Natura*, 5.1297-349—see Rouse trans.). Plutarch also objects to the Stoics' denial of animal-human contracts (*De Sollertia* 999A), as does Porphyry in *On Abstinence*. The idea of animal justice was also a theme in Roman natural histories. Aelian and Pliny (*Natural History*, 8.65—see Rackham trans.) both attributed to animals wisdom, intelligence, and justice. See Gilhus, *Animals, Gods and Humans*, 71-72. For discussion on the debates about animals in antiquity, see the entries by G. Fay Edwards and Devin Henry in this volume.

12. E. Cohen, "Law, Folklore, and Animal Lore," 11.

13. Cohen, "Law, Folklore," 13, recounts that in 1587 flies were sued for ruining vineyards by the syndics of the commune of Saint-Julien-de-Maurienne, and the bishop appointed the flies a lawyer, lest the animals remain defenseless.

14. In one delectable case the lawyer for the rats of Autun pleaded that his clients had not appeared before the court when summoned because of their fear of local cats and demanded that safe conduct be provided, to which the court duly complied (Cohen, "Law, Folklore," 14).

15. *Physics* 199b4.

16. Considering whether the "monstrous races of the East" are human, Augustine describes the tension aptly: "If we assume that the subjects of those remarkable accounts are in fact men, it may be suggested that God decided to create some races in this way, so that we should not suppose that the wisdom with which he fashions the physical being of men has gone astray in the case of the monsters (*monstris*) which are bound to be born among us of human parents; for that would be to regard the works of God's wisdom as the products of an imperfectly skilled craftsman" (Bettenson, *Augustine: City of God*, 663–64; cited in Bildhauer and Mills, *The Monstrous Middle Ages*, 9).

17. Fudge, *Perceiving Animals*, 115.

18. Porphyry, in *On Abstinence from Killing Animals* 3.3, responds that just because we cannot interpret what animals say, it doesn't follow that they are not using

signs in a meaningful way. The Persians and other races, he drolly observes, are inarticulate and yet we do not deny them intelligence.

19. Aristotle's *History of Animals* (8.1, 10.1) represents higher mammals as having the same psychical and human qualities, lesser only in quantity, or as having analogous qualities or the same qualities potentially, much as children do. The list includes temperamental dispositions, cunning, an approximation of sagacity and prudence, crafts (e.g., weaving, house building), the capacity to instruct others (including us), and the capacity to learn and to interpret signs. *Politics* 1332b4–6, however, asserts the primacy of human reason: "Animals lead for the most part a life of nature, although in lesser particulars some are influenced by habit. Man has reason (*logoi*), in addition, and man only."

20. Plutarch, *De Sollertia* 961B.

21. The faculty for animal judgment in Avicenna's terms is an "estimative faculty" (*vis estimativa*). The capacity of animals to learn, to detect the utility or disutility of objects (e.g., the *malicitas* of the wolf), and their quasi-prudential or intentional behavior is a form of judgment. See van Riet, *Avicenna Latinus: Liber de anima* 2:39. Aquinas adopted Avicenna's theory of the internal senses at *Summa Theologiae* I-I, q.83.a.1(see Gilby).

22. Aquinas, *Contra Gentiles*, III.112.2867–68, in Fathers.

23. See Cicero, *De Officiis*, 1.50, 1.11(see Miller trans.).

24. Descartes resided in Saint Germain-en-Laye during 1614–15, where these elaborate hydraulically operated automata appeared in the grottos of the royal gardens. The same automata are described by Salomon de Caus, *Les raisons des forces mouvantes*, 1:27.

25. Descartes's theory of the internal senses represents a mechanization of the sensory processes outlined in medieval theories, particularly those of Avicenna and Aquinas.

26. Gunderson, "Descartes, La Mettrie, Language and Machines," 198.

27. See Copeland, "The Turing Test."

28. See Searle, "Minds, Brains and Programs."

29. Descartes's use of "morally" here signals something less than metaphysical impossibility: a practical or physical limitation. Gunderson, "Descartes," 209, helpfully describes Descartes's distinction between universal and nonuniversal instruments in terms of the difference between *general-purpose* and *special-purpose* instruments. Humans are general-purpose instruments because they can generalize from one task they can perform to indefinitely many related but different tasks, for example, from computing timesheets to budgeting, whereas special-purpose instruments cannot. For reasons outlined below, I am not sure that Descartes consistently draws this distinction. For further discussion see my "Animal Automatism."

30. In acting according to a corporeal principle, animals surpass us in perfection in regard to many actions, but they can act only from instinct or natural impulse (*Oeuvres* 4:575).

31. Cf. *Principles of Philosophy*, II, 54; *Oeuvres* 8A:71.

32. See Staddon, *Adaptive Behavior and Learning.*. As with Descartes's critics, contemporary biologists are disposed to think that such behavior presupposes cognition.

33. In "Animal Automatism" I speculate about what limitations a body exactly like a human body without a soul would possess. If it were restricted to making discriminations only on the basis of sensory images, it would be incapable of acting on the basis of information that exceeded its capacity for sensation and imagination. It would presumably, therefore, be indifferent to the differences between a chiliagon and a myriagon and to any nonsensory differences, including exclusively intensional differences.

34. Rorty, "The Concept of Potentiality," 251–53; Des Chene, *Spirits and Clocks*, 11. Ordinarily Descartes appears to be a reductionist when it comes to explaining nature: "All the variety in matter, or all the diversity of its forms, depends on motion....All the properties which we clearly perceive in it are reducible to its divisibility and consequent mobility in respect of its parts, and its resulting capacity to be affected in all the ways which we perceive as being derivable from the movement of the parts" (*Oeuvres* 8A:52; *Philosophical Writings* 1:232).

35. Draft of a letter from Regius to Voetius, written by Descartes. See also Descartes's letter to Mesland (February 9, 1645; *Oeuvres* 4:166–67).

36. Des Chene, *Spirits and Clocks*, 116–52.

37. Cf. *Principles of Philosophy*, II.8 (*Oeuvres* 8A:44–45; *Philosophical Writings* 1:226).

38. Cf. *Principles of Philosophy*, II.25 (*Oeuvres* 8A:53–54; *Philosophical Writings* 1:233).

39. Descartes rejects any role for ends or "final causes" in physics at *Oeuvres* 7:55, 8A:81, 4:292, 8A:15–16, 7:442; 3:667–68. Des Chene, *Spirits and Clocks*, 132.

40. Des Chene, *Spirits and Clocks*, 132–40. He notes at 140 that "the ban on consideration of ends in natural philosophy must be lifted" in order to understand the operations of organic bodies as Descartes conceives them.

41. Functional attributions are ubiquitous in Descartes's natural philosophy. In the *Meditations* the functions of sensations and passions are defined by their contribution to "the conservation of the healthy human" (*Oeuvres* 7:87–88). *The Passions of the Soul* distinguishes functions that relate to the body, to the soul, and to the whole human being (*Oeuvres* 11:331–33, 342, 351, 359). The organs of the human body are defined by their functions: "That which we call, for example, the arm or hand of a man is that which has the exterior shape, size

and *use* of one" (*Oeuvres* 4:169; my emphasis). The *Treatise on Man* and *Description of the Human Body* explicate the functions of organs of the human body without referring to any animating soul (*Oeuvres* 11:199ff., 223ff.). The organs of animals and proper parts of plants are elsewhere subject to functional analysis (*Oeuvres* 7:230; 4:573–76, 5:276–77).

42. See my "Cartesian Functional Analysis" for an extended discussion of these points.

43. I am grateful to the Social Sciences and Humanities Research Council of Canada for financial support for this project, to Calvin Normore for many illuminating conversations, to Caitlin Prouatt for exceptional research assistance, and especially to the editors of this volume, Peter Adamson and G. Fay Edwards for their expert stewardship and insight.

CHAPTER EIGHT

1. References to Kant's works, other than the *Critique of Pure Reason*, are to the volume and page number of the German Academy Edition (*Kants gesammelte Schriften* [KgS]) of each work. References to the *Critique of Pure Reason* (*Kritik der reinen Vernuft*) are to the standard A and B pagination of the first (1781) and second (1787) editions. Translations from the *Groundwork*, *Critique of Practical Reason*, and *The Metaphysics of Morals* are based upon those in Gregor, *Practical Philosophy*; from Kant's *Critique of the Power of Judgment* (*Kritik der Urteilskraft* [1790] (KgS 5)), [hereafter *Power of Judgment*] those in Guyer and Matthews, *Critique of the Power of Judgment*; from Kant's ethics lectures (when possible) those in Heath and Schneewind, *Lectures on Ethics*; from Kant's lectures on metaphysics those in Ameriks and Naragon, *Lectures on Metaphysics*. For a translation of Kant's *Critique of Pure Reason*, see Guyer and Wood.

2. For an earlier treatment of these issues, with a somewhat different focus, see Kain, "Duties regarding Animals."

3. For helpful discussions of the nature and content of and relationships between Kant's empirical psychology and anthropology, see Frierson, *Kant's Empirical Psychology*; Sturm, *Kant*.

4. The argument of the next several paragraphs is developed in more detail in Kain, "Kant's Defense."

5. VR refers to Kant's "Von den verschiedenen Racen der Menschen, zur Ankündigung der Vorlesungen der physischen Geographie im Sommerhalbjahr" [1775] (KgS 2), "Of the Different Races of Human Beings," which can be found in Louden and Zöller, *Anthropology, History, and Education*.

6. GtP refers to Kant's "Über den Gebrauch teleologischer Principien in der Philosophie" [1788] (KgS 8), "On the Use of Teleological Principles in Philosophy," which can be found in Louden and Zöller, *Anthropology*.

7. Kant eschewed both spermatic and oocytic theories of reproduction, and he offered an innovative "'middle way' between mechanistic epigenesis and strong preformationism" in the theory of reproduction (Sloan, "Preforming the Categories," 238). For important recent work on the place of Kant's theory in the context of eighteenth century debates about generation, see also Sloan, "Buffon, German Biology"; Lenoir, "Kant, Blumenbach"; Richards, "Kant and Blumenbach"; Zammito, "'This Inscrutable Principle.'"

8. BBM refers to Kant's "Bestimmung des Begriffs einer Menschenrasse" [1785] (KgS 8), "Determination of the Concept of a Human Race" (see Louden and Zöller, *Anthropology*).

9. "For one cannot turn a family of animals [*Tiergeschlecht*] into a special kind [*besonderen Spezies*] if it belongs with another one to one and the same system of generation of nature" (GtP 8:165).

10. "For all faculties or capacities of the soul can be reduced to the three that cannot be further derived from a common ground: the faculty of cognition, the feeling of pleasure and displeasure, and the faculty of desire" (*Power of Judgment*, 5:177). See also *Lectures on Metaphysics*, 28:115–17, 274–77, 448–49, 594, 690; 29:906, 1026. On the historical significance of Kant's tripartite psychology, see Hilgard, "The Trilogy of Mind"; Frierson, *Kant's Empirical Psychology*; Sturm, *Kant*.

11. Frierson, "Kant's Empirical Account."

12. LJ 9:64–65; FS 2:59–60; PS 2:285; Handschriftlichen Nachlass (Handwritten Remains) (KgS 14–23), 15:161–62, 713; *Lectures on Metaphysics*, 28:66–67, 78–79, 98–99, 857. (FS refers to Kant's "Die falsche Spitzfindigkeit der vier syllogistischen Figuren erwiesen" [1762] (KgS 2), "The false subtlety of the four syllogistic figures," and PS refers to Kant's Preisschrift—"Untersuchung über die Deutlichkeit der Grundsätze der natürlichen Theologie und der Moral" [1764] (KgS 2), Prize Essay: "Inquiry concerning the distinctness of the principles of natural theology and morality" (for both see Walford and Meerbote, *Theoretical Philosophy*); LJ refers to Jäsche, *Immanuel Kants Logik, ein Handbuch zu Vorlesungen* (reprinted in KgS 9), which can be found under the title "Jäsche Logic" in Young, *Lectures on Logic*; For a careful analysis of Kant's account of the nature and limits of animal psychology, upon which I rely in this paragraph, see Naragon, "Reason and Animals" and "Kant on Descartes." See also Ameriks, *Kant's Theory of Mind*, 242.

13. It is striking how unqualified Kant's basic assertion of minds or souls is, compared to his more qualified commitment to the reality of organisms (*Power of Judgment* 5:379).

14. For additional historical context, see Ingensiep, "Tierseele und tierethische Argumentationen."

15. VPG-Hesse, 122–3. See also VM 28:117. Transcriptions by Werner Stark, translations are my own. (VPG refers to Kant's *Vorlesungen über physischen Geographie* (KgS 26—in progress), *Lectures on Physical Geography* (unpublished)).

16. Anthropology refers to Kant's *Anthropologie in pragmatischer Hinsicht* [1798] (KgS 7), *Anthropology from a Pragmatic Point of View*, in Louden and Zöller, *Anthropology*.

17. There is an ambiguous relationship between this description of the practical predispositions and the description found in the *Religion* (animality, humanity, and personality) (RGV 6:26–28).

18. The second Critique's appeal to the fact of reason marks a "great reversal" from Kant's attempts to establish freedom in the *Groundwork* (Ameriks, "Kant's Deduction").

19. Kant's Physical Geography course originally included some anthropological topics (as did his metaphysics course); by the mid-1770s Kant conceived of anthropology and physical geography as complementary "pragmatic" disciplines, which he then taught alternating semesters (VR 2:443; 10:146).

20. *Anthropology*, 7:322; VPG-Pillau 252, 266.

21. In Watkins, *Natural Science*.

22. VPG-Kaehler 405; VPG-Messina 248.

23. VPG-Pillau 266. The comparison of beavers, monkeys, dogs, and elephants seems to have been a common trope; see for example Buffon's discussion of elephants in Leclerc, *Histoire Naturelle*, vol 11.

24. VPG-Kaehler 401–2. On faithfulness to their master, see also VPG-Hesse 117; *Metaphysics of Morals*, 6:443; *Lectures on Ethics*, 27:459.

25. *Lectures on Metaphysics*, 29:949; 28:116; *Lectures on Anthropology*, 25:1196 (see Louden and Wood).

26. VPG-Pillau 252. The most detailed discussion is found in the parallel Pillau and Barth notes. These are the primary source for the rest of this paragraph, unless otherwise noted. Interestingly, Cicero (*Letters to Friends*, VII.1—for a translation see Shackleton Bailey) also names the elephant as an animal with which humans feel particular sympathy and affinity.

27. VPG-Kaehler 397; cf. *Physical Geography*, 9:328.

28. VPG-Kaehler 396; cf. VPG-Messina 238.

29. VPG-Pillau 253. This is an important contrast with most other animals, which Kant thinks are easily deceived (*Lectures on Metaphysics*, 28:116).

30. Aside from distinguishing discipline from mere learning, Kant does not elaborate. He appears to accept the myth that elephants do not mate in captivity but does not mention Buffon's interpretation of this as a form of modesty or self-control (VPG-Pillau 235). Nor does he elaborate an interpretation of an elephant's desire to avenge itself or resist being duped.

31. See Kain, "Kant's Defense," 82n70.

32. Christine Korsgaard seems independently to arrive at some similar conclusions in "Interacting with Animals."

33. This is not to deny that Kant also draws some distinctions within "price." See, for example, *Groundwork*, 4: 428, 434; *Metaphysics of Morals*, 6:434.

34. RGV refers to Kant's *Die Religion innerhalb der Grenzen der blossen Vernunft* [1793] (KgS 6), *Religion within the Boundaries of Mere Reason* (see Wood and di Giovanni, *Religion and Rational Theology*).

35. Kant rejects the possibility that organisms, in general, could be "final ends" or ends in themselves (*Power of Judgment* 5:425–35), contra Meier, *Philosophische Sittenlehre*, §975.

36. For this idea in the Stoic theory of justice see G. Fay Edwards's chapter in this volume.

37. Lest Kant's use of the word "humanity" here appear to beg all of the relevant questions about the scope of moral status, we must note that Kant often employs the terms "humanity" and "personality" in a technical sense to refer to certain capacities or predispositions of the will, which, so far as that goes, may or may not turn out to be ascribable to all and only human beings. It is the account of animals' natures—described above—that must guide judgments about which kinds of beings have these capacities or predispositions.

38. I have argued elsewhere that Kant has a principled basis for his ascription of moral status to all human beings, even to humans in so-called marginal cases. See Kain, "Kant's Defense," 82–87, 90–100.

39. See also *Power of Judgment* 5: 372, 482n; *Lectures on Ethics*, 27:459, 27:709–10.

40. For an earlier version of the argument of this section, see Kain, "Duties regarding Animals."

41. For more discussion of Kant's derivations of such duties, see Wood, *Kantian Ethics*, ch. 9; Smit and Timmons, "Kant's Grounding Project," 246, 254.

42. Baranzke, "Tierethik, Tiernatur."

43. Denis, "Kant's Conception," 417.

44. Denis, "Kant's Conception," 406–7.

45. The general capacity for love as "delight" (*Liebe des Wohlgefallens, amor complacentiae*), "pleasure joined immediately to the representation of an object's existence," is discussed as part of Kant's treatment of the "moral endowment" of *Menschenliebe*, the latter being either a special instance or a particular development of the former (*Metaphysics of Morals*, 6:402, 449, 450). Although sympathy does not itself appear explicitly on the list of subjective preconditions of duty, it seems to have a similar status. "Sympathetic joy and sadness (*sympathia moralis*) are sensible feelings of pleasure or displeasure ... at another's state of joy or pain"

(*Metaphysics of Morals*, 6:456). Humans, Kant claims, have a natural receptivity to such shared feeling, often called "humanity" or "humaneness" (*Menschlichkeit, humanitas aesthetica*), which is a precondition for the willingness to share in others' feelings. "While it is not in itself a duty to share the sufferings (as well as the joys) of others, it is a duty to sympathize actively in their fate; and to this end it is therefore an indirect duty to cultivate the compassionate natural (aesthetic) feelings in us" (*Metaphysics of Morals*, 6:457).

46. Guyer, *Kant and the Experience of Freedom*, 390. (Although Guyer may not endorse this specific analysis, or the point to which I am putting it.)

47. While Kant does not offer an elaborate justification for or account of the criteria for distinguishing proper and improper or disordered feelings here, his psychological and anthropological theories provide some basis for such distinctions. See Frierson, *Kant's Empirical Psychology*.

48. Denis, "Kant's Conception," 407.

49. Denis, "Kant's Conception," 417.

50. For one way to develop this point, see Calhoun, "But What about the Animals?"

51. Our (proper) feelings here typically make it *seem* that we have duties *to* animals; this illusion is what Kant calls an "amphiboly" (*Metaphysics of Morals*, 6:442; see Kain, "Duties regarding Animals," 231).

52. This alternate interpretation of Kant's position goes back at least to Schopenhauer, *Grundlage der Moral*, §8, in *Die beiden Grundprobleme der Ethik*. For similar criticisms of Kant, see Broadie and Pybus, "Kant's Treatment of Animals"; Singer, *Animal Liberation*; Regan, *The Case for Animal Rights*; Nussbaum, *Frontiers of Justice*; Warren, *Moral Status*. In order to go beyond the brutalization argument, Wood and Korsgaard have each proposed some revisions to Kant's account: Wood, "Kant on Duties"; Korsgaard, "Interacting with Animals"; Korsgaard, "Fellow Creatures." For an assessment of their modified Kantian proposals, see Kain, "Duties regarding Animals," 228–31; Skidmore, "Duties to Animals."

53. Could we reshape our love and sympathy so that cruelty to animals would not have such significance, reshaping our love and sympathy to respond to human beings, but only to human beings? Maybe, though Kant might consider this fairly unlikely. Perhaps acquiring some false beliefs, such as thinking of animals as mindless machines, could help? Supposing we could, *ought* we reshape them like that, or ought we not? Thanks to James Skidmore for pressing such questions in correspondence, and to Josh Folk for helpful critical discussion. Kant himself tended to have significant deference toward our given nature, e.g., his treatment of superficial mutilation (*Metaphysics of Morals*, 6:423), and arbitrarily reshaping our morally significant feelings might be plausibly considered

"damage" rather than cultivation. Nonetheless, on Kant's theory, supposing that we did have or acquire such a different sensibility, our duties regarding animals would be somewhat different, perhaps more closely resembling our duties regarding inanimate nature, which prohibit a "propensity to wanton destruction of what is *beautiful*" (*Metaphysics of Morals*, 6:443).

54. For a critical discussion of some other important objections to this account, see Kain, "Duties regarding Animals," 226–27.

55. While this is a duty to oneself, what the duty requires is *gratitude to the dog, pace* Timmermann, "When the Tail Wags the Dog," at 132; or, if gratitude proper entails respect (which cannot be had for a dog), then what is required is some analog of gratitude to the dog (*Metaphysics of Morals*, 6:454). Kant does condone killing dogs if they become rabid, however (VPG-Hesse, 117).

56. Denis, "Kant's Conception," esp. 413–14. See *Metaphysics of Morals*, 6: 422–24, 434–37.

57. For a sketch of some such arguments, see Denis, "Kant's Conception." Without endorsing all of her conclusions, one can see how this approach might address a remarkably wide range of ethical questions. See also Denis, "Animality and Agency."

58. For further assessment, see Kain, "Duties regarding Animals," 226–32.

59. For an edition of this work, see Leechman, *System of Moral Philosophy*.

60. Kant was likely familiar with Lessing's 1756 German translation of Hutcheson's *System, Franz Hutchesons' Sittenlehre der Vernunft*; the key chapter is on 457–67. Kant also had access to Hutcheson's discussion of animal virtue in the fourth edition of the *Inquiry*, II.vii (1738), via Merck's 1762 German translation, which was part of Kant's library (Merck, *Franz Hutcheson's Untersuchung*, 286–87). On Kant's reception of Hutcheson's ethics more generally, see, for example, Henrich, "Hutcheson und Kant"; Kuehn, "Ethics and Anthropology."

61. Hutcheson endorsed not only the approval of our affections toward animals but also the approval of the (lower) forms of benevolent affection possessed and manifested by animals themselves, which can be called "lower kinds of Virtue," even though he considered animals incapable of universal benevolence and incapable of a reflective "moral sense" (*Inquiry* II.vii.iii, 4th edition).

62. Haakonssen, *Natural Law*, 79–81.

63. For an edition of this work see Leidhold, *An Inquiry*.

64. For Kant's arguments against moral sense theory and appeals to happiness as foundation or moral criterion, see for example *Groundwork*, 4:442.

65. For discussion, see Haakonssen, *Natural Law*, 79; Haakonssen, *Thomas Reid on Practical Ethics*, 254–55; Garrett, "Francis Hutcheson and the Origin of Animal Rights"; Garrett, "Animals and Ethics." For another famous eighteenth-century

claim about animal rights, see the comments of Jeremy Bentham, *An Introduction to the Principles of Morals and Legislation*, XVII.1.4n.

66. More generally "a man hath a *right* to do, possess, or demand any thing, when his acting, possessing, or obtaining from another in these circumstances tends to the good of society, or to the interest of the individual consistently with the rights of others and the general good of society, and obstructing him would have the contrary tendency" (*System* II.iii; cf. *Inquiry* II.vii.vi). While some of Hutcheson's formulations specify "man" or "any person," Hutcheson does not argue for or against this as a formal restriction. Of course most early modern theories of natural rights exclude non-rational beings, despite the authoritative claims to the contrary of Ulpian in Justinian's *Institutes* and *Digest* (Haakonssen, *Thomas Reid*, 254–55).

67. While Kant would agree that we can behave wrongly regarding animals and that the animals are (among) those that suffer when we do, he would insist this is insufficient to establish a right. On Kant's different, and more substantial, conception of rights, rights are essentially concerned with the equal freedom of action of rational beings rather than with anyone's welfare, much less with the "general good," and rights are connected with an authorization for coercion (*Metaphysics of Morals*, 6:230–31, 241). It seems clear why non-rational animals will not have rights on Kant's account.

68. Some, but not all, rights may "reside" in, "belong to," or be "immediately constituted" for some individual's good (*System* II.iv.iii), but it is not clear when or how we would determine this to be the case. In the explication of animal rights, Hutcheson appeals to the good of the whole system and the good of orders or kinds of animals more than that of any individuals (*System* II.vi).

69. Hutcheson insisted, for example, that it is "abundantly manifest" that humans have a right to use animals for food, given our relative positions in the "well-ordered complex system" aimed at the common good of all.

70. For cutting-edge work on this topic, see the essays in Allais and Callanan, *Kant on Animals*. I would like to thank the editors, Lara Denis, and audiences in Skukuza and London for helpful comments on previous versions of this essay.

CHAPTER EIGHT: REFLECTION

1. Schopenhauer, *Parerga and Paralipomena*, § 305, in Del Caro and Janaway, 521.

2. See the report on the conversation with Carl Georg Bähr (May 9, 1858) from Schopenhauer, *Gespräche*, in Hübscher, 254. On the date of the encounter see 316–17.

3. Schopenhauer, *Gespräche*, in Hübscher, 255.

4. N. Mann, *Gabriel von Max: Eine kunsthistorische Skizze*, 5. See also Muther, *Geschichte der Malerei im Neunzehnten Jahrhundert. Erster Teil*, 439–40, where

Max is regarded especially for his original view of art as a medium for philosophical investigation. According to Muther, Max had direct knowledge of Schopenhauer's writings (434).

5. Max was one of the founding members of the Psychologische Gesellschaft, stemming from the Theosophische Sozietät Loge Germania. See Althaus and Böller, "Gabriel von Max (1814–1915)," 31. This essay is contained in the catalogue of the exhibition *Gabriel von Max: Malerstar Darwinist, Spiritist* at the Lembachhaus in Munich (October 2010–February 2011); it is one of the most up-to-date and comprehensive resources available for reconstructing Max's career as a painter in the broad context of his scientific and philosophical interests. Gabriel von Max's *Nachlass* is kept at the Deutsches Kunstarchiv, Germanisches Nationalmuseum, Nuremberg.

6. In a letter Max refers directly to Thomas Henry Huxley's understanding of "the question of all questions" in his *Evidence as to Man's Place in Nature*. See Althaus and Friedel, *Gabriel von Max*, 241.

7. Cf. Althaus, "'Das übrige lese man in Darwin nach,'" 251.

8. N. Mann, *Gabriel von Max*, 24.

9. See Althaus, "Die Affen," 298.

10. For instance, in the poses of the apes in the famous painting *Apes as Art Critics*, one can easily recognize the same apes portrayed as dead in a series of photographs taken by Max. See Althaus, "Die Affen"; Uhlig, "Gegenzauber."

11. On the exchange regarding anthropology and evolution between Max and the influential Jena biologist Ernst Haeckel see Bach, "Über den wechselseitigen Einfluss."

12. On apes as a ridiculous imitation of humans a key source is Galen. See May, *Galen: On the Usefulness of the Parts of the Body*, esp. 108. For discussion see French, *Ancient Natural History*, 192.

CHAPTER NINE

1. Ludwig Büchner, *Force and Matter*, in Collingwood, 85.

2. On these points, I've drawn on Vermorel, "The Drive."

3. Blumenbach, *Über den Bildungstrieb*, 12–13; translation quoted from Richards, *The Romantic Conception*, 218–19.

4. Blumenbach, *Über den Bildungstrieb*, 25–26; quoted from Richards, *The Romantic Conception*, 226.

5. Immanuel Kant to Johann Friedrich Blumenbach (August 5, 1790), in Fischer, *Briefwechsel von Immanuel Kant*.

6. Schelling, *Von der Weltseele (On the World Soul)*, 235.

7. Translations of this work are from Gregor, *Kant: The Metaphysics of Morals*.

8. Translations of this work are from Guyer and Wood, *Critique of Pure Reason.*

9. Translations of this work are from Di Giovanni and Wood, *Immanuel Kant: Religion within the Boundaries of Mere Reason.*

10. This, at any rate, is the way Kant is usually interpreted. For discussion, see Katsafanas, "Nietzsche and Kant."

11. See further Deborah Brown's chapter in the present volume.

12. Cottingham et al., *The Philosophical Writings of Descartes,* 2:161. For earlier discussions of the same example see the chapters by Peter Adamson and Juhana Toivanen in this volume.

13. Cottingham et al., *Philosophical Writings of Descartes,* 1: 108.

14. Compare to Helen Steward's discussion of Morgan's Canon in this volume.

15. Darwin, *The Descent of Man,* ch. 2.

16. Brougham, *Dissertations,* 1:17–18.

17. Darwin, *On the Origin of Species* (New York: Modern Library, 1993), 317–18.

18. Mivart, "Organic Nature's Riddle," 323. St. George Mivart (1827–1900) attempted to reconcile natural selection with the teachings of the Catholic Church. He was in regular contact with the leading figures of the period, including Huxley and Darwin, both of whom responded to his critiques at length in their published works.

19. Mivart, "Organic Nature's Riddle," 323–25.

20. Mivart, "Organic Nature's Riddle," 325.

21. Mivart, "Organic Nature's Riddle," 326.

22. Mivart, "Organic Nature's Riddle," 326.

23. James, *The Principles of Psychology,* 2:387–88.

24. James, *Principles of Psychology,* 2:389.

25. Reid, *Essays on the Active Powers of the Human Mind,* ch. 2.

26. Schneider, *Theirische Wille,* ch. 4.

27. Spencer, *The Principles of Psychology,* §170.

28. Spencer, *Principles of Psychology,* §195.

29. Spencer, *Principles of Psychology,* §195.

30. Spencer, *Principles of Psychology,* §196.

31. "The movement produced in a creature having a rudimentary eye, when an opaque object is suddenly passed before that eye, is more general and more simple than is the movement produced in a creature which grasps the prey passing before it. In the first case the effect is produced whatever the relative position of the object, providing the obscuration be considerable; in the second case it is produced only when the object is just in front" (Spencer, *Principles of Psychology,* §197).

32. Spencer, *Principles of Psychology,* §198.

33. Spencer, *Principles of Psychology,* §205.

34. Spencer, *Principles of Psychology*, §203.
35. Spencer, *Principles of Psychology*, §203.
36. See also Wundt's remarks translated at Judd, *Wilhelm Wundt: Outlines of Psychology*, 281–82: "The attempts to define the relation of man and animals from a psychological point of view vary between two extremes. One of these is the predominating view of the old psychology that the higher 'faculties of mind,' especially 'reason,' are entirely wanting in animals, or that, as Descartes held, animals are mere reflex mechanisms without mind. The other is the wide-spread opinion of representatives of special animal psychology, that animals are essentially equal to man in all respects, in ability to consider, to judge, to draw conclusions, in moral feelings, etc. With the rejection of faculty-psychology the first of these views becomes untenable. The second rests on the tendency prevalent in popular psychology to interpret all objective phenomena in terms of human thought, especially in terms of logical reflection. The closer analysis of so-called manifestations of intelligence among animals shows, however, that they are in all cases fully explicable as simple sensible recognitions and associations, and that they lack the characteristics belonging to concepts proper and to logical operations. But associative processes pass without a break into apperceptive, and the beginnings of the latter, that is, simple acts of active attention and choice, appear without any doubt in the case of higher animals, so that the difference is after all more one of the degree and complexity of the psychical processes than a difference in kind."
37. Collingwood, *Ludwig Büchner: Force and Matter*, preface.
38. Schopenhauer, *The World as Will and Representation*, 2: 533 (hereafter WWR). Translations of Schopenhauer's work are from Payne, *Arthur Schopenhauer: The World as Will and Representation*.
39. WWR, 2:535.
40. WWR, 2:540.
41. WWR, 2:535.
42. WWR, 2:535.
43. WWR, 2:540.
44. Descartes, *Fourth Replies*, in Adam and Tannery, *Oeuvres de Descartes*, VII 246; *Discourse on Method*, in Adam and Tannery, VI 33.
45. Locke, *An Essay Concerning Human Understanding*, II.xxvii.9.
46. Kant, *Anthropology*, 127. Translation from Louden, *Kant: Anthropology from a Pragmatic Point of View*.
47. Hegel, *Lectures on the History of Philosophy*, 3:551–52. Translations of this work are from Haldane, *G. W. F. Hegel: Lectures on the History of Philosophy*.

48. Kant, *Groundwork*, 4:428. Translation from Gregor and Timmerman, *Kant: Groundwork of the Metaphysics of Morals.*

49. Fichte, *The System of Ethics*, in Breazeale and Zöller, 106.

50. Fichte, *System of Ethics*, in Breazeale and Zöller, 106–7.

51. Fichte, *System of Ethics*, in Breazeale and Zöller, 107.

52. Fichte, *System of Ethics*, in Breazeale and Zöller, 101.

53. Friedrich Schiller, *Letters on the Aesthetic Education of Man*, letter 12. Translations of this work are from Dole et al., *Aesthetic and Philosophical Essays.*

54. Schiller, *Letters*, letter 12.

55. Schiller, *Letters*, letter 12.

56. Schiller, *Letters*, letter 13.

57. Schiller, *Letters*, letter 14.

58. Schiller, *Letters*, letter 14.

59. Schiller, *Letters*, letter 13.

60. Kant, *Lectures on Metaphysics*, 28:276. Translation by Ameriks and Naragon.

61. Kant, *Metaphysics of Morals*, 6:442. Although we have no duties *to* animals, Kant allows that we have duties *regarding* animals. For example, Kant claims that we have a duty not to be cruel to animals. He reasons that cruelty toward animals undermines sympathy and love, and this can lead us to violate our duties to human beings. So we should avoid cruelty to animals not because it is bad for them but because it is bad for us. As Schopenhauer describes Kant's view, "One should have compassion with animals just for practice" (Schopenhauer, *The Two Fundamental Problems of Ethics*, in Cartwright and Erdmann, 173). Although this is the traditional way of reading Kant on animals, Kain (this volume) provides a novel argument that Kant requires us to have certain moral emotions directed toward animals (e.g., that we must be sympathetic toward animals and not just, as Schopenhauer puts it, for practice).

62. Schopenhauer, WWR, 2:201.

63. Schopenhauer, WWR, 2:205.

64. Schopenhauer, WWR, 2:275.

65. Schopenhauer, *Two Fundamental Problems*, in Cartwright and Erdmann, 239.

66. Schopenhauer, *Two Fundamental Problems*, in Cartwright and Erdmann, 173.

67. Schopenhauer, *Two Fundamental Problems*, in Cartwright and Erdmann, 242.

68. Schopenhauer, *Two Fundamental Problems*, in Cartwright and Erdmann, 237. Schopenhauer repeatedly emphasizes the superiority of Hindu over Christian thought on animals: in a typical line, he writes that it is "a fitting symbol of the defect of Christian morals...that John the Baptist appears quite like a Hindu Sannyasi, but at the same time—is clad in animal skins!" (242). For a discussion

of Indian approaches to animals, see Amber Carpenter's contribution in this volume.

69. Schopenhauer, *Two Fundamental Problems*, in Cartwright and Erdmann, 253.

70. Büchner, *Force and Matter*, in Collingwood, ch. 19. I am grateful to an audience at King's College London for extremely helpful comments on this material.

CHAPTER TEN

1. Darwin, *On the Origin of Species*, 488.

2. The correspondence from the late 1860s reveals clearly that Darwin and his allies were gratified by many positive responses to his proposals about descent with modification. As is well known, his claims on behalf of natural selection were far more controversial.

3. Perhaps his decision to focus on "a species taken singly" was prompted by Alfred Russel Wallace's "Essay on Man," in which Wallace concluded that natural selection would have only a limited ability to expand the brain beyond its ancestral condition (presumably that of an ape). While showing his usual respect for the co-discoverer of natural selection, Darwin suggests that Wallace has lapsed from the thesis of human connectedness, defended in his "celebrated" earlier article. See Darwin, *The Descent of Man*, 47, esp. n67. Was *The Descent of Man* prompted by a felt need to quell deviation on the part of a prominent ally?

4. As Darwin had explained in advance (*The Descent of Man*, 3).

5. The basic point of Darwin's significance is well made by Regan, *The Case for Animal Rights*, 18–21, although I diverge from Regan's analysis of just how Darwin revolutionized our understanding.

6. Contemporary biology can supplement Darwin's recognition of affinities at the macro level with details at a much finer grain: for example, chromosomal banding patterns and nucleotide sequences.

7. Darwin, *Expression. of the Emotions in Man and Animals* , 77. Darwin in *The Descent of Man* offers a much briefer discussion of the same phenomena (67).

8. Darwin, *The Descent of Man*, 68, 72.

9. "In regard to mental qualities, their transmission is manifest in our dogs, horses, and other domestic animals" (Darwin, *The Descent of Man*, 27). "The lower animals, like man, manifestly feel pleasure and pain" (67). "Only a few persons now dispute that animals possess some power of reasoning" (73).

10. Darwin, *The Descent of Man*, 82.

11. Darwin, *The Descent of Man*, 85, 87.

12. Darwin, *The Descent of Man*, 83.

13. Disputes about generativity pervade the debates about whether apes have acquired linguistic competence. In part this is the consequence of Chomsky's seminal

emphasis on the recursions that underlie syntax. Although studies of Washoe, Lucy, Kanzi, and their successors have sometimes recorded animals combining signs in unprecedented ways, it is well to recall that Herbert Terrace's originally positive verdict about Nim Chimpsky gave way to doubts as his careful analysis of the data revealed important limitations in the creative use of language. See Terrace et al., "Can an Ape Create a Sentence?"

14. Darwin, *The Descent of Man*, 67.

15. De Waal, *Good Natured*, 83.

16. For a fascinating range of examples, see Byrne and Whiten, "Tactical Deception in Primates."

17. Darwin, *The Descent of Man*, 94.

18. Darwin, *The Descent of Man*, 95.

19. Darwin, *The Descent of Man*, 95.

20. The account briefly reviewed here is summarized at *The Descent of Man*, 95–96, and its individual claims are illustrated and supported throughout *The Descent of Man*, ch .4.

21. Peter Singer deploys the image in the title of his book *The Expanding Circle*, but the phrase is significantly older, occurring in Lecky's *History of European Morals* (which Darwin quotes), and can be traced back to the Stoics; see, for example, the fragment from Hierocles that is translated into English in Long and Sedley, *The Hellenistic Philosophers*, 349.

22. Darwin, *The Descent of Man*, 119.

23. Darwin, *The Descent of Man*, 128.

24. Darwin, *The Descent of Man*, 128, also 106.

25. Darwin, *The Descent of Man*, 114–15.

26. This paragraph reflects my own way of articulating what I view as the main insights of Darwin's turn to "natural history." The position outlined here is developed more thoroughly in Kitcher, *The Ethical Project*, and, with some refinements, in my article "Is a Naturalized Ethics Possible?"

27. Darwin, *The Descent of Man*, 122.

28. Darwin, *The Descent of Man*, 606, 613.

29. This vision is advocated explicitly in Regan, *The Case for Animal Rights*, but it is by no means restricted to him.

30. Darwin, *The Origin of Species*, 473.

31. See, for example, the excellent discussions in Gruen, *Ethics and Animals*, ch. 3 Beauchamp et al., *The Human Use of Animals*, chs. 2–4.

32. "Hence it is quite credible that the presence of a feline animal in large numbers in a district might determine, through the intervention first of mice and then of bees, the frequency of certain flowers in that district!" (Darwin, *The Origin of*

Species, 74). The untoward effects of well-intentioned ecological interventions (the introduction of the myxoma virus, the use of DDT) have underscored Darwin's point.

33. It might be argued that some groups of domesticated animals constitute new species rather than new subspecies. Because I shall later appeal to the differences between domesticated animals and their feral relatives, I am being deliberately conservative about the extent of those differences.

34. In a certain obvious sense, they already belong to our moral community. This point will become clearer in the next sections.

35. This is not to exclude another obvious domain in which past human action has affected the organic world, namely our extensive modification of the environments in which organisms live. Because that domain is so vast, any attempt to legislate within it must be selective: we simply cannot attend to the entire collection of species we have affected.

36. See Lee, *The !Kung San*; Boehm, *Hierarchy in the Forest*; Boehm, *Moral Origin*; Knauft, "Violence and Sociality in Human Evolution."

37. The most prominent alternative would be to consider only a subset, and allow those not belonging to it to leave the group. That approach would be at odds with the ties produced by (at least occasional) cooperation, and also risky in an environment containing hostile neighbors.

38. For a more detailed account of this approach to ethical method, see Kitcher, *The Ethical Project*, ch. 10.

39. Again, ch. 10 of Kitcher, *The Ethical Project*, provides more detail. I should also note the affinities with Adam Smith's conception of extended sympathy. For discussion of this, see my essay "The Hall of Mirrors."

40. That form is determined by the character of the problem to which ethical life attempts to provide solutions. Our limited responsiveness to others is addressed by discussions that include the perspectives of those affected, in which factual errors are corrected, and in which participants aim at a resolution all can accept.

41. For more on this, see Kitcher, *The Ethical Project*.

42. This general proposal adapts the approach to well-ordered science I have advocated in *Science, Truth, and Democracy* and in *Science in a Democratic Society*. The idea of selecting discussants with particular qualities of intellect and character is indebted to the important work of J. Fishkin on citizen juries; see his *When the People Speak*.

43. For a lucid and absorbing account of the research that led to this discovery, see Bliss, *The Discovery of Insulin*.

44. It is worth pointing out, however, that the principal animals involved—the dogs—belong to a species with which many human beings have especially close bonds. The "sacrificed" cattle, interestingly, are typically forgotten.

45. I have discussed the need for this type of systematic appraisal a little more extensively in *Science in a Democratic Society* §§19–20.

46. See, for example, Beauchamp et al., *The Human Use of Animals*, ch. 13.

47. They are also legitimately concerned that the framework is inadequately applied in individual cases because of the biased composition of oversight committees. The suggestions of the previous section attempt to address this complaint.

48. Human identification with the fly's "point of view" is not completely unknown, at least in fiction. Tristram Shandy's Uncle Toby releases a fly trapped behind a window, exclaiming, "Go poor devil, get thee gone, why should I hurt thee?—This world surely is wide enough to hold both thee and me." Interestingly, so far as I know, there has been no expressed concern about the names given to some of the *Drosophila* mutants—*Krüppel* (cripple), *hunchback*, *Oskar* (after the central figure of Günter Grass's *The Tin Drum*)—even though these naming practices might seem faintly to echo conduct to which animal rights activists correctly object (a notable instance being the laboratory personnel at the University of Pennsylvania, filmed laughing at the clumsiness of baboons who had been deliberately neurally damaged; see Beauchamp et al., *The Human Use of Animals*, ch. 11).

49. At present the complexities of mammalian genomics have blocked any straightforward extension of Nüsslein-Volhard's experimental approach to mice. As I will emphasize, however, the constant generation of variant strains is a pervasive feature of contemporary biomedical practice.

50. See "Mice and Rats in Laboratories," *PETA*, http://www.peta.org/issues/animals-used-for-experimentation/animals-laboratories/mice-rats-laboratories/.

51. It is worth remarking that young researchers sometimes establish themselves by "designing" a "knock-out" mouse for the exploration of a particular disease. Fashioning a strain that they (and others) can use requires considerable scientific creativity.

52. See, for example, Hedrich, *The Laboratory Mouse*, 10.

53. Of course pain is sometimes an unavoidable feature of the experiment. Modeling some diseases can require that analgesics and sedatives not be administered.

54. See Regan, *The Case for Animal Rights*, 363ff. Lori Gruen conceives animal well-being in different terms, but with similar emphasis on the normal life-cycle; see *Ethics and Animals*, ch. 4.

55. See Hedrich, *The Laboratory Mouse*, 403.

56. Some estimates of the monthly mortality rate for mice in the wild have it that, in any given month, almost half the mice in the population will die. See Collins and Kays, "Patterns of Mortality in a Wild Population of White-Footed Mice."

57. Many protections for lab technicians are already built into the breeding of the mouse strains. The Jax Lab carefully monitors the mice to ensure they are free from diseases that affect human beings.

58. I should add, however, that many writers who campaign for strong reforms of our practices of dealing with animals do not make the mistake just diagnosed. They often write eloquently about their own interactions with domesticated animals (particularly pets). Gruen's *Ethics and Animals* is an outstanding example.

59. Plainly, requirements to provide laboratory mice with comparable lives to those enjoyed by pet rodents would not support experimental procedures on very young mice. Those might be defended in other ways, or perhaps it is possible to breed mouse strains in which the pertinent juvenile features are preserved in adulthood.

60. I am much indebted to Mark Viney and to our many conversations about the ethical treatment of experimental animals (during 2011–12, when we were both fellows at the Wissenschaftskolleg zu Berlin). Many thanks to Patricia Kitcher for extremely constructive suggestions about an earlier draft. I am grateful also to those who discussed my paper at the London conference, and particularly to Peter Adamson for detailed comments that have improved the final version.

CHAPTER ELEVEN

1. Morgan, *An Introduction to Comparative Psychology*, 53.
2. Galef, "Historical Origins," 9.
3. For examples of explicit invocation, see Epstein, "The Principle of Parsimony"; Budiansky, *If a Lion Could Talk*; Karin-D'Arcy, "The Modern Role"; Shettleworth, "Clever Animals."
4. Dennett, "Intentional Systems."
5. Sober, "Morgan's Canon."
6. Fodor, "Not So Clever Hans."
7. Of particular note are those by Fitzpatrick, "Doing Away with Morgan's Canon"; Allen-Hermanson, "Morgan's Canon Revisited"; Montminy, "What Use is Morgan's Canon?"
8. See for example Wozniak, "Conwy Lloyd Morgan."
9. For affirmations that Morgan's Canon continues to play a useful role in psychology, see Karin-D'Arcy, "The Modern Role"; Dwyer and Burgess, "Rational Accounts"; Shettleworth, "Clever Animals."
10. See, e.g., the discussion of reed warblers' inability to detect cuckoo chicks that have hatched in their nest: BBC, *Springwatch* 2014, episode 10. https://www.youtube.com/watch?v=TQYEmhNdjy4
11. Radick, "Morgan's Canon."
12. Fitzpatrick, "Doing Away with Morgan's Canon," 242.
13. This crucial point—that in the absence of empirical reasons to prefer one explanation over another, agnosticism is the appropriate attitude until further empirical

evidence of the sort that might enable a rational preference to be formed—is made by many critics of the Canon, including Sober, "Morgan's Canon," 228: "The canon seems to license inferences in which the proper conclusion is that no inferences can be drawn"; Fodor, "Not So Clever Hans," 12: "A priori, there is nothing to choose between the hypothesis that a certain behavior has a 'higher' sort of mental aetiology and the hypothesis that it doesn't. If you want to know which is true, you just have to go and look"; and Fitzpatrick, "Doing Away with Morgan's Canon," 235: "If the worry about crude anthropomorphism is that it is not sufficiently supported by the data, it is not clear that we are thereby justified in endorsing the least cognitively sophisticated explanation available, since that explanation may not be sufficiently supported by the data either. After all, we could instead simply be agnostic."

14. Morgan, *An Introduction*, 53.
15. Wundt, *Grundzüge der physiologischen Psychologie*.
16. Morgan, *An Introduction*, 59.
17. Morgan, *An Introduction*, 54.
18. Some species of bird defend their eggs and chicks by leading potential predators away from the nest with a display in which they mimic having an injury to a wing. Once the predator has been safely distracted, they are usually then able to fly off to safety themselves.
19. Morgan, *An Introduction*, 59.
20. Morgan, "The Limits of Animal Intelligence," 225. Though Romanes had of course also utilized the word "intelligence" (witness the title of his major work), he appears to conceive of it rather as a rather lowly variety of reason rather than, as Morgan has it, a set of powers deserving of its own distinctive category.
21. To a modern ear it perhaps seems strange to think of explanations that invoke mere instinct as psychological explanations. The invocation of instinct has come to be seen in some contexts as something *opposed* to the invocation of mentality, and often also as something opposed to the existence of real agency in a creature. (For more on the history of the idea of instinct see Paul Katsafanas's contribution to this volume.) But this was not at all how the concept was understood by Romanes, from whose discussion, as already mentioned, Morgan's takes its point of departure. For Romanes, instinct was to be clearly distinguished from mere reflex by "the element of mind" (*Animal Intelligence*, 11). Romanes is clear that instinct "involves *mental operations*" (11), by which he means that a certain degree of consciousness is implied. He is sensible, of course, that in many instances it may be difficult or impossible to decide whether or not the mind element is present, but his considered view is that "this is altogether a separate matter and has nothing to do with the question of defining instinct in a manner which shall be formally exclusive, on the

one hand, of reflex action, and on the other, of reason" (11–12). There is every reason to suppose that Morgan would have adopted the same view. For him, explanations adverting to animal instincts were psychological explanations implying the presence of consciousness—and the hierarchy of powers to which his Canon makes implicit reference is hence an entirely *intrapsychic* hierarchy.

22. Morgan, *An Introduction*, 124, my emphasis.

23. Allen-Hermanson, "Morgan's Canon Revisited," 613.

24. Dennett, *The Intentional Stance*.

25. Sober, "Morgan's Canon," 225.

26. As Fodor points out, all you need to make a Turing machine, in a sense an excellent reasoner, is "two kinds of pebble and an endless roll of lavatory paper" ("Not so Clever Hans," 13).

27. See Hirschfeld and Gelman, *Mapping the Mind*, for a discussion of the phenomenon of domain specificity.

28. Notably Sober, "Morgan's Canon," and Fitzpatrick, "Doing Away with Morgan's Canon."

29. See, e.g., Epstein, "The Principle of Parsimony," 119: "No defense of the principle [of parsimony] . . . is offered, for . . . I believe that no definitive defense is possible. . . . I simply assume it, as did Ockham and others, as a first principle."

30. This point appears to have been first made by Newbury, "Current Interpretation and Significance of Morgan's Canon," 72, who is quoted approvingly by Sober, "Morgan's Canon," 230.

31. Fodor, "Not So Clever Hans," 13.

32. Fitzpatrick, "Doing Away with Morgan's Canon," 231.

33. Morgan, *An Introduction*, 59.

34. See, e.g., Fujiwara-Tsujii et al., "Behavioral Responses"; Mizunami et al., "Alarm Pheromone"; Wyatt, *Pheromones and Animal Behavior*.

35. McMillan, *Mental Health*, 72.

36. Fitzpatrick, "Doing Away with Morgan's Canon," 236.

37. Frisch, *The Dance Language*.

38. Blumberg et al., "Distress Vocalizations," 78.

39. Blumberg et al., "Distress Vocalizations," 78.

40. Blumberg and Sokoloff, "Do Infant Rats Cry?," 86.

CHAPTER TWELVE

1. I am here distinguishing between moral standing and moral status or significance, following Goodpaster, "On Being Morally Considerable." The former I take to mean the existence of *any* degree of direct moral considerability; the latter I take to mean the *degree* of moral worth.

2. See the contributions of Deborah Brown and Patrick Kain in this volume.

3. Ritvo, *The Animal Estate*.

4. Carruthers, *The Animals Issue*.

5. Bentham, *An Introduction to the Principles of Morals and Legislation*, 311.

6. Nozick, *Anarchy, State and Utopia*, 35–42.

7. Phillips, *The Welfare of Animals*, 137–45.

8. Fraser and Weary, "Quality of Life," 40.

9. Rachels, *Created from Animals*, 182.

10. Becker, "The Priority of Human Interests," 235–36.

11. Rachels, *Created from Animals*, 184.

12. Brody, "Defending Animal Research."

13. Magel, *Keyguide to Information Sources in Animal Rights*, 13–25.

14. Singer, *Animal Liberation*.

15. Regan, *The Case for Animal Rights*.

16. See Francione, *Animals as Persons*; Francione and Garner, *The Animal Rights Debate*.

17. Cohen and Regan, *The Animal Rights Debate*, 127.

18. See Clarke and Linzey, *Political Theory and Animal Rights*, 136.

19. Hare, "Why I Am Only a Demi-Vegetarian," 238.

20. Singer, "A Response," 326.

21. Singer, *Practical Ethics*, 27.

22. Act utilitarianism is a theory of ethics which states that a person's act is morally right if and only if it produces at least as much happiness or pleasure or the satisfaction of preferences (for the actor and others) as any other act that the person could perform at that time. Act utilitarianism is often contrasted with rule utilitarianism, which holds that the morally right action is the one that is in accordance with a moral rule whose general observance would create the most happiness or pleasure or satisfaction of preferences.

23. See Frey, *Rights, Killing and Suffering*, 197–203; Regan, "Utilitarianism, Vegetarianism and Animal Rights," 310–11; Regan, *Case for Animal Rights* (2004), 221–23.

24. Regan, "Utilitarianism, Vegetarianism," 311.

25. Rawls, *A Theory of Justice*.

26. Carruthers, *The Animals Issue*, 98–99.

27. Rowlands, *Animal Rights: A Philosophical Defence*; Rowlands, *Animal Rights: Moral Theory*.

28. This of course is to assume that animals are not rational, something we have seen questioned elsewhere in the present volume.

29. Baxter, *A Theory of Ecological Justice*, 95–96.

30. See Garner, "Rawls, Animals and Justice."

31. Other moral philosophers, such as Stephen Clark in *The Moral Status of Animals*, plow a lonely eclectic furrow.

32. DeGrazia, *Taking Animals Seriously*, 60.

33. Steinbock, "Speciesism," 247.

34. See, for example, Steinbock, "Speciesism" Cohen's contribution to Cohen and Regan, *Animal Rights Debate*; Cohen, "The Case for the Use of Animals"; McCloskey, "The Moral Case for Experimentation on Animals."

35. Frey, "Autonomy and the Value of Animal Life."

36. Frey, "Autonomy," 54

37. DeGrazia, *Taking Animals Seriously*, 233.

38. McMahan, *The Ethics of Killing*, 190.

39. Cavalieri and Singer, *The Great Ape Project*.

40. McMahan, *The Ethics of Killing*, 249; van De Veer, "Of Beasts, Persons."

41. Dombrowski, *Babies and Beasts*.

42. Pluhar, *Beyond Prejudice*.

43. Pluhar, "Is There a Morally Relevant Difference between Human and Animal Nonpersons?" 60.

44. McMahan, *The Ethics of Killing*, 192.

45. Carruthers, *The Animals Issue*, 114–17; Devine, "The Moral Basis," 495–502.

46. Cohen, "The Case for the Use of Animals."

47. Nobis, "Carl Cohen's 'Kind' Arguments"; Palmer, *Animal Ethics*, 22; Cohen and Regan, *Animal Rights Debate*, 278–79.

48. Cohen, "The Case for the Use of Animals," 15; Feder Kittay, "At the Margins," 126.

49. McMahan, *The Ethics of Killing*, 44.

50. McMahan, *The Ethics of Killing*, 217–20.

51. Gunnarsson, "The Great Apes," 309.

52. See Hart, "Are There Any Natural Rights?"; Steiner, "Working Rights."

53. See Raz, *The Morality of Freedom*.

54. Cochrane, *Animal Rights*, 42–43.

55. Rachels, *Created from Animals*; Feinberg, "The Rights of Animals."

56. Cochrane, "Animal Rights and Animal Experiments"; Cochrane, "Do Animals Have an Interest in Liberty?"; Cochrane, *Animal Rights*.

57. Cochrane, *Animal Rights*, 17.

58. Rachels, *Created from Animals*.

59. The fully worked out argument can be found in Garner, *A Theory of Justice*.

60. Rachels, *Created from Animals*, 167.

61. Constraints of space prevent me from discussing these approaches here, but on the virtue ethics approach see Hursthouse, *Ethics, Humans and Other Animals*, and on the capabilities approach see Nussbaum, *Frontiers of Justice*.

62. Palmer, *Animal Ethics*, 5.

63. Gilligan, *In a Different Voice*.

64. See Donovan and Adams, *The Feminist Care Tradition*.

65. Becker, "The Priority of Human Interests."

66. See, in particular, Palmer, *Animal Ethics*.

67. Cochrane, "Cosmozoopolis."

68. Donaldson and Kymlicka, *Zoopolis*.

69. Space prohibits me from considering the ensuing debate in detail here but see Cochrane, "Cosmozoopolis"; Per-Anders, "Animal National Liberation?"; Horta, "Zoopolis, Intervention."

70. Donaldson and Kymlicka, *Zoopolis*, ch. 2.

71. Donaldson and Kymlicka, *Zoopolis*, 40.

72. Kymlicka, *Multicultural Citizenship*.

73. See further Garner and O'Sullivan, *The Political Turn in Animal Ethics*.

74. See Sanbonmatsu, *Critical Theory and Animal Liberation*; Hargrove, *The Animal Rights/Environmental Ethics Debate*.

Primary Literature

Adam, C., and P. Tannery, eds. *Oeuvres de Descartes*. 11 vols. Paris: Vrin, 1897–1913/1996.

Adamson, P., and P. E. Pormann, trans. *The Philosophical Works of al-Kindī*. Karachi: Oxford University Press, 2012.

Ameriks, K., and S. Naragon, eds. and trans. *Kant: Lectures on Metaphysics*. Cambridge, UK: Cambridge University Press, 1996.

Anghiera, Pietro Martire d'. *Libretto de tutta la navigatione de re de Spagna de le isole et terreni nouamente trouati*, edited by A. Trevisan. Venice, 1504.

Anghiera, Pietro Martire d'. *De orbe novo decades. I. Oceana decas*. Ed. and trans. B. Gauvin. Paris, 2003.

Anlan, Y., ed. *Huashi Congshu*. Taipei: Wenshizhe chubanshe, 1974.

Annas, J., ed., and R. Woolf, trans. *Cicero: On Moral Ends*. Cambridge, UK: Cambridge University Press, 2001.

Annas, J., and J. Barnes, trans. *Sextus Empiricus: Outlines of Scepticism*. Cambridge, UK: Cambridge University Press, 2000.

Anonymous. "Utrum pygmei sint homines?" Paris BN lat. 15850, fol.16va–17rb.

Aquinas, Thomas. *Quaestiones disputatae de veritate*. Rome: Ad Sanctae Sabinae, 1973.

Aquinas, Thomas. *Sententia libri Ethicorum*. Rome: ad Sanctae Sabinae, 1969.

Aquinas, Thomas. *Sententia libri Politicorum*. Rome: ad Sanctae Sabinae, 1971.

Ariew, R., ed. *G. W. Leibniz and S. C. Leibniz and S. Clark: Correspondence*. Indianapolis, IN: Hackett, 2000.

Armstrong, A. H., trans. *Plotinus: Enneads*. 7 vols. Cambridge, MA: Harvard University Press, 1969–88.

Averroes. *Commentarium in libros Physicorum Aristotelis*. Frankfurt am Main: Minerva, 1962.

Baillet, A. *La Vie de M. Descartes: Extraits*. Paris: Centre national de la recherche scientifique, 1691.

Baltzly, D., and H. Tennant, trans. *Proclus: Commentary on Plato's Timaeus*. Cambridge, UK: Cambridge University Press, 2007.

Bapat, S. *A critical edition of the Brahmasūtras. Sanskrit text with translation into English, critical analysis and notes, with Śaṅkarācārya's commentary Śārīrakamīmāṃsābhāsya*. Delhi: New Bharatiya Book Corporation, 2011.

Barnes, J., ed. *The Complete Works of Aristotle*. 2 vols. Princeton, NJ: Princeton University Press, 1984.

Barnes, J., ed. *Porphyry: Introduction*. Oxford: Clarendon, 2003.

Basore, J. W., trans. *Seneca: Moral Essays*, vol. 1. Cambridge, MA: Harvard University Press, 1928.

Benecke, F., ed. *Hartmann von Aue: Iwein*. Trans. T. Cramer. Berlin: de Gruyter, 2004.

Bentham, J. *An Introduction to the Principles of Morals and Legislation*. New York: Hafner Press, 1948.

Bettenson, H., trans. *Augustine: City of God*. London: Penguin, 1984.

Blake, N. F., ed. *William Caxton: The History of Reynard the Fox*. London: Oxford University Press, 1970.

Blumenbach, J. F. *Über den Bildungstrieb*. Göttingen: Johann Christian Dieterich, 1789.

Boese, H., ed. *Thomas of Cantrimpré: Liber de natura rerum. Editio princeps secundum codices manuscriptos*. Berlin: de Gruyter, 1973.

Borgnet, A., ed. *Albertus Magnus: De anima*. Paris: Vivès, 1890.

Borgnet, A., ed. *Albertus Magnus: De homine*. Paris: Vivès, 1896.

Bougerol, J. G., ed. *John of la Rochelle: Summa de anima*. Paris: Vrin, 1995.

Braakhuis, H. A. G., G. A. Wilson, and G. J. Etzkorn, eds. *Syncategoremata: Henrico de Gandavo adscripta*. Leuven: Leuven University Press, 2010.

Breazeale, D., and G. Zöller, trans. *J. G. Fichte: The System of Ethics*. Cambridge, UK: Cambridge University Press, 2005.

Brougham, H. *Dissertations on Subjects of Science concerned with Natural Theology: Being the Concluding Volumes of the New Edition of Paley's Work*. London: Knight, 1839.

Burlingame, E. W. *Buddhist Legends*, vol. 1. Cambridge, MA: Harvard University Press, 1921.

Bury, R. G., trans. *Sextus Empiricus: Against Professors*. Cambridge, MA: Harvard University Press, 1949.

Campanella, T. *Medicinalia*. Lyon: Pillehotte, 1635.

Caramello, P., ed. *Thomas Aquinas: Summa Theologiae*. Turin: Marietti, 1948–50.

Cartwright, E., and E. E. Erdmann, trans. *Arthur Schopenhauer: Two Fundamental Problems of Ethics*. Oxford: Oxford University Press, 2010.

Cathala, M. R., and R. M. Spiazzi, eds. *Thomas Aquinas: In duodecim libros Metaphysicorum Aristotelis expositio*. Rome: Marietti, 1971.

Clark, G., trans. *Porphyry: On Abstinence from Killing Animals*. London: Duckworth, 2000.

Collingwood, J. F., trans. *Ludwig Büchner: Force and Matter. Empirico-Philosophical Studies, Intelligibly Rendered*. New York: Cambridge University Press, 2012.

Colvin, I. G., trans. *I Saw the World: Sixty Poems from Walther von der Vogelweide*. London: Hyperion Press, 1938.

Cooper, J. M., ed. *Plato: Complete Works*. Indianapolis, IN: Hackett, 1997.

Cormeau, C., ed. *Walther von der Vogelweide: Leichs, Lieder, Sangsprüche*. Berlin: de Gruyter, 1996.

Cottingham, J., et al., trans. *The Philosophical Writings of Descartes*. 3 vols. Cambridge, UK: Cambridge University Press, 1984–91.

Cotton, C., trans. *Essays of Montaigne*. Vol. 4. Revised by W. C. Hazlett. New York: Edwin C. Hill, 1910.

Cowell, E. B., ed. *The Jātaka: or, Stories of the Buddha's Former Births*. Vols. 1–3. Trans. R. Chalmers. London: Cambridge University Press, 1895. Reprint, Delhi: Motilal Banarsidass, 1990.

Cudworth, R. *The True Intellectual System of the Universe*. 2nd ed. London: Royston, 1743.

Darwin, C. *The Descent of Man*. London: Penguin, 2004.

Darwin, C. *Expression of the Emotions in Man and Animals*. Chicago: University of Chicago Press, 1965.

Darwin, C. *On the Origin of Species*. New York: Modern Library, 1993.

Darwin, C. *On the Origin of Species by Means of Natural Selection, or the Preservation of Favoured Races in the Struggle for Life*. London: John Murray, 1859.

de Benito, M. V., ed. and trans. *Al-Rāzī: Libro de la introducción dal arte de la medicina o "Isagoge."* Salamanca: Ediciones Universidad Salamanca, 1979.

de Caus, S. *Les raisons des forces mouvantes, avec diverses machines tant utiles que plaisantes. Aus quelles sont adioints plusieurs desseins de grotes et fontaines*. Frankfurt: Jan Norton, 1615.

De Lacy, P., ed. and trans. *Galen: On the Doctrines of Hippocrates and Plato*. Berlin: Akademie-Verlag, 1984.

Del Caro, A., and C. Janaway, eds. *Schopenhauer, Parerga and Paralipomena: Short Philosophical Essays*. Vol. 2. Cambridge, UK: Cambridge University Press, 2015.

de Rijk, L. M., ed. and J. Spruyt, trans. *Peter of Spain: Syncategoreumata*. Leiden: Brill, 1992.

Diels H., ed. *Aetius: Doxographi Graeci*. Berlin: Weidmann, 1879.

Digby, K. *Two Treatises: In the one of which, the nature of bodies; in the other, the nature of man's soule, is looked into: in way of discovery of the immortality of reasonable soules*. London: John Williams, 1645.

Dods, M., trans. *Augustine: The City of God*. Irvine, CA: Xist, 2015.

Dole, N., ed. *Friedrich Schiller: Aesthetic and Philosophical Essays*. Boston: F. A. Niccolls, 1795/1902.

Eliot, G., trans. *Ludwig Feuerbach: The Essence of Christianity*. New York: Prometheus Books, 1989.

Ernst, G., ed. *Tommaso Campanella: Del senso delle cose e della magia*. Rome: Laterza, 2007.

Fathers, D., trans. *Thomas Aquinas: Contra Gentiles*. London: Burns, Oates and Washbourne, 1938.

Ferro, G., ed. *Cristoforo Colombo: Diario di bordo. Libro della prima navigazione e scoperta delle Indie*. Milan: Mursia, 1985.

Fiedls, K. E., trans. *Emile Durkheim: The Elementary Forms of the Religious Life*. New York: Free Press, 1996.

Fischer, H. E. ed. *Briefwechsel von Immanuel Kant*. Munich: Georg Müller, 1912.

Foerster, W., ed. *Chrétien de Troyes: Yvain*. Trans. I. Nolting-Hauff. Munich: Wilhelm Fink, 1983.

Foresti, F., A. M. N. Patrone, and A. L. T. Budriesi, eds. *Girolamo Manfredi: Liber de homine/Il Perché*. Bologna: Luigi Parma, 1988.

Forrester, J. M., trans. *The De Subtilitate of Girolamo Cardano*. Tempe: Arizona Center for Medieval and Renaissance Studies, 2013.

Gauthier, L., ed. and trans. *Ibn Ṭufayl: Hayy ben Yaqdhân*. Algiers: Imprimerie Orientale, 1900.

Gauthier, R. A. "Notes sur Siger de Brabant (fin) II: Siger en 1272–1275. Aubry de Reims et la scission des Normands." *Revue des Sciences Philosophiques et Théologiques* 68.1 (1984): 3–50.

Gauthier, R. A., ed. *Thomas Aquinas: Sentencia libri De anima*. Rome: Commissio Leonina, 1984.

Gauvin, B., ed. *Pietro Martire d'Anghiera: Décades du Nouveau Monde. Livre 1: La Décade océane*. Paris: Le Belles Lettres, 2003.

Genequand, C., ed. and trans. *Ibn Bājja (Avempace): La conduit de l'isolé et deux autres épîtres*. Paris: Vrin, 2010.

Gertz, S., J. Dillon, and D. Russell, trans. *Theophrastus: Aeneas of Gaza*. London: Bristol Classical Press, 2012.

Gilby, T., ed. and trans. *Thomas Aquinas: Summa Theologiae*. London: Blackfriars, 1968.

Glorieux, P., ed. *Jean Gerson: Oeuvres Completes*. Paris: Desclée, 1962.

Goodman, L. E., and R. McGregor, eds. and trans. *Epistles of the Brethren of Purity: The Case of the Animals versus Man before the King of the Jinn*. Oxford: Oxford University Press, 2010.

Goodwin, W. W., trans. *Plutarch's Morals*. Boston: Little, Brown, 1871.

Grant, M., ed. *Galen: On the Powers of Foods*. In *Galen on Food and Diet*. New York: Routledge, 2000.

Gregor, M., ed. *Kant: The Metaphysics of Morals*. Cambridge, UK: Cambridge University Press, 1996.

Gregor, M., ed. and trans. *Kant: Practical Philosophy*. Cambridge, UK: Cambridge University Press, 1996.

Gregor, M., and J. Timmermann, trans. *Kant: Groundwork of the Metaphysics of Morals*. New York: Cambridge University Press, 1996–98.

Gummere, R. M., trans. *Seneca: Epistles 93–124*. Cambridge, MA: Harvard University Press, 1925.

Guthrie, K. S., ed. and trans. *Pythagoras Sourcebook and Library*. Grand Rapids, MI: Phanes Press, 1988.

Guyer, P., ed. and trans., and E. Matthews, trans. *Kant: Critique of the Power of Judgment*. Cambridge, UK: Cambridge University Press, 2000.

Guyer, P., and A. Wood, eds. *Kant: Critique of Pure Reason*. Cambridge, UK: Cambridge University Press, 1998.

Haakonssen, K., ed. *Thomas Reid on Practical Ethics: Lectures and Papers on Natural Religion, Self-Government, Natural Jurisprudence and the Law of Nations*. Edinburgh: Edinburgh University Press, 2007.

Haksar, A. N. D., trans., *Hitopadeśa*. London: Penguin Books, 2007.

Haldane, E. S., trans., *G. W. F. Hegel: Lectures on the History of Philosophy*. 3 vols. Lincoln: University of Nebraska Press, 1985.

Hayduck, M., ed. Alexander of Aphrodisias. In *Aristotelis Metaphysicam Commentaria*. Berlin: G. Reimer, 1891.

Heath, P., ed. and trans., and J. Schneewind, ed. *Kant: Lectures on Ethics*. Cambridge, UK: Cambridge University Press, 1997.

Helmbold, W. C., ed. *Plutarch: Moralia*. 12 vols. Cambridge, MA: Harvard University Press, 1957.

Henderson, J., trans. *Aristophanes: Clouds, Wasps, Peace*. Cambridge, MA: Harvard University Press, 1998.

Hibbs, T. S., trans. *Aquinas on Human Nature*. Indianapolis, IN: Hackett, 1999.

Hicks, R. D., trans. *Diogenes Laertius: Lives of Eminent Philosophers*. 2 vols. Cambridge MA: Harvard University Press, 1925.

Horner, I. B., trans. *The Book of the Discipline: Vinaya Piṭaka*. London: Pali Text Society, 1942.

Hubbell, H. M., trans. *Cicero II: De Inventione, De Optimo Genere, Oratorium Topica*. Cambridge, MA: Harvard University Press, 1968.

Hübscher, A., ed. *Arthur Schopenhauer: Gespräche*. Frankfurt a.M.: Frommann, 1971.

Jacobi, H., trans. *Jaina Sutras, Part II: Sacred Books of the East*. Vol. 45. Oxford: Oxford University Press, 1895.

James, W. *The Principles of Psychology*. New York: Dover, 1890.

Jansen, B., ed. *Peter of John Olivi: Quaestiones in secundum librum sententiarum*. Florence: Collegium S. Bonaventurae, 1922–26.

Judd, C. H., trans. *Wilhelm Wundt: Outlines of Psychology*. London: G. E. Strechert, 1907.

Kant, I. *Kants gesammelte Schriften*. 29 vols. Berlin: Walter de Gruyter, 1902–.

Kaske, C. V., and J. R. Clark, eds. *Marsilio Ficino: Three Books on Life*. Binghamton, NY: Renaissance Society of America, 1989.

Keyes, C. W., trans. *Cicero: On the Laws*. Cambridge, MA: Harvard University Press, 1928.

Khalidi, M. A., ed. and trans. *Medieval Islamic Philosophical Writings*. Cambridge, UK: Cambridge University Press, 2005.

Khalifat, S., ed. *Yaḥyā Ibn 'Adī: The Philosophical Treatises*. Amman: al-Jāmi'a l-Urdunnīya, 1988.

Khoroche, P. *Once the Buddha Was a Monkey*. Chicago: University of Chicago Press, 1989.

Kibler, W. W., trans. *Chrétien de Troyes: The Knight with the Lion or Yvain*. London: Penguin Books, 1991.

Kirk, G. S., J. E. Raven, and M. Schofield. *The Presocratic Philosophers: A Critical History with a Selection of Texts*. Cambridge, UK: Cambridge University Press, 1983.

Kitchell, K. F., and I. M. Resnick, trans. *Albert the Great: On Animals. A Medieval Summa Zoologica*. 2 vols. Baltimore: Johns Hopkins University Press, 1999.

Koch, K., et al., eds. *Galen: De sanitate tuenda, de alimentorum facultatibus, de bonis malisque sucis, de victu attenuante, de ptisana*. Leipzig: Teubner, 1923.

Kraus, P., ed. *Al-Rāzī: Rasā'il falsafiyya (Philosophical Epistles)*. Cairo: Paul Barbey, 1939.

Kukkonen, T. *Ibn Tufayl: Living the Life of Reason*. Oxford: Oneworld, 2014.

Ladd, J., trans. *Immanuel Kant: Metaphysics of Morals*. New York: Bobbs Merrill, 1965.

Lecky, W. *History of European Morals from Augustus to Charlemagne*. Vol. 1. London: D. Appleton, 1869.

Leclerc, G.-L., ed. *Histoire Naturelle*. Vol. 11, Paris: Imprimerie Royale, 1764.

Leechman, W., ed. *Francis Hutcheson: System of Moral Philosophy*. London: A. Millar, 1755.

Leidhold, W., ed., *Francis Hutcheson: An Inquiry into the Original of Our Ideas of Beauty and Virtue*. Indianapolis, IN: Liberty Fund, 2004.

Lessing, G. E., trans. *Franz Hutchesons' Sittenlehre der Vernunft, aus dem Englischen übersetzt*. Leipzig: Johann Wendler, 1756.

Lévi-Strauss, C. *Totemism*. Boston: Beacon Press, 1963.

Locke, J. *An Essay concerning Human Understanding*. Oxford: Oxford University Press, 1975.

Long, A. A., and D. N. Sedley. *The Hellenistic Philosophers*. Cambridge, UK: Cambridge University Press, 1990.

Louden, R. B., and A. Wood, eds. *Kant: Lectures on Anthropology*. Cambridge, UK: Cambridge University Press, 2012.

Louden, R. B., and G. Zöller, eds. *Kant: Anthropology, History and Education*. Cambridge, UK: Cambridge University Press, 2007.

Louden, R. B., ed. *Kant: Anthropology from a Pragmatic Point of View*. Cambridge: Cambridge University Press, 2006.

Lutz, C. E., ed. and trans. "Musonius Rufus, The Roman Socrates." *Yale Classical Studies* 10 (1947): 3–147.

Magee, J., ed. and trans. *Calcidius: On Plato's Timaeus*. Cambridge, MA: Harvard University Press, 2016.

Mahdi, M., ed. *al-Fārābī: Falsafat Arisṭūṭālīs*. Beirut: Dār Majallat Shiʿr, 1961.

Mahdi, M., trans. *Alfarabi: Philosophy of Plato and Aristotle*. Ithaca, NY: Cornell University Press, 1962.

Maillard, J. F., ed. *Francesco Zorzi: L'elegante poema e Commento sopra il poema*. Milan: Archè, 1991.

Mann, J., ed. and trans. *Ysengrimus*. Leiden: Brill, 1987.

Marc, P., C. Pera, and P. Caramello, eds. *Thomas Aquinas: Liber de veritate catholicae Fidei contra errores infidelium seu Summa contra Gentiles*. Turin: Marietti, 1961.

Marno, C. "Anonymi Philosophia 'Sicut dicitur ab Aristotile': A Parisian Prologue to Porphyry." *Cahiers de l'Institut du Moyen Âge grec et latin* 61 (1991): 140–46.

May, M. T., trans. *Galen: On the Usefulness of the Parts of the Body*. Ithaca, NY: Cornell University Press, 1968.

McConeghy, P. M., trans. *Hartmann von Aue: Iwein*. New York: Garland, 1984.

McGinnis, J., and D. C. Reisman, eds. and trans. *Classical Arabic Philosophy: An Anthology of Sources*. Indianapolis, IN: Hackett, 2007.

McNamee, G., trans. *Aelian: On the Nature of Animals*. San Antonio, TX: Trinity University Press, 2011.

Merck, J. H., trans. *Franz Hutcheson's Untersuchung unsrer Begriffe von Schönheit und Tugend in zwo Abhandlungen*. Frankfurt: Fleischerischen, 1762.

Milanesi, M., ed. *Giovanni Ramusio: Navigazioni e viaggi*. Turin: Einaudi, 1978–88.

Miller, A. V., trans. *G. W. F. Hegel: Phenomenology of Spirit*. Oxford: Oxford University Press, 1977.

Miller, W. ed. and trans. *Cicero, Marcus Tullius, De officiis*. London: Heinemann, 1913.

Minio-Paluello, L., ed. *Anicius Manlius Severinus Boethius Porphyrii Isagoge translatio*. Paris: Desclée de Brouwer, 1966.

Mivart, S. G. "Organic Nature's Riddle." *Fortnightly Review* 44 (1885): 323–37.

Mommsen, T., et al., eds. *Corpus iuris civilis*. Cambridge, UK: Cambridge University Press, 2014.

Montecatini, A. *In Politica Aristotelis Progymnasmata*. Ferrara: Victorius Baldinus, 1587.

Most, G. W., ed. and trans. *Hesiod: Works and Days*. Cambridge, MA: Harvard University Press, 2006.

Moyle, J., trans. *Antonello Gerbi: Nature in the New World. From Christopher Columbus to Gonzalo Fernández de Oviedo*. Pittsburgh, PA: University of Pittsburgh Press, 2010.

Morgan, C. L. *An Introduction to Comparative Psychology*. London: Walter Scott, 1894.

Morgan, C. L. "The Limits of Animal Intelligence." *Fortnightly Review* 54 (1893): 223–39.

Muckle, J. T. "The Treatise *De Anima* of Dominicus Gundissalinus." *Mediaeval Studies* 2 (1940): 23–103.

Nader, A. N., ed. *Ibn Ṭufayl: Ḥayy Ibn Yaqẓān*. Beirut: Dār al-Mashriq, 1993.

Ñāṇamoli, B., and B. Bodhi, trans. *The Middle-Length Discourses of the Buddha: A Translation of the Majjhima Nikāya*. Boston: Wisdom Publications, 1995.

Needham, R., trans. *Claude Lévi-Strauss: Totemism*. Boston: Beacon Press, 1963.

Nicholas of Vaudémont [John Buridan, pseud.]. *Quaestiones super octo libros Politicorum*. Frankfurt: Minerva, 1969.

Nisbet, H. B., trans. *G. W. F. Hegel: Elements of the Philosophy of Right*. Cambridge, UK: Cambridge University Press, 1991.

Oldfather, W. A., trans. *Epictetus: Discourses*. Books 1–2. Cambridge, MA: Harvard University Press, 1989.

Olivelle, P., trans. *The Law Code of Manu*. Oxford: Oxford University Press, 2004.

Olivelle, P., trans. *The Pañcatantra: The Book of India's Folk Wisdom*. Oxford: Oxford University Press, 1997.

Paolella, A., ed. *Della Porta: De humana physiognomonia libri sex*. Naples: Edizioni Scientifiche Italiane, 2011.

Paolella, A., ed. *Della Porta: Della fisionomia dell'uomo libri sei*. Naples: Edizioni Scientifiche Italiane, 2013.

Patillon, M., and L. Brisson, eds. *Longinus: Fragments, Art rhétorique. Rufus: Art rhétorique*. Paris: Les Belles Lettres, 2001.

Payne, E. F., and D. E. Cartwright, trans. *Arthur Schopenhauer: On the Basis of Morality*. Indianapolis, IN: Hackett Classics, 2001.

Payne, E. F. J., trans. *Arthur Schopenhauer: The World as Will and Representation*. 2 vols. New York: Dover, 1969.

Pellizzari, P., ed. *Doni: I Mondi e gli Inferni*. Milan: Einaudi, 1994.

Perry, B. E., ed. *Aesopica: Greek and Latin Texts*. Urbana: University of Illinois Press, 1952.

Peter of Auvergne. *Questiones super libros Politicorum*. Paris BN lat. 16089, fol.274r–319r.

Pliny the Elder. *Histoire naturelle de l'or et de l'argent*. London: Guillaume Bowyer, 1729.

Powell, O., ed. *Galen: On the Properties of Foodstuffs (De alimentorum facultatibus)*. Cambridge, UK: Cambridge University Press, 2003.

Pozzi, M., ed. *Il mondo nuovo di Amerigo Vespucci, Vespucci autentico e apocrifo*. Milan: Serra e Riva Editori, 1984.

Rackham, H., trans. *Cicero: On the Nature of the Gods* and *Academics*. Cambridge, MA: Harvard University Press, 1989.

Rackham, H., trans. *Plinius Secundus, Gaius, Natural History*. 10 vols. London: Heinemann, 1938–1963.

Raimondi, P. F., and M. Carparelli, eds. *Vanini: "De admirandis naturae reginae deaeque mortalium arcanis,"* in *Tutte le opere*. Milan: Bompiani, 2010.

Rawls, J. *A Theory of Justice*. Oxford: Oxford University Press, 1971.

Red Pine, *Laṅkāvatāra Sūtra: Translation and Commentary*. Berkeley, CA: Counterpoint, 2013.

Regan, J., trans. *Commentary on Aristotle's Politics*. Indianapolis, IN: Hackett, 2007.

Reid, T. *Essays on the Active Powers of the Human Mind*. Cambridge, MA: MIT Press, 1969.

Remnant, P., and J. Bennett, eds. *G. W. Leibniz: New Essays on Human Understanding*. Cambridge, UK: Cambridge University Press, 1996.

Roethe, G., ed. *Die Gedichte Reinmars von Zweter*. Amsterdam: Rodopi, 1967.

Ronca, I., and M. Curr, ed. and trans. *William of Conches: A Dialogue on Natural Philosophy* (*Dragmaticon Philosophiae*). Notre Dame, IN: University of Notre Dame Press, 1997.

Rosenthal, F., trans. *Ibn Khaldun: The Muqaddima.* 3 vols. Princeton, NJ: Princeton University Press, 1958.

Rotman, A. *Divine Stories.* Somerville, MA: Wisdom Publications, 2008.

Rouse, W. H. D., trans. *Lucretius: De Rerum Natura.* London: Heineman, 1937.

Ruggieri, R. M., ed. *Marco Polo: Il Milione.* Florence: Olschki, 1986.

Russell, D. A., ed. and trans. *Quintillian: The Orator's Education.* Cambridge, MA: Harvard University Press, 2002.

Ryan, C., trans. *Dante: The Banquet.* Saratoga, NY: ANMA Libri, 1989.

Samaritanus, H., ed. *Giles of Rome: De regimine principum.* Rome: B. Zanettus, 1607.

Schelling, F. W. J. *Von der Weltseele.* Hamburg: Freidrich Perthes, 1809.

Schiefsky, M. J., ed. *Hippocrates: On Ancient Medicine.* Leiden: Brill, 2005.

Schneider, G. H. *Der Thierische Wille: Systematische Darstellung und Erklärung der thierischen Triebe und deren Entstehung, Entwickelung und Verbreitung im Thierreiche als Grundlage zu einer vergleichenden Willenslehre.* Leipzig: Abel, 1880.

Schoeck, R. J., G. Bedouelle, and C. R. Thompson, eds. *Erasmus, Desiderius: Colloquies* I. In *The Collected Works of Erasmus.* Vol. 39. Toronto: University of Toronto Press, 1997.

Schopenhauer, A. *Die beiden Grundprobleme der Ethik.* Frankfurt: Hermannsche Buchhandlung, 1841.

Shackleton, Bailey, D. R. trans. *Cicero: Letters to Friends.* Vol 1. Cambridge, MA: Harvard University Press, 2001.

Sharples, R. W., trans. *Alexander of Aphrodisias: Quaestiones* 1.1–2.15. London: Bloomsbury, 2014.

Sharples, R. W., and P. J. van der Eijk, trans. *Nemesius: On the Nature of Man.* Liverpool: Liverpool University Press, 2008.

Silano, G., trans. *Peter Lombard: The Sentences.* 4 vols. Toronto: Pontifical Institute of Medieval Studies, 2007–10.

Simpson, J. *Reynard the Fox: A New Translation.* New York: Liveright/Norton, 2015.

Singer, P. N., ed. *Galen: Psychological Writings.* Cambridge, UK: Cambridge University Press, 2013.

Singer, C., ed. *Galen: On Anatomical Procedures.* Oxford: Oxford University Press, 1999.

Singer, P. N., trans. "The Thinning Diet," in P. N. Singer ed., *Galen: Selected Works.* Oxford: Oxford University Press, 1977.

Slavitt, D. R., trans. *Boethius: Consolation of Philosophy.* Cambridge, MA: Harvard University Press, 2008.

Spencer, H. *The Principles of Psychology*. 2nd ed. London: Williams and Norgate, 1870.

Spon, C., ed. *Girolamo Cardano: Opera omnia*. Lyon: Huguetan and Ravaud, 1663. 6 vols. Reprint, Stuttgart-Bad Cannstatt: Frommann, 1966.

Staden, H. *Warhaftig Historia und beschreibung eyner Landtschafft der Wilden, Nacketen, Grimmigen Menschfresser Leuthen, in der Newen welt America gelegen....* Marburg: Kolb, 1557.

Stadler, H., ed. *Albertus Magnus: De animalibus libri XXVI*. Münster: Aschendorffsche Verlagsbuchhandlung, 1916.

Stählin, O., and L. Früchtel, eds. *Clement of Alexandria: Stromata*. Books 1–6. Berlin: Akademie-Verlag, 1960.

Stählin, O., and L. Früchtel, eds. *Clement of Alexandria: Stromata*. Books 7–8. Leipzig: Akademie, 1970.

Stoner, J., trans. *Girolamo Cardano: The Book of My Life*. New York: Dutton, 1930.

Sulpicius Severus. *Dialogi libri II*. Turnhout: Brepols, 2010.

Taylor, T., trans. *Porphyry On Abstinence from Animal Food*. London: T. Rodd, 1823.

Taylor, T., trans. *Iamblichus: Life of Pythagoras*. London: J. M. Watkins, 1818.

Terian, A., ed. *Philonis Alexandrini De Animalibus: The Armenian Text, with an Introduction, Translation, and Commentary*. Chico, CA: Scholars' Press, 1981.

Thomas of Cantimpré. *Bonum universale de apibus*. Douai: B. Belleri, 1627.

Thörnqvist, C. T. "Walter Burley's *Expositio* on Aristotle's Treatises on Sleep and Dreaming." *Cahiers de l'Institut du Moyen Âge Grec et Latin* 83 (2014): 379–515.

Tournon, A., ed. *Essais de Michel de Montaigne*. Book 1. Paris: Imprimerie nationale Éditions, 1998.

Vangensten, O. C. L., A. Fonahn, and H. Hopstock. *Leonardo da Vinci: Quaderni d'Anatomia II. Ventiquattro fogli della Royal Library di Windsor. Cuore: Anatomia e Fisiologia*. Christiana: Dwybad, 1911–16.

van Ophuijsen, J. M. *Alexander of Aphrodisias: On Aristotle Topics*. London: Bloomsbury, 2001.

van Riet, S., ed. *Avicenna Latinus: Liber de anima*. Louvain: Peeters, 1968.

Veitch, J., ed. *Rene Descartes: A Discourse on Method*. London: Dent, 1912.

Waley, A., trans. *The Book of Songs*. New York: Grove Press, 1960.

Walford, D., and R. Meerbote, eds. *Kant: Theoretical Philosophy, 1755–1770*. Cambridge, UK: Cambridge University Press, 1992.

Walsh, N., trans. *The Long Discourses of the Buddha: A Translation of the Digha Nikaya*. Boston: Wisdom Publications, 1999.

Watkins, E., ed. *Kant: Natural Science*. Cambridge, UK: Cambridge University Press, 2012.

Watson, B., trans. *The Complete Works of Zhuangzi*. New York: Columbia University Press, 1964.

Wickens, G. M., trans. *Naṣīr al-Dīn al-Ṭūsī: The Nasirean Ethics*. London: Allen and Unwin, 1964.

Wilcox, J. C., ed. *The Transmission and Influence of Qusta ibn Luca's On the Difference between Spirit and the Soul*. Ann Arbor: University of Michigan Press, 1985.

Williams, T., trans. *Augustine: On the Free Choice of the Will*. Indianapolis, IN: Hackett, 1993.

Willms, E., ed. *Lieder und Sangsprüche aus dem 13. Jahrhundert und ihr Weiterleben im Meistersang*. Berlin: Walter de Gruyter, 2008.

Wood, A., and G. di Giovanni, eds. *Kant: Religion within the Boundaries of Mere Reason*. New York: Cambridge University Press, 1999.

Wood, A., and G. di Giovanni, eds. *Kant: Religion and Rational Theology*. Cambridge, UK: Cambridge University Press, 1996.

Wundt, W. *Grundzüge der physiologischen Psychologie*. Leipzig: Engelmann, 1874.

Young, J. M., ed. and trans. *Kant: Lectures on Logic*. Cambridge, UK: Cambridge University Press, 1992.

Zidayah, M., trans. "Ibn Bajja's Book Tadbir al-Mutawahhid: An Edition, Translation and Commentary." PhD thesis, McGill University, 1968.

Zurayk, C., ed. *Miskawayh: Tahḏīb al-Aḫlaq*. Beirut: al-Nadin al-Lubnāniyya, 1966.

Zurayk, C., trans. *Miskawayh: The Refinement of Character*. Beirut: American University of Beirut, 1968.

Secondary Literature

Adamson, P. "Abū Bakr al-Rāzī on Animals." *Archiv für Geschichte der Philosophie* 94 (2012): 249–73.

Adamson, P. "Al-Rāzī, *Spiritual Medicine*." In *The Oxford Handbook of Islamic Philosophy*, edited by K. El-Rouayheb and S. Schmitdke, 63–82. Oxford: Oxford University Press, 2017.

Adamson, P. "Correcting Plotinus: Soul's Relationship to Body in Avicenna's Commentary on the *Theology of Aristotle*." In *Philosophy, Science and Exegesis in Greek, Arabic and Latin Commentaries*, 2 vols., edited by P. Adamson, H. Baltussen, and M. W. F. Stone, 2:59–75. London: Institute of Classical Studies, 2004.

Adamson, P. "The Ethical Treatment of Animals." In *Routledge Companion to Islamic Philosophy*, edited by R. C. Taylor and L. X. López-Farjeat, 371–82. London: Routledge, 2015.

Adamson, P. "Platonic Pleasures in Epicurus and al-Rāzī." In *In the Age of al-Fārābī: Arabic Philosophy in the Fourth/Tenth Century*, edited by P. Adamson, 71–94. London: Warburg Institute, 2008.

Adamson, P. "Miskawayh's Psychology." In *Classical Arabic Philosophy: Sources and Reception*, edited by P. Adamson, 39–54. London: Warburg Institute, 2007.

Adamson, P. "Yaḥyā Ibn ʿAdī and Averroes on Metaphysics Alpha Elatton." *Documenti e Studi sulla Tradizione Filosofica Medievale* 21 (2010): 343–74.

Albala, K. *Eating Right in the Renaissance*. Berkeley: University of California Press, 2002.

Alexander, D. *Saints and Animals in the Middle Ages*. Suffolk, UK: Boydell Press, 2008.

Alexandrin, E. R. "Rāzī and His Mediaeval Opponents: Discussions concerning *Tanāsukh* and the Afterlife." *Cahiers de studia iranica* 26 (2002): 397–409.

Allais, L., and J. Callanan, eds. *Kant on Animals*. Oxford: Oxford University Press, forthcoming.

Allen-Hermanson, S. "Morgan's Canon Revisited." *Philosophy of Science* 72 (2005): 608–31.

Althaus, K. "'Das übrige lese man in Darwin nach': Die wissenschaftliche Sammlung." In *Gabriel von Max: Malerstar Darwinist, Spiritist*, edited by K. Althaus, and H. Friedel, 247–57. Munich: Hirmer, 2010.

Althaus, K. "Die Affen: Studienobjekte und Lebensgefährten." In *Gabriel von Max: Malerstar Darwinist, Spiritist*, edited by K. Althaus and H. Friedel, 295–315. Munich: Hirmer, 2010.

Althaus, K., and S. Böller. "Gabriel von Max (1814–1915)." In *Gabriel von Max: Malerstar Darwinist, Spiritist*, edited by K. Althaus and H. Friedel, 18–37. Munich: Hirmer, 2010.

Althaus, K., and H. Friedel, eds. *Gabriel von Max: Malerstar Darwinist, Spiritist*. Munich: Hirmer, 2010.

Ameriks, K. "Kant's Deduction of Freedom and Morality." *Journal of the History of Philosophy* 19 (1981): 53–79.

Ameriks, K. *Kant's Theory of Mind: An Analysis of the Paralogisms of Pure Reason*. Oxford: Oxford University Press, 2000.

Bach, T. "Über den wechselseitigen Einfluss von Wissenschaft und Kunst: Gabriel von Max und Ernst Haeckel in Briefen." In *Gabriel von Max: Malerstar Darwinist, Spiritist*, edited by K. Althaus and H. Friedel, 282–94. Munich: Hirmer, 2010.

Balasooriya, S., et al., eds. *Buddhist Studies in Honour of Walpola Rahula*. London: Vimamsa, 1980.

Balbir, N., and P. Georges-Jean, eds. *Penser, dire et representer l'animal dans le monde indien*. Paris: Honoré Champion, 2009.

Baranzke, H. "Tierethik, Tiernatur und Moralanthropologie im Kontext von §17 Tugendlehre." *Kant-Studien* 96 (2005): 336–63.

Baxter, B. *A Theory of Ecological Justice*. London: Routledge, 2005.

Bazán, C. "The Human Soul: Form and Substance? Thomas Aquinas' Critique of Eclectic Aristotelianism." *Archives d'Histoire Doctrinale et Littéraire du Moyen Âge* 64 (1997): 95–126.

Beauchamp, T. L., B. Orlans, R. Dresser, D. B. Morton, and J. P. Gluck. *The Human Use of Animals*. New York: Oxford University Press, 2008.

Beauchamp, T. L., and R. G. Frey. *The Oxford Handbook of Animal Ethics*. Oxford: Oxford University Press, 2011.

Becker, L. "The Priority of Human Interests." In *Ethics and Animals*, edited by H. Miller and W. Williams, 225–42. Clifton, NJ: Humana Press, 1983.

Benkheira, M. H., C. Mayeur-Jaouen, and J. Sublet. *L'animal en Islam*. Paris: Indes savantes, 2005.

Bianchi, L. *Studi sull'aristotelismo del Rinascimento*. Padua: Il Poligrafo, 2003.

Biesterfeldt, H. H. *Galens Traktat Dass die Kräfte der Seele den Mischungen des Körpers folgen*. Wiesbaden: Steiner, 1973.

Bildhauer, B., and R. Mills, eds. *The Monstrous Middle Ages*. Toronto: University of Toronto Press, 2003.

Black, D. L. "Avicenna on Self-Awareness and Knowing that One Knows." In *The Unity of Science in the Arabic Tradition*, edited by S. Rahman et al., 63–87. Dordrecht: Kluwer, 2008.

Black, D. L. "Estimation (*Wahm*) in Avicenna: The Logical and Psychological Dimensions." *Dialogue* 32 (1993): 219–58.

Black, D. L. "Imagination and Estimation: Arabic Paradigms and Western Transformations." *Topoi* 19 (2000): 59–75.

Blatti, S., and P. F. Snowdon, eds. *Animalism: New Essays on Persons, Animals, and Identity*. Oxford: Oxford University Press, 2016.

Bliss, M. *The Discovery of Insulin*. Chicago: University of Chicago Press, 1982.

Blumberg, M. S., and G. Sokoloff. "Do Infant Rats Cry?" *Psychological Review* 108 (2001): 83–95.

Blumberg, M. S., G. Sokoloff, R. F. Kirby, and K. J. Kent. "Distress Vocalizations in Infant Rats: What's All the Fuss About?" *Psychological Science* 11 (2000): 78–81.

Boehm, C. *Hierarchy in the Forest: The Evolution of Egalitarian Behavior*. Cambridge, MA: Harvard University Press, 1999.

Boehm, C. *Moral Origin: The Evolution of Virtue, Altruism, and Shame*. New York: Basic Books, 2012.

Bourgeois, A. "Mbawa-Pakasu: L'image du buffle chez les Yaka et leurs voisins." *Arts d'Afrique Noire* 77.1 (1991): 19–32.

Bousquet, G. H. "Des Animaux et de leur traitement selon le Judaïsme, le Christianisme et l'Islam." *Studia Islamica* 9 (1958): 31–48.

Bouttiaux, M. "Guro Masked Performers Serving Spirits and People." *African Arts* 42.2 (2009): 56–67.

Brett, A. *Liberty, Right and Nature: Individual Rights in Later Scholastic Thought*. Cambridge, UK: Cambridge University Press, 1997.

Broadie, A., and E. M. Pybus. "Kant's Treatment of Animals." *Philosophy* 49 (1974): 375–83.

Brody, B. "Defending Animal Research: An International Perspective." In *Why Animal Experimentation Matters: The Use of Animals in Medical Research*, edited by E. F. Paul and J. Paul, 131–47. New Brunswick, NJ: Transaction, 2001.

Brown, D. J. "Animal Automatism and Machine Intelligence." *Res Philosophica* 92.1 (2015): 93–115.

Brown, D. J. "Cartesian Functional Analysis." *Australasian Journal of Philosophy* 90.1 (2012): 75–92.

Budiansky, S. *If a Lion Could Talk: How Animals Think*. London: Wiedenfeld, 1998.

Byrne, R., and Whiten, A. "Tactical Deception in Primates: The 1990 Database." *Primate Report* 27 (1990): 1–101.

Calhoun, C. "But What about the Animals?" In *Reason, Value, and Respect: Kantian Themes from the Philosophy of Thomas E. Hill, Jr.*, edited by M. Timmons and R. M. Johnson, 194–214. Oxford: Oxford University Press, 2015.

Camporesi, P. *I balsami di Venere*. Milan: Garzanti, 1989.

Carpenter, A. D. "Ethics without Justice: Eliminating the Roots of Resentment." In *A Mirror Is for Reflection: Understanding Buddhist Ethics*, edited by J. Davis, 315–35. New York: Oxford University Press, 2017.

Carpenter, A. D. "The Saṁmitīyas and the Case of the Disappearing 'Who?'— A Buddhist Whodunit." In *The Return of Consciousness—A New Science on Ancient Questions*, edited by A. Haag, 211–36. Stockholm: Axson Johnson Foundation, 2017.

Carruthers, P. *The Animals Issue*. Cambridge, UK: Cambridge University Press, 1992.

Cashdollar, S. "Aristotle's Account of Incidental Perception." *Phronesis* 18.2 (1973): 156–75.

Cavalieri, P., and P. Singer, eds. *The Great Ape Project: Equality beyond Humanity*. London: Fourth Estate, 1983.

Cavarzere, A. "Ego Polivi Versibus Senariis: Phaedrus and Iambic Poetry." In *Iambic Ideas: Essays on a Poetic Tradition. From Archaic Greece to the Late Roman Empire*, edited by A. Cavarzere, A. Aloni, and A. Barchiesi, 205–17. Oxford: Rowman and Littlefield, 2001.

Ceyssens, R. *De Luulu à Tervuren: La collection Oscar Michaux au Musée Royal de l'Afrique Centrale. Studies in Social Sciences and Humanities* 172. Tervuren: Musée royal de l'Afrique centrale, 2011.

Chakrabarti, A. "Rationality in Indian Philosophy." In *A Companion to World Philosophies*, edited by E. Deutsch, 259–78. Oxford: Blackwell, 1997.

Chapple, C. K. "Inherent Value without Nostalgia: Animals and the Jaina Tradition." In *A Communion of Subjects*, edited by K. Patton and P. Waldau, 241–49. New York: Columbia University Press, 2009.

Chapple, C. K. *Nonviolence to Animals, Earth and Self in Asian Traditions*. Albany: State University of New York Press 1993.

Charles, D. "Aristotle on Practical and Theoretical Knowledge." In *Bridging the Gap between Aristotle's Science and Ethics*, edited by D. Henry and M. Leunissen, 71–93. Cambridge, UK: Cambridge University Press, 2015.

Clark, S. *The Moral Status of Animals*. Oxford: Clarendon Press, 1984.

Clarke, P., and A. Linzey, eds. *Political Theory and Animal Rights*. London: Pluto Press, 1990.

Cochrane, A. "Animal Rights and Animal Experiments: An Interest-Based Approach." *Res Publica* 13 (2007): 293–318.

Cochrane, A. *Animal Rights without Liberation*. New York: Columbia University Press, 2012.

Cochrane, A. "Cosmozoopolis: The Case against Group-Differentiated Animal Rights." *Law, Ethics and Philosophy* 1 (2012): 127–41.

Cochrane, A. "Do Animals Have an Interest in Liberty?" *Political Studies* 57 (2009): 660–79.

Cohen, C. "The Case for the Use of Animals in Biomedical Research." *New England Journal of Medicine* 315.14 (1986): 865–70.

Cohen, C., and T. Regan. *The Animal Rights Debate*. New York: Rowman and Littlefield, 2001.

Cohen, E. "Law, Folklore and Animal Lore." *Past and Present* 110 (1986): 6–37.

Colle, P. *Les Baluba*. 2 vols. Brussels: A. Dewit, 1913.

Collins, C., and R. Kays. "Patterns of Mortality in a Wild Population of White-Footed Mice." *Northeastern Naturalist* 21 (2014): 323–36.

Copeland, J. "The Turing Test." *Minds and Machines* 10 (2000): 519–39.

Costantino, M. "*Anonymi Philosophia Sicut dicitur ab Aristotile*: A Parisian Prologue to Porphyry." *Cahiers de l'institut du moyen-âge grec et latin* 61 (1991): 140–46.

Cottingham, J. "'A Brute to the Brutes?' Descartes' Treatment of Animals." *Philosophy* 53.206 (1978): 551–59.

Cozzoli, A.-T. "Poesia satirica latina e favola esopica (Ennio, Lucilio e Orazio)." *Rivista di cultura classica e medioevale* 37 (1995): 187–204.

Cummings, B. "Animal Passions and Human Sciences: Shame, Blushing and Nakedness in Early Modern Europe and the New World." In *At the Borders of the Human*, edited by E. Fudge, R. Gilbert, and S. Wiseman, 26–50. Basingstoke, UK: Macmillan, 1999.

Dalal, N., and C. Taylor, eds. *Asian Perspectives on Animal Ethics: Rethinking the Nonhuman*. New York: Routledge, 2014.

Daly, L. W. *Aesop without Morals*. London: Thomas Yoseloff, 1961.

DeGrazia, D. *Taking Animals Seriously: Mental Life and Moral Status.* Cambridge, UK: Cambridge University Press, 1996.

de Heusch, L. *The Drunken King or the Origin of the State.* Bloomington: Indiana University Press, 1982.

Deleanu, F. "Buddhist 'Ethology' in the Pāli Canon: Between Symbol and Observation." *Eastern Buddhist,* new series, 23.2 (2000): 79–127.

De Leemans, P., and M. Klemm. "Animals and Anthropology in Medieval Philosophy." In *A Cultural History of Animals in the Medieval Age,* edited by B. Resl, 2:153–77. Oxford: Berg, 2007.

del Vecchio, L., and A. M. Fiore. "Fabula in satura: Osservazioni su alcuni frammenti delle Satire di Ennio." *Vigilata lucernis* 20 (1998): 59–72.

de Waal, F. *Are We Smart Enough to Know How Smart Animals Are?* London: Granta, 2016.

de Waal, F. *Good Natured: The Origins of Right and Wrong in Humans and Other Animals.* Cambridge, MA: Harvard University Press, 1996.

Denis, L. "Animality and Agency: a Kantian Approach to Abortion." *Philosophy and Phenomenological Research* 76 (2008): 117–37.

Denis, L. "Kant's Conception of Duties regarding Animals: Reconstruction and Reconsideration." *History of Philosophy Quarterly* 17 (2000): 405–23.

Dennett, D. *The Intentional Stance.* Cambridge, MA: MIT Press, 1989.

Dennett, D. "Intentional Systems in Cognitive Ethology: The Panglossian Paradigm Defended." In *The Intentional Stance:* 237–68. Originally published in *Behavioral and Brain Sciences* 6 (1983): 343–90.

Des Chene, D. *Spirits and Clocks.* Ithaca, NY: Cornell University Press, 2001.

Devine, P. "The Moral Basis of Vegetarianism." *Philosophy* 53.206 (1978): 481–505.

Di Martino, C. *Ratio particularis: Doctrines des senses internes d'Avicenne à Thomas d'Aquin.* Paris: Vrin, 2008.

Diamond, C. "Eating Meat and Eating People." *Philosophy* 53.206 (1978): 465–79.

Dombrowski, D. *Babies and Beasts: The Argument from Marginal Cases.* Chicago: University of Illinois Press, 1997.

Dombrowski, D. A. *Vegetarianism: The Philosophy behind the Ethical Diet.* Amherst: University of Massachusetts Press, 1984.

Donaldson, S., and W. Kymlicka. *Zoopolis: A Political Theory of Animal Rights.* New York: Oxford University Press, 2011.

Doniger, W. "A Symbol in Search of an Object: The Mythology of Horses in India." In *A Communion of Subjects,* edited by K. Patton and P. Waldau, 335–50. New York: Columbia University Press, 2009.

Doniger O'Flaherty, W. *The Origins of Evil in Hindu Mythology.* Berkeley: University of California Press, 1976.

Donovan, J., and C. Adams, eds. *The Feminist Care Tradition in Animal Ethics.* New York: Columbia University Press, 2007.

Dorst, J., and P. Dandelot. *A Field Guide to the Larger Mammals of Africa.* Boston: Houghton Mifflin, 1969.

Dover, K. J. *Greek Popular Morality in the Time of Plato and Aristotle.* Oxford: Blackwell, 1974.

Dreyfus, G. "Meditation as an Ethical Activity." *Journal of Buddhist Ethics* 2 (1995): 28–54.

Druart, T.-A. "Al-Rāzī's Conception of the Soul: Psychological Background to His Ethics." *Medieval Philosophy and Theology* 5 (1996): 245–63.

Druart, T.-A. "The Human Soul's Individuation and Its Survival after the Body's Death: Avicenna on the Causal Relation between Body and Soul." *Arabic Sciences and Philosophy* 10 (2000): 259–73.

Druart, T.-A. "Logic and Language." In *The Routledge Companion to Islamic Philosophy*, edited by R. C. Taylor and L. X. López-Farjeat, 69–81. London: Routledge, 2015.

Dundas, P. *The Jains.* London: Routledge, 1992.

Durkheim, Emile. *The Elementary Forms of the Religious Life.* Trans. K. E. Fields. New York: Free Press, 1996.

Durling, R. J. "Galen in the Renaissance: A Chronological Census of Renaissance Editions and Translations of Galen." *Journal of the Warburg and Courtauld Institutes* 24.3 (1961): 230–305.

Dwyer, D. M., and K. F. Burgess. "Rational Accounts of Animal Behaviour: Lessons from C. Lloyd Morgan's Canon." *International Journal of Comparative Psychology* 24 (2011): 349–64.

Edwards, G. F. "Irrational Animals in Porphyry's Logical Works: A Problem for the Consensus Interpretation of *On Abstinence*." *Phronesis* 59.1 (2014): 22–43.

Edwards, G. F. "The Purpose of Porphyry's Rational Animals: A Dialectical Attack on the Stoics in *On Abstinence from Animal Food*." In *Aristotle Re-interpreted: New Findings on Seven Hundred Years of the Ancient Commentators*, edited by R. Sorabji, 263–90. London: Bloomsbury, 2016.

Epstein, R. "The Principle of Parsimony and Some Applications in Psychology." *Journal of Mind and Behavior* 5 (1984): 119–30.

Ernst, G. "L'analogia e la differenza: Uomo e animali in Campanella." In *The Animal Soul and the Human Mind: Renaissance Debates*, edited by C. Muratori, 209–25. Pisa: Serra, 2013.

Evans, E. P. *The Criminal Prosecution and Capital Punishment of Animals.* London: Faber and Faber, 1987.

Feder Kittay, E. "At the Margins of Moral Personhood." *Ethics* 116.1 (2005): 100–131.

Feinberg, J. "The Rights of Animals and Unborn Generations." In *Rights, Justice and the Bounds of Liberty: Essays in Social Philosophy*, 159–84. Princeton, NJ: Princeton University Press, 1980.

Fernandez, J. W. "Meditating on Animals—Figuring Out Humans!" Foreword to A.F. Roberts, *Animals in African Arts: From the Familiar to the Marvelous*, 356–73. Munich: Prestel, 1995.

Fernandez, J. W. *Persuasions and Performances: The Play of Tropes in Culture.* Bloomington: Indiana University Press, 1986.

Fernandez, J. W. "Principles of Opposition and Vitality in Fang Aesthetics." In *Art and Aesthetics in Primitive Societies*, edited by C. Jopling, 356–73. New York: Dutton, 1971.

Findly, E. B. *Plant Lives: Borderline Beings in Indian Traditions.* Delhi: Motilal Banarsidass, 2008.

Fishkin, J. *When the People Speak.* New York: Oxford University Press, 2009.

Fitzpatrick, S. "Doing Away with Morgan's Canon." *Mind and Language* 23 (2008): 224–46.

Flinn, J. *Le Roman de Reynart dans la littérature française et dans les littératures étrangères au moyen âge.* Toronto: University of Toronto Press, 1963.

Fodor, J. "Not So Clever Hans." *London Review of Books*, February 4, 1999.

Foltz, R. C. *Animals in Islamic Tradition and Muslim Cultures.* Oxford: Oneworld, 2006.

Foster, B. R. "The Person in Mesopotamian Thought." In *The Oxford Handbook of Cuneiform Culture*, edited by K. Radner and E. Robson, 117–39. Oxford: Oxford University Press, 2011.

Framarin, C. G. *Hinduism and Environmental Ethics: Law, Literature, and Philosophy.* Abingdon, UK: Routledge, 2014.

Francione, G. *Animals as Persons.* New York: Columbia University Press, 2008.

Francione, G. *Animals, Property and the Law.* Philadelphia: Temple University Press, 1995.

Francione, G., and R. Garner. *The Animal Rights Debate: Abolition or Regulation.* New York: Columbia University Press, 2010.

Fraser, D., and D. Weary. "Quality of Life for Farm Animals: Linking Science, Ethics and Animal Welfare." In *The Well-Being of Farm Animals: Challenges and Solutions*, edited by J. Benson and B. Rollin, 39–60. Oxford: Blackwell, 2004.

Frede, M. "The Stoic Conception of Reason." In *Hellenistic Philosophy*, edited by K. Boudouris, 2:50–63. Athens: International Association for Greek Philosophy, 1994.

French, R. *Ancient Natural History.* London: Routledge, 1994.

French, R. *Dissection and Vivisection in the European Renaissance*. Farnham, UK: Ashgate, 1999.

Freschi, E. "Review of Ellison Banks Findly's *Plant Lives*." *Philosophy East and West* 61.2 (2011): 380–85.

Freschi, E. "Systematising an Absent Category: Discourses on Nature in Prābhākara Mīmāṃsā." In *The Human Person and Nature in Classical and Modern India*, 45–54. Pisa: Fabrizio Serra Editore, 2015.

Frey, R. "Autonomy and the Value of Animal Life." *Monist* 70 (1987): 50–63.

Frey, R. *Rights, Killing and Suffering*. Oxford: Clarendon Press, 1983.

Friedrich, U. *Menschentier und Tiermensch: Diskurse der Grenzziehung und Grenzüberschreitung im Mittelalter*. Göttingen: Vandenhoeck und Ruprecht, 2009.

Frierson, P. "Kant's Empirical Account of Human Action." *Philosophers' Imprint* 5.7 (2005): 1–34.

Frierson, P. *Kant's Empirical Psychology*. Cambridge, UK: Cambridge University Press, 2014

Frisch, K. von. *The Dance Language and the Orientation of Bees*. Oxford: Oxford University Press, 1967.

Fudge, E. *Perceiving Animals: Humans and Beasts in Early Modern English Culture*. Chicago: University of Illinois Press, 2000.

Fujiwara-Tsujii, N., N. Yamagata, T. Takeda, and M. Mizonami. "Behavioral Responses to the Alarm Pheromone of the Ant Camponotus obscuripes (Hymenoptera: Formicidae)." *Zoological Science* 23.4 (2006): 353–58.

Galef, B. G., Jr. "Historical Origins: The Making of a Science." In *Foundations of Animal Behavior: Classic Papers with Commentaries*, edited by L. D. Houck and L. C. Drickamer, 5–126. Chicago: University of Chicago Press, 1996.

Garner, R. "Rawls, Animals and Justice: New Literature, Same Response." *Res Publica* 18 (2012): 159–72.

Garner, R. *A Theory of Justice for Animals: Animal Rights in a Nonideal World*. New York: Oxford University Press, 2013.

Garner, R., and S. O'Sullivan, eds. *The Political Turn in Animal Ethics*. London: Rowman and Littlefield International, 2016.

Garrett, A. "Animals and Ethics in the History of Modern Philosophy." In *The Oxford Handbook on Ethics and Animals*, edited by T. L. Beauchamp and R. G. Frey, 61–87. Oxford: Oxford University Press, 2011.

Garrett, A. "Francis Hutcheson and the Origin of Animal Rights." *Journal of the History of Philosophy* 45 (2007): 243–65.

Gauthier, D. *Morals by Agreement*. Oxford: Clarendon Press, 1986.

Gerhardt, C. "Reinmars von Zweter 'Idealer Mann' (Roethe Nr. 99 und 100)."
    Beiträge zur Geschichte der deutschen Sprache und Literatur 109 (1987): 51–84.

Gilhus, I. S. *Animals, Gods and Humans: Changing Attitudes towards Animals in
    Greek, Roman and Early Christian Ideas.* London: Routledge, 2006.

Gilligan, C. *In a Different Voice: Psychological Theory and Women's Development.*
    Cambridge, MA: Harvard University Press, 1983.

Gliozzi, G., ed. *La scoperta dei selvaggi: Antropologia e colonialismo da Colombo a
    Diderot.* Milan: Principato, 1971.

Goodpaster, K. "On Being Morally Considerable." *Journal of Philosophy* 75 (1978):
    308–25.

Gotthelf, A. "Darwin on Aristotle." *Journal of the History of Biology* 32 (1999): 3–31.

Grass, G. *The Tin Drum.* London: Vintage, 2009.

Greenblatt, S., ed. *New World Encounters.* Berkeley: University of California Press,
    1993.

Gregoric, P. *Aristotle on the Common Sense.* Oxford: Oxford University Press, 2007.

Grendler, P. F. *The Universities of the Italian Renaissance.* Baltimore: Johns Hopkins
    University Press, 2011.

Grieco, A. J. "Food and Social Classes in Late Medieval and Renaissance Italy." In
    Food: A Culinary History from Antiquity to the Present, edited by J.-L. Flandrin
    and M. Montanari and translated by A. Sonnenfeld, 302–12. New York:
    Columbia University Press, 2013.

Gruen, L. *Ethics and Animals: An Introduction.* Cambridge, UK: Cambridge
    University Press, 2011.

Gunderson, K. "Descartes, La Mettrie, Language and Machines." *Philosophy* 39
    (1964): 193–222.

Gunnarsson, L. "The Great Apes and the Severely Disabled: Moral Status and
    Thick Evaluative Concepts." *Ethical Theory and Moral Practice* 11 (2008): 305–26.

Guyer, P. *Kant and the Experience of Freedom.* Cambridge, UK: Cambridge
    University Press, 1993.

Haakonssen, K. *Natural Law and Moral Philosophy.* Cambridge, UK: Cambridge
    University Press, 1996.

Hallet, J.-P. *Animal Kitabu.* New York: Random House, 1967.

Hare, R. "Why I Am Only a Demi-Vegetarian." In *Singer and His Critics,* edited by
    D. Jamieson, 233–46. Oxford: Blackwell, 1997.

Hargrove, E., ed. *The Animal Rights/Environmental Ethics Debate: The
    Environmental Perspective.* Albany: State University of New York Press, 1992.

Harris, I. "Buddhism and Ecology." In *Contemporary Buddhist Ethics,* edited by
    D. Jamieson, 113–35. Richmond, VA: Curzon Press, 2000.

Hart, H. "Are There Any Natural Rights?" In *Political Philosophy*, edited by A. Quinton, 53–66. Oxford: Oxford University Press, 1967.

Harvey, P. *An Introduction to Buddhist Ethics: Foundations, Values and Issues*. Oxford: Oxford University Press, 2000.

Harvey, R. *The Inward Wits: Psychological Theory in the Middle Ages and the Renaissance*. London: Warburg Institute, 1975.

Hasse, D. N. *Avicenna's De Anima in the Latin West: The Formation of a Peripatetic Philosophy of the Soul 1160–1300*. London: Warburg Institute, 2000.

Hassig, D. *Medieval Bestiaries: Text, Image, Ideology*. Cambridge, UK: Cambridge University Press, 1995.

Heath, J. *The Talking Greeks: Speech, Animals and the Other in Homer, Aeschylus and Plato*. Cambridge, UK: Cambridge University Press, 2005.

Hedrich, H., ed. *The Laboratory Mouse*. London: Elsevier, 2004.

Heemskerk, M. T. *Suffering in the Mu'tazilite Theology: 'Abd al-Jabbār's Teaching on Pain and Divine Justice*. Leiden: Brill, 2000.

Heinämaa, S., V. Lähteenmäki, and P. Remes, eds. *Consciousness: From Perception to Reflection in the History of Philosophy*. Dordrecht: Springer, 2007.

Helmig, C. "Plutarch of Chaeronea and Porphyry on Transmigration: Who Is the Author of Stobaeus I 445.14–448.3 (W.–H.)?" *Classical Quarterly* 58.1 (2008): 250–55.

Henrich, D. "Hutcheson und Kant." *Kant-Studien* 49 (1958): 49–69.

Hibbs, T. S., ed. *Aquinas on Human Nature*. Indianapolis, IN: Hackett, 1999.

Hilgard, E. "The Trilogy of Mind: Cognition, Affection, and Conation." *Journal of the History of the Behavioral Sciences* 16 (1980): 107–17.

Hirschfeld, L. A., and S. A. Gelman, eds. *Mapping the Mind: Domain Specificity in Cognition and Culture*. Cambridge, UK: Cambridge University Press, 1994.

Hoffmann, T. "Intellectualism and Voluntarism." In *Cambridge History of Medieval Philosophy*, edited by R. Pasnau, 414–27. Cambridge, UK: Cambridge University Press, 2010.

Hogg, J. "Carthusian Abstinence." In *Spiritualität heute und gestern*, edited by J. Hogg, 5–15. New York: Edwin Mellen Press, 1991.

Holzberg, N. *The Ancient Fable: An Introduction*. Indianapolis, IN: Indiana University Press, 2002.

Horta, O. "Zoopolis, Intervention, and the State of Nature." *Law, Ethics and Philosophy* 1 (2012): 113–25.

Houston, S., and M. Timmons. "Kant's Grounding Project in the Doctrine of Virtue." In *Kant on Practical Justification: Interpretative Essays*, edited by M. Timmons and S. Baiasu, 229–68. New York: Oxford University Press, 2013.

Hursthouse, R. *Ethics, Humans and Other Animals*. London: Routledge, 2000.

Huxley, T. H. "On the Hypothesis That Animals Are Automata, and Its History." *Fortnightly Review* 95 (1874): 555–80.

Ingensiep, H. W. "Tierseele und tierethische Argumentationen in der deutschen philosophischen Literatur des 18. Jahrhunderts." *NTM: Internationale Zeitschrift für Geschichte und Ethik der Naturwissenschaften, Technik und Medizin*, new series, 4 (1996): 103–18.

Jaini, P. S. "Ahimsa and 'Just War' Jainism." In *Ahimsa, Anekānta and Jainism*, edited by T. Sethia, 47–61. New Delhi: Motilal Banarsidass, 2004.

Jaini, P. S. "Animals and Agents in Ahimsa Action and Spiritual Life." *Journal of Dharma* 16.3 (1991): 269–81.

Jamison, S. "The Function of Animals in the *Ṛg Veda*." In *Penser, dire et representer l'animal dans le monde indien*, edited by N. Balbir and G.-J. Pinault, 197–218. Paris: Honoré Champion, 2009.

Jedrkiewicz, S. *Sapere e paradosso nell' antichità: Esopo e la favola*. Rome: dell'Ateneo, 1989.

Johansen, T. K. *The Powers of the Aristotelian Soul*. Oxford: Oxford University Press, 2012.

Joyce, R. *The Evolution of Morality*. Cambridge, MA: MIT Press, 2006.

Kahn, C. H. "Aristotle on Thinking." In *Essays on Aristotle's De Anima*, edited by M. Nussbaum and A. O. Rorty, 359–80. Oxford: Clarendon Press, 1992.

Kain, P. "Duties regarding Animals." In *Kant's Metaphysics of Morals: A Critical Guide*, edited by L. Denis, 210–33. Cambridge, UK: Cambridge University Press, 2010.

Kain, P. "Kant's Defense of Human Moral Status." *Journal of the History of Philosophy* 47 (2009): 59–102.

Karamanolis, G. E. *Plato and Aristotle in Agreement? Platonists on Aristotle from Antiochus to Porphyry*. Oxford: Oxford University Press, 2006.

Karin-D'Arcy, R. "The Modern Role of Morgan's Canon in Comparative Psychology." *International Journal of Comparative Psychology* 18 (2005): 179–201.

Katsafanas, P. "Nietzsche and Kant on the Will: Two Models of Reflective Agency." *Philosophy and Phenomenological Research* 89 (2014): 185–216.

Kaukua, J. *Self-Awareness in Islamic Philosophy: Avicenna and Beyond*. Cambridge, UK: Cambridge University Press, 2015.

King, P. "Aquinas on the Emotions." In *The Oxford Handbook of Aquinas*, edited by B. Davies and E. Stump, 209–23. Oxford: Oxford University Press, 2012.

Kitcher, P. *The Ethical Project*. Cambridge, MA: Harvard University Press, 2011.

Kitcher, P. "The Hall of Mirrors." In *Preludes to Pragmatism: Toward a Reconstruction of Philosophy*, 325–40. New York: Oxford University Press, 2012.

Kitcher, P. "Is a Naturalized Ethics Possible?" *Behaviour* 151 (2014): 245–60.

Kitcher, P. *Science in a Democratic Society*. Amherst, NY: Prometheus Books, 2011.

Kitcher, P. *Science, Truth, and Democracy*. New York: Oxford University Press, 2001.

Knauft, B. M. "Violence and Sociality in Human Evolution." *Current Anthropology* 32 (1987): 391–428.

Knuuttila, S. *Emotions in Ancient and Medieval Philosophy*. Oxford: Clarendon Press, 2004.

Knuuttila, S., and P. Kärkkäinen, eds. *Theories of Perception in Medieval and Early Modern Philosophy*. Dordrecht: Springer, 2008.

Köhler, T. W. *Homo animal nobilissimum: Konturen des spezifisch Menschlichen in der naturphilosophischen Aristoteleskommentierung des dreizehnten Jahrhunderts*. 3 vols. Leiden: Brill, 2008–14.

König-Pralong, C. "Animal equivoque: De Lincoln à Paris via Cologne." In *Mots médiévaux offerts à Ruedi Imbach*, edited by I. Atucha et al., 67–76. Porto: Fédération internationale des Instituts d'études médiévales, 2011.

Korhonen, T., and E. Ruonakoski. *Human and Animal in Ancient Greece: Empathy and Encounter in Classical Literature*. London: I. B. Tauris, 2017.

Korsgaard, C. M. "Fellow Creatures: Kantian Ethics and Our Duties to Animals." In *The Tanner Lectures on Human Values* 24, edited by G. B. Peterson, 77–110. Salt Lake City: University of Utah Press, 2005.

Korsgaard, C. M. "Interacting with Animals: a Kantian Account." In *The Oxford Handbook on Ethics and Animals*, edited by T. Beauchamp and R. G. Frey, 91–118. Oxford: Oxford University Press, 2010.

Kramer, M. "Rights without Trimmings." In *A Debate over Rights: Philosophical Enquires*, edited by M. Kramer, N. Simmonds and H. Steiner, 7–112. Oxford: Clarendon Press, 1998.

Kraus, P. "*Kitāb al-aḫlāq li-Jālīnūs* [Galen's *On Character Traits*]." *Bulletin of the Faculty of Arts of the University of Egypt* 5 (1937): 1–51.

Kruk, R. "Ibn Sīnā on Animals: Between the First Teacher and the Physician." In *Avicenna and His Heritage*, edited by J. L. Janssens and D. De Smet, 325–41. Leuven: Leuven University Press, 2002.

Kuehn, M. "Ethics and Anthropology in the Development of Kant's Moral Philosophy." In *Cambridge Critical Guide to Kant's Groundwork of the Metaphysics of Morals*, edited by J. Timmermann, 7–28. Cambridge, UK: Cambridge University Press, 2009.

Kukkonen, T. "Heart, Spirit, Form, Substance: Ibn Ṭufayl's Psychology." In *In the Age of Averroes: Arabic Philosophy in the Sixth/Twelfth Century*, edited by P. Adamson, 195–214. London: Warburg Institute, 2011.

Kymlicka, W. *Multicultural Citizenship*. Oxford: Clarendon Press, 1995.

Langholf, V. *Medical Theories in Hippocrates: Early Texts and the Epidemics*. Berlin: de Gruyter, 1990.

Laspia, P. "Aristotele e gli animali." In *Bestie, filosofi e altri animali*, edited by F. Cimatti and S. Plastina, 17–35. Milan: Mimesis, 2016.

Lauzi, E. *Il destino degli animali: Aspetti delle tradizioni culturali araba e occidentale nel Medio Evo*. Florence: Società Internazionale per lo Studio del Medioevo Latino, 2012.

Leakey, L. *The Wild Realm: Animals of East Africa*. Washington, DC: National Geographic Society, 1969.

Lee, R. *The !Kung San: Men, Women and Work in a Foraging Society*. Cambridge, UK: Cambridge University Press, 1979.

Lefkowitz, J. B. "Aesop and Animal Fables." In *The Oxford Handbook of Animals in Classical Thought and Life*, edited by G. L. Campbell, 1–23. Oxford: Oxford University Press, 2014.

Lennox, J. "Aristotle on the Biological Roots of Virtue." In *Bridging the Gap between Aristotle's Science and Ethics*, edited by D. Henry and M. Leunissen, 193–213. Cambridge, UK: Cambridge University Press, 2015.

Lenoir, T. "Kant, Blumenbach and Vital Materialism in German Biology." *Isis* 71 (1980): 77–108.

Lestringant, F. *Le Huguenot et le Sauvage: L'Amérique et la Controverse Coloniale, en France, au Temps des Guerres de Religion*. Paris: Klincksieck, 1999.

Lestringant, F. "Le nom des 'Cannibales' de Christophe Colomb à Michel de Montaigne." *Bulletin de la Société International des Amis de Montaigne* 17–18 (1984): 51–74.

Leunissen, M. "Aristotle on Natural Character and Its Implications for Moral Development." *Journal of the History of Philosophy* 50.4 (2012): 507–30.

Lévi-Strauss, C. *The Savage Mind*. Chicago: University of Chicago Press, 1966.

Longrigg, J. *Greek Rational Medicine: Philosophy and Medicine from Alcmaeon to the Alexandrians*. New York: Routledge, 1993.

López-Farjeat, L. X. "Avicenna on Non-Conceptual Content and Self-Awareness in Non-Human Animals." In *Medieval and Early Modern Approaches to Cognitive and Moral Psychology*, edited by J. Kaukua and T. Ekenberg, 61–73. Dordrecht: Springer, 2016.

López-Farjeat, L. X. "The 'Language' of Non-Human Animals in al-Fārābī and Ibn Sīnā." In *The Origin and Nature of Language and Logic in Medieval Islamic, Jewish and Christian Thought*, edited by S. Harvey and N. Germann. Forthcoming.

Loughlin, S. "Similarities and Differences between Human and Animal Emotion in Aquinas's Thought." *The Thomist* 65 (2001): 45–65.

Lowry, R. *The Evolution of Psychological Theory*. Hawthorne, NY: Aldine, 1971.

Lurz, R. W., ed. *The Philosophy of Animal Minds*. Cambridge, UK: Cambridge University Press, 2009.

Magel, C. *Keyguide to Information Sources in Animal Rights*. London: McFarland, 1989.

Mann, J. "Beast Epic and Fable." In *Medieval Latin: An Introduction and Bibliographical Guide*, edited by F. A. C. Mantello and A. G. Rigg, 556–61. Washington, DC: Catholic University of America Press, 1996.

Mann, J. *From Aesop to Reynard: Beast Literature in Medieval England*. Oxford: Oxford University Press, 2009.

Mann, N. *Gabriel von Max: Eine kunsthistorische Skizze*. Leipzig: J. J. Weber, 1890.

Marcondes, D. "The Anthropological Argument: The Rediscovery of Ancient Skepticism in Modern Thought." In *Skepticism in the Modern Age: Building on the Work of Richard Popkin*, edited by J. R. Maia Neto, G. Paganini, and J. C. Laursen, 37–53. Leiden: Brill, 2009.

Marmura, M. E. "Avicenna's 'Flying Man' in Context." *Monist* 69 (1986): 383–95.

Marno, C. "Anonymi Philosophia 'Sicut dicitur ab Aristotile': A Parisian Prologue to Porphyry." *Cahiers de l'Institut du Moyen Âge grec et latin* 61 (1991): 140–46.

Matilal, B. K. *Ethics and Epics*. Oxford: Oxford University Press, 2002.

McCloskey, H. "The Moral Case for Experimentation on Animals." *Monist* 70.1 (1987): 64–82.

McDermott, J. P. "Animals and Humans in Early Buddhism." *Indo-Iranian Journal* 32 (1989): 269–80.

McGinnis, J. *Avicenna*. New York: Oxford University Press, 2010.

McMahan, J. *The Ethics of Killing: Problems at the Margins of Life*. Oxford: Oxford University Press, 2002.

McMillan, F. D. *Mental Health and Well-Being in Animals*. Hoboken, NJ: Wiley, 2008.

Meier, G. H. *Philosophische Sittenlehre*. Halle: Hemmerde, 1753–61.

Mermier, G. "L'Essay *Des Cannibales* de Montaigne." *Bulletin de la Société International des Amis de Montaigne* 7–8 (1973): 27–38.

Meyer, S. S. *Aristotle on Moral Responsibility: Character and Cause*. Oxford: Oxford University Press, 2011.

Milanesi, M. "Arsarot o Anian? Identità e separazione tra Asia e Nuovo Mondo nella cartografia del Cinquecento (1500–1570)." In *Il nuovo mondo nella coscienza italiana e tedesca nel Cinquecento*, edited by A. Prosperi and W. Reinhard, 19–78. Bologna: Il Mulino, 1992.

Mizunami, M., N. Yamagata, and H. Nishino. "Alarm Pheromone Processing in the Ant Brain: An Evolutionary Perspective." *Frontiers in Behavioral Neuroscience* 4.28 (2010): 1–9.

Montanari, Massimo. *A Cultural History of Food in the Medieval Age*. Vol. 2 of
A Cultural History of Food, edited by F. Parasecoli and P. Scholliers. Oxford:
Berg, 2012.

Montanari, M. *The Culture of Food*. Oxford: Blackwell, 1994.

Montminy, M. "What Use Is Morgan's Canon?" *Philosophical Psychology* 18 (2005):
399–414.

Mudimbe, V. Y. "Afterword: The Idea of Luba." In *Memory: Luba Art and the
Making of History*, edited by M. N. Roberts and A. F. Roberts, 244–77. Munich:
Prestel, 1996.

Muratori, C., ed. *The Animal Soul and the Human Mind: Renaissance Debates*. Pisa:
Serra, 2013.

Muratori, C. "Pitagora tra i cannibali: Dieta e ordine dei viventi a partire dalla
letteratura rinascimentale sul nuovo mondo." In *Bestie, filosofi e altri animali*,
edited by F. Cimatti and S. Plastina, 143–60. Milan: Mimesis, 2016.

Muratori, C., and B. Dohm, eds. *Ethical Perspectives on Animals in the Renaissance
and Early Modern Period*. Florence: Società Internazionale per lo Studio del
Medioevo Latino, 2013.

Muther, R. *Geschichte der Malerei im Neunzehnten Jahrhundert. Erster Teil*.
Paderborn: KlassikArt, 2013.

Naragon, S. "Kant on Descartes and the Brutes." *Kant-Studien* 81 (1990): 1–23.

Naragon, S. "Reason and Animals: Descartes, Kant, and Mead on the Place of
Humans in Nature." PhD dissertation, University of Notre Dame, 1987.

Needham, R. *Primordial Characters*. Charlottesville: University Press of Virginia,
1980.

Nelson, L. "Cows, Elephants, Dogs, and Other Lesser Embodiments of *Ātman*:
Reflections on Hindu Attitudes toward Nonhuman Animals." In *A Communion
of Subjects*, edited by K. Patton and P. Waldau, 179–93. New York: Columbia
University Press, 2009.

Newbury, E. "Current Interpretation and Significance of Morgan's Canon."
Psychological Bulletin 51 (1954): 70–74.

Newmyer, S. T. *Animals in Greek and Roman Thought: A Sourcebook*. London:
Routledge, 2011.

Newmyer, S. T. "Animals in Plutarch." In *A Companion to Plutarch*, edited by
M. Beck, 223–34. Oxford: Wiley-Blackwell, 2014.

Nielsen, K. M. "Deliberation as Inquiry: Aristotle's Alternative to the Presumption
of Open Alternatives." *The Philosophical Review* 120.3 (2011): 383–421.

Nobis, N. "Carl Cohen's 'Kind' Arguments for Animal Rights and against Human
Rights." *Journal of Applied Philosophy* 21.1 (2004): 43–59.

Nøjgaard, M. *La fable antique*. 2 vols. Copenhagen: Busck, 1964–67.

Nooter, M. H. "Luba Art and Government: Creating Power in a Central African Kingdom." PhD dissertation, Columbia University, 1990.

Nozick, R. *Anarchy, State and Utopia*. Oxford: Blackwell, 1974.

Nussbaum, M. *Frontiers of Justice: Disability, Nationality, Species Membership*. Cambridge, MA: Harvard University Press, 2006.

Olivelle, P. "Food for Thought: Dietary Rules and Social Organization in Ancient India." In *Collected Essays I: Language, Texts and Society. Explorations in Ancient Indian Culture and Religion*, edited by P. Olivelle, 367–94. Florence: University of Florence Press, 2008. Originally published as the 2001 Gonda Lecture (Amsterdam: Royal Netherlands Academy of Arts and Sciences, 2002).

Olivelle, P. "Talking Animals." *Religions of South Asia* 7 (2013): 14–26.

Orlandi, A. *Le edizioni dell'opera di Della Porta*. Pisa: Serra, 2013.

Osborne, C. *Dumb Beasts and Dead Philosophers: Humanity and the Humane in Ancient Philosophy and Literature*. Oxford: Clarendon, 2007.

Palmer, C. *Animal Ethics in Context*. New York: Columbia University Press, 2010.

Pasnau, R. *Thomas Aquinas on Human Nature: A Philosophical Study of* Summa Theologiae Ia. Cambridge, UK: Cambridge University Press, 2002.

Passmore, J. "Treatment of Animals." *Journal of the History of Ideas* 36 (1975): 195–218.

Pastoureau, M. "Le bestiaire de cinq sens (XIIe–XVIe siècles)." *Micrologus* 10 (2002): 133–45.

Per-Anders, S. "Animal National Liberation?" *Journal of Animal Ethics* 3.2 (2013): 188–200.

Perfetti, S. *Aristotle's Zoology and Its Renaissance Commentators (1521–1601)*. Leuven: Leuven University Press, 2000.

Perler, D. "Why Is the Sheep Afraid of the Wolf? Medieval Debates on Animal Passions." In *Emotion and Cognitive Life in Medieval and Early Modern Philosophy*, edited by M. Pickavé and L. Shapiro, 32–52. Oxford: Oxford University Press, 2012.

Perrett, R. W. "Moral Vegetarianism and the Indian Tradition." In *Ethical and Political Dilemmas of Modern India*, edited by N. Smart and S. Thakur, 82–99. Basingstoke, UK: Macmillan, 1993.

Perry, B. E. "The Origin of the Epimythium." *Transactions and Proceedings of the American Philological Association* 71 (1940): 391–419.

Petridis, C. "Bwadi bwa Chikwanga: A Ram Mask of the Bakwa Luntu." *African Arts* 38.2 (2005): 50–95.

Phillips, C. *The Welfare of Animals: The Silent Majority*. Brisbane: Springer Scientific, 2009.

Pickavé, M., and L. Shapiro, eds. *Emotions and Cognitive Life in Medieval and Early Modern Philosophy*. Oxford: Oxford University Press, 2012.

Pluhar, E. *Beyond Prejudice: The Moral Significance of Human and Nonhuman Animals*. Durham, NC: Duke University Press, 1995.

Pluhar, E. "Is There a Morally Relevant Difference between Human and Animal Nonpersons?" *Journal of Agricultural Ethics* 1 (1988): 59–68.

Pormann, P. E. "Avicenna on Medical Practice, Epistemology, and the Physiology of the Inner Senses." In *Interpreting Avicenna: Critical Essays*, edited by P. Adamson, 91–108. Cambridge, UK: Cambridge University Press, 2013.

Raber, K. *Animal Bodies, Renaissance Culture*. Philadelphia: University of Pennsylvania Press, 2013.

Rachels, J. *Created from Animals: The Moral Implications of Darwinism*. Oxford: Oxford University Press, 1990.

Radick, G. "Morgan's Canon, Garner's Phonograph, and the Evolutionary Origins of Language and Reason." *British Journal for the History of Science* 33 (2000): 3–23.

Rahman, F. *The Philosophy of Mullā Ṣadrā*. Albany: State University of New York Press, 1975.

Raz, J. *The Morality of Freedom*. Oxford: Clarendon Press, 1986.

Reefe, T. *The Rainbow and the Kings: A History of the Luba Empire to 1891*. Berkeley: University of California Press, 1981.

Regan, T. *The Case for Animal Rights*. London: Routledge, 1984. Revised ed. Berkeley: University of California Press, 2004.

Regan, T. "Utilitarianism, Vegetarianism and Animal Rights." *Philosophy and Public Affairs* 9.4 (1980): 305–24.

Resnick, I. M., and K. F. Kitchell Jr. "Albert the Great on the 'Language' of Animals." *American Catholic Philosophical Quarterly* 70.1 (1996): 41–61.

Rich, A. N. M. "Reincarnation in Plotinus." *Mnemosyne* 4.10 (1957): 232–38.

Richards, R. *Darwin and the Emergence of Evolutionary Theories of Mind and Behavior*. Chicago: University of Chicago Press, 1987.

Richards, R. J. *The Romantic Conception of Life*. Chicago: University of Chicago Press, 2002.

Richards, R. J. "Kant and Blumenbach on the *Bildungstrieb*: A Historical Misunderstanding." *Studies in History and Philosophy of Science Part C: Studies in History and Philosophy of Biological and Biomedical Sciences* 31 (2000): 11–32.

Riskin, J. *The Restless Clock: A History of the Centuries Long Argument over What Makes Living Things Tick*. Chicago: University of Chicago Press, 2016.

Ritvo, H. *The Animal Estate*. Cambridge, MA: Harvard University Press, 1987.

Roberts, A. F. *Animals in African Arts: From the Familiar to the Marvelous*. Munich: Prestel, 1995.

Roberts, A. F. "Performing Cosmology: Harmonies of Land, Lake, Body, and Sky." In *African Cosmos: Stellar Arts*, edited by C. M. Kreamer, 184–203. New York: National Museum of African Art, 2012.

Roberts, A. F. "Why the Hero Lost His Teeth: Reflections on the Great Luba Helmet Mask." In *La danse du masque/The Dancing Mask*. Forthcoming.

Roberts, A. F., and E. M. Maurer, eds. *The Rising of a New Moon: A Century of Tabwa Art*. Ann Arbor: University of Michigan Museum of Art, 1985.

Roberts, M. N. "The King Is a Woman: Shaping Power in Luba Royal Arts." *African Arts* 46.3 (2013): 68–81.

Roberts, M. N., and A. F. Roberts, eds. *Memory: Luba Art and the Making of History*. Munich: Prestel, 1996.

Rocca, J. *Galen on the Brain: Anatomical Knowledge and Physiological Speculation in the Second Century AD*. Leiden: Brill, 2003.

Romanes, G. *Animal Intelligence*. London: Kegan Paul, 1882.

Rorty, R. "The Concept of Potentiality in Aristotle and Descartes." PhD dissertation, Yale University, 1956.

Rosenfield, L. C. *From Beast-Machine to Man-Machine: Animal Soul in French Letters from Descartes to La Mettrie*. Oxford: Oxford University Press, 1941. Reprinted in New York: Columbia University Press, 1968.

Rowlands, M. *Animal Rights: A Philosophical Defence*. Basingstoke, UK: Macmillan, 1998.

Rowlands, M. *Animal Rights: Moral Theory and Practice*. Basingstoke, UK: Palgrave, 2009.

Rowlands, M. *Can Animals Be Moral?* Oxford: Oxford University Press, 2012.

Rowlands, M. "Contractarianism and Animal Rights." *Journal of Applied Philosophy* 14.3 (1997): 235–47.

Salisbury, J. E. *The Beast Within*. New York: Routledge, 2011.

Sanbonmatsu, J., ed. *Critical Theory and Animal Liberation*. New York: Rowman and Littlefield, 2011.

Sayeed, A. *Women and the Transmission of Religious Knowledge in Islam*. Cambridge, UK: Cambridge University Press, 2013.

Schmidt-Raghavan, M. "Animal Liberation and Ahiṁsā." In *Ethical and Political Dilemmas of Modern India*, edited by N. Smart and S. Thakur, 60–80. Basingstoke, UK: Macmillan, 1993.

Schmithausen, L. *Buddhism and Nature*. Tokyo: International Institute for Buddhist Studies, 1991.

Schmithausen, L. *The Problem of the Sentience of Plants in Earliest Buddhism*. Tokyo: International Institute for Buddhist Studies, 1991.

Schmithausen, L. "Tier und Mensch im Buddhismus." In *Tiere und Menschen: Geschichte eines prekären Verhältnisses*, edited by P. Münch, 179–224. Paderborn: Ferdinand Schöningh, 1998.

Schmithausen, L., and M. Maithrimurthi. "Attitudes towards Animals in Indian Buddhism." In *Penser, dire et representer l'animal dans le monde indien*, edited by N. Balbir and G.-J. Pinault, 47–115. Paris: Honoré Champion, 2009.

Schoffeleers, M. "Twins and Unilateral Figures in Central and Southern Africa: Symmetry and Asymmetry in the Symbolization of the Sacred." *Journal of Religion in Africa* 21.4 (1991): 345–72.

Schuster, M. *Untersuchungen zu Plutarchs Dialog De sollertia animalium, mit Besonderer Berücksichtigung der Lehrtätigkeit Plutarchs.* Augsburg: Himmer, 1917.

Searle, J. "Minds, Brains and Programs." *Behavioral and Brain Sciences* 3 (1980): 417–57.

Seyfort-Ruegg, D. "*Ahiṃsā* and Vegetarianism in the History of Buddhism." In *Buddhist Studies in Honour of Walpola Rahula*, edited by S. Balasooriya et al., 234–50. London: Gordon Fraser, 1980.

Shettleworth, S. J. "Clever Animals and Killjoy Explanations in Comparative Psychology." *Trends in Cognitive Sciences* 14 (2010): 477–81.

Shields, C. "Aristotle's Psychology." In *The Stanford Encyclopedia of Philosophy*, edited by E. N. Zalta. Spring 2015 edition. Online.

Simpson, J. "Beast Epic and Fable." In *Medieval England: An Encyclopaedia*, edited by P. E. Szarmach, M. T. Tavormina, and J. T. Rosenthal, 111–12. New York: Garland, 1998.

Simpson, J. "Consuming Ethics: Caxton's *History of Reynard the Fox*." In *Studies in Late Medieval and Early Renaissance Texts in Honour of John Scattergood*, edited by A. Fletcher and A.-M. D'Arcy, 321–36. Dublin: Four Courts Press, 2005.

Simpson, J. R. *Animal Body, Literary Corpus: The Old French Roman de Renart.* Amsterdam: Rodopi, 1996.

Singer, P. *Animal Liberation: A New Ethics for Our Treatment of Animals.* New York: Random House, 1975. 2nd edition printed in London: J. Cape, 1990.

Singer, P. *The Expanding Circle: Ethics, Evolution, and Moral Progress.* Princeton, NJ: Princeton University Press, 2011.

Singer, P. *Practical Ethics.* Cambridge, UK: Cambridge University Press, 1993.

Singer, P. "A Response." In *Singer and His Critics*, edited by D. Jamieson, 269–335. Oxford: Blackwell, 1999.

Skidmore, J. "Duties to Animals: The Failure of Kant's Moral Theory." *Journal of Value Inquiry* 35 (2001): 541–59.

Sloan, P. R. "Buffon, German Biology, and the Historical Interpretation of Biological Species." *British Journal for the History of Science* 12 (1979): 109–53.

Sloan, P. R. "Preforming the Categories: Eighteenth-Century Generation Theory and the Biological Roots of Kant's *a priori*." *Journal of the History of Philosophy* 40 (2002): 229–53.

Smit, H., and M. Timmons. "Kant's Grounding Project in the Doctrine of Virtue." In *Kant on Practical Justification: Interpretative Essays*, edited by M. Timmons and S. Baiasu, 229–68. New York: Oxford University Press, 2013.

Sober, E. "Morgan's Canon." In *The Evolution of Mind*, edited by D. D. Cummins and C. Allen, 224–42. Oxford: Oxford University Press, 1998.

Sorabji, R. *Animal Minds and Human Morals: The Origins of the Western Debate.* Ithaca, NY: Cornell University Press, 1993.

Staddon, J. E. R. *Adaptive Behavior and Learning.* Cambridge, UK: Cambridge University Press, 1983.

Steel, C., G. Guldentops, and P. Beullens, eds. *Aristotle's Animals in the Middle Ages and Renaissance.* Leuven: Leuven University Press, 1999.

Steinbock, B. "Speciesism and the Idea of Equality." *Philosophy* 53 (1978): 247–56.

Steiner, G. *Anthropocentrism and Its Discontents: The Moral Status of Animals in the History of Western Philosophy.* Pittsburgh, PA: University of Pittsburgh Press, 2005.

Steiner, H. "Working Rights." In *A Debate over Rights: Philosophical Enquires*, edited by M. Kramer, N. Simmonds, and H. Steiner, 233–301. Oxford: Clarendon Press, 1998.

Stewart, J. "The Question of Vegetarianism and Diet in Pāli Buddhism." *Journal of Buddhist Ethics* 17 (2010): 100–138.

Sturm, T. *Kant und die Wissenschaften vom Menschen.* Münster: Mentis, 2009.

Sung, H.-M. *Decoded Messages: The Symbolic Language of Chinese Animal Painting.* New Haven, CT: Yale University Press, 2010.

Sung, H.-M. "Fish (Yu 魚)." In *Decoded Messages: The Symbolic Language of Chinese Animal Painting*, 207–44. New Haven, CT: Yale University Press, 2010.

Terrace, H. S., L. A. Petitto, R. J. Sanders, and T. G. Bever. "Can an Ape Create a Sentence?" *Science* 206 (1979): 891–902.

Theuws, T. "Le Styx ambigu." *Problèmes sociaux congolais* 81 (1968): 5–33.

Thomas, E. C., trans. *F. A. Lange: The History of Materialism and Criticism of Its Present Importance.* New York: Humanities Press, 1950.

Thorpe, W. H. *Learning and Instinct in Animals.* London: Methuen, 1956.

Timmermann, J. "Kant on Conscience, 'Indirect' Duty, and Moral Error." *International Philosophical Quarterly* 46 (2006): 293–308.

Timmermann, J. "When the Tail Wags the Dog: Animal Welfare and Indirect Duty in Kantian Ethics." *Kantian Review* 10 (2005): 128–49.

Tlili, S. *Animals in the Qur'an.* Cambridge, UK: Cambridge University Press, 2015.

Toivanen, J. *Perception and the Internal Senses: Peter of John Olivi on the Cognitive Functions of the Sensitive Soul*. Leiden: Brill, 2013.

Toivanen, J. "Perceptual Self-Awareness in Seneca, Augustine, and Peter Olivi." *Journal of the History of Philosophy* 51.3 (2013): 355–82.

Tuominen, M. *Apprehension and Argument: Ancient Theories of Starting Points for Knowledge*. Dordrecht: Springer, 2007.

Uhlig, F. "Gegenzauber: Gabriel von Max' Interesse für Affen." In *Gabriel von Max: Malerstar Darwinist, Spiritist*, edited by K. Althaus and H. Friedel, 316–29. Munich: Hirmer, 2010.

Vallely, A. "Being Sentiently with Others: The Shared Existential Trajectory among Humans and Nonhumans in Jainism." In *Asian Perspectives on Animal Ethics*, edited by N. Dalal and C. Taylor, 38–55. London: Routledge, 2014.

van De Veer, D. "Of Beasts, Persons and the Original Position." *Monist* 62.3 (1979): 368–77.

van Dijk, G.-J. *ΑΙΝΟΙ, ΛΟΓΟΙ, ΜΥΘΟΙ: Fables in Archaic, Classical, and Hellenistic Greek Literature*. Leiden: Brill, 1997.

van Ess, J. *Theologie und Gesellschaft im 2. und 3. Jahrhundert Hidschra: eine Geschichte des religiösen Denkens im frühen Islam*. 6 vols. Berlin: de Gruyter, 1991–95.

Vargas, I. "Snake-Kings, Boars' Heads, Deer Parks, Monkey Talk: Animals as Transmitters and Transformers in Indian and Tibetan Buddhist Narratives." In *A Communion of Subjects*, edited by K. Patton and P. Waldau, 218–40. New York: Columbia University Press, 2009.

Venkatesananda, S. *Vasistha's Yoga*. Albany: State University of New York Press, 1993.

Vermorel, M. "The Drive [*Trieb*] from Goethe to Freud." *International Review of Psycho-Analysis* 17 (1990): 249–56.

Waldau, P., and K. Patton, eds. *A Communion of Subjects: Animals in Religion, Science, and Ethics*. New York: Columbia University Press, 2009.

Walker, P. E. "The Doctrine of Metempsychosis in Islam." In *Islamic Studies Presented to Charles J. Adams*, edited by W. B. Hallaq and D. P. Little, 219–38. Leiden: Brill, 1991.

Walters, K., and L. Portmess. *Ethical Vegetarianism: From Pythagoras to Peter Singer*. Albany: State University of New York Press, 1999.

Warren, M. A. *Moral Status: Obligation to Persons and Other Living Things*. Oxford: Oxford University Press, 1997.

Weghsteen, J. "Haut-Congo: Foudre et faiseurs de pluie." *Grands Lacs* 167, new series 3 (1953), 22.

Wild, M. *Die anthropologische Differenz*. Berlin: De Gruyter, 2006.

Wilkins, J. "The Contribution of Galen *De subtiliante diaeta* (*On the Thinning Diet*)." In *The Unknown Galen*, edited by V. Nutton, 47–55. London: Institute of Classical Studies, 2002.

Willis, R. G., ed. *Signifying Animals: Human Meaning in the Natural World*. London: Unwin Hyman, 1990.

Wilm, E. C. *The Theories of Instinct*. New Haven, CT: Yale University Press, 1925.

Wojciehowski, H. C. *Group Identity in the Renaissance World*. Cambridge, UK: Cambridge University Press, 2011.

Wolfson, H. A. "The Internal Senses in Latin, Arabic and Hebrew Philosophical Texts." *Harvard Theological Review* 28 (1935): 69–133. Reprinted in *Studies in the History of Philosophy and Religion*, edited by I. Twersky and G. H. Williams, 1:69–133. Cambridge, MA: Harvard University Press, 1973.

Wood, A. W. *Kantian Ethics*. Cambridge, UK: Cambridge University Press, 2008.

Wood, A. W. "Kant on Duties regarding Non-Rational Nature I." *Proceedings of the Aristotelian Society*, supplement 72 (1998): 189–210.

Wood, A. W. *Kant's Ethical Thought*. Cambridge, UK: Cambridge University Press, 1999.

Wozniak, R. H. "Conwy Lloyd Morgan, Mental Evolution and the *Introduction to Comparative Psychology*." In C. L. Morgan, *Introduction to Comparative Psychology*, vii–xix. London: Routledge, 1993.

Wyatt, T. D. *Pheromones and Animal Behavior: Chemical Signals and Signatures*. Cambridge, UK: Cambridge University Press, 2014.

Zafiropoulos, C. A. *Ethics in Aesop's Fables: The Augustana Collection*. Leiden: Brill, 2000.

Zammito, J. H. "'This Inscrutable Principle of an Original Organization': Epigenesis and 'Looseness of Fit' in Kant's Philosophy of Science." *Studies in History and Philosophy of Science* 34a (2003): 73–109.

Zhang, Q., ed. *Zhongwen da Cidian* [The Encyclopedic Dictionary of the Chinese Language]. Taipei: Chinese Cultural University, 1990.

Index of Animal Names

FANTASTIC BEASTS

Index of Authors and Texts

Index of Key Terms